Making *Ubumwe*

STUDIES IN FORCED MIGRATION
General Editor: Dawn Chatty

Volume 1
A Tamil Asylum Diaspora: Sri Lankan Migration, Settlement and Politics in Switzerland
Christopher McDowell

Volume 2
Understanding Impoverishment: The Consequences of Development-induced Displacement
Edited by Christopher McDowell

Volume 3
Losing Place: Refugee Populations and Rural Transformations in East Africa
Johnathan B. Bascom

Volume 4
The End of the Refugee Cycle? Refugee Repatriation and Reconstruction
Edited by Richard Black and Khalid Koser

Volume 5
Engendering Forced Migration: Theory and Practice
Edited by Doreen Indra

Volume 6
Refugee Policy in Sudan, 1967–1984
Ahmed Karadawi

Volume 7
Psychosocial Wellness of Refugees: Issues in Qualitative and Quantitative Research
Edited by Frederick L. Ahearn, Jr.

Volume 8
Fear in Bongoland: Burundi Refugees in Urban Tanzania
Marc Sommers

Volume 9
Whatever Happened to Asylum in Britain? A Tale of Two Walls
Louise Pirouet

Volume 10
Conservation and Mobile Indigenous Peoples: Displacement, Forced Settlement and Sustainable Development
Edited by Dawn Chatty and Marcus Colchester

Volume 11
Tibetans in Nepal: The Dynamics of International Assistance among a Community in Exile
Anne Frechette

Volume 12
Crossing the Aegean: An Appraisal of the 1923 Compulsory Population Exchange between Greece and Turkey
Edited by Renée Hirschon

Volume 13
Refugees and the Transformation of Societies: Agency, Policies, Ethics and Politics
Edited by Philomena Essed, Georg Frerks and Joke Schrijvers

Volume 14
Children and Youth on the Front Line: Ethnography, Armed Conflict and Displacement
Edited by Jo Boyden and Joanna de Berry

Volume 15
Religion and Nation: Iranian Local and Transnational Networks in Britain
Kathryn Spellman

Volume 16
Children of Palestine: Experiencing Forced Migration in the Middle East
Dawn Chatty and Gillian Lewando Hundt

Volume 17
Rights in Exile: Janus-faced Humanitarianism
Guglielmo Verdirame and Barbara Harrell-Bond

Volume 18
Development-induced Displacement: Problems, Policies and People
Edited by Chris de Wet

Volume 19
Transnational Nomads: How Somalis Cope with Refugee Life in the Dadaab Camps of Kenya
Cindy Horst

Volume 20
New Regionalism and Asylum Seekers: Challenges Ahead
Edited by Susan Kneebone and Felicity Rawlings-Sanei

Volume 21
(Re)constructing Armenia in Lebanon and Syria: Ethno-Cultural Diversity and the State in the Aftermath of a Refugee Crisis
Nicola Migliorino

Volume 22
'Brothers' or Others? Propriety and Gender for Muslim Arab Sudanese in Egypt
Anita Fábos

Volume 23
Iron in the Soul: Displacement, Livelihood and Health in Cyprus
Peter Loizos

Volume 24
Not Born a Refugee Woman: Contesting Identities, Rethinking Practices
Edited by Maroussia Hajdukowski-Ahmed, Nazilla Khanlou and Helene Moussa

Volume 25
Years of Conflict: Adolescence, Political Violence and Displacement
Edited by Jason Hart

Volume 26
Remaking Home: Reconstructing Life, Place and Identity in Rome and Amsterdam
Maja Korac

Volume 27
Materialising Exile: Material Culture and Embodied Experience among the Karenni Refugees in Thailand
Sandra H. Dudley

Volume 28
The Early Morning Phone Call: Somali Refugees' Remittances
Anna Lindley

Volume 29
Deterritorialised Youth: Sahrawi and Afghan Refugees at the Margins of the Middle East
Edited by Dawn Chatty

Volume 30
Politics of Innocence: Hutu Identity, Conflict and Camp Life
Simon Turner

Volume 31
Zimbabwe's New Diaspora: Displacement and the Cultural Politics of Survival
Edited by JoAnn McGregor and Ranka Primorac

Volume 32
The Migration-Displacement Nexus: Patterns, Processes and Policies
Edited by Khalid Koser and Susan Martin

Volume 33
The Agendas of the Tibetan Refugees: Survival Strategies of a Government-in-Exile in a World of Transnational Organizations
Thomas Kauffmann

Volume 34
Making Ubumwe: Power, State and Camps in Rwanda's Unity-Building Project
Andrea Purdeková

Making *Ubumwe*

POWER, STATE AND CAMPS IN
RWANDA'S UNITY-BUILDING PROJECT

By
Andrea Purdeková

berghahn
NEW YORK • OXFORD
www.berghahnbooks.com

First published in 2015 by
Berghahn Books
www.berghahnbooks.com

© 2015, 2018 Andrea Purdeková
First paperback edition published in 2018

All rights reserved.
Except for the quotation of short passages
for the purposes of criticism and review, no part of this book
may be reproduced in any form or by any means, electronic or
mechanical, including photocopying, recording, or any information
storage and retrieval system now known or to be invented,
without written permission of the publisher.

Library of Congress Cataloging-in-Publication Data
Purdeková, Andrea, author.
 Making ubumwe: power, state and camps in Rwanda's unity-building project / by Andrea Purdeková.
   pages cm. -- (Studies in forced migration; volume 34)
 ISBN 978-1-78238-832-6 (hbk: alk. paper) -- ISBN 978-1-78920-072-0 (pbk: alk. paper) -- ISBN 978-1-78238-833-3 (ebook)
 1. Conflict management--Rwanda. 2. Conflict management--Government policy--Rwanda. 3. Peace-building--Rwanda. 4. Rwanda--Politics and government--1994- 5. Civil society--Rwanda. I. Title. II. Series: Studies in forced migration; v. 34.
 HN795.Z9C7378 2015
 303.6'90967571--dc23

2015003001

British Library Cataloguing in Publication Data
A catalogue record for this book is available
from the British Library

ISBN 978-1-78238-832-6 (hardback)
ISBN 978-1-78920-072-0 (paperback)
ISBN 978-1-78238-833-3 (ebook)

Contents

Acknowledgements	vii
Abbreviations	ix
Glossary	xi
Figure 1. Map of Rwanda indicating the location of *ingando* camps visited during fieldwork.	xiii
Figure 2. A sketch of the Nkumba *ingando* camp.	xiv

Part I: Introduction

1. *Kubaka Ubumwe*: Building Unity in a Divided Society	3
2. Settling the Unsettled: The Politics and Policing of Meaning in Rwanda	33

Part II: The Political Process

3. The Wording of Power: Legitimization as Narrative Currency	63
4. The Presencing Effect: Surveillance and State Reach in Rwanda	89
5. Incorporation, Disconnect: The Embodiments of Power and the Unworking of Contestation in Rwanda	113

Part III: Making *Ubumwe*: The Imageries, Planning and Performances of Unity in Rwanda

6. Unity's Multiplicities: Ambiguity at Work — 133

7. Performances and Platforms: Activities of Unity and Reconciliation in the Contexts of Power — 152

8. *Ingando* Camps: Nation Building as Consent Building — 174

9. Rights of Passage: Liminality and the Reproduction of Power — 203

Part IV: Conclusions

10. The Yeast of Change: Civic Education, Social Transformation and the New Development Corps — 225

11. What Kind of Unity? Prospects for Coexistence, Social Justice and Peace — 244

Bibliography — 251

Index — 275

Acknowledgements

First and foremost, I owe a debt of gratitude to all the people in Rwanda who have agreed to share their time and thoughts with me, whether in formal interviews or informal exchanges. Without them, this work would simply not have been possible. Most of them would not want to be mentioned by name and hence my acknowledgement must take a general form – this should not however detract from the centrality and value of their contribution. The National Unity and Reconciliation Commission (NURC) and its employees have taught me much about the official vision of unity building and the challenges that the project faces. Thanks to them, I have also been able to observe how policy is made and put into action and to participate in many events and activities that would otherwise remain out of reach. Besides NURC, there were hundreds of other people – employees at associations, research institutes, local administrators, coordinators and participants at different activities, students, neighbours, friends and casual acquaintances – all of whom helped me understand the political and social dynamics unfolding around me. I would like to extend special thanks to my Rwandan friends and my housemates in Nyamirambo who volunteered advice, support and countless hours of discussion. I hope that the book can serve to expand such discussion in new ways and into new spaces, both within Rwanda and without. Despite the critical importance of my interlocutors in forming my knowledge, any errors of fact or interpretation are naturally solely my own.

The fieldwork for this project has been undertaken during my study at Oxford and I would like to extend my sincere thanks to Dr Patricia Daley and Professor Roger Zetter for their unwavering support over the years. A travel grant from Oxford's Department of International Development has contributed to the costs of fieldwork and a publication grant from the same department has allowed me to start transforming my research into a book. A two-year scholarship from the Harold Hyam Wingate Foundation has been crucial in extending my research and thinking on the topics discussed here and in preparing the book for publication. I am extremely grateful to those who have read the whole manuscript or its parts – in particular I would like to thank Professor Jocelyn Alexander, Professor Johan Pottier as well as the anonymous reviewers of Berghahn Books for their extremely valuable comments. Portions of the manuscript have been previously published and I am again very grateful to the reviewers, as well as the editors of the Journal of Modern African Studies and Palgrave Macmillan for their permission to reproduce the work here. An earlier version of Chapter Four has appeared under the title '"Even If I Am Not Here, There Are So Many Eyes": Surveillance and State Reach in Rwanda' in 2011 in *JMAS* (Volume 49, Issue 3, Cambridge University Press) and a shorter and modified version of Chapter Ten has been published as '"Civic Education" and Social Transformation in Post-Genocide Rwanda: Forging the Perfect Development Subjects' in a 2012 edited collection by Palgrave Macmillan called *Rwanda Fast Forward: Social, Economic, Military and Reconciliation Prospects*.

My colleagues at the African Studies Centre in Oxford have been a source of great inspiration and I am immensely grateful for having had the opportunity to work with them and learn from them over the past two years. The students I supervised and taught as part of the MSc in African Studies at Oxford have also inspired me in no small measure and for that equally I owe them my thanks. At home, I owe an immense debt of gratitude to my husband and to my parents, who have steadfastly supported me in my academic endeavours, nudged me on in difficult times and borne my absences when I was finishing the manuscript.

My daughter Dominika has been a constant source of life-affirming joy and it is to her that I dedicate this book.

Abbreviations

AERG	*Association d'Etudiants Rescapés du Génocide* / Genocide Survivors Student Association
AFDL	Alliance of Democratic Forces for the Liberation of Congo
CNDP	*Congrès National pour la Défense du Peuple* / National Congress for the Defence of the People
DRC	Democratic Republic of the Congo
DFID	Department for International Development (UK)
EAC	East African Community
EPRDF	Ethiopian People's Revolutionary Democratic Front
ES	Executive Secretary
FAR	*Forces Armées Rwandaises* / The Armed Forces of Rwanda
FARG	*Fonds d'Assistance aux Rescapés du Génocide* / Victims of Genocide Fund
FDLR	*Forces Démocratiques de Libération du Rwanda* / Democratic Forces for the Liberation of Rwanda
GNU	Government of National Unity
HPG	Humanitarian Policy Group
HRW	Human Rights Watch
ICG	International Crisis Group
ICTR	International Criminal Tribunal for Rwanda
IDP	Integrated Development Programme
IO	International Organization
IRDP	Institute of Research and Dialogue for Peace
KIST	Kigali Institute of Science and Technology
LDF	Local Defence Forces
LDGL	*Ligue des Droits de la Personne dans la Région des Grands Lacs* / Great Lakes Region Human Rights League
MDR	*Mouvement Démocratique Républicain* / Democratic Republican Movement

MIGEPROF	Ministry of Gender and Family Promotion
MINAGRI	Ministry of Agriculture and Animal Resources
MINALOC	Ministry of Local Government, Community Development and Social Affairs
MINECOFIN	Ministry of Finance and Economic Planning
MINICOM	Ministry of Trade and Industry
MTN	Mobile Telephone Networks
NDI	National Democratic Institute
NGO	Non-Governmental Organization
NUR	National Unity and Reconciliation Commission
NRM	National Resistance Movement (Uganda)
NTK	*New Times Kigali* (daily newspaper)
PARMEHUTU	*Parti du Mouvement de l'Emancipation Hutu* / Party of the Hutu Emancipation Movement
PL	*Parti Libéral* / Liberal Party
PRI	Prison Reform International
PSD	*Parti Social Démocrate* / Social Democratic Party
RANU	Rwandese Alliance for National Unity
RCD	Rally for Congolese Democracy
RDRC	Rwanda Demobilization and Reintegration Commission
RPA	Rwanda Patriotic Army
RPF	Rwanda Patriotic Front
RwF	Rwandan Franc
SCUR	Student Clubs for Unity and Reconciliation
TIG	*Travaux d'Intérêts Généraux* / Community Service
ULK	*Université Libre de Kigali* / Kigali Independent University
UN	United Nations
UNDP	United Nations Development Programme
UNHCR	United Nations High Commissioner for Refugees
US DOS	United States Department of State
USAID	United States Agency for International Development

Glossary

abakangurambaga – 'those who wake up the masses'/local 'promoters'
abaturage – population
abunzi – informal dispute settlement system at village level
agasozi ndatwa – exemplary hills
akarere (pl. uturere) – district
amacakubiri – divisionism
amajyambere – development
gacaca – 'popular'/community courts (justice 'on the grass')
icyunamo – mourning period
imihigo – annual 'performance' contracts
ingando – camps or retreats for selected populations
ingengabitekerezo ya jenoside – genocide ideology
intara (pl. intara) – province
interahamwe – 'those who work/attack together' (name of genocide militias)
intwari – heroes
inyangamugayo – gacaca judges
itorero – 'advanced' ingando
kubohoza – coercion to join a political party
njyanama – sector assembly of all adults
ubudehe – 'mutual assistance' programme at cell level
ubumwe – unity
ubunyarwanda – Rwandanicity
ubusabane – a community 'get-together' festival
ubwiyunge – reconciliation

umudugudu (pl. imidugudu) – village (referring both to an administrative level and to planned villages constructed after the genocide)
umuganda – community works (one Saturday per month)
umurenge (pl. imirenge) – sector
umuryango – family
umusanzu – contribution
umuyobozi – an official/head of
umuzungu (pl. abazungu) – white person

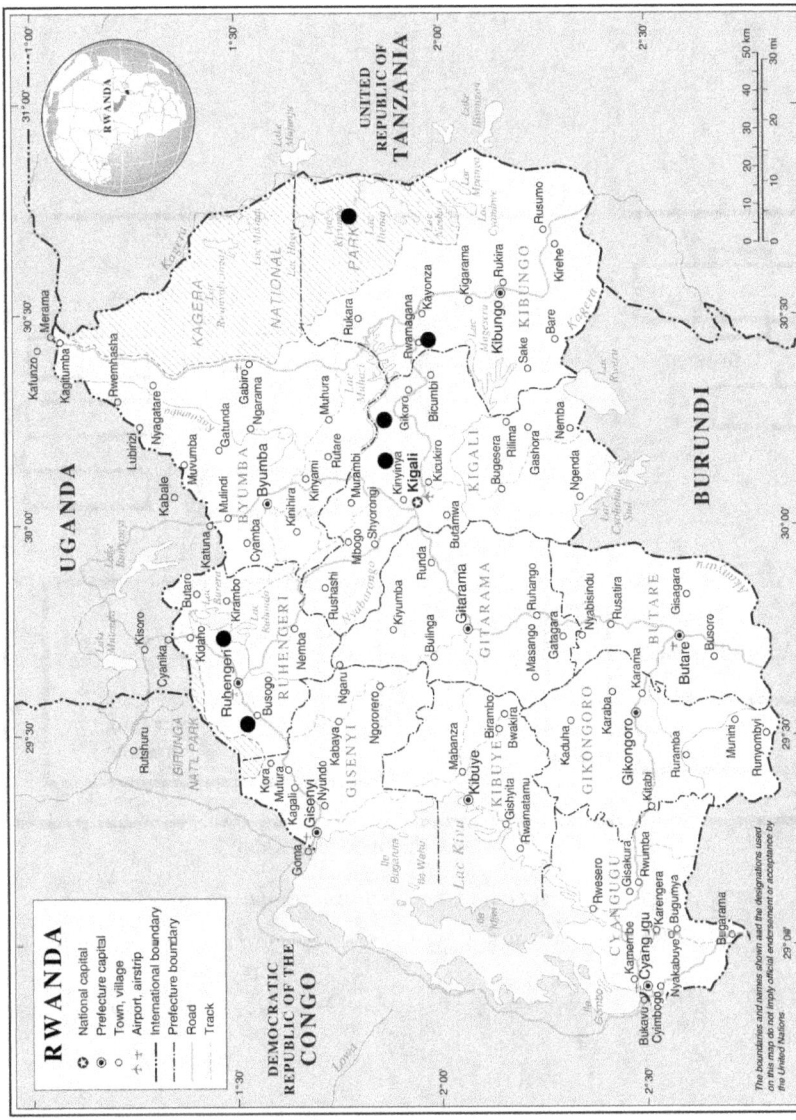

Figure 1. Map of Rwanda. Location of *ingando* camps visited during fieldwork marked by solid black dots. The indicated location is approximate only.

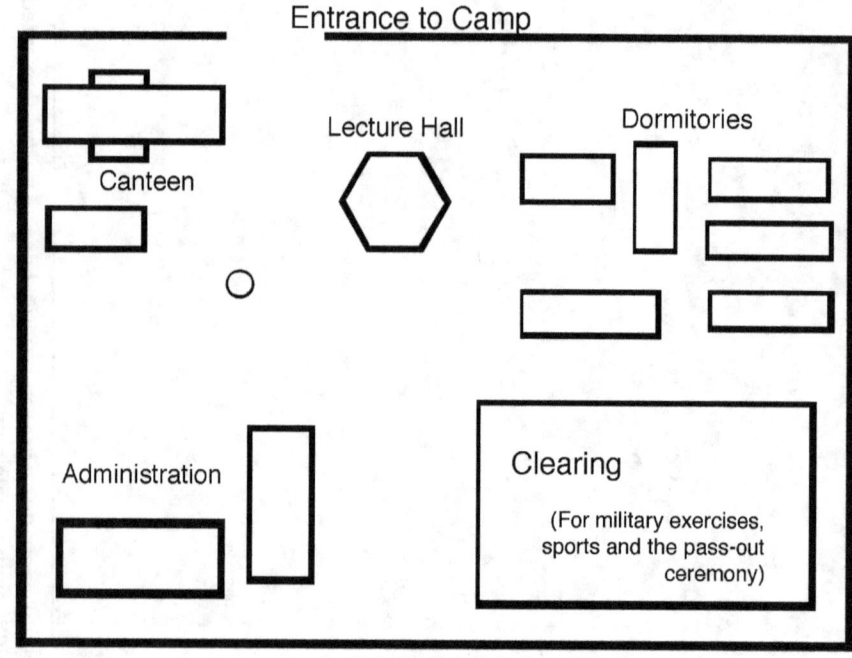

Figure 2. A sketch of the Nkumba *ingando* camp.

Part I
Introduction

1
Kubaka Ubumwe
Building Unity in a Divided Society

Near the village of Kageyo, in the unspoilt darkness of an Akagera night, a late visitor addresses the crowd of assembled young men and women. 'Can someone tell me what unity is?' asks the employee of the National Unity and Reconciliation Commission from the makeshift podium. After a silent pause, an *animateur* of the crowd takes the lead. 'There is you and there is me, and there is no difference between us, that is unity', he suggests, to the general contentment of the speaker. But unity or *ubumwe* in Kinyarwanda is not only a discussion point in the remoteness of an *ingando* camp. The term has a wider public presence, being deployed and redeployed in media, meetings, activities, policy documents and happenings in rural and urban Rwanda. In the parlance of the commission that bears its name, the shorthand 'u&u' – short for *ubumwe n'ubwiyunge*, unity and reconciliation – is suggestive of the common currency that the term has become and points to its bureaucratization and status as a 'social project' of the state.

In one reading then, what follows is a study of an exigent social engineering project of coexistence in the aftermath of mass violence. How does a government approach the task of building a social togetherness and a cohesive social whole after genocide? Why and how does such a project take the shape it does? How do nationwide and state-directed social projects align with, negotiate or override the needs of local communities into which they insert themselves? What is the ultimate goal of social togetherness on a large, nationwide scale? Who makes it, how and with what effects?

This book takes the opportunity to start exploring this complex social process, at once very abstract and quite concrete. On one side lies the abstraction of unity, a discursive domain responding to complex fields of meaning that are not readily visible. This contrasts with the almost mundane nature of the execution of unity as a project – there is an actual government institution in charge, there are specific individuals in it, and there is the work that they do to make this happen.

In its exploration of *kubaka ubumwe* (unity building), the book opens the enquiry beyond the subject's typical disciplinary 'location' – reconciliation and transitional justice – considering instead the broader social and political field within which the process is embedded. Such expansion better reflects the fact that unity building is merely one aspect of a wider transformation project of the state, a project that is unique in its intensity and its targeting of all aspects of society (Straus and Waldorf 2011; Reyntjens 2013). An expanded inquiry also better mirrors the nature of power itself, which, as a structuring force of possibility (Foucault 1982; Hayward 1998; Stewart 2001) does not conform to social science disciplinary ontology, cutting instead through all categories of inquiry. The issue here is not only ontological, however. It reaches method too. Power is an insurgent force, an opportunist flow. Conceptualizing power as insurgency is key to unlocking the logic of social transformation in Rwanda where 'thematic' boundaries (between politics, development and unity and reconciliation) are blurred as diverse spaces and platforms are often appropriated for broader, overarching aims. But in order to trace power, the study itself has to simulate its manner of propagation, it has to become contingent and opportunistic, an ambush on openings and leads as these arise.

In another reading then, the book is a tracing. The study does not presume what *ubumwe* should be about, rather it tries to approach unity building as an unknown object and learn about its different aspects anywhere where the term is invoked or deployed intensively, looking at what people do when the term 'applies'. The strategy leads the researcher through diverse contexts, from the textual to the voiced and the performed, from logical frameworks and conceptual notes, from the office of the National Unity and Reconciliation Commission (NURC) to the placing of diverse bodies 'together', to role play and enaction, to the makeshift and transient *ingando* camp at the Tanzanian border, a work camp for released prisoners at Gasabo, to the festivals of *ubusabane* outside Nyanza, or the *umuganda* community works in Gikondo. The result is not a fine contour but a sketch outlining the life and anatomy of unity as an idea and a political project. It is a story of the many ways in which an idea is conceptualized, operationalized and performed in very specific settings inside Rwanda, and the ways in which the word's interpretive latitude invites creative manipulation.

Finally, we might say the book is ultimately not about unity, despite the title proving that it indeed is. Perhaps unity is best understood as a frame, a window to understand the wider state-society relations and the process of creating a new political community in post-genocide Rwanda. Perhaps what is most important is not the particular 'what' of unity but the 'how' – how a social togetherness is envisioned on a mass scale – how the state imagines social transformation, how it approaches its citizenry, in fact what type of citizen it seeks to create. Languages of unity can serve as powerful openings to discussions on the appropriation of the symbolic in determining political inclusion and exclusion, the making and remaking of social roles and bonds, and the fashioning of the public self and the collective corps.

Locating the Subject: Post-Conflict Reconciliation

The project of social unity is typically narrated as one aspect of much broader processes of post-conflict reconciliation, a topic that has received intense scholarly attention in the past two decades (Shaw et al. 2010; Wilson 2000 and 2001; Minow 1998; Minow and Chayes 2003; Huyse and Salter 2008; Hayner 2010; Clark and Kaufman 2008; Pankhurst 2008; among others). Reconciliation is typically understood as a multidimensional project comprising justice or retribution, restitution (whether reconstitutive, rehabilitative or symbolic), truth telling, commemoration and other memory-related performances, as well as unity or nation building. The latter aspect has received relatively little academic attention – in the Rwandan context, it is overshadowed by a vast literature on the *gacaca* courts and the International Criminal Tribunal for Rwanda (ICTR) – and this despite unity building being a uniquely pressing and challenging task in so-called violently 'divided societies' where perpetrators and victims of violence live in close proximity, and where people struggle to re-imagine and reconstruct their political and moral community.

Rwanda is a unique case in this respect. The degree of disruption that the 1994 genocide caused is hard to overstate. The unprecedented scale of the event demanded creation of a new term to describe it – *jenoside*. The *jenoside* claimed up to a million lives,[1] produced millions of refugees and spawned a continental war, touching every life inside the country and beyond. It has been a tragedy of mass proportions, not only in terms of victims but also perpetrators. The genocide was locally carried out, often by 'intimate enemies' (Theidon 2006; Straus and Lyons 2006). The result is a society where the dividing lines run through every community and are themselves complex. Far from a simplistic account of a bipolar society of Hutu and Tutsi struggling to be reconciled, the society represents a complicated web of tensions between survivors, *genocidaires* and moderate Hutu,[2] between those who suffered, those who saved, those who killed or simply stood by and that 'segment of the population that blurs the [victim-perpetrator] dichotomy, inhabiting Primo Levi's (1989) grey zone of "half-tints and complexities"' (Theidon 2006: 436). Further to this, since the end of the genocide close to forty per cent of the present population have returned from various countries in the diaspora and tensions exist among Tutsi returnee groups as well as between returnees and those who stayed behind (the *Sopecya*).

Into this context comes a government dominated by the Rwanda Patriotic Front (RPF) in which Tutsi returnees from Uganda are overrepresented[3] (Ansoms 2009; Reyntjens 2004 and 2006; Zorbas 2004; Prunier 2009) and which oversees a strong state, a minority government that is nonetheless set to deliver 'unity'. 'Rwandan officials are prompt to point out that the aim of the state at this critical juncture is to build a nation' (Lemarchand 2009: 65). But what does unity mean, and to whom? In the complex social context delineated above, how do today's Rwandans learn to 'live together again'? Since living 'side by side' is not a choice but a given, what does the state's social engineering project consist of?

Re-locating the Subject: Power and the State

The Rwandan government has certainly not stayed with mere rhetoric. One cannot but notice the vast labour spent on production of activities created in the name of unity and reconciliation, many of which lay claims to traditionality and connection to the local. Thousands of local *gacaca* courts have tried millions of accused. In an attempt at de-ethnicization, the government has abolished the mention of ethnicity and is promoting the building of Rwandanness and Rwandanicity. A score of allegedly 'local', 'participatory' and 'traditional' unity and reconciliation activities and institutions have been set up, including *abunzi* mediation committees, *ubusabane* community festivals, *ubudehe* development schemes, *itorero* schools and *ingando* camps, among others. A new history has been drafted and is being disseminated (see Melvin 2013). The National and Unity Reconciliation Commission (NURC), stipulated under the 1993 Arusha Accords and established in 1999, has been promoting 'civic education' in *ingando* camps and urging Rwandans to ask for and grant forgiveness. The sheer scope of activity in Rwanda contrasts starkly with neighbouring Burundi, where it is activity's absence instead that is noticeable. In the light of production alone, Rwanda indeed seems remarkable.

But appearance has its own politics. Official characterization abides by its own political economy – naming and description can themselves mask and perform political work. The state and political power work on the premise that tokens – formalities and formulations – are substances in their own right and they are exploiting this 'parallel occurrence' or 'doubling' (formal discursive roster and actual tangible practice). In Rwanda, systematic discrepancies exist between how activities are depicted and their observed content. The systematic 'production of gaps' thus needs to be explored alongside the logic that underlies specific labelling and the labels' sanctioning power.

Treating characterization as a strategic tool has implications for method. Just as I decided not to presume what things are, I did not want to presume what the effects ought to be. Noting the 'dynamics of gaps' and the delicate politics of characterization, I decided to proceed away from discussions of 'effectiveness' to discussions of 'productiveness' of social events. Rather than asking 'Are these activities achieving what they say they want to achieve?' I asked 'What are the different effects that are actually produced and why?' The productive aspect of social events is often overlooked, with the result that activities might be outright dismissed as ineffective. For example, referring to the Rwandan prohibition on the mention of ethnicity, René Lemarchand exclaims: 'As if one could change society by decree!' (2009: 106). Naturally, society cannot be changed by decree, neither has it been, and even government officials acknowledge this. Hence the more interesting query becomes 'What if any ends are nonetheless served?' Mere discursive or surface-level enactments, whether enforced articulation or active silence, are acts useful to the government, with containment as a wider strategy. 'Shallowness' or 'failure' to achieve intended, programmatic goals can still result in 'useful production' for the regime.

The dynamics of gaps is just one aspect of a broader politics of reconciliation in Rwanda. Understanding the full extent of politicization has been a gradual process, one that ultimately shifted the key themes and vocabularies of my inquiry. When I was setting out for my first fieldwork trip to Rwanda in 2008, none of the terms that are part of the book title featured prominently in my research design. Originally, I set out to study the making of the new official history, a story of the past highlighting unity of all Rwandans and the imposed nature of divisions. I wanted to see how this history was being transmitted, received, reworked and renarrated on the ground. I was also particularly interested in the settings of the *ingando* camps – painted by the government as 'solidarity' and nation-building tools while critics dismissed them in broad strokes as political re-education or brainwashing. But soon after coming to Rwanda, much broader themes of power, the state and 'unity' repeatedly appeared in my notes and transcripts, and it is around these that my research ultimately got re-centred. I understood that without placing my endeavour in relation to these themes, it would be impossible to understand construction of historical or any type of narratives, the space of *ingando* and in fact any other type of performance.

Not only were these key themes, they were clearly interconnected. State building and unity building in Rwanda are not easily separable. Once in the field, it soon became clear to me that one could not study the myriad official activities called 'unity and reconciliation' activities without seeing these as yet another encounter with the state and power at the local level. Contrary to the dominant image of a 'weak' African state, the state in Rwanda is dense and intricate, which is not to say that it is all-powerful. Many people might eye it with suspicion or as something to be avoided, but this does not mean the state is not present in their lives, that it is easy to escape its reach, or that it indeed does not have important effects in the sphere of the everyday.

As a result of this re-centring, I reformulated and broadened my interest. Beyond simply focusing on official versus counter-narratives or claimed versus actual effects in unity building and reconciliation, I found it meaningful to go deeper and ask questions about power and the state: How is power organized and legitimized in post-genocide Rwanda and how does this affect how 'unity' and 'reconciliation' are construed and pursued? How does politics inscribe itself into the very conceptualization of unity (in the official discourse) and in what ways does it determine the nature (not only possible outcomes) of unity and reconciliation activities? How, to what extent, and to what ends does the government appropriate the wider discourse of 'unity and reconciliation' and the activities organized in its name? Besides studying the way in which power works at the macro level, I also wanted to see how it functions at the micro level: How do the political dynamics determine what can be achieved through purportedly local, traditional and grassroots activities? What does participation in these activities mean in the context of a 'strong state' equipped with an intricate system of surveillance and a tight management of voice and silence?

The Politics of Ambiguity

'Unity' is an ambiguous term. In line with its semantic allusions to encompassment, unity is expansive, open to more than one interpretation. Since it does not have one obvious meaning, the word is 'uncertain' when standing on its own. Ambiguity nonetheless differs profoundly from vacuousness. The word does not mean 'everything and nothing'. There are both constraints on possible interpretations, and very particular interpretations actually at play and in tension. For most people unity does not carry a 'neutral' tinge but the semantic prosodies (associations) are both negative and positive, adding yet another layer of ambiguity that can be politically exploited.

Language is contingent on context and the best way to find out what unity means and is in a particular setting is to trace its use. To understand the 'lived' reality of language means it has to be effectively 'decenter[ed] onto other dimensions and other registers' (Deleuze and Guattari 1987: 8). One of the key projects of the book is to decentre unity onto the political realm. The argument I make is as follows: unity has a political life of its own. It not only has a long political history in Rwanda and the region, but it is a politicized idea in the current public discourse that performs political work. More importantly, unity as a political idea cannot be divorced from unity as it is understood by people outside of officialdom, or from unity as deployed in the discourses and practices of transitional justice. The political sphere fundamentally shapes any action in these arenas.

As suggested above, unity's ambiguity is particularly productive politically and has been appropriated many times by centres of power, in Africa and beyond, simultaneously cast as for the social good and appropriated for respective political ends. After independence in the 1960s, African leaders have deployed discourses of unity as a way to legitimize the erection of one-party states and a way to excuse the erosion of political space. With the distinctive connotations attached to 'unity' as a state-sponsored ideology, *ubumwe* is reminiscent of the Slovak word *jednota*, which to this day carries a strong tang of pompous collectivist ideals, disciplined bodies[4] and the grandiose propaganda of the communist regime. Rwanda's context is of course unique – the official meaning of unity here arises in the securitized, tense environment of a post-genocide society. But what is perhaps similar is that in the public sphere *ubumwe* is not an obscure word but a charged notion, along with its opposite – division. In fact, it is against this prominent notion of division and divisionism that a specific and powerful political notion of unity arises.

Unity as deployed in Rwanda's public realm is a fundamentally politicized word, not a neutral term. Yet in the international arena of post-conflict reconstruction and peace building, unity represents what Renner (2014) called (in reference to reconciliation) an 'empty universal' – 'a vague yet powerful social ideal'. Unity building arises as an 'essentially defined concept' (Nordstrom 1997: 115) and one a priori defined as positive. It is knowledge 'always already there' in certain social epistemologies, knowledge from which technical questions arise (e.g., How to best build unity?) but which is not questioned itself. The findings presented here will unsettle this notion. The languages and projects of unity are fundamentally politically ambiguous, and it is only through the observation of their concrete deployments and enactions that we can come to learn about the type of social and political work that these perform.

Rather than as a challenge, I take ambiguity as a central opening to analysis, exploring the productiveness and political uses of both unity's semantic latitude and semantic prosodies. I want to see how political actors borrow from and dialogue with 'alternative' interpretations, layer and fragment the notion themselves through their discourse, policy and practice, how they play off the wider unquestioned (and positive) associations of the term, and how, despite the 'multiplicities of unity', a very specific official version nonetheless results. Drawing on communications and organizations studies literature, and taking inspiration from Eisenberg's (1984) influential concept and findings regarding 'strategic ambiguity', the present research will show that 'unity's multiplicities' are far from a paradox, but rather a 'working tension', a dynamics that operates in particular ways and to particular interests.

A 'Politography' of Unity

This is not a book 'about' Rwanda, and yet it is. It studies the way in which a government is trying to create a Rwanda, it is about the imagined unit(y) and how this is produced from the centre and applied at the margins. It is about a project of 'rooting' identity in a place that is in flux and whose history is in dispute. Rather than carefully observing a given community, I trace and observe actors who nurture an idea, what this idea means to them, how they transmit it to others in disparate corners in disparate social situations, how the idea transforms into policy practice and action and, finally, how it is performed.

Hence the study is best understood as one 'grounded in a topic and a process rather than a place' (Nordstrom 1997: 10). Topicality as an organizing principle is well expounded by Nordstrom's 'ethnography of a warzone' (1997) or Crewe and Harrison's 'ethnography of aid' (1998). Processuality on the other hand is perhaps best captured in Malkki's (1995) study of the construction of political subjectivity, collective identity and historicity in the context of displacement, or in Ferguson's (1999) 'ethnography of decline' on the Zambian copperbelt. Topic- and process-centered approaches seem especially well suited to conflict-affected settings as they divert attention from certainties and taken-for-granted unities ('The Nuer', 'The Banyarwanda'), transforming the task instead into one of trying to capture the uncertain and contested process of their creation. In the context of conflict and war – both being social disruptors and transformation 'intensifiers' – this approach has been employed by Sharon Hutchinson (1996) in her study of the Nuer of Southern Sudan. Hutchinson has challenged Evans Pritchard's celebrated 1940 study of the Nuer, a classic of anthropology, on the grounds that it produces 'an illusion that Nuer culture and social life are somehow above history and beyond change'. Rather than focusing on 'unity, equilibrium and order' and 'things shared', Hutchinson's *Nuer Dilemmas* analysed 'confusion and conflict among the Nuer' and the 'conflicts of interest, perspective and power' among various sub-groups, thus 'call[ing] into question the very idea of "the Nuer"' (ibid.: 28–29). Hutchinson shows how money and commodification of values, war and the state fundamentally transformed Nuer communities.

Just like the Nuer of Southern Sudan, Rwandan societies have undergone profound change over the past centuries – ever greater incorporation into a centralized polity, colonial encounter, capitalism, genocide, mass outmigrations, mass returns. These historical dynamics also brought changes to Rwanda as a unit(y) (Vansina 2004; Des Forges 2011). An approach emphasizing process thus seems sensible not only in a divided, post-genocide society, but also a social geography where historically, just as in many other places, peripheries were often forcibly incorporated into the centralizing and expansionary central kingdom, ruled by the Nyiginya dynasty (C. Newbury 1988; D. Newbury 2001; Pottier 2002).

A unity cannot be conceptualized without the unifier, or a polity without power. Even on a small territory such as that of Rwanda nation is not something that is 'ever there' but rather an unstable and evolving political project linked to the (expansionary) state (Vansina 2004; Des Forges 2011; Newbury 1988). Hence rather than 'a people', the book takes 'labor in production of a people' as its topic. By looking at the social processes and agents involved, it approaches 'a people', 'unity' and 'reconciliation' as an enterprise. This means that it treats the appeals to 'unity of culture' as themselves contestable and political (e.g., 'we all speak Kinyarwanda, we are one').

Approaching unity building as a political project and process might tempt us to narrate it against the tension between homogeneity and difference. The stress on things shared, after all, clashes with the diversity, disruption and movement on the ground. This tension, present in all state-directed social engineering projects has now been well explored, most prominently by James Scott (1998). Scott's close-up study of the top-down revealed homogenization as a key project of the 'high modernist' state, whose ways of seeing and search for order and legibility fundamentally undermine the local, contingent ways of knowing and being he called *métis*.

Rwanda is a high modernist state par excellence, and what could be a better social engineering project to demonstrate the tensions between homogenization and difference than unity building? The reality, of course, is more complex. The simple opposition between state and society, and the logic of homogeneity versus diversity, do not hold up to scrutiny. As will be shown, even the project of unity itself is not 'one' and multiplicities and fragmentation are built into it. At the same time, the state, far from 'hovering' above society is embedded within it in multiple ways and borrows from its cultural registers (see also Purdeková 2013). Finally, the simple opposition between the local as a 'site of resistance' and the state as a 'site of control' is oversimplified. Yet, despite the blurring of boundaries, a very specific version of 'unity' is asserted, at different levels and in different social situations; it is the purpose of this book to explain how and why this happens.

Since the (re)fashioning of a social whole is fundamentally a political project, what follows is a 'politography' of sorts – not a full political ethnography but a study 'with an ethnographic aspect' (Ferguson 1999: 21). Altering the name is not only a way to emphasize the difference. More importantly, dropping the 'ethno-' prefix but keeping the 'graphy' is a way to combine the useful methodological aspects of ethnography emphasizing participant observation, thick description and the actors' point of view with the very different ontological focus on the 'making' of unities, without presuming that these do in fact exist (that there is, literally, an identity). Polity refers to a political form (and formation) of a union, whereas ethnos refers to a people, a nation, a community.

With regard to key terms, the reader might still wonder why the more familiar term of 'nation building' should not suffice, instead of unity building. I have previously carried out such more conventional analysis exploring the Rwandan project as a 'state-to-nation' nation building, exploring its inbuilt paradoxes of inclusion and exclusion, as well as de- and re-ethnicization (see Purdeková 2008a). The nationalism framework is useful but ultimately limiting. For one, nation building encloses us within a very specific debate on collective identities (where Anderson's 'imagined communities' or Brubaker's notion of 'groupness' undoubtedly offer key and innovative analytical tools) and it presupposes a very specific notion of unity as nationalist or cross-ethnic loyalty. But such pre-filled meaning precludes our understanding of alternatives and additional, even conflicting layers of meaning. The frame of unity has a much stronger analytical purchase. Unity is a broader term than nation and cannot simply be equated with de-ethnicization. The term directs us to imaginaries and production of 'social wholes' and 'togetherness' whatever form these may take. Focus on unity thus allows for a richer, more emplaced and closer look at the project unfolding in Rwanda. Most importantly, unity – *ubumwe* – is the term of choice on the ground. It derives from the word *umwe* or 'one', hence its literal translation is 'oneness'. In contrast, *igihugu cyacu* (our nation, country) is most often used in reference to development (as in *kubaka igihugu* or building our country), patriotism (*rukundo rw'igihugu*), or when underlining the oneness of the people of Rwanda by highlighting that they have *igihugu cimwe* (one country), *umurima umwe* (one language) or *umuco umwe* (one culture). These expressions are part of the broader unity-building discourse but do not represent it in its totality. At its core, *ubumwe* is tied more to popular expressions such as *twese hamwe* (all of us together) or the greeting *turi kumwe* (we are together). Unity is fundamentally the oneness of 'being together' and it is the aim of the project to find out what sort of 'togetherness' the state promotes.

Importantly, the present book cannot and does not explore all there is to learn about unity in contemporary Rwanda. Nor is it an exhaustive study of 'multiplicities of unity' – it does not cover in sufficient depth alternative 'imaginings' of unity on the ground. The full 'life' of *ubumwe* and its appropriations by political actors will require further historical and ethnographic work. The key aim here is to uncover the broad driving forces, the key logics, and some of the core imaginaries underlying the official unity-building project. The official project is indeed key since the 'policing of unity' and the rallying of people around a particular notion of unity makes the notion of 'separate', 'non-state', 'grassroots' or 'genuine' field of action a problematic proposition. Though multiple initiatives are initiated outside of the state framework, the search for the 'truly grassroots' obscures the way in which actors at all levels have to negotiate power and the state in their daily lives.

The Politics of Depoliticization

Though transitional justice entered academic 'fieldhood' only recently (Bell 2009), it has already produced voluminous scholarship investigating the ways in which societies struggle with a history of injustice in the context of regime transition. It was in post-1989 Central and Eastern Europe where a very specific query arose: 'How should societies undergoing political transition deal with a past of violence and human rights abuse?' Besides this specific historical context, transitional justice was narrowly constituted as a legal discipline and has largely remained 'abstract[ed] from its political context' (Thomson and Nagy 2010: 12). Only recently has the legal stronghold started to be 'de-colonized' by permeation of other disciplines, including anthropology and political science (Bell 2009: 6) slowly producing a 'thicker' understanding (McEvoy 2007).

The evolving field needs to continue moving beyond regime transition (e.g., South Africa, post-Soviet Europe, El Salvador), making its considerations and solutions relevant to contexts of community violence (e.g., Rwanda, Burundi) and political environments where the state and the regime type have not been fundamentally reworked, what has recently been coined as the problem of 'new beginnings' (Anders and Zenker 2014). In such contexts, political analysis is indeed indispensable and needs to revolve around a unique set of questions, among them: What happens when projects predicated on 'transformation' (such as unity building after conflict) are executed by political regimes that embody continuity (in form) rather than change? What happens to social projects revolving around 'inclusion' (the new rules and forms of social togetherness, new imaginaries of belonging) when these are executed by a regime that constrains political space? More broadly, what is the relationship between political process (of regime production and reproduction) and national-level social processes such as unity building? Does one 'shape' the other, are they co-constituted, or is the causality more complex? Further research is necessary if we are to successfully answer these questions. In the context of Rwanda, political analysis of reconciliation has been limited almost exclusively to *gacaca* trials and courts (Thomson 2011; Ingelaere 2009; Chakravarty 2014), omitting key aspects of the broader process and thus precluding more integrative analysis.

The present project aims to at least partially fill the gaps in knowledge identified above by politicizing or else 're-politicizing' our reading of Rwanda's unity-building process. There are diverse ways in which one can launch such analysis, but three are especially useful for the context of Rwanda

– to critically investigate the depoliticized language enveloping the 'unity and reconciliation' activities, to open to view the genealogies of unity building as a political tool in Rwanda and the wider region, and finally, to consider the appropriations of unity building and transitional justice processes for political ends. In each case, the linkages between social process and political regime will be explored.

In the broadest sense, politicization refers to making the underlying political forces visible. Their invisibility has political implications in itself. Discursive exclusion of topics such as nationalism, unity building and justice out of this sphere makes these arenas more open to manipulation (without repercussion) and pushes these processes out of the 'contestation sphere' – the space where people can legitimately challenge, criticize and rework a process or an institution – thus indirectly aiding the consolidation of authoritarian rule.

Rwanda's multiple unity and reconciliation activities – the *gacaca*, *ingando*, *itorero*, *abunzi*, *ubusabane*, to name just a few – are invariably presented as traditional and as located close to the people – both conceptually and physically. Yet the traditionality label as well as the very framework of transitional justice through which these activities are often glanced are fundamentally depoliticizing, obscuring how these spaces double as platforms of control, governance and symbolic production of power.

The post-genocide production of neo-traditionality in Rwanda has to be placed in the wider context of resurgence and rather uncritical embrace of 'traditionality' in the sphere of reconciliation (for a recent critical analysis see Allen and Macdonald 2013; Allen 2010). Recourse to 'traditional' solutions or 'hybridized' processes (a combination of local and Western approaches) became popular in conflict-affected countries such as Sierra Leone, Rwanda and Uganda as it represented an antidote to the universalisms of development and promised to draw on more authentic sources. Rwanda is a perfect example of this phenomenon with tens of self-professedly 'home-grown' unity, reconciliation, justice and development activities springing up over the past ten years. Locally sourced activities adapted to specific and contemporary needs are certainly required. However, as will be shown, in the case of Rwanda 'traditionality' is imposed on communities from above and the very label of 'traditional' performs both intentional and unintentional political work.

Politicization also involves uncovering the dependence of unity approaches on the formation and types of regimes that instituted them, and the subsequent political uses and utility of the languages of unity. At the macro level, the pathways to peace and the nature of political/regime transition determines the type of unity-building strategies that result. In South Sudan, decades of civil war resulted in secession but the war has also created profound internal divisions, not least about the very idea of 'unity' with the

North (Johnson 2003; Deng 1995). In Eritrea, the struggle for independence from Ethiopia has fostered a distinct oppositional unity – cohesion sourced from the fight against an outsider (Tronvoll 1998). In Burundi, on the other hand, a negotiated settlement between an incumbent and rebel movements, and the resultant power sharing, have produced a distinct version of unity building based on ethnic accommodation (see Vandeginste 2014 for a detailed description). Rwanda presents a different macro context yet again, one where central power was captured through military victory by an exile political front and its armed wing, and hence where fewer compromises had to be made in pushing a dominant vision of unity through. The result is an approach to identity politics that is distinctly 'abolitionist' (Purdeková 2009; as in literally putting an end to something through official decree) or, in a more recent formulation, 'integrationist' (Vandeginste 2014), focused on suppression of difference and cultivation of nationalist loyalty.

The politics of unity has a long pedigree in Rwanda and is grounded in particular production and interpretation of the country's history. The early Rwandan historiography (from the colonial period up to the First Republic), exemplified by the work of Abbé Alexis Kagame and Jacques Maquet, has elaborated a distinctly court-centric view of the past, a centralized and unified picture of the pre-colonial kingdom (Pottier 2002), a picture that has re-emerged since the genocide. Despite evidence of very discordant local readings of the past (Chakravarty 2014; Watkins and Jessee 2014), the story of pre-colonial unity constitutes the core of the official history today and underpins the policy of de-ethnicization (Purdeková 2008a and 2008b). But the notion of unity has also been reappropriated as an explicit political platform by the Tutsi exiles, fleeing Rwanda in successive waves since 1959. Both the Rwandan Alliance for National Unity (RANU), created in 1979, and the Rwanda Patriotic Front (RPF) into which RANU was transformed in 1987 highlighted Rwandan unity. The political platform of the newly created RPF, the so-called '8 Point Plan', included as the most important among its points the promise of 'inter-ethnic unity'. An RPF soldier recites an exile mobilization song with nostalgia: *Humura Rwanda nziza, humura ngaho ndaje!* (Don't be afraid good Rwanda, don't be afraid I am coming), *Isoko y'ubumwe na mahoro* (The source of unity and peace) (Stearns 2011: 75).

The broad outlines of the new 'consensus on history' date to the politics of the Tutsi diaspora but they were defined more clearly and formally after the genocide. Following the establishment of the transitional government in July 1994, the *Guverinoma y'Ubumwe bw'Abanyarwanda* or 'The Government of Rwandan Unity', grassroots consultations were held in 1996/97 where people across Rwanda were asked to name the main reasons for Rwandan 'disunity'. Later came the more decisive 'Urugwiro Meetings' at the Office of the President (May 1998 – March 1999) where the discursive consensus was finally cemented by eminent personalities of the state – political authorities, religious figures and academics, among them the RPF founder Tito Rutaremara and Professor Paul Rutayisire (Director of the Centre for Conflict Management).

The aim of the high-level meetings was to arrive at 'a consensus on the priority programmes and issues necessary for reconstruction of Rwanda as a country' (ibid.), the first agenda item being the 'rebuilding of national unity'. Two documents exist summarizing the meetings, one specifically dealing with the 'Unity of Rwandans' (*Ubumwe Bw'Abanyarwanda*).[5] Briefly, it was settled that 'before Europeans' arrival, the country was characterized by unity' (Office of the President of the Republic 1999a: 11), that 'the unity was for all Rwandans: Hutu, Tutsi and Twa' (Office of the President of the Republic 1999b: 4) and that 'White People' were the usurpers of that unity. 'When Europeans came, the seed of hatred and disagreement started being sown among Rwanda's children' (Office of the President of the Republic 1999a: 10). In the last chapter, we learn that 'the Society, RPF *Inkotanyi*' (ibid.: 12) is set to restore this (merely dormant) unity. This narrative has formed the core of the 'official history' propagated ever since.

But unity discourses have been utilized elsewhere in the region and beyond. Under the successive Tutsi-dominated regimes in post-independence Burundi, talk of unity (also *ubumwe*) served effectively to paper over divisions and concentrations of power in the hands of a minority (Lemarchand 1994; Daley 2006). President Jean-Baptiste Bagaza (1976–1987) stressed national unity and banned all references to ethnicity. Bagaza's successor Pierre Buyoya (1987–1993) has further stepped up the rhetoric under his 'National Unity Policy'. A Charter of National Unity was drafted and adopted by popular referendum on February 5 1991, the day itself remaining a national holiday. In addition, 'every educated person had to engage in lengthy propaganda sessions to explain to the farmers the notion of unity' (Uvin 1999: 261). A unity monument was erected in Bujumbura, a unity anthem composed, even 'unity caps' went on sale (Naniwe-Kaburahe 2008: 150). As opposed to Rwanda, the talk of *ubumwe* under Burundi's Buyoya-led regime was accompanied by a move to political liberalization, which was as promising as it was short-lived. In 1993, shortly after the inaugural democratic elections, the first ever Hutu leader to assume the presidential post was assassinated, ushering in a fifteen-year-long civil war.

The distinct vagueness and yet political expediency of *ubumwe* has been immortalized in a small monument at the centre of a roundabout in the Burundian town of Rushubi, in Bujumbura Rural. Alongside Prince Louis Rwagasore, the 'hero of independence' and the assassinated President-elect Melchior Ndadaye, the 'hero of democracy', I noted a quote on unity by President Pierre Buyoya: 'The unity of the Barundi is the greatest wealth and it cannot be replaced if lost', read the plaque (*Ubumwe bw'barundi ni itunga ridasumbwa kandi nidashumbushwa*). The words today stand both as a paradox, since unity was all but lost shortly after this pronouncement, and as a testament to the ever-inventive survival of unity as a political ideal-cum-tool.

Whether couched in nationalist terms as in Burundi and Rwanda or ideological terms as in socialist Somalia (1969–1991) where mention of ethnicity, clan or lineage was forbidden and effigies of 'tribalism' burned under Siad Barre's rule (Lewis 1988; Besteman 1999), unity has been cast as a progressive form of belonging opposed to and replacing the atavistic loyalties of region, class or kinship. In all of these cases it also proved no more than surface-level engineering that all but silenced continued and multiple exclusions from power, some of which operated along the very lines discredited through official ideology (see e.g., Lemarchand 1994; Lyons and Samatar 1995; Besteman 1999 and 1996). In the case of Somalia, however, Besteman argues that the effects were more profound yet: 'The law that redefined bodies and identities as Somali by eradicating the recognition of racial, status, or kinship distinctions was a first step in establishing state dominance over people's actions, discourse, and interactions' (Besteman 1996: 589). The result was a more pervasive social control of everyday life.

This type of political past has certainly given 'unity' discourses, which are read against historical precedents, an unpopular undertone, a tag of suspiciousness, paradoxically even triggering notions of exclusion at the same time as they discursively revolve around the very idea of inclusion, integration and cohesion. In other words, there is a historical pattern pointing to the usefulness of political discourses of unity, as well as to the limits of their acceptance. This also suggests that unity building has to be placed within the wider context of 'the moral discredit incurred by the state' in Africa (Lemarchand 1992) and incurred precisely through such practices of inversion.

A growing body of more contemporary research demonstrates how governing elites, through the use of the state, can appropriate unity and reconciliation processes to other-than-stated ends. Work by Alexander, McGregor and Ranger (2000) and Alexander and McGregor (2006) on Zimbabwe, Bozzoli on South Africa (2006), Longman and Rutagengwa on Rwanda (2004 and 2006) and Tronvoll, Schaefer and Alemu on Ethiopia (2009) show this specifically with regard to memory. Their studies demonstrate how:

> the state through its organs, or through the ruling party, [is] intent on shaping memory to its own vision and interests [producing] political constructions that were not only inaccurate but alienating to the people whose history they were meant to represent. A close look at these cases suggests that the provision of an accurate historical account is at best secondary to the transformative goals of the politics of state. (Bay and Donham 2006: 13)

Within the context of post-genocide Rwanda, additional work on appropriations of memory and crafting of useful histories include Pottier

(2002), Lemarchand (2009) and Hintjens (2009). While these works focus primarily on the new 'narrative closure', the present book tries to delve beyond these well-researched topics and explore in detail how the whole unity and reconciliation process (from concept and policy to execution in activities) is politicized and what ends it comes to serve as a result. The transformative drive of the Rwandan government can hardly be overstated and, as will be shown, unity building is certainly subsumed to the goal of creating a Rwandan citizen best suited to fit the exigencies of authoritarian development.

The notion of political 'appropriation' has to be used carefully though – not all effects that result from so-called 'unity and reconciliation' activities that might be incongruous with their official identity are the result of 'planned' manipulation by government-cum-state machinery. As Ferguson (1990) has observed with regards to the development projects in Lesotho, 'outcomes of planned social interventions can end up coming together into powerful constellations of control that were never intended and in some cases never even recognized' but are nonetheless 'the more effective for being "subjectless"' (ibid.: 19). Ferguson found that the machinery of international development can be instrumental in 'expanding the exercise of a particular sort of state power while simultaneously exerting a powerful depoliticising effect' (ibid.: 21). James Ferguson's work is an important starting point, but it needs to be modified if it is to explain and document how a process generally perceived as 'well-meaning' interlaces with etatization, control and surveillance, or the consolidation of non-contestation in Rwanda. For the process in Rwanda is one that combines both intention and 'instrument effect', and infrastructural and embodied power in addition to 'subjectless discourse' (each of these three spheres of power will be discussed in separate chapters).

The Arts of Presence(ing): The State in Society

Contrary to the dominant model of the African state centred around weakness and fragility (Herbst 1996 and 2000; see also Menkhaus 2010; Bertocchi and Guerzoni 2010; Sogge 2009), the Rwandan state comprises working and sprawling formal institutions; it makes its presence felt in multiple ways, in people's daily lives, and at the most local level. As such, it falls entirely outside the evolving debates on 'the crumbling institutional environment of contemporary Africa' (Meagher 2012: 1074), the 'retreat of the state', alternative systems of order (Bierschenk and Olivier de Sardan 1997; Titeca and de Herdt 2011) and 'hybrid governance' (Hagmann and Péclard 2010; Menkhaus 2008; Raeymaekers et al. 2008; Boege et al. 2008). It opens inquiry of a new kind, questioning the causal relation between state density, formal and informal institutional infrastructure and presence on the one hand, and developmental outcomes, stability and social justice on the other. It equally shifts the state-building debate from discussion of challenges to such projects amidst violence or non-recognition (Smaker and Johnson 2014; Hills 2014; Menkhaus 2008), or the limits and unintended consequences of international state-building paradigms (Curtis 2013; Autesserre 2010) to the study of meaning and effects of 'home-grown' and illiberal state 'reach and overreach' (Ingelaere 2014). The book thus hopes to add to discussions on the nature of the post-colonial state in Africa by exploring a unique case that diverges starkly from the dominant paradigm and mainstream debates on weakness, failure and collapse of the state in Africa (see Migdal 1988; Reno 1998; Zartman 1995 for works in this tradition).

Importantly, the notion of a 'strong' state should not connote a state's capability to deliver on its social transformation goals; it refers to a dense and intricate structure exerting a variegated presence in people's everyday lives, resulting in a complex framework of social control. Such definition leaves any effects, whether positive or negative, open to question and investigation. It does beg the obvious query though: Is such a state uniquely capable of delivering the tasks it sets out for itself?

The Rwandan state has consolidated gradually, and it is meaningful to argue that the genocide presents another important watershed in the trajectory of state consolidation. It was in the mid-eighteenth century when the Nyiginya kingdom was 'beset by serious military challenges' (Des Forges 2011: 6) that the king Rujugira introduced 'social armies' positioned at the borders, which triggered not only expansion of the state into peripheral areas but also its institutional development. Later under kings Rwabugiri and Musinga (1896–1931) 'the state greatly expanded, as well as deepened', becoming 'extraordinarily complex' (ibid.: 11) even if not uniformly imposed. While the Rwandan state has been historically relatively intricate and centralized when compared to other states in Africa, we witness greater etatization of society after the 1994 genocide. There are three key and interconnected reasons for the 'densification' of the Rwandan state at this historical juncture. The destruction and political shifts accompanying the genocide ushered in reconstruction and the 'application' of state in most arenas of life. The existential insecurity on the back of which the regime has been built has also opened space for further securitization and increased surveillance of local life. This tendency has been strengthened further by the developmentalist outlook of the current government, its accent on rupture with the past and the wholesale transformation of Rwandan society in most arenas of life including the household economy, agriculture, political values, coexistence, health and hygiene, among others. The process of decentralization initiated in 2000 also contributed. It represented a 'profound and relatively rapid institutional change' whereby 'the role of the local level has been expanded to an unprecedented degree in Rwandan history' (Chemouni 2014: 248). The fact that the state has been de facto captured by one political party aids etatization, though it is not a unique factor in the post-genocide period.

Importantly, the state 'densification' occurs despite the official abolition of the previously lowest administrative unit of the *nyumbakumi* and despite the fact that a well-known state activity – the *umuganda* community works – reappeared after the genocide in a less intense form. These developments have to be placed into a wider context of increased local devolution and multiple new activities and platforms of very local state presence, explored fully in Chapter Four. A number of important questions then arise: What does it mean that Rwandan society has become increasingly etatized? How does the benevolence of the rationale ('serving the population') square up with the effects on the ground? Finally, what lessons flow from this for the three grand projects of our time – state building, peace building and nation building?

The state is a key asset to the government in the execution of the *ubumwe* project, and is so at a very local and tangible level. But besides simply helping to 'unroll' activities and programmes, in fact through this very unrolling, it further increases its presence in the lives of ordinary Rwandans, with important political effect. The state after all is not only an institution 'substantiate[d] in people's lives in the sphere of everyday practices' (Sharma and Gupta 2006: 11), it is such day-to-day stateness that makes politics feasible: 'At one level, [state] proceduralism is so thoroughly commonplace and ordinary to be [considered] uninteresting ... At another level, it is these putatively technical and unremarkable practices that render tenable the political tasks of state formation, governance and the exercise of power ... they provide important clues to understanding the micropolitics of state work, how state authority and government operate in people's daily lives' (ibid.). Observation of 'mundane stateness' has certainly proved key to my own understanding of the nature of power and politics in post-genocide Rwanda. In my attempt to understand the interface between unity building and power/state making, I observed the presence of the state everywhere I went – on the streets of Kigali, in the permanent structure of the Nyakabanda cell office, or in a transient rural-based activity.

Despite the availability of empirically rich case studies exploring state-society relations in Africa (Leonardi 2011 and 2013; Ingelaere 2010 and 2014; Lefort 2010; West 2005; Bierschenk and Olivier de Sardan 2003; among others) one struggles to find a more integrated analysis focused specifically on state presence, its perceptions by people and its effects. Even anthologies explicitly on the anthropology of the state (i.e., Sharma and Gupta 2006; Das and Poole 2004) fail to explore state 'presencing' techniques and their links to governance and control (for recent exceptions exploring surveillance in the African context, see McGregor 2013 on Zimbabwe and Bozzini 2011 on Eritrea).

With regards to the anthropology of power[6] and politics,[7] a number of recent works have provided useful insights into the everyday negotiation and interpretation of the state, power and national belonging (e.g., Wedeen 2008 and 1999; Mbembe 2001; Navarro-Yashin 2012). The anthropology of the political can mean many things from studying politicians 'in their natural habitat' or 'face to face' (Schatz 2009: 1) or observing the operation of bureaucracies or special units 'up close' (Bierschenk and Olivier de Sardan 2014) or it might involve the project of exploring the 'instance' and insertion of power and the state in the space of the everyday. Anthropological methods are indeed irreplaceable for all these tasks. They are 'uniquely positioned to explore informal dimensions of power (Abeles 2004), hidden faces of power (Lukes 1974; Gaventa 1980), ... ostensibly inconspicuous resistance to power (Scott 1990), [or] ambiguous effects of [the] power exercise (Wedeen 1999) (Kubik, in Schatz 2009)'. Observation and participation allow for reading of behaviour in its context and can uncover the way in which power is mapped onto relations, spatial arrangements, procedures and protocols, moods or speech.

The present book uses these methods to study the interface between the Rwandan state and society, paying attention to the ways in which power and the state materialize on the ground, and to what effect. The limits and subversion of state power will also be explored. As will be shown, power does not only work through 'physical' presence, but more broadly, through the perceived potential of such presence. The book thus calls for a 'thicker' reading of the state, one that reaches beyond the official structure and encompasses the varied infrastructures of its power, including spaces nominally outside of its reach, its 'overspilling' effects, and the perceptions of its presence and control.

Ingando Camps: Separation and Transformation

A distinctive feature of the unity and reconciliation process is the multitude of activities sanctioned in its name. But whereas the community *gacaca* courts have captured the attention of the world and engendered academic debates, few people know of and even fewer people have studied the official initiatives (over a dozen in number) created under the banner of unity and reconciliation. Nonetheless it is precisely these activities that might be uniquely positioned to help us understand the exigent project of social transformation unfolding in Rwanda with all its discrepancies and paradoxes. The present book places special accent on one among these activities: the *ingando* camps, retreats offering informal 'civic' education to different segments of the population in the name of building Rwandanness. The book offers the first in-depth study of the camps as well as the wider project of shaping a new form of political subjectivity and membership into which they offer an irreplaceable insight.

The *ingando* camps are part and parcel of an intense 'civic education' drive, an initiative into which the government has invested heavily since the genocide. The initiative centres on building a new Rwandan citizen or *Umunyarwanda* and revolves around rupture with the past and alignment with the current needs of the development-centred state. Rwanda is perhaps unique in today's Africa in terms of the sheer scope and ambition of the political education project, the wholesale deployment of informal, often camp-based education said to build patriotism and a sense of being Rwandan, and easing integration into the rules and logic of the RPF-led Rwanda. *Ingando* reaches the diaspora where camps are organized in countries with sizeable Rwandan migrant populations such as Belgium and India. Most recently, the *ingando* model has been vastly expanded and decentralized to the smallest of administrative levels through the introduction of the *Itorero ry'Igihugu* (The National Academy) education programme (approved in 2007 and launched in 2009). Hundreds of thousands of Rwandans have already passed through *ingando* and *itorero*, only further showing that the activities are hardly negligible, whether from the viewpoint of ambition or actual reach.

The use of camps for purposes of control, separation and transformation has a long history on the African continent, and of course beyond it as well. Searching for other exemplars of political camps aimed in one way or another at 'transformation', one quickly notes just how often the camp has been used as a very modern and collective technology of power. From the Mau Mau 'rehabilitation' camps in late colonial Kenya (Elkins 2000 and 2005) and FRELIMO's re-education camps in late 1970s and 1980s Mozambique (Manning 1998; Sumich 2011; Nordstrom 1997), to more recent examples of Uganda's *Chaka Mchaka* political education camps and the *Kyankwanzi* Academy, or indeed further afield to South Korea's *Hanawon* or 'House of Unity' for the *saetomin* (new settlers) from North Korea (Southcott 2011), the examples abound. These diverse instances are yet to be tied together through a proper comparative analysis. Such analysis should certainly be pursued as the camp proves one of the most potent examples of 'social ordering', even as it places in order the imagined 'matter out of place' (Malkki 1995, referring to refugees). Camps such as *ingando* emblematize the dominant form of state-led social engineering today, its accent on immobilization, its drive for legibility, homogeneity and control, and its uses of formal and informal education to foster not only a sense of collective belonging but also a specific sense of self.

In Africa, camps have been mostly studied in the contexts of displacement. There is now a vast literature on refugee camps, IDP sites, transit camps or regroupment sites. Much less attention has been afforded to the distinct type of 'confined spatiality' studied here – the political education, re-education and reintegration camp, the use of camps not primarily for physical control and separation, but rather transformation and social engineering. Separation and control afforded by 'confined spatialities' are certainly useful and utilized in camps such as *ingando*, but they are means rather than ends. In a reversal, where the refugee camp revolves around the production of non-citizens and represents a space of exclusion, camps such as *ingando*, far from signalling spaces of sovereign 'abandon' (Agamben 1998) are instead spaces of 'intense application' – institutions using concentrated efforts to produce a particular citizen/subject/member. Despite being about a particular form of 'incorporation' rather than exclusion, I hope to show that this type of camp is as much a 'nomos of the modern' (ibid.) as refugee camps are. Refugee camps might represent spaces of exception, exclusion and production of bare life (though ultimately, in no more than a stylized form) but camps such as *ingando* reflect as powerfully on modern sovereignty, this time on forms of 'sovereign inclusion' (an idea further explored in Chapter 9).

The study of government-organized camps should also offer unique insight into the political uses and political dimensions of space-time dislocation, liminality and simulation. Within the context of Rwanda specifically, the camps offer insights into the government's accent on 'mindset change' and fashioning of the ideal citizen, which lie at the heart of its governance. The camps also bring forth discussions on the state's strategic dissimulations and politics of characterization. In addition to this, the different strategies of unity building interlock in the space of *ingando* and the camps also allow insight into the important uses of spatiality, symbolism and enaction to achieve desired ends.

The book is thus also an attempt to revive debates on liminality. The focus on contemporary, state-directed and collective rites of passage offers an opportunity to explore certain questions afresh: What can the profoundly political use of encamped spaces tell us about the liminal? Is the liminal ever outside power and politics? In which sense, if at all, is liminality an 'interstructural' space? Fundamentally, as I hope to show, *ingando* camps lend a fascinating insight into the ways in which liminality is harnessed by governments for the purposes of change by suspending the familiar and dislodging a person from routine in an isolated setting of a total institution. But change is not what such stylized enactions are solely 'about'. *Ingando* are ultimately about the reproduction of political power.

In fact, it is a broader goal of this book to demonstrate the multifaceted consolidation and reproduction of the current political system. Increasingly, rich empirically-based studies show how Rwandans are narrating alternatives to accepted versions of history (Chakravarty 2014; Watkins and Jessee 2014) and defying policies imposed from above (Van Damme, Ansoms and Baret 2014; Thomson 2013 and 2011). The focus here is different as the book seeks to understand how political power seeks to entrench itself despite or perhaps alongside these divergences and resistances, through both expected and less expected avenues – linguistic practices of the regime, the infrastructure and presence of the state, proliferation of platforms and activities and participation in these, as well as spatio-temporal, symbolic and performative dimensions of camps. Unity itself is a potent symbolic device for narrating and ushering such reproduction – not despite, but because of its ambiguity. In fact, ambiguity itself emerges as a key tool of manoeuvre, not only on behalf of the state but also for those who try to navigate it.

The book does not only demonstrate broad 'politicization' where yet another outwardly benign project comes to serve other than stated aims and interests of power, as Ferguson (1990) has demonstrated with regards to development or Carrier and Klantschnig (2012) with reference to drug control. It hopes to add value by its careful tracing of the multiple levels and concrete instances through which reproduction of power takes place, by focusing on the play with potent images, the 'sanctioning' power of such images, their malleability and the multiplicity of uses to which they can be put and that defy and often directly counteract the positive connotations of the label. The book shows how the developmental and post-conflict paradigms open the space for and further justify the insertions of state into the social body, with the result of increased etatization, and how notions of unity, nation and cohesion aid in that process. The analysis will also explore the fundamental limits of state power thus produced, and the repercussions of this vis-à-vis social justice and peace.

All in all, the book will ask us to reassess and nuance our approach to state and state building in post-conflict and divided societies. The view of the state as a neutral service provider and guarantor of welfare needs to be abandoned for a more balanced and political conception. In other words, a shift is necessary from a technocratic conception of the Rwandan state as (whether successfully or unsuccessfully, or to what degree) giving, producing and promising public good to a more complete conception of state that is also (whether successfully or unsuccessfully, or to what degree) extractive, oppressing and erosive of trust, producing public bads as well as 'regime goods' through its framework of coercive *eu*topia[8] – the transformative rush to the 'good place' envisioned in the government's development plans and programmes and to which today all, including unity, must be subsumed.

Notes on Method: Sources and Sites

The present book draws on seven months of fieldwork carried out in Rwanda between March 2008 and April 2009. The book tries to open to view two hitherto under-studied spaces – the *ingando* re-education and reintegration camps, and the government commission tasked with 'unity and reconciliation'. While the significance of studying *ingando* has been explored above, the look at a key government actor is no less important. Thus far little if any political analysis draws on direct observation of the Rwandan government 'at work' and from the inside. The insider perspective unworks the conception of a state as a cohesive machinery and policy, even when the state is less than democratic and repressive, hence posing a seeming paradox between micro process and macro effect that the book will foreground and address. These two original empirical bases are carefully complemented with perspectives and views from other spaces and actors.

The research draws on a range of methods from observation to interviews, from informal discussions to questionnaires. Altogether, I gathered approximately 230 formal and informal interviews and questionnaires (160 interviews, 70 questionnaires) from a diverse set of people: participants at government-based 'unity and reconciliation' activities, government officials at different levels, NGOs, researchers, journalists, students as well as many other Rwandans I met during the main activity of fieldwork – the getting to and by – the constant and time-consuming search for places and access, and waiting. Perhaps unsurprisingly, I had some of the most insightful conversations while travelling and 'hanging around'.

Overall, the less structured was the encounter, the more open and forthcoming was the speaker. Equally, the fewer traces that remained of the encounter, the more openings it offered. As a rule, I refrained from audio recording, and quickly understood that less or no note taking eased tension and produced more insight, albeit at the cost of an imperfect 'trace'. Similarly, the fewer external elements that were introduced into the encounter, the less uncertainty and suspicion were produced. Because of this I tried (where possible) to source interpretation and translation from within the setting that I studied, and it is also for this reason that I at times forewent understanding completely in exchange for confidence.

Key data were undoubtedly drawn from participant observation, which offered rich contexts to words and actions. I had the opportunity to participate at multiple activities from *ingando* to *umuganda*, *ubusabane*, official genocide commemoration events, prison visits and more. At the Commission, I sat at planning, review, coordination meetings, or more informal happenings such as the entertainment of the Chinese donor delegation. But many more events proved key, from the 2008 state-organized protests, to participation at a 'Wedding Planning Committee'. As most researchers, I learned in unexpected places and from unconventional sources, from jokes, gestures, off-hand remarks, changes of mood, or seating arrangements. Official and unofficial learning blended into each other. Nonetheless, combining methods and different levels of 'structured' encounter was enlightening in itself. It modulated disclosure and offered insights into when, how and what people felt comfortable speaking about – these important insights are discussed in the next chapter.

The *ingando* camps form a key case study and hence much of my research has revolved around trying to understand these spaces from different perspectives and positions – from the inside and the outside, from participants, organizers and non-participants. I combined visits to camps and observation of lessons and activities with formal interviews, informal discussions, questionnaires, as well as primary and secondary materials. Almost all of the formal and informal interactions have involved a discussion of *ingando*, whether it was a central discussion point or one of many. I have spoken to past and present *ingando* organizers, participants of different backgrounds in terms of age, education, region, ethnicity, occupation and language, as well as diverse people in the government, NGOs and more. The responses of more than 110 participants from three types of *ingando* (for university entrants, ex-combatants and released prisoners) have been an especially rich source of information as have been the *ingando* visits.

In order to get a better understanding of *ingando* as a social event, I placed accent on gaining access to different types of *ingando*. The NURC only organized *ingando* for university entrants, which I visited three times, sitting through fourteen hours of class and participating in the closing graduation ceremony. A broader remit required negotiating access from three additional government institutions: The Ministry of Gender and Family Planning (MIGEPROF), The Community Work (TIG) Headquarters, and the Rwanda Demobilization and Reintegration Commission (RDRC). In the end, I was able to visit six different types of *ingando*, though never for more than two days at a time: five state-organized camps (for students, released prisoners, street children, youth ex-combatants and adult ex-combatants) and one non-state organized *ingando* (for Adventist youth). Importantly, the book in no sense offers a full depiction of *ingando* in all its forms. This is in part due to the nature of access and in part due to the occasional or even ad-hoc organization of the camps. Nevertheless, the study draws on a large amount of new information. There are two chapters dedicated exclusively to the camps, but moments and insights from *ingando* appear throughout the book.

Another key aspect of my fieldwork, mainly in the first three months, has been the observation of the work of the National Unity and Reconciliation Commission (NURC) up close, from the daily happenings at the office, internal meetings and meetings with other stakeholders and donors, to participation in activities organized by the commission. NURC was not only the gatekeeper to the field that I wanted to explore, it was also a key part of it, being the shaper and 'keeper' of the official discourse, and organizer of many activities. The insider perspective on NURC proved important but was not completely planned. I wanted to access *ingando* camps and other activities, not necessarily to be affiliated with the commission. After the first weeks in the field, marked by slow progress, the 'breakthrough' finally came.

The Director of Civic Education at NURC offered me entry – I was told that I could participate in different activities and visit *ingando* camps but in exchange I had to spend 'some days of the week' at the office 'working'. Though I agreed, no assignments were given to me. Initially, I did nothing for hours on end, feeling I was wasting my time. My first assignment was a comprehensive edit of a commissioner's master's thesis. This made me wonder whether it was really me who 'managed to enter' or whether it was them who managed to capture me.

Gradually, I sensed a transition. Even though I was not given any tasks and my official role was left undecided – at different points I was called 'cross-cutting staff', 'volunteer staff', a *stagiaire* and a researcher in residence – I seemed to have turned from an ambiguous figure to an expected and accepted 'member' and learned to understand and make the most of my NURC role by chatting with and shadowing its employees. My role felt frustrating at first, but ultimately proved to be a rich register of learning. I had the opportunity to travel across the country on 'official business', participate in activities, meetings and observe informal interactions. Equally, my careful attempts to extricate myself from the commission's oversight taught me valuable lessons about political control. Since my goal was to explore a wide range of perspectives, I had to carve my own research space at the same time as I could not afford to (as I quickly realized) break my relations with the Commission. Since the beginning of my fieldwork, I took off on independent trips and set up and conducted interviews with associations, NGOs, religious authorities, policy makers, local administrative officials, and importantly, *ingando* participants and participants at other activities outside the purview of NURC.

During my time in Rwanda, I befriended many commissioners who treated me warmly and often sought me out for a chat or told me to accompany them on travel, and yet I felt that a degree of institutional distrust surfaced intermittently and eroded the personal rapport and camaraderie that had been established. But this was, after all, a government institution and I was a researcher, and one that was gently but persistently disobedient to boot. The tension between the personal and official was undoubtedly present, and I felt I came to be embedded in something akin to, if not an outright bad-faith economy (Scheper-Hughes 1992: 111), then certainly a half-faith one where both sides were inevitably 'tricking each other'. I sensed my host had to maintain a level of (at times unwilling) helpfulness and I had to maintain a level of (at times unwilling) aloofness – placing a guard on my opinions and not being too assertive about my interests as this might raise suspicions. Ultimately, discreetness proves an asset as well as a cost; it is disclosure of opinions that officially marks you as a political friend, and it is the guardedness and unwillingness to 'pass judgements' that distances you and raises suspicions.

Even under a repressive regime, fieldwork is a complex tangle of facilitative as well as obstructive relationships (Hammersley and Atkinson 2007: 58). In Rwanda, institutions rarely refuse to let one in, they rather prefer to monitor research at close quarters. As a result, I had to learn how to meet controlling manoeuvres and indirect management with equally gentle and indirect ducking. Just as there was a clear gatekeeper in my case, there was an appointed 'overseer', a young NURC employee who was genuinely friendly but also genuinely interested in the details of my whereabouts and opinions: 'Purdeková, it is better if we always know where you are', he told me, 'it is for your safety. It would be better if you give me a list of organizations you see each week and when'. I also received lessons about 'protocol', including the very importance of protocol itself. 'It is better to follow protocol', I was disciplined softly but firmly on one occasion. My 'guardian' also urged me to submit the final report, first explained to me as 'an assessment on your stay, because people do not know what is in your head, if you do not write it, they might think there is something confidential'. Control might also work through 'suggestions' – the passing of comments insinuating that you know enough (e.g., 'Ah, by this time you know everything!' or 'You know enough, no?') or that your work is superfluous ('Purdeková, did you see the assessment we [NURC] did on *ingando* ... you did not even have to do your research!'). In Rwanda, you are 'let in' but there is a strong attempt to control what you learn (or at least diffuse). The fitting notion here is *être amené à la compréhension* – be almost literally 'led to understanding'.

My involvement with a government institution was certainly the ethical and methodological issue I struggled with the most. On the one hand, NURC was key to my study. It offered access to official unity and reconciliation activities, to learning about the policy and its implementation, about the setting up and carrying out of activities. On the other hand, this naturally brought trade-offs, dilemmas and complications. Would people automatically associate me with the government? Aware of this possibility, I tried to carefully manage my image. Most of my interviews were set up on my own and outside of the NURC context, with the obvious exception of conversations and discussions during the NURC-organized activities, interviews with NURC employees and government officials. Even when I mentioned that I was observing the work of NURC at close quarters (quite literally), I always tried to convey the message that I was an 'independent' researcher, protective of information and open to hearing all views.

Ingando camps clearly proved to be the most complicated research spaces. To get to *ingando*, I either went with NURC employees or, more often, travelled alone but still needed special permits from different government institutions. Eventually, however, I came to sincerely doubt that the 'permission' (or my insistence on 'independence') could add or subtract much in terms of informants' carefulness in what was ultimately a bounded, surveilled space run by government agents. I was a conspicuous presence who raised questions and suspicions, not all of which could be known to me or be defused by my brief discourse of assurances. Nonetheless, different types of participants were not equally guarded. The broader nature and meaning of such 'variability of voice' will be discussed in the next chapter.

During my time at NURC, I also struggled with the potential symbolic service I rendered the commission on various occasions. I often wondered what my presence at activities itself might accomplish – an additional leverage to support the weight of the government's words, a level of legitimization however transient and small? The notion that I was 'shadowing the Commission' was clearly misplaced when it came to public events. I was rarely in the commissioners' 'shadow', rather always visible, occasionally even seated in the first row during events. I understood that this symbolic service as well as the guard over my feelings and opinions was an inevitable trade-off. Most researchers experience it to some degree and a subset of them is directly asked to by their profession. As Rabinow (1977: 47) describes in his *Reflections on Fieldwork in Morocco*, a researcher struggles with the dictum of 'being [constantly] on one's guard', always ready to 'suspend disbelief'. In a way, this makes the researcher a 'non-person' or else a 'total persona', 'willing to enter into any situation as a smiling observer and carefully note down the specifics of the event' (ibid.). Like Scott (1985: xviii) I found such 'judicious neutrality' both useful and an 'enormous psychological burden' resulting in 'my own hidden transcript'.

Seeking informed consent was as important as it was complicated. Even the researcher's transparency and the participant's agreement do not defuse the wider political contexts that can still make this exchange problematic, and potentially costly. My own research was always preceded by an introduction – I told potential participants who I was, where I studied, what my topic was, why I found it important and why they were invited to participate. Especially in large group situations (e.g., *ingando*), this coincided with the way visitors (*abashyitsi*) are expected to behave. I stood up in front of the gathering, usually the whole camp, and made an introductory speech. In one-on-one interviews, the introduction was made when I first approached the person. All in all, some participants were talkative and eager to explain while others were reticent, some declined outright, and yet others agreed with an ambivalently pronounced *nacyibazo* ('no problem' meaning 'OK' but in this sense more like 'ah, oh well, OK').

In Rwanda, one has to seriously consider the stakes involved in a research encounter. Association with inquisitive *bazungu* (whites) can create complications vis-à-vis one's community or the government. Protection of informants and data is key, and yet it is difficult to gauge what exactly is safe. What can be safely said on the phone or in an email? What is a safe place to hold an interview? Offices might not be safe, especially if someone wants to convey sensitive information. But is a cafe or a restaurant or one's house safe? Is a full restaurant or an empty restaurant safer? My sense after seven months in the field is that it is almost impossible to find a place where an informant feels completely at ease divulging very sensitive information.

My own home was certainly a complicated space. Its owner, as I learned after coming to Rwanda, was the former president of the Islamic Democratic Party (PDI) – a Muslim dominated organization and part of the RPF alliance – and former Minister of Foreign Affairs, Andre Habib Bumaya. Though Bumaya 'fell from grace to grass' (NTK, March 22, 2006), having been dismissed from his position in 2006 by the RPF-led government,[9] leaving for a temporary stay abroad, the house was managed in his absence by his brother – a *Mudepite* (member of parliament) at the time. *KwaBumaya* (*chez* Bumaya), the name by which the house was commonly referred to, was located in Nyamirambo, an area where few *bazungu* lived. The residents were researchers and development workers and the house received many Rwandans, including research assistants. Nonetheless, when it came to sensitive matters, informants were not sure whether the house was safe (Could it be bugged? Was the security guard a spy?) and I could not completely assure them.

As a rule, the more time one has spent in the field – which correlates with more insight, more relationships, more accumulated disclosure, and more experience of disciplining and surveillance – the less faith one has in creating a 'safe' encounter. This means that research relationships at times have to be cut short and that the informants' demands to 'jealously guard all that' have to be taken with utmost seriousness. Fortunately, none of my informants were threatened or punished in any way for their association with me (while I was in Rwanda, or afterwards, as far as I know).[10] To protect my informants, their identities have been anonymized; the names that do appear are pseudonyms that bear no relation to informants' real names. The only exceptions to this rule are high-ranking civil servants who have spoken to me on record. I also include names or positions of those who have spoken in public.

Finally, let me briefly but explicitly reflect on the aims of this project as a whole so that these cannot be misunderstood or misappropriated. This book is not policy-oriented and offers no actionables at the end. Neither is it politically motivated, with no presumptions that precede it. Its main research questions emerged in the field itself. The main task of the book is to offer an in-depth, field-based study of the process of unity building in post-genocide Rwanda. The key words are witness, document and comprehend. *Kumva* is the Kinyarwanda verb that combines the empirical of see, hear, touch with the metaphysical of understand. I want to see what happens and why, part of which is to understand why there might be distortions in the representation of certain processes, events and activities, and why some things are silenced, by whom and for what purposes. The aim is to unlock the complexities of a social process that has not received the attention it deserves. At the same time, the study makes no claim to total insight or to being a closed product. This better fits the 'unfinished realities of everyday life' (Finnström 2008: 28) and the coexistence of versions of past, present, even self. This approach is likewise better placed to acknowledge our ability to transcend and alter our contexts, our potential to expand what is possible by doing something new or unexpected (viz. Arendt's notion of 'action' or praxis, 1958).

The book is divided into three sections. The introductory section closes with a chapter on the 'structure of voice' – a reflection on what is knowable and how in a context where voice itself is a complex field of action and a key sphere of power's assertion. Following this, Section II offers an in-depth analysis of political dynamics in post-genocide Rwanda, delineating the intricacies of state and social control. Chapter Three focuses on legitimizations of political power, scrutinizing the nature and impacts of three different legitimization narratives and how these themselves form and reform what unity 'means'. Chapter Four, in turn, explores the nature of the Rwandan state and the extent to which it is present in people's lives. The chapter explores the intricate administrative and information apparatus, the spectrum of state-led activities, as well as the effects that such structure produces in terms of surveillance and indirect control. Chapter Five considers the micro-dimensions of power in contemporary Rwanda, more specifically the individual and societal 'embodiments' of power as well as its subversion. The section closes by exploring the implications for the unity-building process.

Section III focuses on the performances of *ubumwe* – on the making of unity through unity and reconciliation activities, specifically (but not exclusively) *ingando* – and how political dynamics fundamentally mould the very constitution as well as effects of these activities. Chapter Six explores the 'multiplicities of unity', contrasting the government's view with alternative conceptions, and details the various government-employed 'strategies' of unity. Chapter Seven looks at activities themselves, analysing (among other things) the purpose and accurateness of the characterization of activities as 'grassroots', 'participatory' and 'traditional'. The chapter also studies the contents of selected activities and shows the different manners in which these are politicized. Chapters Eight and Nine focus specifically on *ingando* camps. As mentioned, more than any other activity, *ingando*'s spatial, symbolic and performative nature, in addition to particular texts being disseminated, make it a key example of the intended social transformation attempted by the government. It is a space where the different dynamics of this wider project converge and can best be glanced.

Finally, Section IV focuses on what the performances and broader discourses of unity tell us about the way in which the Rwandan government conceptualizes and approaches social transformation and delineates the broader goals to which the process of *kubaka ubumwe* is subsumed. Chapter Ten tries to understand the 'new Rwandan' that is to be reconstructed in the liminality of *ingando*. The chapter focuses on the government's overall social transformation objectives – the creation of 'perfect development subjects' – and how this overall objective translates into the conceptualization and practices of unity and reconciliation. Chapter Eleven offers final reflections on unity building and the nature of the state, and considers the prospects for political stability, social justice and peace.

Notes

1. The exact number of victims is not known. Estimates by NGOs, researchers and the government span from 500,000 to a million victims.
2. Many of them showed 'proactive resistance' (Lemarchand 2009).
3. For quantification of this claim see Ansoms (2009: 294; the numbers were gathered over the years by Marysse and Reyntjens).
4. The national gymnastic event in Czechoslovakia called Spartakiáda and held every five years showcased perfect physical coordination of a mass of bodies.
5. The second report was the more general one: 'Report of the Reflection Meetings Held in the Office of the President of the Republic from May 1998 to March 1999' (Office of the President; Kigali, August 1999).
6. e.g., repression, co-optation, resistance.
7. e.g., legitimation practices, governmentality or the rationalities of rule.
8. This term is inspired by Michael Jennings's (2009) use of 'coercive utopia' in his analysis of development projects of the late colonial period in Africa. I use eu-topia (the Greek word for a 'good place') instead to indicate that the vision might be indeed attainable and yet its costs and alternatives must be discussed.
9. After being dismissed from his position, Bumaya left for the United States but he returned while I was still doing my fieldwork. I had the opportunity to talk (informally) with Bumaya about reconciliation and unity when he visited the house in early 2009.
10. I was very fortunate to escape some unpleasant realities that other researchers had to face. I heard first-hand accounts of blackmail, open dissuasion, threats and/or arrests of informants.

2

Settling the Unsettled
The Politics and Policing of Meaning in Rwanda

After a lengthy interview on the history of RPF in exile, as we stand in the buzz of the street in front of Irindi House, my informant states matter-of-factly: 'Ah, so you will become one of those specialists on the region'. I quickly express my uneasiness with the label, but he continues with a serious tone: 'Be careful which camp you end up in … people will always group you'. My appeals to ignorance bring forth an unpleasant but revealing conversation about two 'camps', one of which is clearly to the dislike of the government. 'Some [critics] even say this government is a Tutsi government, [they] do not believe there can be a nation here, that we can live together, but you know we are trying to build one Rwanda'. As he proceeds to discuss specific academics, I keep thinking how paradoxically the prerogative of 'faith in unity' is used to divide academia into friends and critics. The conversation is finally cut off as an acquaintance of my informant approaches us smiling. He works at the Revenue Authority and exclaims as he vigorously shakes my hand: 'Pay your taxes, build the nation!' Though the mood lightens up, the earlier exchange leaves an unpleasant aftertaste, but as all unpleasantness, it comes and goes, or better, it goes and then comes again.

'Politics is not merely about material interests', writes Lisa Wedeen in her political ethnography of Hafiz al-Asad's personality cult in Syria, '[it is also] about contests over the symbolic world, over the management and appropriation of meanings' (1999: 31). This expansive reading of the political could hardly be more relevant than in the study of contemporary Rwanda where symbolic struggles over 'knowing' and representing the country place the researcher in the midst of a struggle over signification. It is not only the domain of the said that needs to be carefully policed, but equally, if not more so, the entrepreneurship of the written word. Different accounts from the field speaking of accusations, revocation of permits, expulsion, surveillance and threats to informants attest to this powerfully (Begley 2009 and 2012; Thomson 2010 and 2013). But what are the broader political techniques of control over narrative and truth, and how do they manifest? What 'landscape of voice' emerges as a result – what, where and how do people choose to disclose, and is the notion of public voicelessness useful? Finally, what are the political effects? Does the resulting anatomy of voice and silence, broadly speaking, offer service to power?

The formulation of research as part and parcel of a struggle over meaning provides an opportunity to pursue a more systematic political study of Rwanda's post-conflict knowledge making than hitherto attempted. The analysis here builds on empirically rich tomes of interconnected and overlapping literature – the writing on research challenges in conflict, post-conflict and 'violently divided communities' focused on ethical prerogatives of 'do no harm' and the foregrounding of marginal voices (Lundy and McGovern 2006; Smyth and Robinson 2001; Nordstrom and Robben 1995), research in 'highly politicized research settings' focused on trust, access and the uses of data sourced under repression (King 2009; Thomson 2010; Fujii 2010; Chakravarty 2012; Begley 2012; Ansoms 2012; Bouka 2012), critical approaches to oral accounts produced under power asymmetries and by those relatively powerless, centred around the notion of narrative spheres, 'narrative inequality' and the very 'hearability' of certain transcripts (Blommaert, Boc and McCormick 2006; Scott 1990; Zorbas 2009; Ingelaere 2009; Burnet 2012), and finally literature on post-war elite instrumentalization of historical narratives, memories, information and disinformation (e.g., Pottier 2002). The aim here is to garner the rich insights from these studies and combine them with my own observations in an attempt to derive a 'structure of voice' framework – both a concrete (even if partial) depiction of degrees and rules of narrative 'opening' in Rwanda, and a more general tool to assess the politics of knowledge in similar settings.

Post-genocide Rwanda, as a key example of a country that is at once post-conflict, divided, and highly politicized, poses important challenges to the researcher: How do we represent a society divided over meaning and interpretation of the past and present? And how do we research, and what can be found out in the context of a politicized epistemic space? This raises classic methodological questions related to impartiality, representativeness and the truth, but also political questions related to indeterminacy and intelligibility. The present chapter makes the politicized research context and its challenges explicit but it does not aim at a 'resolution'. Rather, it is the very tension of contradictions and divergences that is a key site of learning and that is productive of analysis. In multiple senses, intermediacy rather than finalities, process rather than product offer useful insight. In a society where image and appearance are coveted capital, seemingly insulated spaces of method and data production become themselves settings of politics, and hence sources in their own right. Far from being mere 'means to findings', research methodology and the actual conduct of research become key sites of learning, a meta-finding on the political process itself. The process and result merge and thus lend renewed importance to 'experiential data' in social science (Strauss 1987; Yates 2003).

In order to properly 'embed' both my own research and the politics of knowledge and voice, the chapter first delineates the historical and political dynamics at the time of fieldwork, exploring the notion of the 'post-genocide present', and places the unity project within a broader context of lingering tensions and divisions as reflected through the unsettled nature of key narratives, including those on history and identity. The chapter then delves deeper to investigate how voice and silence are managed in an attempt to 'settle the unsettled'. Finally, the chapter will try to propose a method cued to the politics and contradictions of research in settings such as Rwanda, a method that reaches beyond a critical scrutiny of specific testimonies or novel ways of reading the uncertain, invented or untrue (White 2000) to the investigation of a 'structure of voice'. Such analysis is not only possible or enlightening but ethically required, and it asks that the researcher poses a set of key questions about the field encounter: Who speaks, who can speak, and whose voices are sidelined or silenced? Is there a politics to knowledge production, and how does power write itself into narratives themselves? We need a critical scrutiny of the very endeavour of 'giving words to things' – labelling, characterization, narration, word display, disguise and omission. The study of these questions also forms a key aspect of the present study, helping us to isolate the dynamics and silent rules of narrating unity in post-genocide Rwanda, the way in which narratives are woven, how narrativity is policed and to what extent people can or do bend the rules of public voice.

A last note on the unsettled and divided nature of academic narratives themselves. To say that method is finding means that the very way we look powerfully shapes what we see. It is easy to get tangled up in appearances or the lull of the mundane, the calm and clean face of a powerful order. But as Linda Green (1999) highlights in her political ethnography of the Guatemalan Highlands, a politicized society divided by violence, the researcher needs to scratch beneath the surface of normalcy. It is only outside the daily goings-on and the casual encounters that distrust, uncertainty and fear emerge as a powerful presence and a structuring force in society. Importantly, this is not to say that Rwanda today is characterized by a 'culture of terror' (Taussig 1984; Sluka 2000) or is 'engulfed in fear'. That would be a misreading of much subtler dynamics. Such characterization assigns fear a strange permanency and saliency that it often does not have under repression. The emergence and occasional presence of fear nonetheless has a powerful effect on people as they embark on the path of avoidance. They might become more careful, measured, or evasive in order to avoid fear. Hence often what we observe is not fear itself but its fruit, tension and anxiety, suspicion and distrust, skilful navigation of mostly unwritten rules and risks, as well as silences and a particular structure to expression.

The 'Post-Genocide Present' and the Disunity of Narratives

The Rwandan political economy of meaning, knowledge, and, by extension 'disclosure' and voice, arises at the historical crossroads of a post-genocide society and a repressive regime. The first task thus must be to 'emplace' the current research in this wider setting, a setting that can be meaningfully characterized as 'post-genocide' beyond a simple chronological sense, and where the government project can best be captured under the heading of 'settling the unsettled'.

In late 2008, when my fieldwork began in earnest, genocide remained a salient structuring force of politics, relationships, settlement, narratives. Rwandans could still 'remember and see'.[1] Besides the ubiquitousness of official memorials or *inzibutso* ('there are as many of those here as there are MTN shops'[2]) and the memories and stories evoked by most places, there were scars, disfigurements and screams to serve as reminders. Pink and orange prison uniforms of genocide detainees and dark fuchsia overalls of TIGists (those serving alternative punishments) appeared everywhere. Genocide exerted immense gravity on life stories, dividing narrative time into its 'befores' and its 'afters'.

The broad political dynamics also drew on genocide for their force, legitimization and meaning. In late 2008, parliamentary elections had just concluded (September 2008) producing a staggering voter turnout of 98 per cent and a 78.7 per cent electoral victory for the RPF alliance.[3] The victors of the 1990–1994 war thus reaffirmed their unbroken hold on power. Despite this, battles – both physical and ideological – continued. 'Genocide ideology' was presented as a resurgent threat ('genocide ideology is slowly creeping back into society'[4]) and became a prominent item on the government's agenda. Additionally, Rwanda renewed its involvement in the DRC via the proxy of the National Congress for the Defence of the People (CNDP) and its leader, Laurent Nkunda, a Congolese Tutsi with 'a long track record as Kigali's man' (Prunier 2009: 297). In late October 2008, Nkunda initiated an offensive in North Kivu allegedly to protect the Tutsi minority from continued FDLR[5] threat – an entry legitimization that Rwanda had used repeatedly over the past fifteen years.[6]

The recurrent Rwandan presence in the DRC toughened the stance of the international community (Prunier 2009: 324). In 2008, despite Kigali's assurances of non-involvement, diplomatic convoys flew to both DRC and

Kigali for pressure talks. Increasingly critical reports on the human rights situation led to suspension of aid by Netherlands and Sweden. This further hastened the transformation of Rwanda's image abroad. Immediately after the genocide, the international community was overwrought with guilt for not intervening to end the hecatomb, which translated into financial generosity and leniency in judgement ('the genocide credit'; Reyntjens 2004). But a decade later, the world was not so unequivocal about the RPF legacy. The 2006 'Brugière Report' (still reverberating in Rwanda at the time of my fieldwork) calling for the indictment of top RPF officials accused of shooting down President Habyarimana's plane in 1994 was a negative 'culmination' of sorts. This report by a French judge effectively proclaimed the president and other top government officials to be criminals and called for arrest warrants to be issued against them. In November 2008, the Head of Rwandan Protocol – Rose Kabuye – was arrested in Germany on official business. The event triggered large state-organized protests in Rwanda and an outpouring of anger against Germany, France and Europe more broadly.

The geopolitical shift that commenced after the genocide – 'the policy to exit the "Francophony" and to enter the "Anglophony"' (Ansoms 2009: 295) – continued. Rwanda entered the East African Community (EAC), made an application to enter the Commonwealth and made an abrupt transition by introducing English as an official language of instruction from January 2009. Though the constitution clearly posited the legal existence of three official languages in Rwanda, it increasingly appeared that there were only two. The name of a *salon de coiffure* (hair salon) in Nyamirambo perfectly demonstrated the state of linguistic transition – the painted sign read 'Familly' – not the French *famille* anymore and not the English *family* yet.

But there is more to the post-genocide present and it reaches beyond specific political dynamics. Besides being a witness generation still weighed down by memory, this is fundamentally a generation of both disruption and reconstitution, where people are 'recreating worlds' rather than just 'fine-tuning' them (Nordstrom 1997: 13). The genocide has redrawn multiple maps – of settlement, land, relations – and produced a continued impact on feelings, attitudes and behaviour. The mass 2009 *icyuriro* commemoration at the Amahoro stadium underscored the continued preoccupation with the backward spirals of memory. As dusk was falling over the Amahoro stadium, filled with thousands of people, a string of screams like an instant plague plunged people to the floor as they relived scenes from the past. They were held and carried away. Only the raised volume of the music flowing from the loudspeakers managed to halt the propagation of traumatic memory around us. This occurrence, not uncommon at commemorative events, contrasted starkly with the purposeful symbolism of the candle-lighting ceremony at the close of the evening. The large sign made of candles was lit by fifteen-year-old girls and boys – all children born just after the genocide. The sign read *icyizere* (hope) and meant to symbolize the new beginning represented by those without the 'lived memory' of genocide. Yet even the government realizes that the transmission of the past is more complex, and it is ever mindful to prevent the 'passing on' of certain narratives, memories and beliefs across generations.

Family or familiar setting has been broken for many and it has been reconstituted in alternative ways. Child-headed households and *mayibobo* groups (street children) emerged. The number of street children has itself been much reduced by their forced incorporation into the institutions of the state – the 'family' of rules and roles. 'Artificial' families (Sezibera 2009) were created by orphaned students grouped under the umbrella student survivor associations AERG and FARG.[7] The families assign roles ('mother', 'father', 'uncles'), organize and participate in community events, and take *noms guerriers* of symbolic importance such as 'Intwari' (heroes), 'Imanzi' (deceased heroes showing extreme bravery), 'Inganyi' (victorious) or 'Isonga' (first, top, highest). The post-genocide returnees also re-established familial ties by replanting refugee camp networks in the planned villages known as *imidugudu*.[8]

Mass movements of people contributed to disruption. Although forced mass migration has been part of life throughout remembered history (Vansina 2004; Pottier 2002), the post-genocide in- and out-migrations stand out due to their sheer diversity and scope. The RPF inherited not only a devastated but literally a 'displaced' country, part of which it itself helped to dislocate.[9] Precise figures do not exist, but approximate counts remain instructive: up to 1.5 million Hutu internally displaced;[10] up to three million mostly Hutu refugees abroad in the DRC and Burundi, fleeing from a mix of pressure and fear of revenge (so-called 'new-caseload' refugees; Reyntjens 2004: 15), two million of whom returned in 1996/97 (HPG 2007: 1); and 0.7 million Tutsi returning immediately after the RPF takeover in 1994/95 (so-called 'old caseload'; HPG 2007: 1). Since 1994, about 2.1–3.4 million refugees[11] have been repatriated and resettled, a 'record in world history' (Kaiza 2003). The result is that 25–40 per cent of the population[12] is constituted by post-genocide returnees. In some areas, a third of the population is new and in two prefectures half of the inhabitants arrived recently (De Lame 2004: 4).

In a certain sense then, there has been a transition from a life in exile, on the move, in camps, to a more settled, constant and controlled 'dwelling'. But the notion of overall 'settling down' should not conjure up 'return' to pre-genocide settlement patterns. Really 'another war'[13] unrolled as Tutsi returnees took over abandoned houses – of those dead or those across in the DRC – some of which they claimed belonged to their families in the first place, before they were pushed to exile (HPG 2007). After Hutu returned en masse, 'land sharing' agreements had to be struck in many localities (ibid.). Parts of the Akagera Park have been degazetted to accommodate Tutsi old-caseload returnees. A large-scale *imidugudu* villagization programme was initiated.

The government has also commenced large-scale expropriations, mostly of poor neighbourhoods in Kigali (e.g., lower Kyovu Hill, Kimicyanga).

Thousands of detainees (*abafungwa*) from across the Rwandan prisons commenced their own 'return' in 2003 when the government initiated *gacaca* and started provisionally releasing detainees charged with lesser crimes. To my questions about life after the 'alternative' punishment of TIG (literally 'public interest works'), many of my respondents said they will finally go back to 'normal life' (*buzima busanzwe*). This return to normalcy, not unexpectedly, profoundly shook the survivors' hard-won semblance of calm. In their own words, this happened just as 'we were rejoining life ... household chores were sweeping bad thoughts into the hole of forgetfulness' (Hatzfeld 2007). Disruption returned – 'it was 1994 all over again' – and survivors fell into a state of shock (ibid.).

Besides 'disruption', the generation is characterized by multiplicities originating from dispersion (living in multiple exiles), violence and varied responses to both. Identities in Rwanda have always been more complex than the Hutu-Tutsi binary suggests,[14] but they are even more so post-genocide. Besides 'Tutsi victims' and 'Hutu perpetrators', there are also Hutu victims and Tutsi perpetrators. There are people of mixed Hutu-Tutsi descent or marriage (the 'Hutsi', see e.g., Hilker 2012) who have been facing their own complicated predicament of distrust and at times double persecution. There are Hutu who saved, who saved for money and who both saved and killed. There are Tutsi who killed (some were even members of *Interahamwe*) and Hutu that were mistaken for Tutsi and killed. There were extremist Hutu and moderate Hutu, the latter of which were targeted to be killed. There are the unacknowledged Hutu and Twa victims of RPF crimes. Though most killings were carried out by men (e.g., Hogg 2010), women killed too (Leggat-Smith 1995) and many women were complicit as silent bystanders (Hatzfeld 2005b). Rwandans also distinguish between the 'ordinary people' who carried out violence and intellectuals who were the masterminds (Hogg 2010: 76). Alongside these fine-tuned distinctions, the grand labels of 'Hutu' and 'Tutsi' survive and are put to use in daily life. The Twa continue to live on the margins of society – physically, politically and economically.

Post-genocide Rwanda also comprises multiple returnee groups. There are the 'Uganda Boys' or *Abasaja* or 'those from U-G'. There are the 'Dubais' or *Abacongo* from the DRC, the *Abarundi* from Burundi. Others came from Tanzania and Kenya but also further afield, from other countries of Africa, Europe, North America, Asia. Many returnees did not speak Kinyarwanda when they arrived or spoke other languages better. In fact, 'most of us are still learning Kinyarwanda'.[15] As a result of the recent returns, Kigali represents a mix of cosmopolitan histories that speak not only of dispersed pasts but also transnational presents. Some people think of themselves as 'Ugandan' or 'Congolese' first. Luganda, Kirundi, Swahili or Lingala can be heard spoken on Kigali streets and many people still compose sentences in two or three languages, a mix known as 'Kinyafranglais'. A returnee friend confessed he speaks English at home, Swahili with friends and Kinyarwanda at work. The way one speaks Kinyarwanda also divulges one's returnee 'origin'.[16] Those who dominate Kinyarwanda behold it with pride. Rwandans who fall short of fluency are corrected and can even be looked down upon. Though Kigali remains the 'hot spot for languages', *Icyongereza* (English) is the fever of the day. It is the new language of power and opportunity. It is the language of the future: 'Vision 2020[17] needs people who speak English', proclaims a painted sign in Biryogo, Kigali.

Networks based on country of exile survive but their exclusiveness is seen to have diminished. 'Just after the genocide … every person was tagged [and people did not intermix]', a Hutu returnee confessed, 'that place was for survivors, that place was for Hutu, that place for the Ugandans … today, there is no place I cannot go'.[18] The Tutsi returnees and those who stayed behind (the *Sopecya* or *Abajepe*) still struggle with relating to each other. There are also tensions between the various returnee groups, and between the dominant networks of Uganda returnees (perceived to hold both economic and political power) and the rest (Ansoms 2009; Reyntjens 2004; Zorbas 2004). In survivors' eyes, the returnees are 'running the show', 'they govern the country' (Hatzfeld 2007: 90). 'Some say this ethnic thing has been replaced by division of returnees. One of the most hated groups are the Ugandans, how do I say … they are in power'.[19]

The divergence is also reflected through the unsettled nature of key narratives – those of 'history', 'identity' and 'conflict'. The government highlights the necessity of 'finding a consensus to make a nation'[20] (*ukuri rwacu* – our truth; or *ukuri kurwanda rwacu* – the truth about our country) but even members of the government do not fully agree on the seemingly compact key narratives of the official discourse. A veteran of the RPF told me quite bluntly that 'Rwandans are divided on everything'.[21]

With regard to identity, a number of researchers have discussed the ban on ethnicity (and in fact expression of any 'divisionist' identity and ideology) and the promotion of *Banyarwanda* identity (the two parts constituting the strategy of 'de-ethnicization'; see also Purdeková 2008b or Lemarchand 2009). However, this identity discourse is much more complex, contradictory and unfinished than readily admitted, starting from the verbal acknowledgements that the genocide was a 'genocide against the Tutsi' to the open pronouncements of many people, including officials of the government, that the official accent on non-existence of ethnicity is 'non-sense'.[22]

An important step towards dismantling of the tight prohibition on voicing ethnicity came when the term 'genocide against Tutsi' (*jenoside yakorewe abatutsi*) was introduced in the constitution as the official term for the 1994 genocide.[23] The move created confusion and a multiplicity of interpretations.

If there is 'genocide against the Tutsi', there must be 'Tutsi'. This in turn brought the following retort from the officialdom: 'There are Tutsi and Hutu but we should not make them the core of our loyalty'. NURC's Director of Civic Education confessed that 'Rwandans can distinguish between Tutsi and Hutu, these are ethnic groups, but we should not accentuate that, we should try and foster the feeling of being Rwandan'.[24] This goes against earlier (and still prevalent) pronouncements that ethnicity does not exist.

As a rule, the adherence to the official public 'speech protocol' is in an inverse relationship to the power of the interlocutor and the knowledge they have of the researcher. The resulting inevitable 'public prudence' leads to indirect references to 'ethnies', 'ethnism' or 'the two groups' rather than Hutu, Tutsi and Twa. The 'HMG' ('historically marginalized groups') or *les potiers* (potters) is also an acceptable reference specifically to the Twa. After a longer time in the field, the actual speech protocol shows inconsistencies. While it is an unspoken norm that Tutsi and Hutu should not be mentioned, Twa can be spoken about. This last group is small, almost negligible and hence does not matter politically, only inasmuch as the civilizing mission to 'integrate' them matters. But even the word 'Tutsi' could often be heard around NURC ('These Europeans, why do they hate the Tutsi so much?'[25]). The word 'Hutu', on the other hand, is never spoken publicly. It is mentioned and remains meaningful privately. Officially, the word emerges strictly as part of an ideological discourse meant to negate it or belittle it as identity. Use of the term is perceived as politically threatening, possibly pointing to concentrations of power. Outward accentuation of Hutu identity, especially in politics, almost inevitably brings on accusation of 'divisionism'. In the words of one of my long-term informants, one result is that 'Tutsi is often mentioned with pride, whereas a Hutu is ashamed of revealing who they are'.[26] The recent government programme of Ndi Umunyarwanda (I am Rwandan) asking Hutu to personally apologise for the crimes (*icyaha*) of their parents might further contribute to these dynamics surrounding collective worth and guilt.

This official dance-around comes in stark contrast to common daily practices whereby people of all backgrounds still talk of and distinguish 'Hutu' from 'Tutsi'. Racial 'body maps' (Malkki 1995) are still part of life's orientation. Off-hand remarks about types of noses and skin tones figure in informal conversations. Sipping on the popular Ugandan *waragi* liqueur in a small corner shop, the leader of my cell (a state official) inquired laconically: 'What is your tribe?'[27] People pronounced sentences such as: 'A Hutu can spot a Tutsi at fifty metres, and vice versa;[28] or 'We [Hutu] look a certain way'.[29] Many other researchers noted the currency and salience of racial and ethnic markers in daily social life post-genocide (Hilker 2009; Buckley-Zistel 2009; Zorbas 2009; Hatzfeld 2007 and 2005a). Not only are the labels present, but many people believe they are meaningful and important if we are to interpret both the past and the present (Chakravarty 2014).

Similarly, despite the existence of an official history, which is put in circulation through the increasingly controlled press, formal and (especially) informal education and other state-organized activities, the new historical consensus is far from universally accepted. Counter-narratives or perhaps 'side-histories' exist (see also Chakravarty 2014; Watkins and Jessee 2014). Paradoxically, the divergences come out clearly even from interviews with the elite. In the whitewashed building of the RPF Secretariat, that symbolic centre of power itself, an RPF veteran and spokesperson, and a well-known intellectual suggested that 'we [Hutu and Tutsi] have opposed memories'.[30] The main points of disagreement (corroborated by Chakravarty 2014) include, among others, the role and legacy of the Nyiginya monarchy (was it unificatory, as NURC highlights, or exploitative?), the interpretation of the 1959 events, the year when the monarchy was abolished, Tutsi rule ended and a Hutu-dominated republic was established (was this a 'revolution' as passed on during the two republics, or the actual beginning of genocide as, again, the NURC suggests?). Finally, there is no settled history of political violence. Specifically, there is the non-addressed and extremely sensitive issue of Hutu civilian victims that died at the hands of the RPF. This active omission creates a large pool of enforced silence and a potentially damaging though quiet discontent (Burnet 2012; Chakravarty 2014).

To sum up, two opposed dynamics intertwined in the Rwanda I entered and created the political context to meaning making. On the one hand, there was the vibrancy and multiplicities of difference and division – the clashes and coexistence among self-ascribed, witnessed and proscribed identities, serious divergences in historical narratives and multiple grievances. Into all these multiplicities created by disruptions and restorations came a powerful state firmly set to create an overarching identity of *Munyarwanda* (a Rwandan), and more broadly, set to make 'one' out of many. The way in which this is attempted, the policies and activities that are to deliver it, and the effects that are produced, is the focus of the rest of the book.

Naturally, it would be fallacious to assume that while Rwanda brims with difference, the state and the government are monolithic, a notion cemented by references in the literature and by informants to 'the government' or 'elite Tutsi'. After all, even the very organization in charge of unity and reconciliation – the National Unity and Reconciliation Commission (NURC) was not 'unified'. Besides the issues of hierarchies and official versus personal agendas, NURC also reflected much wider and key tensions in the post-genocide society. There was a clear distinction between the 'core' employees and other workers, where the former seemed much more identified with the ideologies underpinning the work of the commission, holding higher posts and having spent a longer time in the institution, usually being present since NURC's inception. During my fieldwork, the head and 'face' of the NURC wasn't its president but rather its Executive Secretary, Fatuma Ndangiza, a post-genocide returnee from Uganda. Ndangiza was a 'big personality', known by everyone in the field and beyond. Many referred to NURC informally as chez Fatuma or *kwa* Fatuma. Fatuma's presence at events instantly raised their profile. 'Fatuma is arriving, I will have a story!' exclaimed a young journalist after a whole day spent at a unity and reconciliation activity. Fatuma was soft-spoken and solemn but had a powerful presence. She exuded the air of a wise matriarch and many commissioners and NURC partners looked at her with respect akin to reverence. But NURC also mirrored wider social exclusions and tensions. During my time in Rwanda, I came to know most of the commissioners. Although genocide survivors and Hutu were present among them, most employees and most of those who held power were Tutsi returnees, predominantly from Uganda and to a lesser extent from the DRC. This fact made it hard to dispel the notion that a 'minority vision' of unity was being promoted in Rwanda.

Neither did the commission – the body meant to be quintessentially about social cohesion, a broader vision and the 'greater good' – manage to bridge social divides or, unsurprisingly, prevent personal interest eroding or overriding the public interest, or prevent many from considering it as a station 'on the way' to elsewhere. While the monthly *umuganda* works, however brief and perfunctory the effort, did succeed in getting office workers to 'dirty' their shoes descending steep hills with heavy hoes, planting trees and fertilizing them with dung, they rarely interacted with the TIGists (the released prisoners serving commuted sentences in labour camps) who silently ferried dung up and down the steep hills. The commissioners also heartily rewarded themselves with an *ubusabane* right after – skilfully applying their own 'u&r' terminology to a several-hours-long restaurant lunch filled with a profusion of drinks, meat and merriment. As anywhere else, some minded their *agasozi ndatwa* – their 'example hill' (pointing to the belly) – a play on another of the government's many new development schemes.

Political graft is the pinnacle of the personal overshadowing the official, and the commission could not claim an unblemished record here either. During the 2009 Unity and Reconciliation Week, as we were entering the Ruhengeri prison to give a lecture on the week's topic, I saw my NURC companion in an intimate discussion with a prisoner, suggesting prior acquaintance. The irony of the situation only became apparent later when I learned that the man used to hold a relatively high-up position in the commission, that is, before his attempt to embezzle a large sum of money.

In informal conversations, many of the lower ranked staff or interns also freely spoke of futures elsewhere. Jean-Claude, a recent hire fresh out of university, said his dream was to be at a law firm. David, an intern, planned for a Master's degree in business administration in Bangalore because 'that is where the *amafaranga* [money] is'. When I jokingly asked who will be left to run the country, he playfully replied pointing to another intern: 'Jeanette!'

Jeanette's own dream was to work for an international NGO (a number of years later she was still in the government, though now in a different department).

Distrust, suspicion and the presence of serious divides running within the 'unifier' itself came to a most dramatic head just before I left. An employee who had worked at NURC for a long time was accused of participation in the genocide and was swiftly imprisoned. I was told that 'suspicion was there all along' but now there was 'proof'. I remembered the bespectacled Remi, a Hutu man responsible for the monthly office *umuganda*, and his quietness at gatherings. 'Someone in prison has finally spoken', I was told. This person had implicated Remi, accusing him of drawing up a list of Hutu and Tutsi students at a secondary school during the genocide. Whether true or false, the story spoke loudly about the ongoing distrust and the fractures that lay just under the surface *kwa biro* (at the office).

Importantly, the fact that a commission or even a policy is internally fragmentable into different motivations and tensions should not create the impression of an ineffectual or weak state machinery or be confused with a lack of very real effects on the ground. But how can this paradox be resolved? How can we skirt a totalizing and reifying anthropomorphism of the state (Migdal 2001) whilst not denying some degree of state selfhood (or 'personhood', Wendt 1999, 2004)? Making a broad use of Wendt's notion of state 'self' as a 'narrative structure' might be useful. Though the concept was developed in international relations, it proves productive in interpreting the state facing 'inward' to society as much as facing 'outward' to other states. It also helps to demonstrate that the same political logic applies within officialdom as it does outside – the founding narratives (and hence also goals) of governance are publicly upheld, even if privately unworked. Difference and division on important issues exists in Rwanda (even within officialdom) but it is a key project of the government to obscure this, to regiment the surface and make way for official narratives. The next section explores how this is attempted specifically through the management of voice and silence.

The Management of Voice and Silence in Rwanda

Can public voice and silence become the handmaidens of political regimes? The answer to this question is far from straightforward, and needs to be based on a more general query: How do power and voice interact? Drawing out the rules of voice and mapping its landscapes is a crucial task, but also a perilous one due to the complexity of the topic. To begin with, what I witnessed in Rwanda did not always fit with the received academic 'truths' about the Rwandan culture of communication. Ethnographic accounts speak of reticence, secrecy and the importance of keeping appearances (De

Lame 2005 and 2004; Ingelaere 2009). Already the first Europeans noted Rwandan 'reliance on ambiguous language and the employment of ruse' (Des Forges 2011: 13). The concept of *ubwenge* is often cited, highlighting the value of public 'self-control', as are Rwandan proverbs highlighting duplicity such as 'the mouth does not always say what lies in the heart'.

These observations, however, cannot easily explain why some people willingly volunteered sensitive information to me and to others (see Chakravarty 2012 and 2014). Placidity and obedience do not explain why some are not afraid to talk critically (for example, telling me that *ingando* is teaching 'biased history' or is 'brainwashing', or that the government is a 'dictatorship'), or the occasional occurrence of open resistance; they explain neither its forms, nor its bounds. The supposed demure and composed behaviour of Rwandans does not explain why some actors chose to shock and unsettle. In a transgressive performance at an *ingando* camp, a liminal space whose purpose is to unhinge, a speaker questioned and probed all that is 'sacred' – God and the Bible, the distinction between human and animal, even the sanctity of the private parts by insinuating the naked buttocks of a woman in squat. Events such as these are completely unaccounted-for in portrayals that highlight cultural norms and continuity.

The post-genocide transitional space is both one of repressed emotion and voice, and also one where disparate actors work on effecting a transformation. The very unworking of the received culture of voice is, after all, the cornerstone of small healing initiatives that avowedly try to break with containment by 'raising dead emotions', 'making men cry' and 'discussing what our parents told us'.[31] But people cut different shortcuts to 'out'. 'Nail your suffering on a cross' is an initiative that includes pinning messages on crosses as a way to relieve suffering. Not everything needs to be said 'openly' to liberate or to speak to a 'powerful other'. In the aftermath of genocide, Rwanda has also been awash with researchers, focus groups and their icebreaker tricks, and in return many local people skilfully learned to navigate the worth of their voice. But Rwanda is also the site of Potemkin villages – ideological showcases of peace and reconciliation, and of innumerable stages and ceremonies of official voice.

The fact that people 'speak' says little about the topics, the places and the manner in which they are willing to disclose information, especially if it is perceived as politically sensitive. Who deploys the transgressive performance and to what effect? Who opens up and at what perceived cost? Leaving the field of voice unconceptualized, failing to acknowledge that there are rules and relations, has a direct link to placing it outside power, which is to say, to depoliticizing it. What we need is a dynamic approach foregrounding the politics or structure of voice – the political management of expression, and the limits of this endeavour. Repression in Rwanda is present and has real repercussions. But rather than producing generalized 'voicelessness', repression in Rwanda creates both 'gradated' spaces of constriction in practice and a clear asymmetry and suppression of the unofficial in the public realm. Some people speak their opinion, but many do not. Some spaces 'open up' voice more than others. There are no assurances of punishment, but power works through expectation and possibility.

Though power and the state will receive in-depth attention in the coming chapters, suffice it to say that an intricate system of surveillance in Rwanda not only produces a generalized state of suspicion, it also structures the space of the said and the unsaid. Surveillance made me and my informants change the topic of conversation or stop talking; in some cases it made us progressively diminish contact. But in its essence, surveillance is meant to restrict the very access to certain scripts and, ultimately, to prevent those scripts from arising in the first place. Fundamentally then, the discussion on management of voice is a broader analysis of power – the power to represent, to stake out, to assert.

The Rwandan government tries to carefully manage what outside visitors learn about Rwanda; the attempt is to shape access and replicate the opinion of those in power as fact, to spread the appropriate versions of 'each and every thing'.[32] Little is written about how this is attempted, however. To begin with, not all government employees agree with or in fact are the 'keepers' of the official truth. Just like in pre-colonial Rwanda, where there was a class of people – the 'specialists of history' including the *abiiru* ritual council, the *abacuranwenge* genealogists or the *abateekerezi* memorialists – who together preserved the official history of the kingdom (Vansina 1985, 1994, 2004)[33] and thoroughly shaped the first generation of scholarship on Rwanda (Vansina 1994: 66), so today there exists an informal protocol for the propagation of official voice. The right to speak is concentrated and belongs to select guardians. Depending on the theme, there seem to be specialized collectives that hold the *ijambo*, the authoritative voice, being the *isoko*, the source of authoritative information on a given subject. Even within these institutions or collectives, there might be authorized spokesmen. On the themes of unity and reconciliation, I was repeatedly referred back to the National Unity and Reconciliation Commission (NURC) as the ultimate and authoritative source of information. I met with this type of response at government ministries and commissions, NGOs and associations. At the commission itself, I was told a number of times that 'NURC is the best place to get information'. NURC was the official source, and it was the protocol for me to work, if not solely 'within' them, then definitely 'through' them (I gently disobeyed this tacit norm). The constant referral back to the *isoko* underlined the wider tendency to point in the right (i.e., safe) direction, to converge to the appropriate centre.

Although this kind of management of official voice represents a real challenge for the researcher, and requires careful navigation, we need to look at this phenomenon more closely. Despite the fact that official voices are less likely to criticize the government and more likely to outwardly second its policies, they still have a potential to 'reveal'.[34] Voice, even if 'official', can still produce a richly detailed and insightful account when read 'along the grain' (Stoler 2010). One realizes this when orality is taken away, and replaced with the ultimate 'fixed voice' – the written word. It is in fact the written narratives, produced in the desired neoliberal language of donors, and largely for their consumption too, that diverge most from reality. It is the looking glass of text that has the best potential to lock the observer in a parallel world. The fixed voice is also a strategy for distancing the researcher. At the Rwanda UNDP office, once I finally managed to secure a meeting to discuss *ingando* due to sheer persistence, I was told in person that I would be sent a document 'containing everything concerning [their support to] civic education'. The one-page document was an exemplar of generic and non-specific text that said something and revealed nothing. On another occasion, at the Mutobo camp for ex-combatants, as soon as I started asking questions, the registrar gave me an inquisitive look over his glasses: 'Are you a reporter or something?' After I explained my background, he pointed me to the blackboard: 'The schedule of classes is there, also the timetable, you can copy these down'. No further elaboration was to be offered.

Though accessing multiple 'official' voices in their diverse settings can indeed be enlightening, the researcher must inevitably extricate herself from it. Only the simultaneous access to unofficial transcripts allows one to discover counter-narratives or else the 'full' story of the governing structure, to contextualize the official transcripts gathered, and perhaps most importantly, to offer an in-depth analysis of the wider political implications vis-à-vis silence and voice. The entrapment of many foreigners in the official and the 'fixed' (the written rendering of the official story) may result in a sense of helplessness on behalf of many Rwandans when they are faced with the result – the perceived erroneous or simplistic rendering of the political situation. When I posed some of my 'naïve' questions (i.e., very general, non-leading questions about political dynamics), one of my informants would respond frustrated: 'You can spend your whole life here and not understand what is going on'. Or 'I have been telling you, you cannot catch the reality as it is, but for us…' '[Me:] Do all Rwandans know?' 'They all know, but they prefer to keep quiet'.[35]

The stated preference for silence indeed gets to the core of the problem. 'It happens that people get punished by leaders for talking', suggests a rural farmer, expressing a much more widespread sentiment (in Berglund 2012: 12). In other words, what modulates voice and silence and assures that the latter prevails is the perceived cost associated with 'speaking up' against the official version, and increasingly the perceived cost is narrated as imprisonment. This suggests a number of important things. First, people themselves must navigate the risks, which both explains varied levels of opening (and yet the broader tendency for silence) and puts a price tag on research itself. Moreover, this shows that far from 'obedience', what we witness is an active preference for silence. The preference to keep quiet or replicate the official, just like the different degrees of opening, is filled with agency, it is a calculation based on perceived risk and personal motive.

The control over voice, besides leading to a lopsided account (with official reality being overrepresented) also results in structural violence, constrictions on participation and usurpation of the domains of 'authority' and 'validity', with the resulting downgrading of the non-agreeable. Fear, for one, pushes people into quietness, often a humiliating silence:

> You [the government] proclaim that unity is there, [that] we are reconciled, but I sit in the office and I do not utter a single word. Just imagine sharing an office with two, three compatriots and all day what they talk about is just insulting you, provoking you, and if you dare to respond, you are automatically accused of *ingengabitekerezo* [ref. to genocide ideology]. To avoid that, you just decide to keep quiet.[36]

But it is not only self-imposed silence that can be perceived as degrading, so can self-imposed voice be, the open replication of official dictums and formulas. In this sense, not all spaces are 'equal'. Inside an *ingando* for students, for example, the ability and willingness of people to speak was noticeably greater than in a TIG labour camp where most questions produced the expected echoes of the official transcript. But this is not simply to highlight a difference that most might expect, it is also to draw attention to a much broader issue – the concrete pressures and emotional effects that a research encounter might engender, and the further symbolic violence done when the echoes of the official are treated uncritically or taken as fact. This also shows that not all space is equally disempowering and all groups equally disempowered, that indeed there is a variance in voice and voicelessness.

The existence of a carefully defended official story also means that while discussion forums might exist and people might 'talk' and even 'complain', not everything can be discussed. There are numerous taboo subjects in Rwanda. 'There are two things we don't talk about – the army and the succession of Kagame',[37] one of my informants, an NGO researcher, tells me. Themes such as ethnicity, governance and poverty are considered outright 'sensitive' (Ingelaere 2010: 42). To this must be added topics such as 'Rwandan citizenship, non-selective justice, as well as strategies for addressing reconciliation, impunity, and human rights abuses' (NDI 2003: 10). Third and finally, the fact that voice has its designated and concentrated authority means everything that counters the official narrative can not only be punished, but is also pushed into the informal sphere from where it has to be retrieved, and in this case it is dismissed as 'bar talk' or 'gossip'. When unofficial voice is retrieved, it is stripped of authority.

In Rwanda, we can thus speak about a public silence, and importantly, it is structural. The general and indirect structuring force – the perceived cost of speaking up – is compounded by the government's 'tight control' of public outlets of voice including media, television and radio (see Freedom House 2014 for detail), but also conferences, debates or various government-created platforms and activities. Burnet's (2012) ethnographic research spanning more than a decade offers a detailed look at one particular aspect of this – what she calls 'amplified silence' or 'intensive public silence' surrounding experiences of violence, individual, familial, communal that fall outside the 'RPF's rigorously-policed discursive regime' (Watkins 2013: 1). The dominant narrative of the genocide renders 'almost invisible the civil war' that preceded it and the RPF crimes perpetrated before, during and after genocide (Burnet 2012: 111). 'The inherently political nature of nationalised, state-sponsored mourning practices and the RPF's paradigmatic history of the 1994 genocide have pushed individual memories and interpretations of the genocide and civil war into hidden places'. But what Burnet finds especially troubling is that silencing happens on a daily basis within families and communities, the result of 'anxiety created by fear of RPF reprisals' (ibid.). Amplified silence is thus not simply a by-product, it is not simply what is left out. 'Fear is its foundation' (Burnet 2012: 112). While Burnet focuses specifically on past violence – one of the most sensitive topics – the sphere of silence, actively produced through internalized fear, is much broader and includes topics such as identity, unity and reconciliation, history and political governance.

The flipside of silencing is the purposeful 'urging to voice'. Most clearly, this refers to the government's push for reproduction and thus validation of the official scripts through various activities and platforms but also research (which induces affirmation and 'preference falsification', Kuran 1995). Less apparent is the role of the non-governmental sector (IOs, NGOs and associations). Through a myriad of 'participatory' activities, this sector urges 'free expression' and 'personal opinion'. But these efforts might create the false impression that locally sourced and 'encouraged' voice is indeed an authentic reflection of opinion. The perceived ubiquitous surveillance, however, makes this a problematic proposition. Non-governmental 'spaces of voice' can also create a false sense of security. As an example, a Kigali-based research institute held consultative meetings and debates with the population on themes such as rule of law, peace and democracy. To my question on whether people are not afraid to speak out, the researcher replied: 'Well, we use audio-visual material [to break the ice], we film people and then show it to other groups. When people see others talking, they talk too ... Even on the issue of arbitrary power, they are scared to talk first – [after all] the authorities are present at all the forums; but eventually, they do talk'.[38] Such 'icebreaking' is in fact a common strategy in focus group research.

Not all in Rwanda at the time of fieldwork, however, concerned the management of voice. An equally important struggle revolved around the breaking of silence. 'That is the problem, to make those in prisons talk', a NURC employee tells me.[39] The government has tried hard to break the silence among prisoners, not only for the purpose of clarifying the crime they have committed but also in order to speed up the process of justice, to bring closure to families of victims, and to implicate others who have participated. A set of incentives was created for this purpose: a detainee who admitted to a crime and repented was released and passed through a local *gacaca* court, which either acquitted them, commuted their sentence to communal labour (TIG) or sent them back to prison. The system created unique distortions and manipulations of voice (see e.g., Ingelaere 2009, 'Does the Truth Pass Across the Fire Without Burning?') and instead of 'truth', *gacaca* is widely considered to have produced half-truths and lies (Rettig 2008; Burnet 2008; Thomson and Nagy 2011; Reyntjens 2013). The *gacaca* process has also been accompanied by a 'conspiracy of silence' in the countryside. Informal organizations among relatives of detainees (such as *Ceceka!* (Be silent!) and *Ntubavemo* (Don't betray them!)), composed predominantly of women, urged others to vow silence at *gacaca*. In this way, they not only restricted the courts' operation but contributed to the build-up of negative social capital (Rettig 2008: 38).

Ultimately, political power itself can be conceptualized through the language of voice. The concept of *uruvugiro* – the right to speak – is relevant here. We can say that though in Rwanda there might be many physical places where discussions take place, it is only a small minority who today possess *uruvugiro*. Those in power, rather than speaking on behalf of all or many, try hard to make all or most 'speak with their mouths and see with their eyes'.[40]

From Narratives to a Structure of Voice: The Politics of Indeterminacy

The context of a tight management of voice and silence described above raises the important question of intelligibility of our interlocutors and more broadly yet, the issue of indeterminacy of what we observe. Perhaps most profoundly, it cautions that our research too can become a service rendered to the powerful. In what follows, rather than focusing on the notion of public 'voicelessness', I focus on a strategy I believe to be more productive – on the types of voices that emerge, across people and within different settings. The inference of 'structural aspects' of voice requires observation of its varied performance. Attention to the 'variance of voice', the anatomy of narratives, and a multi-method sourcing of data all offer further insights into the *politike y'okwihisha* – the politics of concealment – and the politics of display in today's Rwanda, and into the ways of counteracting it.

Speaking of facts as incontestable and replicable truths is always difficult ('all cultural facts are interpretations', Rabinow 1977: 151) but this is especially so in a setting that combines political repression, a legacy of mass trauma, imperfect information flows (rumour and distrust) and an oral society tailoring messages both to the interlocutor's interests and the addressee (De Lame 2005; Ingelaere 2009). Eliciting knowledge can thus mean forming knowledge – instead of 'getting to', we might be producing meaning (Davies 1999). Narratives are acts, not just 'information' or 'knowledge' (Theidon 2001: 26). There is thus always a degree of uncertainty and in fact fleeing from certainty seems to be a tactic unto itself. In settings where information flows imperfectly and yet is key (e.g., in war, under repressive regimes), often a surplus of meaning is produced in society (see Theidon 2001: 27 on 1990s Peru); there is 'duplicity' or doubling – the rustling of the leaves can be the wind but also a possible *Senderista* attack, a rock thrown on the tin roof of a Kigali house can be children's play but also disgruntlement of a neighbour or a warning.[41] In a society where press, radio and television, even email and phone are, or are believed to be, controlled, further uncertainty arises when a researcher enters this imperfect information economy in search of 'what really happens'. They find they depend on informal talk, hearsay, rumour, just as most Rwandans do. Indeterminacy is worked into the structure of society, performs political work (fosters deniability), and cannot be easily 'designed out' of the research encounter.

One's particular positioning vis-à-vis one's addressees naturally also 'inflects' responses. People saw me as an outsider – a *muzungu* (white person) and a foreign researcher. The latter can be both an asset and a hindrance in research. On the one hand, as a newcomer you are treated like (and in fact are) a child – you are seen as naïve, you know and understand little about the cultural landscape that surrounds you, you stumble across norms and social rules. This is a position to embrace – people heed your bottomless inquisitiveness, they feel the necessity to guide you and show you how things work. Perhaps more importantly, if you know all the norms, you are expected to follow them. It is the liminal position of an outside visitor (*umushyitsi*) that gives one the freedom to get away with social blunder, which would otherwise not be tolerated. The indirectness of speech and guiding also open space for dissent, though it is a precarious type of balancing. Indeed as an entrant you are 'blind', which correlates with determination. The more informed you become, 'seeing' the rules, the less resolve you have to pursue certain questions, the more self-editing and self-constraining you become.

On the negative side, the position of an outsider and a researcher elicits suspicion. A long-term informant later admitted that 'suspicions are there at the beginning, [I was thinking] isn't she recording me?' Another informant in the beginning openly expressed his worry about my possible 'hidden agenda'. When I mentioned I wanted to talk to student *ingando* participants, he said: 'It may work, it may not, there might be mistrust, what does this *muzungu* want, the issue of spies...'[42] He went on to explain: '*Muzungu* is seen with suspicion, even in my ministry when a *muzungu* would come to visit, they say what does he want, what do I tell to this *muzungu*, he came to destroy us. But it is not only *muzungu*, even someone from Gabon, who speaks French, what do they want, they must be connected to the French ... it is a wider problem'.[43]

Partiality and distortion are built into the research encounter. Certain points are omitted, others overemphasized and, finally, unfinished stories are produced. Such accounts are still meaningful and enlightening both for what they reveal and omit. These after all are the 'data' of qualitative research, the fuzzy accounts closest to lived experience, a performed mix of the thought, the felt and the reflected-upon, a mix of imperfect understanding, desire, anxiety, belief. Naturally, partiality cannot be embraced entirely. Observation is a political act of registering and witnessing and has to bear this responsibility. It is not enough to see, one has to look for. In politically tense, repressive and divided contexts, it is hence imperative to ask: 'Whose voices do we listen to and how do we get to them?' (Nordstrom 1997: 45).

In a research context of stark power asymmetries, sourcing the offstage narratives, or what James Scott (1992) famously called the 'hidden' transcripts, is especially important. The word 'hidden', however, might obscure a more gradated reality of levels of openness and a diversity of spaces where people 'speak up'. It is not quite true that Rwandans 'remain strong opponents but only in the remotest corner of [their] backyard' (Lefort writing with reference to Ethiopia, 2010: 454). Some people do open up in public places, including in government offices, bars, restaurants, but they rarely do so directly, though even here there are exceptions. People typically mix direct statements with linguistic strategies that are 'cryptic and opaque' (Scott 1992: 137), that 'reveal and conceal at the same time' (Ingelaere 2010: 54) such as, from my experience, parables, metaphors, facial expressions and answers in the form of rhetorical questions. Conversely, though many people indeed express the preference to 'talk in private', even homes might not be safe if identities and loyalties of those present (or in the vicinity) remain uncertain.

From the bulk of the 'multi-sourced' data that form the empirical basis of this book, a small proportion of voices directly challenged official scripts on the most sensitive topics. Greater trust and a longer acquaintance certainly played a role but could not be the full explanation. During my fieldwork, people of very different backgrounds critiqued the government or explained the reasons for lack of such critique during our first or second encounter, where notions of trust or even 'partial trust' (Chakravarty 2012) were not quite applicable. Those occasions showed at least two things – that some people took charge of the encounter by purposefully volunteering information meant to 'correct' the dominant view, and that they actively took a calculated risk to share. Nonetheless, there were two long-term informants in particular – both Hutu men – whose insights provided depth that the shorter encounters could not offer and as such proved key to my understanding of Rwandan political dynamics. Why trust these sources? First, these men critiqued at high potential cost to themselves with no gain back.[44] Second, these two informants had 'insider' backgrounds. At the time of my fieldwork, one was still working for the government (I refer to him as 'Bernard' and 'civil servant'), the other had recently left the government to work at a research institute (I refer to him as 'Augustin' and 'employee at a research institute').

From all of the above, we can safely deduce that in a post-genocide society governed in an authoritarian way, most social research will involve the gathering of politicized information. The same question can produce a different answer depending on the interlocutor and the setting. Public and private transcripts might be discordant, even irreconcilable. Indeed, depending on the place, some people would talk differently to me ('in the office I could not tell you, but here, as a friend…'). How do we approach this quandary methodologically? In other words, how do we assess the reliability of information? As far as possible, I tried to achieve this by employing a mixed- and multi-method approach combining observation, immersion, semi-structured and unstructured interviews, questionnaires, informal exchanges and analysis of primary and secondary materials. Side-by-side employment of diverse methods is said to allow for 'cross-checking' or 'triangulation' of findings but can be also extremely useful in uncovering divergences. This includes, for example, divergences between official and unofficial scripts and settings, or different costs and incentives applying to the two types of script as reflected in the frequency with which they get narrated.

With regard to specific types of method, one naturally needs to obtain as much detail as possible on the 'variability of voice' – not only in the sense of plurivocality/variety of opinion but also degrees of openness – through interviews, discussions and questionnaires. But rather than presenting either position as the 'more complete truth', a more productive approach might be to focus on the forces underlying the production of these different narratives. This is the 'data' we need to elicit and it cannot simply be 'asked'. It can only be produced after months of observation, offhand remarks, snippets of life stories, gestures and grimaces, manners in which questions are asked, and assumptions that are never questioned. As Fujii (2010) showed, different ways exist to learn from an 'unfree' testimony (e.g., prisoners accused of participation in genocide). Diverse 'metadata' including rumours, inventions, denials, evasions and silences – help us decipher 'the conditions and circumstances in the present that colour and shape what people are willing to say' and the 'power relations that shape informants' current lives'. Behaviour and broader cultural and power contexts, as well as the performance of voice itself (fitted with gestures, movements, pauses, accents) make us learn about that which is not and cannot be said, and that which is said.

Yet it is undoubtedly immersion that proves to be the most meaningful and authentic learning – the very assumption of the role of researcher on a sensitive topic opens a unique window to studying politics. Immersion also helps one understand why Rwanda might profoundly divide those who come to 'understand' it, why we come to 'see' and say different things of Rwanda. The key is that, indeed, power works on the inside and in embodied ways, its public displays are uncertain and often couched in personalized messages delivered to those who need to hear them. Fear does not reside in public spaces, but is nurtured through encounter; fear is a form of knowledge and a form of relation, it is not a visible token exchanged like money, though it certainly can be passed on. Many visitors to Rwanda get dazzled by the economic achievements, the order and security, the talk of hope and progress, and these are all real. But it is the sites and roles we inhabit, and more profoundly, the questions that we ask that determine what and how we come to see and say.

What should we then conclude with regards to credibility and a 'trust' in narrative? With relevance to all sources undermining the official picture, while there might not always be a way to corroborate a specific claim or figure, the broad underlying claims (e.g., 'people self-restrict' or the government has spun intricate webs of control') can be cross-checked through employment of multiple methods. Second-hand narratives need to be accompanied by observation of self-restriction, of differential opening across situations, and by immersion – the first-hand experience of 'guiding', control, pressure, obstruction or threats. In addition, the observation of events and contexts (the structuring of space) and a more formal analysis of political dynamics (the set-up of an institution, the profiles of employees, etc.) can also prove useful in trying to corroborate what the government tries so hard to make unprovable.

Nonetheless indeterminacy needs to be taken far more seriously. For a while now researchers have struggled to make sense of uncertainty and the limits of both access and connection. They relentlessly try to domesticate the indeterminate, defend its usefulness; the uncertain is still 'productive of knowledge'. Lee-Ann Fujii (2010) when faced with the silences, evasions, rumors, denials and inventions that marked the narratives relayed to her, deciphered these for the wider messages that they contained and incorporated them into meaning-production. She talks of 'metadata' that 'speaks'. Not only are these data that speak, or rather are made to speak through the ever more creative interpretive manoeuvres of the researcher, they might even be 'telling [us] more' (White 2000). Louise White persuasively shows how lies and secrets, despite distorting and concealing, can be 'extraordinarily rich historical sources', pointing to structures of feeling and attitudes, containing indirect social commentaries, uncovering the logics and social practices surrounding the making of narratives. These are extremely valuable and valid points. Nonetheless, they do not detract from the fact that certain narratives do still hide and do still conceal, making 'finding out' a task that is difficult ethically and uncertain epistemologically, and making uncertainty and asymmetries in voice a form of political power. Rather than simply 'domesticating indeterminacy', a task that can never be complete, we need to acknowledge it as a broader force with political currency.

The Way Forward: A Critical Method for the Study of Voice and Power

In settings of high social control, power creates a field that warps narratives. Being unaware of this puts us at risk of reproducing interests and images of those who dominate the field. It can result in replication of voice that is not people's 'own', or it might reify silences. Only a direct and explicit study of voice as a political 'field' can help avoid such an outcome. A critical technique should combine inductive and deductive tools, and involve broad analysis of relations between research, voice and power, as well as the observation of voice as performed across different settings, the multilayered 'contexting' to each voiced account, as well as the study of the anatomy of each particular narrative.

Settings of high social control not only create a powerful asymmetry of information, they might also undermine our 'trust' in narrative. Can we be sure that what people say is not just a safe version of official scripts? And if they do replicate the official, how do we know if they do not actually believe it? The 'structure of voice' approach postulates uncertainty and does not necessarily resolve it in each particular case. It lays accent on uncovering forces and relations – laying bare the spoken and unspoken norms of permissible and desirable speech on a particular theme (or themes). Through this, the technique both helps to give depth to the questions above, namely by highlighting the simple but poignant point that people inevitably find 'safety' in the official and risk by breaking with it, but it also helps us to answer these questions on a broader scale too. With sufficient study of structure and context, and the variability across and between people, even particular narratives can be analysed for the credibility of their content. Inevitably, this will not always be the case and not all narratives can pass such a test. But the first important point is this: with very careful work of situating and modulating voice – listening to people in different settings or witnessing self-censure – the rules of 'voice' can be inferred. In other words, we need to achieve not only 'plurivocality' but study the 'variability of voice'.

As much as we should try and place the same 'voice' into many different contexts, so each research encounter should be richly contexted through the deployment of 'thick reading'. This refers both to the peeling-off of different forces constituting an encounter, as much as these can indeed be uncovered, but also uncovering the many layers of meaning or 'communicators' of meaning within each narrative, including silences, omissions, emphases, gestures, openness or distance, digression, hesitation, allusions, turns of phrase and more. 'Variability of voice' and 'thick reading' are inferential techniques and a deductive method must accompany them. An equally key 'site of learning' is the macro nexus between power and voice, which helps us to generate broad questions that can be applied to particular research encounters. Such an approach requires asking the following questions: Is there a politics to knowledge? Which research subjects are sensitive and why? How is one's research interpreted by important actors in the field? Is there a chance of 'capture'? Who speaks, who can speak and whose voices are sidelined or silenced? What is the risk of replicating some of these patterns? What are the ways of counteracting them? What does greater inclusion, representativeness and insight mean? Do they equate access to a more diverse set of people, or do they also require the study of different public and private spaces, and different moments and moods? In Rwanda, such broader structures and dynamics go to the core of discussions on power, and in fact serve as a window to reflect on all the different themes discussed in this book. Yet again, this highlights the importance of method as an end, not simply a means. The process and findings fold into each other.

Without a space of visibility, a 'whispered truth' or a dissonant narrative cannot effectively compete with the echoes of the official. The hallmark of the government's power, but also the distinct mark of its fragility, is the ability to make others speak its truths. This, together with the control of access and capture of attention, assure that those looking from the outside in, or those who come on short visits to Rwanda, will find it difficult if not impossible to reach beyond the official. Andrew Mitchell's visit to Rwanda during the twentieth commemoration of genocide in April 2014 demonstrates this well. His commentary for the Think Africa Press entitled 'Rwanda's 20 Year Miracle'[45] detailing the country's awe-inspiring social and economic developments has to be carefully situated – quite literally we have to pay attention to where and when he made his sojourn to Rwanda. Not only is the commemoration period a tense time of careful containment, and a time when everything is 'on display', and not only suffering but also RPF-led achievements, it is also noticeable that Mr Mitchell made a visit to NURC as well as a 'model village' of reconciliation called Rwera. Disentangling the official from that which lies alongside and beneath is not just a task for 'field research' as it is Rwanda itself that contains and stages both. One can be 'removed' while 'right there'. Similarly, the power of emotion stirred at commemoration ceremonies, the palpable distance traversed from an unassimilable horror can 'carry one away', it can make one less than fully present and attentive to the social and political complexities that are unfolding.

It is only through this critical 'situational' analysis of voice that we can render 'talk about talk' meaningful, systematic and political at once. Such analysis suggests that the current structure of voice, the attempts to settle the unsettled, supplies further power to the powerful. It might be a shallow type of controlling power, an image-setting power vis-à-vis the outsider that barely papers over the open secrets and the divergences of interpretation, but it is still power that has effects, both on the people who bear the containment and those who consume the public voice without delving deeper, with a final pay-off to the regime itself.

Notes

1. Informal discussion with an administrative officer at KIST, 9 March 2009.
2. Informal discussion with a journalist, Gitarama, 21 November 2008.
3. RPF runs as an alliance of six parties, including the Christian Democratic Party, the Islamic Democratic Party, Rwandese Socialist Party, Prosperity and Solidarity Party, Party for Progress and Concord and the Democratic Union of the Rwandese People.
4. NTK 17 January 2008.
5. Democratic Forces for the Liberation of Rwanda (ex-interahamwe).
6. The RPA had used proxies to operate in the DRC on at least two other occasions, working through and alongside the AFDL in the 'First Congo War' and RCD (later RCD-Goma) in the 'Second Congo War' (Prunier 2009). History was to repeat itself after 2009 as well.
7. Sezibera (2009), Presentation at the International Symposium on Genocide, Kigali, 4 April 2009.
8. Jackson, S. (not dated), p. 10 [accessed February 2009].
9. Most IDPs were people fleeing from the advancing RPF (Stockton 1994; Reed 1996).
10. Some estimates as low as 0.5 million have been proposed. It is possible that some IDPs have been double-counted as refugees.
11. This includes 0.5–1.5 million IDPs in addition to 1.1 million 'new-caseload' Hutu, and 0.5–0.8 million 'old-caseload' Tutsi.
12. The article refers to a 2006 population figure of 8.7 million.
13. Interview with a university student, returnee from Uganda, 2 February 2009.
14. Authors such as Vansina 2004, Newbury, D. 2001 and Pottier 2002, among others, point to the importance of clan, regional and lineage affiliations.
15. Informal discussion with a NURC employee, 17 November 2008.
16. Informal chat with a house employee, Nyamirambo, 29 October 2008.
17. Vision 2020 is a key government document outlining Rwanda's development strategy. The key objective is to transform Rwanda into a knowledge-based economy and a middle-income country.

18. Interview with a research institute employee, Kigali, 6 April 2009.
19. Ibid., 21 January 2009.
20. Interview with a RPF Communications Advisor, RPF Headquarters, 23 March 2009.
21. Ibid.
22. Ibid.
23. This came in response to allegations of double genocide.
24. Informal discussion, 22 November 2009.
25. NURC employee commenting on arrest of Rose Kabuye in Germany; 8 December 2008.
26. Informal interview with a MINALOC employee, 18 March 2009.
27. Informal chat at a local store, 10 April 2009.
28. A Tutsi survivor interviewed by Hatzfeld (2005a: 77).
29. Informal discussion with a government employee, MINALOC, 26 February 2009.
30. Interview with a RPF communications adviser and author of two books on Rwandan history and development, 23 March 2009.
31. Interview with a workshop facilitator at World Vision, 31 October 2008.
32. A way to say 'everything' (literal translation from buri byose).
33. Vansina (2004: 4) calls these 'courtiers who were official ideologues in charge of giving meaning to history and of elaborating the official version of its details. It was their task to set it forth, to hold it, to defend it against heresy, to elaborate on it, and to apply it to all the historical genres practiced at the court'.
34. In my experience, only a few people were extremely measured in their response or taciturn. Most people were willing to talk, and in some cases, these people turned into great informants, spending hours with me explaining details of programmes, policies or activities, such as the coordinator of the Muhazi *ingando* camp minutely detailing his own system of 'indirect control' in the camp.
35. Interview with Bernard, 18 March 2009.
36. Ibid., 22 February 2009.
37. Interview with Augustin, 22 January 2009.
38. Interview with the Communication and Public Relations Officer at a research institute, Kigali, 3 November 2008.
39. Informal interaction with a survivor and NURC employee, 17 March 2009.
40. Excerpt from 'Christophe's Story' by Nicki Cornwell (2006: 3), where the child's father comments on a pre-genocide kubohoza group coming to his house, pressuring him to switch party allegiance.
41. In fact, throwing rocks on the roofs of houses is a widespread strategy of harassment in Rwanda and also Burundi.
42. Interview with a research institute employee, 21 January 2009.
43. Ibid.
44. The perennial worry is that these informants might have a hidden agenda. Why do they talk at length if most people keep silent? This is a difficult question, but not because it is unanswerable but rather because it is complex and person-specific. Suffice it to say that one informant suffered harassment in the workplace and close family members repeatedly suffered from unfair

hiring practices. This informant was secretive about his critique (he was still working for the government). The other informant was not so guarded and was heard openly criticizing the government at donor meetings and other public occasions. This open behaviour puzzled me but it is possible he drew some degree of protection precisely from being known to outsiders. Due to aid dependence and preoccupation with image, the Rwandan government prefers to deal with dissidence in a more indirect manner.
45. 'Rwanda's 20-Year Miracle: "We Had Nowhere to Go but Up"', Think Africa Press, 7 April 2014.

Part II
The Political Process

'Rwanda is you and me' – the large sticker sign made of dark purple letters on a glittery background adorns a Nyamirambo-bound bus, colourful inside and blasting hip hop music as it makes impossible swerves around the potholes past the Biryogo mosque. Many signs like this give a unique identity to buses shuffling squeezed passengers to their destinations in this part of the town, a temporary togetherness of bags, bodies, babies and ware, all glued together with loud tunes and the heat. Knock knock, the coins for the fare hit the roof as a passenger announces their separation.

The 'you and me' in the slogan, the togetherness to which it appeals is the *turi kumwe* – we are together – told to a friend as you part, it is the tender holding of someone's hand or arm as you meet and chat on the street. Rwanda is 'you and me', concrete people even if strangers, navigating the uphill climb to Tapis Rouge. But of course, a powerful ambiguity lies at the core of that message. The story is not only one of circles of connection. A young girl holding her nose as the cabbage sellers enter the bus taints the rosy allegory. There is the talk of 'them', 'the others' (*abandi*). 'Watch out for the boys running the *inkweto* repair at the corner', 'I do not like the man you have been talking to', or 'Why would you want Congolese music burnt on a CD?' Some people(s), concrete and imagined, escape the circles and the embrace. There is also the ingrained distrust and the public façade of friendship. Determining who is the *nshuti nyanshuti* (real friend) is important and yet such a shifty ground.

There is also the abstract and official engineering of a 'you and me' by the elite, the outlines of a you that will make an us, the drawing of a new circle to which entry has to be earned, a distinct kind of political friendship. If politics is about the drawing of distinctions between the friend and the enemy, the dangerous other and the desired us, as Carl Schmitt (1927) has famously argued, then unity as officially pursued in Rwanda is deeply political. The project's inclusive roster hides a side of exclusion, and its integrative attempts uneasily coexist with disintegrative dynamics.

The key aim of this section is to demonstrate how post-genocide unity building and reconciliation are embedded within a broader political context from which they cannot easily be extracted. Three chapters study three different political aspects – the legitimations of power (focusing on discourses), the presence of the state (focusing on the structure) and the micro effects of power (focusing on emotions, attitudes, expectations) – to uncover in detail the profound impact of the political on the way in which unity is construed discursively, pursued strategically and enacted through performance as well as to understand the prospects of this process in achieving its stated goals.

The chapter on legitimization analyses issues of the greatest political 'currency' post-genocide around which tacit bargaining revolves (i.e., the political 'promises' to people) – security, prosperity and social harmony. The subsequent chapter then explores a theme that consolidated after mere weeks in the field, namely the presence of the state in people's lives. This is studied through apparatuses of power, specifically the administrative and information-based infrastructures of the state. The section closes with analysis of micro-power strategies and the feelings, attitudes, behaviours and resistances that the political system engenders.

Overall, the chapters will try to demonstrate how the political machine today moulds what unity and reconciliation mean, determines what can be achieved through unity and reconciliation activities (e.g., What kind of participation can result in this political setting?) and purposefully appropriates the unity and reconciliation process as a whole, shaping its nature in view of the government's broader social re-engineering goals. The chapters draw on a diverse evidence base: study of the official discourse, observation of political dynamics and semi-structured interviews with government employees across different ministries, RPF members, local state administrators as well as Rwandans outside of the officialdom.

The 'insertion' of the political machine into all social change processes, unity and reconciliation notwithstanding, creates its own important effects. This led me to conclude that the question 'Is the unity and reconciliation process successful?' is not the right question. It produces a misguided methodology, measuring results that we expect should be taking place. Instead, I observed the activities and realized that they are not only politicized but might at times have other-than-expected objectives and thus other-than-expected outcomes.

This set of chapters is crucial because here we delve beyond concrete policies, activities and subjects (the social ontology of the unity-building process) by studying the forces that shape these and put them into action. After all, how different people understand social categories that surround them cannot be extracted from political dynamics. The same is true for 'unity' – the way in which it is understood, used and pursued is part and parcel of the political process.

3

The Wording of Power
Legitimization as Narrative Currency

Many observers have noted and commented on the increasingly authoritarian political system in Rwanda, hidden under a mere 'façade of pluralism' (ICG 2002: 10; see also Mamdani 2001; Lemarchand 1997 and 2009; Reyntjens 2004, 2011a and 2013). The political analysis that follows takes a slightly different approach. It is not predominantly an analysis of concentrations of power or the structure of the political system (e.g., Is this an authoritarian system, and if so of what kind?). Rather, the focus here lies on the government's constant preoccupation with legitimation. Even the most repressive states lean on and exploit the language, whether direct or indirect, of reasons why they are in power and should stay there, often to an overall regime stabilizing (persistence) effect (Kailitz 2013; Gerschewski 2013; Grauvogel and von Soest 2013; Whaites 2008). While the emerging and largely comparative literature offers important insights into the role of legitimization in authoritarian regimes, we need more in-depth qualitative studies explaining the ways in which legitimization 'works'. With special relevance to the current project, paying close attention to the Rwandan government's legitimization practices and the language games of power proves extremely revealing of the political undertones and meanings attached to unity in contemporary Rwanda.

The question here is not 'Is this system legitimate?' but rather 'What kinds of legitimation are at work and to what effect?' and 'What do languages of legitimacy betray about "unity" as imagined and pursued by the government?' Fundamentally, the chapter aims to explain the manner in which the Rwandan government negotiates these basic political texts and subtexts – the languages it uses, the inconsistencies and thus instabilities that appear between discourse and fact, the manipulations that result. The title phrase 'wording of power' is not meant to suggest that legitimization is all about words, far from it. Authoritarian legitimation is 'no "cheap talk"' (Grauvogel and von Soest 2013: 8) and has 'fundamental political repercussions' (ibid.). But the title phrase does aim to highlight how wording and narration – the specifics of text – seek to structure the field not only of the possible, but the logical, the desirable, the excusable (see Foucault 1972 and 1980a; Hall 1997; Phillips and Hardy 2002; Fairclough 1989). Such structuring, however, means that regimes themselves can get 'entangled' in words, reflecting that political discourses create constraints, not only possibilities, for the powers that be.

Legitimation narratives are ones that revolve around promises, trade-offs, fears and hopes. Fundamentally, the word play is not only about excusing or making desirable. At its core, it is also a play of political intimacy with the constituency, a political communication of care, a dialogue that shares the keywords even if the resulting script is produced from the side of power. Importantly, the strong extraversion and masterful management of dependence of the Rwandan regime makes the dialogue a three-way process with the international community as a key implicit interlocutor in the structuring of legitimation narratives.

This chapter addresses three key legitimations used by the Rwandan government – the guarantee of security, the provision of welfare, and the delivery of unity as social harmony. Each of these languages of care will be analysed for the discrepancies and counter-readings that it obscures. Each legitimation will also bring us closer to the manner in which 'unity' is discoursed and the types of unities that Rwandan politics encourages and discourages. The analysis will expose a security narrative that hides its double and widens the scope of the regime's power, a development promise that cultivates both a pluralist façade and a need for consent in an ultimately weak attempt to 'work it all ways', and a claim to re-established political unity that disarms the government in dealing with the social and political fractures and exclusions that persist. Discourses indeed have real effects but they might not always or equally fortify the regime that deploys them.

Guarantors of Security: The Uses of Fear

'I am not asking you to love me, or even to like me, I just want security for everyone.'
Employee at the Ministry of Youth explaining Kagame's approach, 2009

'The word "protection" sounds two contrasting tones.
One is comforting, the other ominous.'
Charles Tilly, 'War Making and State Making as Organised Crime'

The core legitimation technique in Rwanda today revolves around discourses of security. Understandably, security is a salient issue in a post-conflict society. The notion that, if nothing else, the RPF is to be credited with the re-establishment and maintenance of a peaceful order in Rwanda is fed by but also feeds power. 'Security of the nation is primordial,' suggests President Kagame, 'no matter the price'.[1] The legitimation is so powerful that it becomes especially important to deconstruct. The production of security in Rwanda reaches beyond the concept of public good as it also serves as a political currency and a 'regime good'. The concept of 'double-edged protection' (Tilly 1985: 170) is useful here, urging us to consider carefully the interplay between the comfort and fear of securitization, and between the reality and fiction of threats that are used to rationalize it. It is indispensable to ask at what point does security stop being an indisputable achievement and an innocuous promise and become a powerful tool for a government in assuring its continued grasp on power. The chapter first unpacks the claim that the RPF is the guarantor of security before turning to the way in which the meaning of 'unity' is profoundly affected by a securitization of political discourse.

The Foundational Violence of Post-Genocide Security

In July 1994, the Rwandan Patriotic Front halted the genocide and restored calm on most of Rwanda's territory. Full pacification was achieved only four years later in 1998 when the insurgency in the 'explosive' Northern and Western provinces was defeated (Kinzer 2008: 365, 215). The story of ending the hecatomb omits RPF's own role in increasing insecurity upon their 1990 invasion of Rwanda, their use of violence over four years to achieve military objectives, the killing of civilians in that process, the retaliatory violence[2] that resulted, and the contribution to the radicalization of the Hutu regime (Kinzer 2008; Lemarchand 2009; Kuperman 2001). However hard we look and think, we cannot avoid the fact that the RPF inhabits a grey zone.

In post-genocide Rwanda, however, morality does not operate with greyscales. The RPF paints its campaign in a heroic light as 'liberation', it exalts militarism and the 'ultimate sacrifice', pushing masses through exercises of gun demystification and, importantly, it draws distinction between legitimate and illegitimate violence. Naturally, the drawing of such distinction, along with the appropriation and even proselytization of justified violence is key for a government that captured power through military victory. While those who get to power through the deployment of force simply rule, 'heroes' discursively create a right to rule. This dynamic is directly connected to the wider problem of the belittling of and exceptionalism with regard to RPF crimes. While the genocide is undoubtedly a unique crime, this does not detract from the fact that tens of thousands of civilians died at the hands of the RPF (Lemarchand 2009; Prunier 2009; UN 2010) and that, nonetheless, the victims have no redress and no place in public debate. At the macro level, *jenoside* remains an exclusive horror. At the individual level, scales drop their meaning, and all killing becomes injustice in need of recognition.

During my stay in Rwanda, a number of my informants, some of them students, revealed to me somewhere in the threads of our conversation, that their families were killed by the RPF yet 'we were not allowed to bury them, not even to mention them'.[3] This literal obscurity of the Hutu remains contrasts starkly with the televized and populous ceremonies for the reburying of Tutsi remains in mass graves and their amassing on shelves in multiple memorials such as those in Gisozi or Ntarama (Collins 2004; Hatzfeld 2005a: 148). Walks to memorials and their cleaning (*gusukura*) are staple activities during unity and reconciliation events or commemoration months. Rwanda is also the only country where remains can be legally buried only in officially designated mass sites. Yet both mass burials and display of remains clash with cultural norms. People fear that such practices might prevent souls from finding rest, bring misfortune, and result in what forensic anthropologists refer to as irreversible 'co-mingling' of remains. More importantly yet, these sites are also unacknowledged depositories of unearthed Hutu remains of RPF crimes, which, passed off as 'genocide victims' are thus doubly erased from history (Burnet 2012). The differential treatment of violent death – on one side ostentatiously displayed and thus affirmed, on the other side adamantly albeit shallowly buried and thus 'nonexistent' – is one of the key forces a priori undermining any process of reconciliation.

Besides the foundations of insecurity on which today's security in Rwanda is guaranteed, the Rwandan government also remains a major exporter of insecurity in the region. It destabilizes the DRC in the name of securitizing Rwanda. The RPF has initiated two invasions in 1996 and 1998 as well as more recent proxy wars in 2008 and 2012 to neutralize the enemy – the remnants of the genocidal *interahamwe* militias, which fled to then Zaire in the aftermath of the genocide and reorganized there under the banner of ALIR and later the FDLR. The invasions led to regional involvement and the 'first African World War' (1998–2003) and resulted in a death toll many times higher than that of the Rwandan genocide itself. Academic literature and international reports (Prunier 2009; Reyntjens 2011a; UNSC 1998, 2001, 2008 and UNHCHR 2010) however increasingly support the claim that 'the government uses *interahamwe* to achieve other objectives in the DRC'.[4] Rwandan exploitation of natural resources in the DRC, coordinated by the government (UN 2001) was used initially to 'finance their [military] operations' (Prunier 2009: 220). Eventually, however, 'preserving their stake [mining interests] and control in Eastern Congo became a domestic necessity' (ibid.: 274).

Security suffuses the political discursive space in Rwanda for a number of reasons. Threats are said to emanate from the outside – the FDLR most visibly. Eriksen (2005) has argued that the external security threat has been key in 'strengthening' the Rwandan state after the genocide. But there are internal dynamics at play as well that are equally important. The political discourse highlights a continuous threat on the inside in the form of 'genocide ideology' and this today forms the cornerstone of the 'unfinished battle' narrative and the continuous pointer for the value of RPF's labour in security production. Presence of both internal and external enemies repeatedly underwrites the need for the guarantor (i.e., continued presence in power of the RPF), the high level of securitization within the country, as well as the repeated interventions in the DRC. In Rwanda's play of legitimizations, security needs to be seen as both tangibly present and potentially precarious. It is not a given and has to be repeatedly protected from threats. In other words, security needs to remain a salient issue. Excessive control over the populace is thus legitimized explicitly through the security card. For securitization, after all, order is needed as is surveillance. Among other things, this justifies the maintenance of a sizeable corps of internal security and policing personnel.[5]

The Securitized State and Discourse: The Friend-Enemy Distinction as an Ordering Subtext in Rwanda

The security discourse shapes internal political dynamics in yet a more fundamental way. Lodging of legitimacy in the sphere of security introduces dichotomous, even Manichaean thinking to political practice and wider social relations. The security discourse is based on a powerful dichotomy of 'friend' versus 'enemy' and this division matches the discursive distinction between 'unity' and 'division' in Rwanda. 'Division' as deployed in Rwanda today connotes a political enemy. 'Friends', on the other hand, are loyalists, active promoters or simply those who do not stray out of line.

The enemy category is deleterious, and its persistence today worrying. During the genocide, the RPF invasion was reported on the radio as 'aggression by the *inyangarwanda*', the enemies of Rwanda or literally 'those who hate Rwanda'.[6] Symbolically, genocide emerged when a particular race was conflated with the enemy and thus thrown to the realm of exception. Yet the logic of categorical murder is not only the logic of genocide but it is, more widely, the logic of war. If we drill to the core, it is the logic emerging during times of perceived existential insecurity. War is nonetheless the trigger par excellence of a state of exception, permitting all those in the category of enemy/foe to be liquidated in order to preserve the corpus of the 'legitimate', sovereign 'self'. What exactly falls into the category of enemy though is open to manipulation. In Rwanda during the genocide, a purposeful 'extension fallacy' (Purdekova 2009) equated all Tutsi with enemy or accomplice (*icyitso*; also Hutu who refused to cooperate; Straus 2006). Killing the Tutsi was relayed as an act of war (ibid.), a pre-emptive action to protect oneself in a state of generalized insecurity, called the 'programme of civilian self-defence' by the administration (Stover and Weinstein 2004: 50).

But even outside of war and thus more generally, 'threat' and 'enemy' and 'insecurity' have triggered states of exception, where otherwise unacceptable methods and trade-offs might be legitimized. In one understanding, the realm is created by the sovereign power (hence 'sovereign exception') which can lift specific laws, or which can transcend law (and 'sacrifice without killing', Agamben 1998) in the name of public good, typically security. Today, the Rwandan government holds the power to relegate people and groups of people into spaces of exception by implicitly labelling them 'enemies' and 'threats' through explicit labelling as 'divisionists', those who possess 'genocide ideology' or, most recently, 'terrorists', or those associated with terrorists (accomplices). The head of state is unequivocal about the treatment of the latter: 'This is not a threat but a warning: do not stand idly by as if your indifference, or worse, your complicity has no consequences'.[7]

Almost twenty years after the genocide, enemies (*abanzi b'igihugu*) have not disappeared from within Rwanda. In the official discourse, they continue to exist in the disguise of 'divisionism' (*amacakubiri*) and 'genocide ideology' (*ingenga bitekereezo ya jenoside*). At the time of fieldwork, these terms have been staples in the political vocabulary and daily political communication. In fact, the 'home front' has become more salient than the foreign front vis-à-vis security legitimizations. Pointing out the internal threats that the government can master enhances its security-based legitimacy claims. Though genocide ideology is said to be 'slowly creeping back into the society' (Kezio-Musoke for NTK, 2008), the government claims it can manage the threat. Kagame warns those who 'sow the seeds of divisionism': 'We have enough machines to crush the grains'.[8]

The campaign against 'divisionism' took off in 2002, 'transforming by 2004 into a campaign against "genocide ideology" as well' (HRW 2008: 37). Since this time four separate parliamentary commissions (2003, 2004, 2006 and 2007) investigated and condemned alleged cases of both crimes, reporting a large prevalence of genocide ideology in secondary schools across the country. The then-Minister of Education was sacked, and all teachers in secondary schools were forced to attend lengthy *ingando* camps of up to three months. An internal war of sorts began and the struggle reached all the way to children and to relations between children and parents. The fight literally happens 'at home': '[We realized] that besides the people we are already dealing with, FDLR, prisoners, maybe we have to do something at home'.[9] The reality is that 'hatred goes on and it is taught in families'.[10] A parliamentarian and proponent of the 'law fighting against genocide ideology' explained to me that 'there is genocide ideology among the population, particularly youth. But how is it possible? You were born after the genocide! It is possible only through your parents ... The children [we talked to] promised to be separated from their parents in terms of genocide ideology'.[11] To 'separate' them, the state takes charge. Children as young as nine have been detained and the press reported that 'two primary school girls were jailed over genocide ideology' (Ngabonziza for NTK, 2008). Children and youth thus accused are sent to correctional facilities or prisons. Besides punishment, children are targeted for training and are politicized. The Fourth Children's Summit held on 11 November 2008 in Kigali was organized under the banner 'Child Participation in the Fight Against Genocide Ideology'.[12] With the help of activities such as this, the direction of parent-child authority is partially reversed as children become additional government campaigners: 'Sometimes our parents or other grown-up people have tendencies to grow seeds of discrimination into us. We need to say no and sensitize them against it' (Kwibuka for NTK, November 14 2008).

Divisionism and genocide ideology, however, are only vaguely defined (Reyntjens 2013; Waldorf 2011; AI 2010; HRW 2008). Phrases such as 'stirring [sic] ill feelings', 'propounding wickedness' or phrases referring to acts that 'divide people or spark conflicts or cause uprising based on discrimination' assure that the two terms are 'replete with ambiguity' (AI 2010: 17). 'Rwandan judges interviewed by HRW themselves cannot define what divisionism is, despite the fact that each has adjudicated and convicted on these charges following the "I know it when I see it approach"' (HRW 2008: 34). The vagueness became apparent in many of my own interviews too. Paradoxically, the lawmakers gave me the broadest definition, speaking of 'any form of discrimination'[13] or 'exclusion'.[14] Despite being 'broad and ill-defined' (HRW 2008: 7) or perhaps precisely because of this, these terms are useful and widely used political tools. They have been used to get rid of political opposition ('criminalizing criticism', HRW 2010a: 7), business adversaries or to resolve personal disputes. Over the past years, the government used the charge of divisionism to attack any remaining organized opposition (*opozisiyo*) and to silence critical reporting. In fact, it has been used as a mechanism to 'silence *any* opposition' (Buckley-Zistel 2006: 110). 'Divisionism is basically when you are criticizing the government, that is it',[15] summed up one of my informants. This applies to critique by researchers, which is presented as 'rooted in genocide ideology and revisionism'.[16] But it is not only open critique that is targeted. 'The accusation can be and has been arbitrarily used for anyone who is not walking in the lines of the ruling RPF party' (RMP 2003: 7). This has included 'dissent from government plans for consolidating land holdings'.[17] The result is the criminalization of any insubordination and the subsequent use of prosecution to quell it.

The discourse of security, based on the meta-structure of friend-enemy, brings a specific logic to legitimation. If the life of the regime is equated with (made indispensable for) the life of the people, then a threat to that regime becomes a threat to the people (and in need of being 'cleared'). Through this discursive manoeuvre, security exception is extended to preservation of power. Since divisionism and genocide ideology are now the enemy, the source of insecurity, they are created as a space of exception and a powerful space of decontestation. Additionally, an independent and powerful social dynamic results. All that is successfully associated with 'divisionism' can be cleared, all that is successfully associated with 'unity' prospers. As mentioned, people can be framed as divisionist not only if they are dangerous politically, but also if they are threatening economically, or for other reasons. 'Divisionism' and 'genocide ideology' become avenues manipulated from below; accusations of divisionism become a broadly used political tool. Accusations indeed reach all levels of society and different social situations. They even structure quarrels among survivors in *gacaca* courts. On at least one occasion, a survivor was accused of genocide ideology by other survivors because he decided to tell the truth in *gacaca*, going against a broader collusion to indict a prisoner.[18] If the struggle against genocide ideology is a war of sorts, then just as with other wars it produces a wide space for the implication and clearing of social adversaries. The 'struggle' thus becomes not only a regime good, it also becomes a government-instigated public bad.

At a more symbolic level, the manner in which this discourse 'clears' social space can be seen through personal name change. *Izina ry'irigenurano* (pl. amazina y'amagenurano), explained to me as given names carrying negative connotations meant to divide or segregate people, are the only names that can be changed without a problem and their holders are encouraged to do so. The examples of such names include *Mbarimombazi* (I am with you but 'I know you', meaning I am watching you, I do not necessarily trust you, I am vigilant) *Tubanambazi* (I live with you but I know you) or *Mvukamubanzi* (I am born among the enemy). However, simply 'harsh' names such as *Ntamuhe* (I have no pity) are not considered divisionist. This is relevant because it reflects that 'unity' in Rwanda does not necessarily correlate with peace. In fact, large military campaigns or small hits against individual enemies can be powerful tools of unification. State assassins targeting 'traitors' (*ingambanyi*) – dissidents who break ranks with the government – are promised to be treated as 'heroes', the exemplary types of political friends (see York and Rever 2014).

The fact that names draw the state's attention reflects their importance in Rwandan society. Given names are imbued with meaning, they refer to important contexts of birth that are believed to determine the future of the child. They might also be wishes for the future or warnings about it. Names are a concentrated knowledge and an opening to a personal historical narrative. Therein also lies their danger. At NURC, a young employee explained:

> For example, children who were born while their father is at prison and who gives the child a negative, divisionist name ... later the child asks the mother 'Why am I called like this?' [and she says]: 'This name was given to you by your father, who is in prison.' 'Why is he in prison?' Then the story comes out. You see, the name can be a lasting memory, a trigger of negative ideology.[19]

Since names are seen as triggers of memory and openings to a narrative, the extension and application of the unity/division discourse is again meant to suppress certain narratives, as it does also more widely in press or academic, especially historical texts, but also speeches or songs. 'Renaming' always follows regime changes. But in its essence, it is only one means of control over language and the way in which language is allowed to reflect on society and its history, literally to 'constitute them'. In Rwanda, the expressions *izina ni ryo muntu* (or *ni ryo kintu*) suggests that 'the name is the very man' (or 'the very thing'). The name is supposed to contain in itself 'much of the meaning'.[20] But the presupposition can create political utility as naming might lead to masking, especially when it comes to naming (or labelling) the political.

Security's Rule: The Rule of Fear?

Rwanda's security is one of social control, producing a repressive order. The government polices the country so tightly that crime levels are low, there is little organized protest (or any spontaneous mass protest) and the return of *genocidaires* from prisons and exile has taken place without any major outbursts of conflict. Despite the heavy securitization, 'unnecessary deaths'[21] continue to legitimize further surveillance by the state through official police, Local Defence Forces (LDFs) and plain-clothes police ('community police'). At the lowest administrative levels of village and the cell, the recently established Community Policing Committees (CPCs) organize additional security mechanisms such as the night patrols (*irondo*) and the Neighbourhood Watch programme (*ijisho ry'umuturanyi*, literally 'neighbour's eye'), urging community ownership of monitoring and reporting on 'security incidents'.

Who is really 'safe' in Rwanda is a political question that gets to the core of the very partial endeavour of security production. Certain insecurities are emphasized in government rhetoric (e.g., *interahamwe*, genocide ideology) and portrayed as manageable, the capability to dominate them being the mainstay of the government. But other insecurities are simply left aside or silenced. Many survivors repeatedly relive scenes of terror in their traumatic episodes, which increase during *icyunamo* commemoration ceremonies, in *gacaca* court hearings, and upon meetings with killers on the tiny paths that criss-cross rural Rwanda. Many others live in insecurity, in fear and paranoia for holding certain political opinions, 'sensitive information', or for questioning the authority of the government, or for simply being framed or perceived as such. The threats issued to them might never translate into direct and visible physical violence. Arbitrary arrest and ill-treatment in detention, even disappearances are all certainly present too, even if pushed out of sight (AI 2012; US DoS 2014; HRW 2014, among others).

What is thus at stake is not simply a narrow definition of security but the direct production of insecurity. In today's Rwanda, threat has transformed from an imminent threat of an invasion or group uprising to a day-to-day mix of security tasks with the ultimate outcome of regime protection. And to protect itself, the regime metes out its own violence. The insecurity produced at the 'centre' is the most invisible and normalized (Scheper-Hughes 1992). It does not operate through mass purges or killings and yet it is still 'physical', creating concrete symptoms on the body and the mind. What is at work are thus not simply actions, but a structure of experience.

All in all, the power of the Rwandan security discourse lies in the fear that it both stirs and assuages – the threats against security it can manipulate and master but also through the fear it creates itself, a fear more general and dispersed, which helps it to rule unopposed. Ultimately, the government is not immune to fear itself – some would say it is built on fear's very back. According to one of my informants, politics today is based on *l'équilibre de la peur* – the equilibrium of fear:[22] a small minority is ruling over the vast majority because they are afraid of what would otherwise ensue. A powerful distrust of the Hutu masses (their feelings and intentions) underlies this fear, which, due to repression, can neither be affirmed nor diffused.

By surrendering to this fear, the government ignores not only the wider scholarship on causalities of violence but even its own analyses showing that genocide did not result from primordial identity-based hatred but mainly from 'bad governance'. The nationwide grassroots consultations of 1996/97 aiming to identify 'causes of disunity' among Rwandans found the top three reported causes to be *inda nini* (greed; literally big stomach), a non-participatory political system (exclusion) and *ubujiji* (ignorance) (Musoni 2003: 6), none of which is a characteristic of 'a people', whatever name we give them.

Guarantors of Prosperity: Consent for Development

> 'We are herded like cows, we just hope that the place to which they lead us has greener grass.'
> A Rwandan university student

Security is not a sufficient legitimization, and it is the potent promise of prosperity that is skilfully used to extract further political credit. As a developmental state (Booth and Golooba-Mutebi 2012) and 'comparable to other settings where liberation movements have come to power, the promise of development [is] deployed as a legitimisation strategy for the state' (Muller 2008: 112). The Rwandan government has to offer a strong enough compensation – promises and tokens of pay-off – to its people, most of whom live in poverty and without a number of political rights. But people's expectation of a dividend is also compounded by the heavy taxation of every person in the first place. In other words, the government is 'promising developments' (Pells et al. 2014) because people themselves are made into unwilling shareholders to a particular state-led campaign of wholesale social and economic transformation (see the following two chapters on a more encompassing conception of 'tax').

In what follows, I want to argue that the centrality of development in the government's legitimization corpus explains two key and contradictory political dynamics: on the one hand, the belabouring of images of a benevolent and liberal government that do not fit with reality – a whole 'dynamics of gaps' – and, on the other hand, the contradictory dynamic of practising and cultivating 'consent for development'. The reality-to-please contrasts quite starkly with the oft-emphasized need for economic and political independence, thus highlighting a key tension in today's Rwanda – one between the desire for autonomy and the reality of dependence. In the words of one of my informants, 'Today we are officially a democracy. Before everyone knew it was a one-party state, but today we say multiparty democracy … There is a gap between speech and facts.'[23] Why is image so important in today's Rwanda? Why belabour and carefully protect images so contrasting with realities on the ground? Most obviously, this relates to the reality of economic dependence on liberal democratic states. At the time of fieldwork, about half of the government budget came from the outside (48 per cent in 2009/2010 according to the government's own estimates; MINECOFIN 2010b). As a result, it has been important to present a pleasing and satisfactory façade to the donors. But the image is crucial for a more general reason – to attract investment capital to Rwanda from all possible sources. This has resulted in a gap at many levels between the government's self-portrayal as a democracy and a more complicated and definitely discordant reality.

Preoccupation with a democratic image feeds, perhaps paradoxically, into the government's general repressive tendencies. It directly strengthens anxiety over critique and its subsequent suppression. Desirable representation is essential and those who highlight the discrepancy are undermining the project. Researchers are thus also potentially dangerous, and there is palpable nervousness about what they will 'find'. Research is welcome and supported as long as it 'spreads the good news'. Reports prepared in conjunction with foreign experts are manipulated and re-edited into more 'acceptable' forms (e.g., the case of the Joint Governance Assessment (JGA) report). The worry over image also leads to belabouring of image-relevant cultural aspects (cleanliness; umuganda's nature as a large clean-up exercise) and governance styles (order and discipline).

Besides the fundraising-friendly and investment-friendly profile, another important reason for the gap is tied to internal constituencies rather than external benefactors: the RPF presents itself as the 'liberator' of Rwanda and its armed struggle as a 'liberation struggle'. Indeed, when the RPF formed, its platform extended beyond the core principle of a right of return for refugees and all Rwandans to their country (which really gave rise to the movement in the first place). Realizing this was not sufficient either to form a broad enough base of power inside Rwanda, or prevent mistreatment and discrimination towards the returnees, the RPF opted to include the 'removal of the dictatorship' (i.e., removal of Habyarimana's government) and fostering of unity among all people. Indeed, in an interview with Senator Inyumba, the RPF war was called 'the struggle for democracy' (Kwinjeh for NTK, 23 August 2008). Both of these reasons powerfully show that legitimation under authoritarian regimes can produce its own discursive 'binds' (Grauvogel and von Soest 2013).

The Contours of 'Feigned Plurality': Making Multipartyism Within Consensual Politics

The official discourse claims that 'leaders are in the hands of the people'.[24] Indeed, not only is the whole democracy-relevant developmentalist language ('the right buzzwords', Prunier 2009: 294) present but so is the whole institutional façade. Rwanda 'has parties' and 'holds elections' and has 'separation of powers'. It is involved in 'decentralization' and carries out 'grassroots consultations' and multiple 'local participatory activities'. Yet, despite the government's claims to the contrary, the Rwandan political system is an authoritarian one (Prunier 2009; Roth 2009). Power is centralized – the executive reigns and one party dominates. Elections are no more than rites of 'continuation'. This has been well documented by researchers and my own fieldwork certainly supports these claims. The paragraphs that follow will only briefly explore the façade of pluralism versus the reality of severely obstructed opposition.

First, Rwanda demonstrates well that the mere existence of multiple parties is an insufficient marker of a democracy. Rwanda has parties and yet no meaningful formal political opposition. Real opposition is either in exile[25] or is severely suppressed.[26] Parties that exist are either part of the RPF 'united front'[27] or its puppet parties.[28] The RPF-dominated government carefully balances 'pluralism for show' and its maintenance of control. The game is useful: 'There are no political parties as such', suggests one of my informants, 'They are there in the writing, but we really have just one party, we just want to fool you, then you provide support.'[29] On another occasion, we continue the discussion: 'The other parties are not really parties, [they are] not serious. In fact it is a way of fooling the international community, our godfathers. [Since] they are accusing us of monopartyism, dictatorship, what do we do? [We] tell A, who is a member of our party [RPF] to create her own party',[30] which will be separate but friendly, aligned and not very active. The result is the desired simultaneity of multiple parties and a lack of multipartyism.

There are various mechanisms to assure the desired result of non-threatening opposition. First, a new organic law introduced in 2003 'allowed political parties to be registered only under certain strict conditions. This new law imposed tight restrictions on all political parties, stipulating that they must "reflect the unity of the Rwandan people" and would be "prohibited from disseminating information [of] a denigrating and divisive nature" … It is not hard to see such sweeping clauses as giving incumbents a means of holding on to power, by harassing and intimidating their political opponents and perceived enemies' (Hintjens 2008: 88). Second, to be legally active all parties are required to be members of the 'Forum of Political Parties' (US DoS 2008: 13), a component of the RPF ruling party, which takes decisions by consensus and has the power to interfere with the internal working of other parties.

The core issue is that opposition (understood as divergence of political programmes and a political process involving contentious debate) is viewed in an a priori negative light, as counter-productive. It 'divides' attention, effort and thus energy that should be spent entirely on following a common goal, the political consensus to achieve economic development. Alternatively, opposition figures are seen as political opportunists trying to rally people behind a common 'shield',[31] 'stealing' constituencies or simply trying to 'bring down a strong party'.[32] The claim that multipartyism in Africa is fundamentally divisive, together with the vague threats of 'divisionism' and 'genocide ideology' are useful tools to mould, obstruct or destroy opposition. But the process of undermining opposition begins long before any formal, organized party makes their appearance, and works through general suppression of voice and 'groupness' (Brubaker 2004).

Just as it is insufficient to have parties, Rwanda demonstrates that regular elections are not indicative of the strength, or really, the existence of democracy. Observers have proclaimed Rwandan elections to be neither fair nor free (e.g., Reyntjens 2009). The 97 per cent turnout in the 2003 elections, along with the results, has been called truly 'soviet-style' (Roth 2009). In the 2008 parliamentary elections, the government allegedly inflated the figures for the opposition to avoid an even more embarrassing RPF acclamation (the official result was a 92 per cent win for the RPF; ibid.). All this massive support in a country that, according to its own line, is pervaded by *ingengabitekerezo ya jenoside* (genocide ideology). In general, election results are 'known' – election confirms appointments.

But what happens at the local level, in what manner are people stripped of their power to demonstrate a free choice? Some believe that the results themselves are manipulated: 'All ballots were poured into toilets, some were kept locked in rooms, [they] banned the real votes,'[33] suggests one informant.

'I can give you names,' swears another, 'names of young people stamping voting cards with their thumbs all night.'[34] Whether these comments on the 2008 elections are true or false, election observers reported that those responsible 'did not initially seal ballot boxes' (US DoS 2009: 16) and that this happened in 76 per cent of the observed stations (Reyntjens 2009). It is crucial to mention that the mission observed 576 stations out of a total of more than 15,000 (ibid.). Votes might indeed have been 'stolen' from the people. But it is important to understand that this can be achieved through ways other than the manipulation of results. The management of the very act of voting might be where the theft begins. Voting presupposes a choice and a freedom to make it. Rather than looking at the holding of elections or turnouts, it is the nature of participation that we have to analyse. To begin with, it is mandatory to vote (one cannot 'signal' by absenting); all the while there are hardly any parties and all serious contenders are attacked during pre-election time (HRW 2010a and 2010b). The RPF is the only party active locally, they are not only 'present' (with local offices), they are an active recruiter – there is a pressure to join. The absence of real alternatives can also be readily observed by marking the monopolized 'political display'.[35]

The dynamics of voting itself further constrains choice: 'I've been in those places where they make us line behind the candidate of "choice"', writes a Rwandan blogger, 'At night or the previous night, the local liaison will go from house to house directing villagers to vote for an RPF operative. These poor villagers know what would happen if they tried to demonstrate their democratic rights.'[36] Essentially, this is selection that has to appear as election: 'They say we choose them [district mayors] but we do not. The political machinery is made in such a way that from top to grassroots, there are structures responsible for choosing people, because they have to make a campaign for them. [You] tell people if you do not choose these [preselected candidates], you will get what you deserve.'[37] The allegations of surveillance in the voting process suggest much more indirect and diffuse dynamics might be at play. As regards the 2001 elections of local officials, 'there was no privacy, as everyone had to cast his vote in the presence of a "helper", right inside each polling booth' (OPJDR 2001). But even more broadly, if in Ethiopia (Lefort 2010) 'local residents [in Amhara state] believed that the authorities have unknown means of tracing everybody's vote', this kind of profound distrust in the possibility of 'anonymity' must only be more pronounced in Rwanda where both distrust and surveillance are deeply entrenched.

Finally, and again despite surface appearance, there is alignment rather than separation of powers in Rwanda – all powers align with the dominant executive. 'I remember in 1996/97 or even later, Kagame was defining [to us] "participatory democracy" [as a situation] where RPF defines priority actions and then … sensitizes people to implement them.'[38] Commandment

(Mbembe 2001) in Rwanda operates through 'order' or 'instruction'.[39] Rwandan judges see a discrepancy between laws as they appear on paper and the reality of judicial independence (HRW 2008): 'The principle is one of separation but the executive wants to control everything.' Another judge suggested that independence 'is a state of law, but in fact it is the word of the chief that rules' (HRW 2008: 45).

The judiciary is not only non-independent but the lower-end state executives often mete 'justice' extra-judicially. A 2007 HRW report describes collective punishments ordered (outside of their official capacity) by local authorities, which included fines, involuntary labour and beatings. Local HR NGOs also reported that local officials briefly detained individuals who disagreed publicly with government decisions or policies. Security forces are known to arrest and detain persons arbitrarily and without due process (US DoS 2009; Prunier 2009).

When one digs deeper, a slightly different official narrative emerges, one that does not defend democracy but authoritarianism instead. The current government believes that pluralism divides and that 'consensual' politics is best suited to sustain peace and development in Rwanda. According to a female member of parliament, what Rwandan politics needs is 'one vision, one direction' whose absence 'makes it hard to talk of reconstruction of the nation'.[40] The democratic process is believed to be a priori 'disuniting' – elections might invite rupture, parties might invite subversion, separation of powers might spell non-alignment. This belief is openly expressed in the official transcript: 'While the RPF agreed to work within a multiparty framework, some of its leaders expressed serious misgivings about the risks posed by such a system. In 1995, Kagame told a journalist that unbridled multipartyism would result in "dividing people who are already divided"' (HRW 2002: 4). Rwanda's electoral law, an MP told me, is an example of a 'unity and reconciliation legislature' because, historically, elections have been 'one of the disuniting factors'.[41] In general, an NGO director suggested, 'there is a consensus to build the nation and to oppose [this] is not good'.[42] It is not only the threat of instability, the need to build a nation, but also the imperative of economic development that are all used to legitimize authoritarian rule: 'About six years ago, when we got materials from Singapore,' a former government insider tells me, 'there was a consensus – let's forget politics, let's focus on economics, there will be outcomes benefiting everyone. The [agreed upon] consensus was to be implemented in an authoritarian way. [But] it was not meant to be implemented [by] a little group around Kagame [as it turned out to be]'.[43]

Guarantors of Social Harmony: The Layers of Political Unity

In June 2009, I had the opportunity to serve as an expert witness on a Rwandan national's asylum case. One of the lawyers, who had recently overseen similar cases in US courts, told me to expect the following retort from the presiding judge: 'But Rwanda has officially restored ethnic harmony'. This was a powerful reminder of the success of the power's own representation and the invisibility of the gap between this image and the events on the ground. This experience, along with a more recent case requesting my assessment of the past and present state of the 'ethnic conflict in Rwanda' reflect how outsiders often judge identity politics. The official absence of discrimination seems comforting if not sufficient as a proof of unity, and what seems to matter is specifically ethnic hatred and discrimination. The latter of the two testifies to an adamant bias to 'ethnicize' conflict and social diversity in Rwanda and Africa more broadly. Both of these dynamics produce a degree of external credit to the government. Nonetheless, as will be argued here, the legitimation is ultimately one which enfeebles the regime.

In the RPF political discourse, unity has also been approached principally through the lens of ethnicity, as 'inter-ethnic' unity. The formation of the RPF in exile in December 1987 was accompanied by a revision of its political platform. The new 'Eight Point Agenda'[44] included as the most important among its points the promise of 'unity'. At the RPF Headquarters, it was emphasized to me that 'the first point of RPF politics [was and remains] to reinforce national unity'.[45] In fact, the claim to a restored inter-ethnic unity is used by the Rwandan government as a powerful legitimization of rule and a chip to gain foreign support. But what type of unified community has the government created? In what follows, I will try to critically address claims to political 'unity' by looking at, and beyond, the dominant project of 'de-ethnicisation'. I would like to offer a broad genealogy of post-genocide political unity (union), critically exploring the formation of one state, inclusive national citizenship and de-ethnicized politics.

To Have One State: Forced Migration as a Political Tool

The basic post-genocide decision to continue living together in one political community was not as commonsensical a proposition as it might first appear. The calls for creation of a separate 'Hutuland' and 'Tutsiland' have never gained traction but certainly have a history. At the RPF headquarters, a senior spokesperson of the party[46] recounted how 'the President of Kenya, Daniel Arap Moi, found a genius response to genocide, to separate the Tutsi and the Hutu! There is also a professor in the US who proposed it. [But] you know, [President] Bizimungu's wife is a Tutsi. Well, she would have to go to Tutsiland, her husband to Hutuland, and their children to ... no man's land [laughing]'. Another veteran of Rwandan politics suggested that the idea predates the genocide: 'This was long ago, [President] Kayibanda was proposing it, some stupid idea, before independence, he was sending messages to the UN that there should be Hutuland and Tutsiland because they cannot live together. Lemarchand, writing on the history of Burundi and Rwanda, he was quoting it, but Lemarchand did not know the irony, that Kayibanda was a Hutu with a Tutsi wife [giggling]'.[47]

However unviable and undesirable was the idea of two official entities, it is hard to deny that de facto and informally, the refugee camps formed in the DRC just after the genocide (1994–1996) became a 'Hutuland' of sorts, a state within a state with all the 'trappings of sovereignty' (Prunier 2009: 47). In the camps, millions of people – the vast majority of them Hutu – were organized administratively, governed by their previous authorities and terrorized by militia and soldiers, which coerced them into military exercises and prevented them from leaving. Rwanda itself at that time was depopulated, it was 'empty of everything', as one of my informants suggested.[48] 'From the camps, the genocidal leader Jean Bosco Barayagwiza boasted that "even if [the Tutsi-led Rwandan Patriotic Front] has won a military victory it will not have power. We have the population"' (Lischer 2005: 1). This meant that the 'unified' state that the RPF envisioned had to be literally forced into life. In 1996, the first invasion of the DRC had as its main aim the destruction of the militarized camps and forced return of their inhabitants back 'home'. This invasion was preceded and followed by other forced returns and re-populations of Rwanda – from Burundi, Tanzania, and Uganda (Whitaker 2002; UN News Service 2005; Pambazuka 2010; APA-Kigali 2010).

The manipulations of 'return' did not only concern the Hutu. In fact, right after the genocide, a mass of old-caseload Tutsi refugees returned from Uganda, when, as some recount 'the city still stank, there was blood mixed with stale water and there was the stench of dead people'.[49] Why did so many return immediately after the genocide? 'You see, it was a policy of the RPF,' a returnee suggested. 'Although the UNHCR said that resettlement assistance will be planned and phased, the RPF told people "first come, first serve", and so they all returned at once.'[50] In the politically unstable post-genocide climate, RPF needed to surround itself with loyal constituencies, but it also needed instant legitimizations – after all, the front had fought for the possibility of return and needed to demonstrate the masses returning home from exile, rather than a gradual, hesitant trickle. The government also needed people who were willing and trustworthy to rebuild the country, starting with burying the dead.[51] The actual, physical 'coming together' in Rwanda thus in itself betrays the fragile basis of the post-1994 union.

The Blurry Borders of Rwandanness: The Politics of Inclusion and Exclusion

As mentioned previously, the RPF political programme of 'cross-ethnic unity' predates the genocide. In the diaspora, the call to 'unity' was a useful and necessary platform for the RPF. It served to broaden the political base at the same time as it bolstered the discourse of legitimacy. The platform of unity was not only about the return of all Rwandans (Hutu and Tutsi) from abroad but also about the replacement of the 'discriminatory dictatorship' of Juvenal Habyarimana with one that disregarded ethnicity. As a historian of the RPF explained:

> Already Pasteur Bizimingu[52] said that we are not a syndicate of refugees, ours is a political organization meant to remove from power a dictatorship and then set up a new, well-governed system. RPF could mobilize, sure, because many wanted to return, but they had to shape it as a political organization that could speak more widely, to the people inside.[53]

The unity platform stressing Rwandanness nonetheless sits uneasily with the post-genocide government's practices of inclusion and exclusion from citizenship. The exclusions put a dent in the official narrative of inclusion, betraying political dynamics that work in the opposite direction. Powerful evidence here includes the recent cancellation of passports of dissidents and the differential treatment of Kinyarwanda-speaking migrants since the RPF takeover. With regard to the latter dynamic, while some incoming migrants became 'returnees', others became 'refugees'. In the immediate aftermath of the genocide, besides old-caseload returnees (referring to 1959 mainly Tutsi refugees) and new-caseload returnees (referring to the 1994 mass Hutu out-migration), Rwanda saw the return of both Hutu and Tutsi from much older waves of emigration. They were coming from North Kivu, South Kivu (the *Banyamulenge*), other parts of the DRC such as Katanga and beyond. Later on, however, as ethnically-framed tensions heightened in the Kivus and Rwanda faced large inflows of Kinyarwanda speakers (persecuted Tutsi who had lived in the DRC for generations), these came to be branded and treated as 'refugees'. As mentioned, people from these areas were initially welcomed as 'Rwandan' in the sense that they were free to move and settle. But when the inflow surged, the same people from the same areas, victims of action based on exclusionary citizenship rhetoric, even persecuted as 'friends of Kagame', fleeing the same fighting that has not yet stopped a decade later, were treated officially as 'Congolese' and placed in refugee camps.

'By February 1996, according to UNHCR, there were 37,000 Tutsi refugees in Rwanda' (Prunier 2009: 57). The refugees have been doubly excluded, called Rwandese in Congo and Congolese in Rwanda. A Banyamulenge returnee and a good friend of mine explained: 'It is politics, the [territorial] boundaries are what they are and he [Kagame] has to say that, but me, I know that behind all that, there is something, everyone knows they are Rwandese'.[54] A Kinyarwanda-speaking Congolese migrant from North Kivu put forth a different interpretation: 'These refugees [in Rwanda] they are not Rwandan, they were there when Germany divided Rwanda, [they are] Congolese who speak Kinyarwanda. They are fleeing the *interahamwe*. When I asked how come he was never in a refugee camp, he told me that 'for us, [there were] not many [of us] in 1996. But they came late, in 2001, they came [and] there was no place for them [land here in Rwanda]. So let's take them to refugee camps because there were a lot of them'.[55] Politics clearly intercedes and explains why the same people matter differently to the Rwandan government depending on whether they are inside or outside Rwanda. While useful outside (invoked as Rwandans that require intervention to protect), they are excluded on the inside (invoked as refugees, Congolese).

The full contradiction becomes clear when one puts this issue in the context of the *irredentist* discourse in contemporary Rwanda. The references to 'Greater Rwanda' appeared on at least a couple of occasions during my fieldwork. In an *ingando* history class, the professor did not hide his chagrin at the losses Rwanda incurred to its territory when the borders were officially fixed in 1910 in Brussels:

> The word 'Rwanda' comes from the word *kwaguka* – to get larger and larger, to spread, like the plant of pumpkin. Pre-colonial Rwanda was bigger than Rwanda is today. It included parts of Congo, Tanzania and Uganda. On 14.5.1910 we lost all of these areas because of the Brussels Conference. Every time I remember that, I want to cry. Kivu used to be ours. We lost a third of our current area. Regarding Congo, why cannot we pose this question to Europe, these used to be our areas ... Look at Rwanda [now], how small it is, can you be proud? [a low hum rises from the thousand strong audience][56]

A similar story transpired in a completely unsolicited manner on another occasion but this time I was the only spectator. At the brand new Ministry of Youth, a young and friendly returnee from Canada, elegantly dressed and with a Blackberry as his aide, explained as he sketched borders and regions hastily on the back of the Youth Action Plan:

> There is this part of the country that was giving us a headache since the end of the war [he cross-shades the northwestern region]. In the past, the Rwenzori mountains [in today's Uganda] were the national border. Masisi and Rutshuru [in North Kivu, DRC] were more committed to the king [than the current Rwanda volcano area – the northern region] ... People at the volcanoes, you could not trust them fully ... All these areas [he points them out on a map] speak Kinyarwanda. It should have been a normal process to stay with Rutshuru and Masisi areas, they are also good for grazing, rather than Gisenyi and Ruhengeri.[57]

These reveries about 'Greater Rwanda' suggest that foreigners are 'Rwandan' when this suits the government in Kigali. When Kinyarwanda speakers try to flee the insecurity that Rwandan soldiers help to maintain in the Eastern DRC, they are treated as refugees. They come to an overpopulated country when they are meant to be a solution to 'overpopulation' by staying where they are, acting as dummies marking the historical sphere of Rwandanness.

Identity in Politics: Official De-ethnicization, Silent Engineering

Besides the issues of a 'unified state' and 'equal citizenship', political unity can also be meaningfully analysed (and complicated) through the familiar notion of identity politics or more narrowly 'identity in politics'. The 1993 Arusha Accords became the basis of the Rwandan state, the basic political power-sharing settlement later translated into the constitution. However, the official identity politics did not follow a power-sharing model but rather 'de-ethnicization'. The decision was to omit all mentions of ethnicity from political and public life and to accompany this with criminalization of divisionism and genocide ideology. The idea was to work against categories such as race, ethnicity or region becoming organizing principles in politics, and to simultaneously build a 'common Rwandanness' (*ubunyarwanda*). Rwanda was then, seemingly, to chart a starkly different route from neighbouring Burundi, where explicit accommodation between ethnic groups became the basis of post-conflict governance (Lemarchand 2007; Vandeginste 2014).

But Rwanda's refusal to stipulate and entrench ethnic ratios in politics simply meant that there would be no official balancing and counting of any sort, because any accusation, including that this is a 'minority government' could be deemed divisionist. This not only foreclosed official debate and the criticism of the government, the approach also became toothless, unable to solve problems of politicized ethnicity and other identity-based tensions and divisions that persisted or emerged after the genocide. The official identity politics resorted to denial and suppression.

While a transformative identity politics working against ethnic reductionism and emphasizing connections among a diverse people is certainly necessary, it has to actively acknowledge and address existing issues rather than papering them over or worse, leaving them 'to themselves'. At the level of written law, discrimination has indeed disappeared from Rwanda. Under the legal façade, it persists in various forms. At a general level, most people within Rwanda today are excluded from political power and the resulting tensions cannot be simply viewed as a Hutu-Tutsi issue. However, here I want to focus specifically on Hutu and Tutsi in order to interrogate the claim that 'ethnic harmony' has been restored in Rwanda. This does not mean that I believe that ethnicity causes conflict or that it is the only important social division from the viewpoint of social justice. Nonetheless, 'ethnicity' continues to matter on the ground in Rwanda in terms of how politics is interpreted, and it matters to many of those who try to 'read' Rwandan politics from the outside.

Paradoxically, an identity politics based on suppression or abolition of ethnic difference, by the very fact of its inevitable failure – it suppresses but does not destroy difference, and does not transform it either – gets caught up in 'ethnicization'. First, the regime and its actions continue to be perceived along 'ethnic lines' ('Ugandan Tutsi' or 'Tutsi' have power). 'Ethnicization' proves to be a persistent interpretive lens when it comes to politics. Second, the government itself starts thinking and discoursing in this manner (in a double manoeuvre, addressing the perception it knows is there). In other words, the official discourse is de-ethnicized, but everyone 'talks ethnicity' and judges the government on these terms. The current identity politics, claiming so vociferously to destroy this particular sphere of difference, has in fact not succeeded in challenging the interpretive model where ethnicity remains the salient frame. A reworked identity politics – a method of directly approaching issues of identity – is necessary but is only a partial solution. It needs to be coupled with a political environment of equal inclusiveness that would make such a method seem legitimate.

Besides the fact that 'ethnic unity' remains a useful fiction at present, it is difficult and uncertain even as a proposition. The war, genocide and even post-genocide justice (see Chakravarty 2014) polarized Hutu and Tutsi as identities by heightening the sense of being one or the other and strengthening the separation between the two. Equally important is the fact that for many, ethnicity remains an important and meaningful way to interpret the past and the present (ibid.). Anyone who investigates and observes Rwandan life notes that 'ethnicity remains pertinent in both social and political life'.[58] 'Government says "we are all Rwandan" but in reality … it is still fresh. It is not enough for the President and Fatuma to come and say you are Rwandan … Segregation is still there, everywhere.'[59] What is at stake is the official logic of 'ethnic unity' itself. Notably, the actual talk of 'restored unity' is often confined to demonstrations of peaceful 'coexistence' – a moot point in a tightly policed country, a repressive regime that intensifies 'preference falsification' (Kuran 1995) and where coexistence preceded genocide. More importantly, the assumption that ethnicity and other identities have to give way and cannot coexist alongside Rwandanness is one open to question; in fact it is one that, due to the reasons given above, needs to be reconsidered.

As has been mentioned already, the nature of the political system excludes most of the population, Hutu and Tutsi alike, from political power. Discrimination and exclusion in Rwanda have many forms and levels, but there are also ethnicity-specific exclusions. Due to particular dynamics, Hutu[60] are categorically and disproportionately excluded, albeit informally. Most clearly, it is harder for the Hutu to network themselves into the Anglophone returnee power core. They are also at greater risk of injustice because they are more easily suspected as having (and more easily framed as having) participated in the genocide (since not all perpetrators have been identified and brought to justice), maintaining links to the 'enemy' (i.e., the FDLR), sympathizing with perpetrators in their families, feeling rancour at punishment or harbouring 'negative ideologies'. The fact that the Rwandan genocide involved participation of almost 200,000 people, most of them Hutu, contributed to a categorical distrust of them. The fact that not all perpetrators have been identified and the (inflated and mal-construed) hype surrounding the various threats of 'negative ideology' contribute to the persistence of such suspicions.

A final paradox of this 'abolitionist' identity politics is that despite the rejection of power sharing, 'balancing' tactics still enter the scene through the back door. The Director of a Rwandan NGO suggested without hesitation that 'there is a transition situation – yes, [we want] a nation but also power-sharing'.[61] A young Rwandan female researcher explained that 'even in politics, ethnicity is a consideration. You don't mention ethnicity out loud but when the government is put together, the inclusion of different groups is taken into account ... it is done but not talked about'.[62] Another researcher at the same organization suggested that if you engage in it, at least be transparent: 'What is it? What does it involve? Among whom do you share?'[63] This again demonstrates how an outwardly 'ethnically-blind' government falls prey to ethnicized political practice and the negative repercussions of this unfortunate manoeuvre – the government not only undermines its claims to a 'non-identity-based' conceptualization of power but undermines its attempt to appear 'representative', merely further highlighting the concentration of power.

Any real 'balancing' hardly happens though, and the 'de-ethnicized' state does not create pressure to reach specific ratios. The result is strategic inclusion that satisfies the need for selective showcasing or 'pinpointing as proof'. Such play of appearances was in evidence right from the start of the new dispensation. The first post-genocide president – Pasteur Bizimungu – was a Hutu man but real power lay in the hands of the 'strongman', Minister of Defence Paul Kagame. Most cabinet ministers were Hutu but the really important posts 'were assigned to RPF militants and deputies' (Kinzer 2008: 192). The calculus of appointments continues to suggest that if the 'minister is Tutsi, the assistant to the minister will be Hutu, everyone knows it'.[64] But the perception is that if Hutu are in power, they hold posts of lesser authority: '[There are] thirty ministers, Hutu are not more than five per cent'.[65] Some dismiss the Hutu in power as *Hutu de service* or 'Hutu for hire'. All in all, even if the notion of 'balancing' were a thin internal façade and the notion of restored 'ethnic unity' a thin external one, that minimalist effort is still useful for the government as a form of dissimulation.

As should be apparent from the analysis above, a number of contradictions arise between the rhetoric of restored unity and the actual political practices as they unfold. The first contradiction arises when we counterpose the beaming of images of re-established unity (political currency more for the outside audience) with the simultaneous pointing to the unconquered and serious enemy within and without (political currency spent mainly on inside constituencies). The second contradiction arises by the simultaneous deployment of the discourse of 'de-ethnicized' politics (again more useful to broker favour from the outside) and the actual 'silent engineering' undertaken by the government. The third point is a paradox really and concerns the surprising political value that can be extracted from mere official 'banning' of ethnic discourse. A university student proudly relayed how a recent 'visitor from abroad' commended about Rwanda: 'Here you do not talk about Hutu and Tutsi, you are so developed!'[66] The Rwandan government is exploiting the fixing of African social discourse into an ethnicized straightjacket. If ethnicity is agreed to be the problem, then removing it even just officially creates a notion of improvement. The ethnicized discourse directs the way we perceive the making of political claims in countries like Rwanda. It attunes us to issues of cultural difference and similarity, making them salient, and it eclipses issues of political exclusion and social equality.

Conclusion: Implications for Unity and Unity Building

The above analysis has implications both for the notion of unity – adding to the baggage that is its meaning – and unity building as a process. To begin with, in post-genocide Rwanda, unity is a securitized concept overlaid with the notion of friend versus enemy. Unity is defined as 'against an enemy'; unity means being on the 'right side'. As such, unity is never all encompassing but rather partially inclusive. It is merely the 'politically safe' double of division. Division/divisionism is itself an intensely deployed category. Labelling someone 'divisionist' is both a manner of deterring enemies and a tool for neutralizing enemies by depositing them into a space of exception – one that might be discursively created but that nonetheless bears real effects.

The meaning of unity also arises against the background of and is worked into the logic of the political regime, legitimizing consent (in rule) and alignment (of powers). Unity means showing a friendly roster, 'unifying' oneself with the wider policies and ideologies of the government; it implies non-dissention. Unity is thus opposed not only to conflict-prone division but any division and even difference if the latter is perceived as opposition (as politically threatening difference). Unity as consent (and opposed to plurality or critique) is presented as necessary for stability, peace and prosperity. It is in this manner that the discourse of unity in today's Rwanda lends legitimacy to authoritarian rule.

Interestingly, when it comes to explicit talk of unity, the government presents it largely as a supra-ethnic identity and as something 'natural', a characteristic of a pre-colonial society temporarily arrested during colonial rule and the two republics that followed it. This discourse obscures a number of important historical and political dynamics, namely that the idea of 'unity' itself has a (political) history, that there was a consensus on the 'story of unity' that can be traced to specific meetings of specific people, that a 'unified state' had to be literally forced into life, or that there is no unity if defined as the ability of people to either disregard ethnicity or get equal access to power and political opportunity. Even if shallow and ultimately self-conflicted, the narrower and de-politicized 'cross-ethnic' paradigm still seems to have political value. But the discrepancies and contradictions of key legitimization narratives also demonstrate that 'the wording of power' can both fortify and enfeeble. While securitisation narratives seem to widen the scope for repressive control, de-ethnicisation in the end weakens the ability of the government to address the social and political divisions that persist. The political system in Rwanda is indeed built on hope and promise in a most fundamental sense; the government suffuses the public sphere with narratives about unity and progress with the expectation that the word will, indeed, become the thing.

Notes

1. A preamble to an interview with Paul Kagame, explaining his approach to 'terrorism', published by the government-leaning NTK on 16 June 2014 under the title 'Kagame on Terrorism – I am Not Threatening, I am Warning'.
2. The four-year invasion has led to at least four distinct waves of retaliatory violence against Tutsi civilians (before the genocide) (Kinzer 2008: 99). This has created tensions between the Tutsi within the country and those invading. Also highlighted by Lemarchand (2009: 70).
3. Interview with Bernard, 22 February 2009.
4. Informal discussion with a Rwandan student at a university in Leipzig, Germany, 20 April 2009.
5. MINECOFIN's (2010a: 30, Figure 13) own budget tables clearly show that a full third of the government's budget goes to 'general public service, defense and public order and safety'.
6. Interview with Bernard, 13 February 2009.
7. Interview with Kagame, NTK, 16 June 2014, op. cit.
8. Speech by Paul Kagame, Rebero, 31 March 2003.
9. Interview with a mobilization expert, Ministry of Youth, 16 February 2009.
10. Interview with the head of the Centre for Conflict Management, Butare, 4 February 2009.

11. Interview with Evarista Kalisa, Rwandan Parliament, 9 December 2008.
12. For an official overview of the summit, consult the MIGEPROF website at <http://www.migeprof.gov.rw/index.php?option=com_content&task=view&id=75&Itemid=131>
13. Interview with MP Connie Bwiza, 23 March 2009.
14. Interview with Kalisa, op. cit.
15. Interview with Augustin, 21 January 2009.
16. NTK, 6 September 2010.
17. HRW quoted in an interview with Afrol News, 2 July 2004.
18. Informal discussion with an anthropologist studying *gacaca*, Kigali, 4 April 2009.
19. Informal discussion with a NURC employee, 7 January 2009.
20. Mukarutabana, 'Gakondo: The Royal Myths'.
21. This refers to the hundreds of survivors killed since the 1994 genocide (IBUKA – the survivors' umbrella organization gives a figure of 168 killed between 2002 and 2014).
22. Interview with Augustin, 25 February 2009.
23. Ibid.
24. Interview with the Administrator of the Muhazi Lake *Ingando*, 28 January 2009.
25. Most Rwandan opposition, in fact, resides in exile. Approximately twenty opposition parties were created in exile since the 1994 genocide (GLCSS 2006).
26. In Rwanda, parties that are deemed threatening can be dissolved, as was the case with the MDR of Tswagiramungu, which was accused of divisionism. More recently in the run-up to the 2010 presidential elections, three new parties critical of the government were not able to stand for election. FDU-Inkingi and the Democratic Green Party of Rwanda were 'obstructed from holding meetings necessary to register' (HRW 2010b). Only PS-Imberakuri was allowed to register though was unable to stand for election after Ntaganda was arrested on June 24, 2010 and accused of 'divisionism'.
27. Seven out of the nine parties formed a 'coalition', a euphemism for what is really a united front of RPF party factions.
28. These other two parties are Parti Liberal (PL) and Parti Social Democrat (PSD), who some allege are headed by people active in the RPF.
29. Informal discussion with Bernard, 18 March 2009.
30. Interview with Bernard, 22 February 2009.
31. Interview with a linguist and director of a language centre, Kigali, 10 March 2009.
32. Ibid.
33. Interview with Bernard, op. cit.
34. Second-hand account of an informal discussion, 15 January 2009.
35. RPF flags hang outside local offices, people wear RPF shirts and Kagame smiles down from framed pictures everywhere. In the world of display, no other party competes.
36. Nkunda Rwanda, an anonymous blogger, has left this message on her discussion page entitled 'The Ironies of Voting in Rwanda'.
37. Interview with Bernard, op.cit.

38. Interview with Augustin, who used to be a civil servant and worked on decentralization, 25 February 2009.
39. This not only includes presidential orders, ministerial orders, instructions of ministers but also laws and many indirect/unofficial prohibitions and prescriptions (e.g., no walking barefoot, no street selling).
40. Interview with Bwiza of the Chamber of Deputies, 23 March 2009.
41. Ibid.
42. Interview with the Director of an NGO, 6 November 2008.
43. Interview with Augustin, a research institute employee, 6 April 2009.
44. For more detail, see for example Maundi et al. (2006: 35).
45. Interview with the Head of Diaspora Department at the RPF Headquarters, 23 January 2009.
46. Servillien Sebasoni is the author of two books on Rwanda's history and post-conflict reconstruction. Interview in Kimihurura, Kigali, 23 March 2009.
47. Interview with Tito Rutaremara, Kigali, 14 January 2009.
48. Interview with Bernard, 13 February 2009.
49. Informal discussion with an NTK reporter (a Ugandan returnee), 14 November 2008.
50. Interview with a Ugandan returnee (NURC employee), Nyanza, 17 November 2008.
51. Informal chat with a Ugandan returnee (another NURC employee), 22 November 2008.
52. A Hutu member of the RPF, later the first post-genocide President.
53. Interview with an 'independent consultant' and author of a manuscript on RPF history, Kigali, 22 January 2009.
54. Informal discussion in Kigali, 19 December 2008.
55. Informal discussion in Kigali, 11 March 2009.
56. *Ingando* class at Nkumba, 17 December 2008.
57. Interview with a mobilization expert, Ministry of Youth, 16 February 2009.
58. Ibid.
59. Interview with a communications officer at an NGO, Kigali, 23 February 2009.
60. What follows also pertains to persons of mixed Hutu-Tutsi background.
61. Interview held in Kigali, 6 November 2008.
62. Interview in Kigali, 3 November 2008.
63. Interview in Kigali, 21 January 2009.
64. Interview with Augustin, a researcher, 21 January 2009.
65. Interview with Bernard, a civil servant, 22 February 2009.
66. Kigali, 26 January 2009.

4
The Presencing Effect
Surveillance and State Reach in Rwanda

> *'Government of Rwanda is like MTN–everywhere you go.'*
> A joke passed around Kigali

In sub-Saharan Africa,[1] one typically discusses the empirical 'weakness' of states, their inability to extend authority, legitimate use of force, administration and services over the whole territory or the whole territory equally (Jackson and Rosberg 1982; Widner 1995; Herbst 1996 and 2000). This has become a true 'meta-narrative' of stateness in Africa. The difficulty has been traced to the 'non-territorial nature of power'[2] (Herbst 2000: 35), which presented most African leaders with the fundamental problem of 'how to broadcast power over sparsely settled lands' (ibid.: 3). However, as most analysts briefly mention in a side note, there are exceptions to this rule. In a few places in Africa, including the Great Lakes region and the Ethiopian highlands, 'there are ecologies that have supported relatively high densities of people' and it is these areas that 'have been periodically able to exercise direct control over their peripheries' (Herbst 2000: 11).

Rwanda is the most densely populated African state and it comprises a small territory without any sparsely populated areas. The state's reach is extensive and governments, besides the issue of control over the population, are preoccupied by the issue of territory (manifested in the rise of an irredentist rhetoric). These dynamics are in stark contrast to the recent empirical research of Bierschenk and de Sardan (1997, 2003) in countries such as Benin and the Central African Republic where the state is rather absent in local political milieus, these being instead suffused by a tangle of alternative authorities. Rather than asking 'What makes states weak?' and 'What actors take the place of the state and how?' Rwanda as a case of a 'strong' state makes us pose a different set of questions altogether: What are the different apparatuses through which the central power reaches people and how 'thick' are they? How do they saturate lived time and space? What is the space of the 'non-state'?

Many researchers have noted the strength and intricacy of political administration in Rwanda and how its reach to the lowest levels contributed to the 'effectiveness' and mass nature of the 1994 genocide (Uvin 1998; Stover and Weinstein 2004; Straus 2006). Though governments replace one another, this type of intricate organization, while modified, has remained fundamentally unchanged. In fact, the most recent 2006 decentralization reforms have made state reach more profound than ever before (Chemouni 2014). What are the effects of this expansion? Rather than focusing on the planning and implementation of policies, my core aim is to explore wider effects with regards to social control and state-society relations.

In what follows, I study the reach of central power post-genocide through the analysis of the administrative apparatus and the information apparatus that lies at its disposal, as well as through the spectrum of grassroots activities which it not only organized but through which it governs and finally through the analysis of the structural 'counter-weights' to the state. The analysis is crucial if we are to understand how 'local' official activities (e.g., *umuganda*, *gacaca*, a score of unity and reconciliation activities) are perceived in today's Rwanda, and what can be and is achieved through them. Ultimately, the chapter outlines a pervasive state of social control achieved through multi-level 'presencing' of the state. In this, Rwanda seems unique, even when compared to other African countries with similar political geography and/or administrative structure. The implications of this 'state of (in) society' with regards to social transformation, legitimacy, stability and social justice will be explored in later parts of the book.

Administrative Apparatus

> *'Even if I am not here, there are so many eyes.'*
> Coordinator of an *ingando* camp

The Vertical Structure: From Gihugu to Mudugudu

The administrative apparatus of the Rwandan state is characterized by clear hierarchies and an intricate organization leading from *gihugu* (country) to *mudugudu* (village) and, informally, even below. After two recent rounds of revamping, the official structure has the following five levels: 4 *intara* (provinces), 30 *uturere* (districts), 416 *imirenge* (sectors), 2,146 *utugari* (cells) and 14,876 *imidugudu* (villages). In 2006, the previously lowest administrative unit of the *nyumba kumi* – a grouping of ten households overseen by non-salaried representatives (comprising some 150,000 people altogether) – was officially replaced by the larger units of *imidugudu*. However, there are reports of *nyumba kumi* being active informally even after this date (USAID 2008). The intricate state organization has roots that reach to the pre-colonial Nyiginya kingdom.[3]

The intricate administrative web, however, does not inspire complex mapping. Rather than spatial representations, the primary governance tool for orientation and targeting is 'tracing' through the spreading webs of people that make up the administration. The structure is conceptualized as a chain, with 'cascade' potential and its multiplicatory effects capture people's imagination. The snowball effect of this structure also means that directives and information in general reach large numbers at all levels fast. More than control over territory (though this aspect also matters), administrative governance emphasizes the direct and indirect control over people produced through access. Official power has to be 'felt', it has to be localized and intimate rather than simply decreed from a faraway centre.

Let me first approach the 'presence' of the state through the physical presence of administrative structures (offices) at the lower levels.[4] The sector-level administration has the most physical presence and all its buildings are easily recognizable on the landscape: they are low, red brick buildings with a sign at the entrance, a clearing of red earth in front, an annex of wooden benches (sometimes fitted with an orange tarpaulin roof), a pole with the Rwandan flag, and usually people queuing in front of the *umuyobozi*'s office waiting for an 'audience'. This is the space where *gacaca* and other important meetings and activities take place. Cell offices, usually comprised of a single small room, are included in the space of the sector. In the *Nyakabanda ambere*[5] (first Nyakabanda) cell, papers pinned to the wall list the constituent 'villages' (in cities these are really quarters). 'Village' *ibiro* (offices), however, are spread across the communities themselves. They usually comprise a single room with a small tin sign above the door signalling its purpose.

Which is the most important administrative level? All in all, and from a global perspective of power in a highly centralized and authoritarian state, 'no one takes decisions at the lowest level ... you wait for instructions'.[6] But looking more closely and moving from the top down, all decisions at the district level are taken by the mayor. At levels below this, decisions are taken by the sector head rather than the *Njyanama* council (the sector assembly of all adults) as officially decreed. Meetings and *imihigo* goals [annual targets], for example, should be decided by the council 'but it is never the case ... They speak of a "council" but it is never there'.[7] In fact, it is the military and police who seem to have more clout than administrative decision makers. 'It is the "Brigade CO" that is the highest actual authority at district level – the general/colonel that is [stationed] there'.[8] When it comes to *gacaca*, an anthropologist studying the courts found that the police superintendent is more important than the *inyangamugayo* (*gacaca* judge), especially when it comes to backstage 'preparing' of witnesses.[9]

While directives and power might be handed from the top down, surveillance and control begin at the smallest, most intimate levels, with reports and requests trickling up:

> All of them are important administrative levels. [But] at the low[est] level, they know the people. If you don't pay your taxes, they know. If you are a drunkard, they know. The policing committees start there. If I want a passport I go to the village authority, who says I am a good citizen, I love my neighbours, pay my taxes … Everything begins there, in the village. They [village leaders] give a paper to the cell authorities, then the sector and it ends there. But if there are difficult decisions, there is intervention from the district mayor.[10]

If the sector complex (which includes cell offices) is where a common person normally 'encounters' the state, officially it is the *akarere* (the district) that is the main political-administrative unit. All 'resident citizens' aged above 18 are members of the district council called *Njyanama,* which is responsible for 'mobiliz[ing] residents, discuss[ing] and prioritiz[ing] problems and tak[ing] decisions for their resolution'.[11] *Njyanama* is a 'consultative council' (*conseil consultatif*) on top of which sits the executive council called *Nyobozi*. As described above, *Njyanama* seems to take hardly any decisions of importance, as all are essentially communicated from above. 'The main decision-making power lies with an administrative person (the Executive Secretary) who is appointed by the central administration and thus not elected by the population' (Ansoms 2009: 307).

The trickle-down system can create a paradoxical inflexibility and confusion. Local administration, which is 'close' to the people and should theoretically be able to decide fast and best manage its tasks, in fact becomes paralysed and ineffective because it waits until vital information makes it down the tree-like 'plumbing' of the state: 'At *umudugudu* level, I am sure they [usually] don't know until Friday midnight what to do at *umuganda*, until the decision from cell level and higher [is communicated] … The people don't know what tools to bring … half the people show with machetes when we need hoeing to be done!'[12]

The cell itself has a careful structure of its own. The coordinator of my cell, an *abakangurambaga*,[13] explains that his is a '*travail de bureau*'. 'I sign official documents, take care of all the politics, organize village meetings and I work with the cell committee.' The committee or *komite* is composed of ten people – the coordinator, secretary and persons in charge of education, health, security, development, finance, training, women and youth. The youth representative, for example, 'organizes the youth, and for the moment, is involved in combating ideologies that separate the youth [such as] regionalism, racism'. The coordinator also explains to me that the cell committee members 'are elected by the population, it is not voluntary'. The only member of the cell who is paid is the 'ES' (Executive Secretary), the rest of the cell personnel along with all the village administrators are 'volunteers' (corroborated by Ansoms 2009).

'Umuryango RPF': The Parallel Structures of the Party

Just as the local administrative offices are easily recognizable when you pass them in the countryside, so are the little satellite 'FPR' *ibiros* (RPF offices). No other party has local presence. More importantly, the hierarchies of the RPF mimic those of the state ('at all administrative levels the two structures are there'[14]) with the result that the lines between ruling party and state are blurred. Already in 1995, HRW (1995: 15) noted the existence of *abakada* (cadres) – 'an organized group of powerful young people … political officers attached to the RPA … responsible for supervising local political life'. They were 'operat[ing] parallel to the usual legitimate authorities' (ibid.). In 2007, the informal parallel institution was made public when the ban on 'political party structures at the grassroots' was lifted and the RPF became the first and thus far the only party to elect officials at the *umudugudu* level. The elected seven-person committees then allegedly proceed to elect[15] cell representatives and so on all the way to the district level (NTK 9 July 2007).

Besides its parallel nature, it seems 'the party is more powerful than the state. The party controls the state'.[16] RPF structure controls the administrative structure because, after all, the administrators are party members:

> Informant: I lost my job in 2005 because I refused to become a party member. You cannot become employee of government if [you are] not party member.

> *Me: Is the same person responsible for the two aspects?*

> Informant: [Generally speaking] chairman of administration at *umudugudu* level is in charge of the RPF at *umudugudu* level. You find that it is almost the same people [at the two levels], go to cell, sector, almost the same, district, members of the district council, all members of the RPF … not necessarily the same people, but that is a gentle way of hiding of what is really going on.

> *Me: What do RPF representatives at local levels do?*

> Informant: I used to be a member of my RPF *umudugudu* committee, recruited by force – 'nominated' … The [2010] presidential election campaign has already started and those guys are told to make it happen. As secretary of the *umudugudu* level, you have to assume those responsibilities, strategies for voting campaign, for member recruitment, to deal with defectors – those

who just move away from the party, [and make sure] that you know each and everybody.[17]

The pro-government NTK reported that 'it is amazing but not a surprise to find that all residents of some areas are members of RPF' (NTK 9 July 2007). The reason is that 'the party machinery is very strong and very harsh. Here we are forced to become members of the ruling party ... In the countryside, there is almost 99 per cent if not 100 per cent membership. In town maybe it is little lower, but not below 90 per cent.'[18] Pre-1994, with the advent of multipartysim, the MDR is known to have organized *ukubohoza* ('liberation', literally 'to help untie the yoke') – dispatches of party members to a person's home for forced, and often violent, recruitment (Pinchotti and Verwimp 2007: 16). After the genocide, forced recruitment continued. Before the 2003 elections:

> local officials or party organizers called people to meetings at sector offices where they were publicly pressured to join the RPF. In one case, approximately half the group agreed. Officials continued to 'persuade' those who refused to join ... In a sector in another province, people were told that they should aim to make 90 per cent of their neighbours into RPF supporters. (HRW 2002: 3)

Membership of the party is couched in the soft and encompassing language of 'family'. The full name of the RPF is *Umuryango* RPF-*Inkotanyi*. *Umuryango* has different shades of meaning, it can mean 'association' but is used most often to mean 'extended lineage' or simply 'family'. The RPF's self-presentation using the totalist and exclusivist language of a 'front' or 'family' (HRW 2002; NDI 2003) shows the skilful use of indirect language (an outsider might not recognize coercion in it) and the use of discourse surrounding family to solidify its vision of political 'unity' and 'division'. According to an RPF recruit,

> those who taught me said that the RPF is not a party but rather a family and that all Rwandans should be part of [it]. Those who don't join are outsiders. They are the ones who cause instability in the country. We should build the family to prepare for elections. It would be dangerous to be governed by someone from outside the family. (HRW 2003: 3)

People were afraid that if they did not join, they would be labelled as subversives, as supporters of 'divisionist' parties or as those who refuse to 'build the country together' (ibid.). People are pressured in a more indirect way too:

> At the local level, the authorities were going from house to house handing out forms ... [asking for] name, and then there was a question 'When did you join the *umuryango*?' What do you mean? I joined my family when I was born [laughing] ... no, the *political umuryango*, they meant *ishaka* by it, the party. It is

called *umuryango* because it should be a 'family for everyone' ... You see, it is a demagogic approach. It is tricky, because they ask them [the people they visit] 'Why don't you participate in government programmes?' What do you mean, but this is not national programme, this is RPF![19]

Membership in the 'political family' literally comes with a price. Rwanda is not only a new land of fines, it is a land of 'exactions' couched in the language of 'contributions' (*umusanzu*). Raising money and other resources (such as labour) in the community is a changing but ancient practice and it is done on a small scale everywhere. However, the notion of 'contribution' in Rwanda has been hijacked by the state and transformed into multiple exactions such as *umuganda* (labour) or *icyunamo* (in cash) contributions. While non-state organizations such as churches also have their exactions,[20] these are more than overshadowed by the diverse demands of the state. The 'unity and reconciliation' activities are also couched in the language of *umusanzu*, whereby *chaque doit donner sa contribution*[21] (everyone must make their contribution).

The RPF structure is unquestionably the most widespread and effective fundraising mechanism in Rwanda. It is a *gutwerera* writ large. *Gutwerera* is the process of raising money from family, friends and the wider community (including co-workers) to pay for a wedding, the financing of which is seen not as a private but a community responsibility. If the RPF is the *umuryango*, then elections are the perfect occasion for the political *gutwerera*. Trying to explain the intricate reach of the party, an informant tells me that 'all they [RPF] need is money':

> For parliamentary elections, every government employee, or let's say RPF member, was forced to contribute a third of his salary. If you don't have a job, [there is] still something to contribute, they fix a minimum contribution. For next year [2010], each employee who is a member of the RPF will contribute half of their salary, that is 125,000 RwF [$220 USD]. But every month I also contribute 5,000 RwF to the party, that means every year the contribution to the party is 60,000 RwF.[22]

The Lateral Structure: Multiple Responsibilities and Indirect Control

But there is more to the 'dense' administrative apparatus. First, the state achieves control of the whole machinery through co-optation of multiple people into its 'responsibilities'.

> The whole thing is copied from Mao Tse Tung. In my *umudugudu*, there are 235 families, 3 people in charge of *mutuelle de santé*, 5 on official committee, 3 in community policing, 3 in gender-based violence committee, 5 in *imihigo* committee, I am one of them, 5 education officers, there is also hygiene people responsible for that ... there is a minimum of 50 people responsible

for something. This is a way of ensuring ... you cannot have any 'opening', [space for] opposition there. In Tung's China, the idea was to have two thirds of people busy with different responsibilities.[23]

At the cell level, responsibilities multiply further – there are youth representatives, *ubudehe* committees, and more. 'But was not this administrative structure there before?' 'It was there but we did not have all those small committees, commissions ... that makes it effective and efficient.' Indeed, responsibilities as well as activities have exploded in the past decade. Institutions like *imihigo, ubudehe, itorero* (and their administrative structures) being recently added to the mix.

To 'co-optation through responsibility' should be added the system of lateral (as opposed to simply hierarchical or vertical) controls, whereby there is an 'eye on everybody'. The *itorero* graduates along with local teachers, for example, are part of a so-called 'consultative group' at the cell level. *Itorero* and teachers both have 'their own identity, their structures, their priorities on which they are required to report', but they also 'advise the executive committee'. They have 'legal power to give ideas to the cell, and to be an eye on the executive secretary for example'.[24]

In the Muhazi *ingando* camp for child ex-combatants, the administrator has established a complex indirect system of rule, a society apart from society, where he is the sovereign. His pupils discipline themselves through a carefully constructed political governance system, which includes a leader and a disciplinarian as well as a *gacaca* court to resolve disputes. The children are separated into 'sectors' with rotating duties. Most importantly, 'everybody has an eye on his fellow ... even the leader is looking [at] *gacaca*; *gacaca* is watching the leader, everyone is watching their fellow'.[25]

As becomes clear from the above, the state system creates indirect control through widespread and locally embedded webs of administration and through co-optation of multiple people into its ranks. To break possible dissent and mobilization, the system offers a number of the dispossessed and disempowered just a little more authority over the rest. But it is really the acceptance (even if unwilling) of the 'role' that transforms, not necessarily the possession of more power.

Imihigo *Performance Contracts: Incorporating Family and Individual into the State Structure*

The recently introduced *imihigo* contracts also reflect the increasing permeation of people's lives by the state. *Imihigo* were introduced in 2006 by MINALOC and, as many other activities before and since, they have been presented as a restored 'tradition', specifically as 'a long-standing cultural practice' of accountability where two parties agree to work towards a stated goal.[26] Though there has been no in-depth analysis of this process or its wider political effects, *imihigo* did receive wide acclaim, being called a 'formidable measure of accountability', 'a valuable example to other countries in Africa struggling to implement a truly decentralised approach' (McConnell 2009: 14).[27] This is worrisome because, upon close analysis, *imihigo* brings deeper permeation of society by the state and openings for increased coercion.

Imihigo today are annual public pledges of performance, they are official contracts at different levels stating what that particular administrative unit will achieve and how that fits within the broader development agenda of the state (Vision 2020). *Imihigos* started at the level of district, but in 2007 were extended to all lower administrative levels. At district level, *imihigos* are signed by the mayors in front of the president himself. In 2008, *imihigo* was extended to the family level: each family head signs their own *imihigo*. The plan for 2009 was to extend the *imihigo* practice to every individual.[28] 'What do family heads promise to achieve?' 'For example, [to] send all kids to school, [to] assure that everyone has a health insurance, that all join some kind of cooperative, [that] all fight corruption.'[29] *Imihigo* appears to be a very localized public pledge of compliance with national policies.

But *imihigo* not only permeates the social structure vertically, it is meant to do so horizontally as well. Groups of *itorero* graduates formulate their own *imihigos*. Some NGOs decide to speak of their annual achievement goals in the same language, such as the Rwandan Red Cross (see Wynter 2009). Religious leaders too 'have resolved to adopt performance contracts ... Their contracts will highlight, among other things, interventions in matters of health insurance and fight against genocide ideology' (NTK 24 June 2008). Most recently, an article published by the NTK (Asiimwe 2009) suggests that private businesses should sign *imihigo*:

> We should be looking at how to stretch these performance contracts across all boundaries. They should not only be a thing for the public sector. It could take the form of private, public partnership. For example, MTN, Rwandatel and TIGO could sign annual *imihigo* with the regulatory agency. Private newspapers, radios and television stations could do the same. Private Sector Federation could cluster different businesses and sign performance contracts with members of each cluster.

Every three months, there is an *imihigo* evaluation. At the end of the stated period, reports detailing achievements are prepared at all levels. The district mayors attend a televized event called *kuvuga ibigwi* or *kurata imihigo* (MINALOC 2008), presided over by the president, where they present their performance reports. There are also consultations in which 'people debate why [they] have not finished and accomplished all goals and what have been the obstacles [they] encountered' (ibid.).

What are the effects of *imihigo*? First, through *imihigo*, families are effectively incorporated into the administrative hierarchy and come to form its 'smallest administrative unit' (NTK 10 November 2008). Effectively though, all individuals are meant to make their 'contribution'. Second, *imihigo* is a top-down mechanism of control. It not only further strengthens surveillance, it is also a mechanism for measuring alignment with the government's policies. Local authorities have to 'guide' residents not only to 'embrace' the idea of *imihigo* (NTK 10 November 2008) but also to embrace the policies that are promoted through it (such as 100 per cent enrolment in *mutuelle de santé* schemes) and the labour that leads to achievement of some of the goals.

The pressure to achieve goals can result in coercion (see also Chemouni 2014). 'If [*imihigo*] targets are not met, district authorities can expect their careers to be negatively affected. Not surprisingly therefore, local authorities use measures such as fines and destruction of property to ensure targets are met' (Huggins 2009: 299). Another report also states that 'households that failed to meet their performance targets were fined and could be imprisoned for non-payment at local detention centres called *cachots*' (Thomson 2008: 8). 'In an independent survey commissioned by the Organization for Social Science Research in Eastern and Southern Africa (OSSREA) from mid-2007, more than half of the respondents confirmed some form of compulsion had been used to achieve the *imihigo* targets' (Huggins 2009: 299).

In this context, achievement of a target, whether in form of a quantity or a deadline, becomes more important than quality of output: The *imihigo* for *gacaca* at district and sector levels was that it would finish by 2007. 'Such a target', suggests a PRI report (2007: 6) 'runs in the face of serenity and fairness of the hearing as the courts are under pressure and cannot examine the cases before them in detail'. The proof comes from reading a select *raporo y'imihigo* (*imihigo* report). The District of Ngoma (2009) report on 2008 achievements might present figures without any sources and yet what it does include and how is already telling. The report focuses on 'adherence' to state policies (*umuganda* participation, enrolment in *mutuelle de santé*), state 'extraction' (taxes collected) and 'production' (TIG labour value). Participation at *umuganda* (given at 73 per cent) is included under 'good governance'. The only input under 'justice' is the monetized value of TIG labour.

In addition, rather than promoting local priorities as it claims, *imihigo* assures mainstreaming at all levels into the national development plan. 'I thought it [*imihigo*] was a way to improve the coherence of the planning process, national and local interests, but within the first months it became clear that government promoted the national, not the local priorities.'[30] While my informant agreed that the activity does promote 'some kind of local decision making', often what results is a plan to please the centre: 'The mayor on his own is able to raise 20 per cent, maybe 30 per cent of his budget, the rest comes from the ministries, so of course he thinks "I will look at the priorities [of ministries], and will persuade my people these are their own priorities."[31]

Decentralization: Dispatching of Control?

Based on all the above, it appears the state system effectively 'dispatches' rather than 'decentralizes' control. The latter would suggest that the centre loses some of its hold but what we witness is not devolution of power to conceive and decide, just the devolution of implementation. Sprawling administration, multiple responsibilities and *imihigo*, in the final balance, do not point to decentralization of power, but rather to dispatching of power through which, sure enough, control becomes more effective and compliance increases.

The effects are the exact opposite to the discourse: 'decentralization' has not only not led to democratization, it has also directly strengthened authoritarian rule. This brings to mind Habyarimana's aim to transform the communes into 'motors of development' (Uvin 1998: 24). The attempt meant that 'after years of work, communal development projects served to allow the burgomestres to *better control* their population' (Voyame et al. 1996 and 1999, in Uvin 1998: 25).

The former National Coordinator for Decentralization supports the above verdicts:

> The World Bank has claimed that we have better performance on this [decentralization] than other African countries … But despite this talk and despite this attempt [the official process of decentralization], the majority of decisions concerning the lives of the people come from the centre. Decentralization has not transferred authority to local levels of government. [Rather], it is a way of management of the country, having structures to transmit information more directly to the people, for them to understand what the government wants. Kagame himself said this in a meeting.[32]

During meetings at the ministry, Augustin supposedly raised the point of lower administrative levels adopting the priorities of the centre:

> When I had these comments, the Minister like[d] to talk of 'unicity' – 'The state is one [he would say], why do you differentiate the national and the local?' I said it should be the electorate, the people [who defines priorities] … When it became apparent that I had ideas that contradict my own minister, I left in 2007, I resigned. I said it was for family reasons, health reasons. So [please] do not tell them the truth! [laughter].[33]

Information Apparatus

The administrative and information systems are interdependent but they do not completely overlap. The system of spreading, getting and blocking information is even more widespread, and to a large extent informal. The flows of information lead from the top down as well as going in the opposite direction. The top-down flow will be addressed later in the discussion on 'sensitization' and 'mobilization'. Suffice it to say that for this flow, the administrative system proves a highly useful 'irrigation' scheme. The focus here is instead on the bottom-up system of information gathering.

The state not only dispatches control through creating a widespread network of indirect rule, but also through its network of 'eyes and ears' that is much more 'present' on a daily basis. Both public and some private interactions are surveilled. 'There are some reports that the government monitored homes and telephone calls' (US DoS 2009: 10). During the November 2008 state-organized protests against the arrest of Rwandan Head of Protocol in Germany, MTN sent everyone the same messages in Kinyarwanda, urging people to gather at specific places and times. The US government has also allegedly sold Rwanda an email tracking system, which has been misused by the government to check on its critics, opponents and other 'suspicious' individuals.

Regarding informers (i.e., authorities' spies):

> they are almost everywhere. [They] work closely with the police, intelligence and the army. [They] are recruited mainly from the youth, [they are] trained in Akagera Park, between 6 and 12 months. Some state employees at district, cell level [have been trained]. Once they approached me and tried to convince me but I refused. [Those that approach you] promise you will get a job, and they do [indeed] get appointed first.[34]

People suggest there is a spy per organization and perhaps per office and in fact that all newcomers (to an organization), foreigners and Hutu are given someone to 'watch' them. '[There are] so many staff in government who are not paid for what they have in job description, but for intelligence. The guy next to me ... if you are a Hutu, it is compulsory, you are given someone to watch you. In many places, [there are] people who do not talk, because every word you say is analysed by those guys.'[35] The Department of Military Intelligence (DMI) and the Presidential Protection Unit (PPU) seem to be involved in their own tracking and are said to possess lists of people to be 'watched' and potentially targeted.[36]

Surveillance is not only present inside organizations and government administration, but at the lowest levels of the administrative hierarchy, where those responsible after all 'know the people', and where the two compulsory daily district reports on security source their material. Besides the administrative apparatus, the policing apparatus is also key. The latest addition to the police, *irondos* (daily civilians' night patrols) and Local Defence Forces (LDF) is the so-called 'community police'. But what is the function of yet another 'police' body? Community police are officially selected by the people in the community, they are unarmed and are not paid. People explained them to me as 'plain clothes police', or as not really policemen but simply 'party cadres' selected by the party leadership:

> Community policing is about information. Other countries do not have this system but we do because of the past of genocide. It is to prevent crimes before they happen. You don't want to arrive when somebody is already killed, you want to know about the plan before. People are chosen by others in the community on the basis of their integrity and that they like to talk, that they are not silent ... There are about 10 community police per 150 people say, so you have people in all corners.[37]

Informers are indeed believed to be everywhere, and many people can simply be used for that purpose when and as necessary. To trace teachers harbouring divisionist ideologies, 'well, there are the students, they know and say what the teachers are teaching, [for example] with regards to history, what kind of examples they are using'. 'Problematic' individuals can be traced in bars and restaurants because 'even waiters, they can be intelligence'.[38] The way in which surveillance happens is described in detail by Begley (2009) who, during her field research on the contribution of Rwandan Muslims to the reconciliation process, found out from one of her informants that 'not just one, but five different men have been following our movements' (ibid.: 4). This included 'the waiter from the restaurant [who] hired a couple of street kids to follow us [and who in turn] reported to another man on the street who then contacted the Chairman of the RPF' (ibid.).

It is difficult to know exactly who represents the 'ears and eyes' of higher authorities, and who is merely curious, a gossip, or generally suspecting, or whether those who observe from a distance do in fact understand anything being said and whether they pass it on. Notwithstanding all this, the perception remains that surveillance and locally traced intelligence are ubiquitous and the effects of this on behaviour are very real. Every researcher in Rwanda either experiences or hears stories of surveillance and notices the resulting self-editing behaviour. It is certainly true that neither email nor phone nor even certain occasions at home are considered safe for discussing political or otherwise 'sensitive' issues. 'No one really talks on the phone anymore, just the basics and that is it. You only start commenting on something and people stop you.'[39]

The Spectrum of State-Led Activities

While the administrative and information systems describe the general physical 'presence' of the state and its penetration of people's lives for the purpose of extracting loyalties, contributions (monetary and non-monetary), information and specific conducts, the present sub-section looks in more depth at that aspect of state presence that can be called 'saturation' of people's time with multiple state-ordained activities. First, the section shows that the difficulty of taxation in subsistence economies can be and is resolved by the introduction of alternative but not less potent forms of non-monetary taxation. Second, the actual tax has two components: production for state (labour) and non-production due to state (opportunity cost of time spent on all state-designed activities). Though this requires a much broader analysis than what can be offered here (How much exaction is acceptable and in fact economically viable?), it is important to think of the activities in today's Rwanda in this way – in lieu of finances, it is people's time and energy that are appropriated in the production of public goods (the effectiveness of which is to be disputed vis-à-vis evasion, perfunctory effort or lack of necessary skill).

The intricate administrative and information networks together with the imbrications of the party at every level harness the ability of the Rwandan state to 'mobilize' bodies to a political effect or to disperse them with the aim of preventing political expression. The ability of the state to mobilize its citizens is shown perfectly in the example of the state-organized protests in late 2008. In response to the arrest of Rose Kabuye in Germany, the government organized people from the cell level up. To this end, they used state administrative officials, car patrols mounted with megaphones and text messaging. The result was a flood of people organized in their cell units and merging in the centre, clogging Kigali streets with their banners, slogans and songs. But in the north[40] too (and apparently across the whole country) people were gathered at sector level, either sitting on clearings in front of the administrative offices and listening to officials' speeches or marching (rain or no rain) on parts of the Kigali-Ruhengeri road.

Effective 'dispersion' of bodies, on the other hand, was demonstrated not too long after, during the refugee protests in Kiziba and Gihembe camps. In January 2009, upon hearing that the leader of the CNDP ('protector of Congolese Tutsi') was arrested by Rwandan agents, who were supporting him all along, the refugees within Rwanda staged demonstrations. 'It was hundreds of refugees pretty much just marching around their own camp.'[41] However, 'the government thought that it could get out of hand or turn violent so they entered and sought measures to quell the situation. This included no refugees being allowed in or out of the camp until the situation was normalised ... Refugees were encouraged ... to refrain from any further demonstrations or protests and that's where it stands now'.[42]

Due to the effectiveness of physical mobilization, people not only have to but actually do participate in a myriad of activities, some of which are periodic and others ad-hoc. First, there are multiple unpaid administrative and policing duties (e.g., *irondo* – the local nightly patrols composed of village members). Second, there are general activities, which are costly in terms of time (as opposed to labour). Meetings happen both periodically (such as mandatory weekly security meetings) and on special occasions (e.g., on 'Hero's Day', before elections), during commemoration (e.g., the annual official ceremonies and related activities) or for 'political happenings' (state protests; local RPF meetings). The *gacaca* is convened once a week, which can require extra sessions if a particularly complicated case is being heard.

Third, there are the most clearly labour-exacting duties. The last Saturday of every month is devoted to *umuganda* or 'community work'. *Umuganda* lasts from around eight in the morning until the early afternoon and is followed by a meeting. But 'voluntary' community work does not really have a clear limit. Local leaders have a leeway in trying to enforce extra work, especially in the countryside, where 'surprise *umugandas*' are not uncommon.[43] 'It is in Kigali that there is only one day of *umuganda*. So many districts have [it] even two times.'[44]

Work and meetings are also required as part of the *ubudehe* scheme. In *ubudehe*, cells receive small funds (i.e., 1,000 USD) that they complement with their own resources (i.e., labour) to carry out locally designed projects such as upgrading or formation of anti-erosion terraces, upgrading or construction of roads, construction of schools, etc. *Umuganda* and especially *ubudehe*, where costs are 'matched' by provision of labour for what are often public infrastructure projects,[45] show perhaps most clearly the indirect but effective (in terms of mass targeting and capture) taxing of people in Rwanda.

In addition to the above, increasing amounts of people undergo *itorero* training (similar to *ingando* camps), which involves participation in public works (e.g., construction of a road). *Itorero* graduates draw up group *imihigos* that they pledge to fulfil, which usually means offerings of further free labour for a variety of projects. The pressure to fulfil sector or district *imihigo* goals translates into local authorities' ever greater (ab)use of people's labour. There is also pressure to be an *Agasozi Ndatwa* (example hill) and *indashyikirwa* (the best of the best[46]). 'Because [the leaders] want this [these awards], they impose some kind of meetings and work every week, even two times a week.'[47]

The result is that 'the poor do not have time'.[48] Due to varied exactions and insertions of the state, 'people are not doing what they should be doing [farming]. An agronomist [farmer], on Monday he had to go to see if the *gacaca* will continue, Tuesday was the RPF meeting, then other day some other meetings, plus all the social obligations'.[49] Survivors and women who have male relatives in prisons or TIG camps are perhaps impacted the most. The latter not only lack the extra labour force and have to divide their time between field, children and state activities, they have the added responsibility of trekking to prisons, bringing their husbands, brothers or fathers food and other basic necessities. At the National University of Rwanda (NUR) in Butare, one girl answered my question on the most pressing social problems in Rwanda in the following way:

> Poverty is increasing, especially in the countryside. These days there are a lot of government programmes from *umuganda, gacaca, ubudehe* ... *Umuganda* and *gacaca,* there is no benefit, *ubudehe* at least it brings something to the person ... Tuesday is *gacaca,* Saturday *umuganda,* Thursday *gacaca* ... 3 out of 6 days [there is something] because Sunday does not count ... Plus a lot of meetings. Today at night we have a meeting with the executive secretary of *umurenge,* you cannot resist [refuse to go], otherwise you go to prison ... [There is a] lot of government programmes these days.[50]

The manner in which the government 'makes' people comply with different types of exactions from conduct to labour, how and to what extent people try and manage to evade them, and what type of participation and production actually results, will be discussed in the next chapter. For now, we merely note that the state is 'overbearing' in both its penetration and extraction. Multiple activities exist that make their claim on people's resources. The extent is such that public goods and programmes might today be taking precedence over private welfare of subsistence farmers. The attention to the former might already be at the cost of the latter – the relative inattention to private production on farms, with rural impoverishment as a result.

Lastly, there is reason to believe that the rural areas are disproportionately affected – there is greater surveillance and enforcement. 'Not many people go to *umuganda* here in the city, but in the countryside, eh, can you dare not to go even once? You are fined!'[51] Also, in the cities, there is the least need to build basic infrastructures and it is costly to transport city dwellers to work on rural projects, though terrace upgrading and ditch digging are not uncommon during *umuganda.* Also, office work dictates that in cities all state activities happen during the weekends and after work.[52]

What Counterweights to the State?

At this point, there are two questions of interest: What is 'non-state'? What is a 'bulwark' to the current penetrating party-state? The reason why it makes sense to ask these questions in Rwanda is that the intricate and penetrating state system (increasingly so) has been wholly captured by a specific party with an ideology that aims no less than to transform the society from above. In this goal, the state aims at 'totality' of influence. The state's aspiration is not to annihilate non-state organized life (church sermons, self-help groups, lunch discussions) but rather to have a degree of control and influence over all of these forms.

Importantly, this is not my attempt at discussion of 'civil society', an ambiguous, highly Europe-indigenous term (Mbembe 2001; Uvin 1998). Even if we adopt a clear proxy – associational density – we find that in the case of Rwanda 'dense associational fabric' did not prevent fast disintegration of society in genocide (Uvin 1998: 163–179) and clearly proved an ineffective bulwark against, on the other hand, the extreme asset that the state proved to be. This is because the mere existence of NGOs and other formal or informal groupings does not highlight how the government fundamentally moulds these: i) attacking them for perceived dissention; and ii) urging them to cooperate in the work of the state.

With regard to suppressions of the non-state, we have already discussed the strategies of curbing opposition and of managing dissent and the resulting restrictions on groupness[53] (e.g., political parties, media outlets, but also cultural and human rights organizations that can be and have been attacked as 'divisionist'). With regard to cooperation with the state, *imihigo* contracts are perhaps the best formal demonstration of this phenomenon. They are applied both horizontally and vertically, targeting all possible non-state spheres including the family and the private sector.[54]

Most recently, Gready (2010: 641) has detailed the specific mechanisms in which civil society gets 'managed' by the centre of power:

> The government employs various strategies of management and control ... Legislation enacted in April 2001 gave the government powers to control the management, finances, and projects of national and international NGOs. From the government's perspective, the legislation represents a requirement 'to be organized, to report'. New legislation is in the pipeline, which seeks greater control over NGO activities. In this context, RPF cadres, or those with close ties to the government, have infiltrated the top jobs in local NGOs, 'umbrella' groups, and collectives.

'Opposition', 'dissent' or simply 'unofficial scripts', from which alternative groupness might arise, certainly do exist in their many shades. There are also bulwarks that are more institutionalized or organized than mere 'critique', 'apathy' or 'avoidance'. In a semi-organized but underground form, a bulwark against the state exists in the Hutu 'conspiracy of silence' in *gacaca* (Rettig 2008). In addition, personal networks offer a rather fluid and informal bulwark against the state. People of mixed background, whose affiliations cross ethnicities, are a good example of this phenomenon. While their background exposes them to distrust and even government persecution, they might at the same time get potentially life-saving information just in time from an old acquaintance within the RPF establishment.[55]

Despite these and other dynamics that can 'undo' the state, the increasing permeation of the state into all aspects of life reflects the preoccupation with assuring alignment. As a result of this dynamic, neither religious organizations, schools, nor associations nor even private sector and the family escape the state's reach. Some of these certainly constitute an alternative source of authority, attention and ideology, but they cannot openly oppose and often are urged to align and assist the state.

The Uses of the State: Government's Goals

To what effects and for what goals is the state's overbearing presence used? Is it simply to keep people 'in line'? Analysing the evolution of practice and thinking on 'government' in Europe, Foucault (1991) note a transition from 'sovereignty' (whose end is circular, i.e., the exercise of sovereignty) to government with a 'whole set of specific finalities'[56] (Foucault reprinted in Sharma 2006: 137). In this new 'biopolitical' context, 'government has as its purpose not the act of government itself, but the welfare of the population' (ibid.: 140). In Rwanda, sovereignty and welfare coexist as the ultimate ends of government. Government is about 'care' but also about the survival of this particular political project. Additionally, there is also an interim layer of government that joins the preservation of power with social transformation – governmentality – understood here as the art of producing citizens who not only fit the government's policies but who are also capable of accomplishing them. In general, governmentality encompasses 'the techniques and strategies by which a society is *rendered governable*' (Jones 2007: 174). The focus here is on two governmentality styles that best characterize post-genocide Rwanda at the time of fieldwork – the simultaneous accent on 'containment' and 'transformation.'

Containment

There are various strategies that governments employ to create more governable subjects. 'Socio-scapes' need to be ordered and legible, and this in Rwanda is achieved through intricate administrative, information and physical infrastructure, and a small total area with high population density and almost no uninhabited land. The state's intricate reach also allows for mass gathering and dispersion of bodies. It eases 'tracing': persecuted individuals, whose names are often on lists, cannot easily 'hide'; in addition tools such as 'mobility cards'[57] effectively trace spaces of reintegration; and 'social maps'[58] effectively outline spaces of development insertion. In addition, 'social engineering', including identity engineering, is intensely deployed.

But the integrating theme, encompassing many different control-enhancing techniques, seems to be 'containment'. This strategy broadly relates to the technique of discipline Foucault (1975: 166) named *clôture* or 'enclosure'. But containment in Rwanda goes beyond physical enclosure in the Foucauldian sense (as 'capture' in convents, factories and military barracks of eighteenth-century Europe). Neither does it simply mean capture through improved organization of analytical space whereby individuals are 'placed' so that they can be more easily seen and reached (thus preventing their disappearance, their 'diffuse circulation', their 'dangerous coagulation', ibid.: 168). Containment in Rwanda not only intensifies 'overseeing,' it is also meant to cover up and remove from sight certain undesirable aspects of social reality.

At a physical and visible level, containment is reflected through multiple strategies of controlled and forced movement and stasis. Even at the level of government, one needs 'movement orders' to officiate;[59] here surveillance and legibility are achieved through a centralized signature and stamp. All traders are to be contained in markets – street selling is forbidden. All poor rural farmers are to be contained in rural areas to limit unchecked urbanization. This is achieved through, for example, restrictions on the type of house that can be constructed in urban areas and the consequent tearing down of sub-standard structures (i.e., mud-brick houses).

Another strategy is expropriation. In Kigali, expropriation involves destruction of 'slums' built on potentially lucrative land and the transfer of former residents to the outskirts. With regard to the countryside, in May 2009 the Minister of Natural Resources announced the eviction and relocation of Ruhango (Gishwati Forest) residents and their relocation to a place 'the residents say is a barren and small land compared to Gishwati which has fertile soils'.[60] Additionally, there is containment in villagization schemes (*imidugudu*). The creation of artificial villages (*imidugudu*) completely changes the traditional settlement scheme in Rwanda from 'dispersed' settlement to a 'regrouped' one (HRW 2001), the latter of which is easier to 'read' and control (Jackson for the IFC, no date). The 1996 National Habitat Policy gave as one reason for the establishment of *imidugudu* that 'regrouping residents counters the[ir] dispersion, which makes it difficult to "persuade" (sensitize) them' (in HRW 2001). Besides people, even the genocide human remains are 'contained'. These are gathered in official memorial sites – the only spaces where they, by law, can be laid to rest.

The government's technique of containment reaches beyond Rwanda's territory and comprises forced return of Rwandan asylum seekers. For example, in December 2009, 'the Interior Minister [of Burundi] Nduwimana ordered police to return 103 asylum seekers to Rwanda. Burundi's decision came days after an official delegation from Rwanda told the Burundian government that recently arrived Rwandans should be sent back to Rwanda' (HRW 2009). The goal was to contain unpleasant impressions about RPF-led Rwanda: 'Officials were quoted as saying that they wanted to protect Rwanda's international image as a peaceful country that does not produce refugees' (HRW 2009).

Importantly, containment reaches beyond physical manifestations. At the level of voice and action, it refers to all that, as a result of power's varied interventions, has been left unsaid and that has not been pursued. The attempt is to contain expression of unofficial scripts, of undesirable opinions, emotions, even identities inside persons and inside unofficial and private spheres. Why such a degree of containment? One answer is certainly increased control. But containment's accent on removal of 'symptoms' (of dirt, poverty, frustration, trauma, voiced ethnicity) is also telling. Such acts might seem ultimately shallow (as they do not remove the underlying problems) but they nonetheless hold value for the government – they increase the coveted control over image and impression.

Transformation

The Rwandan government does not, however, only aim at control and containment. It also seeks to change mentalities and transfer knowledge that will help transform people into subjects capable of catalysing change and fulfilling the development plans set forth in official documents. This transformation is to be achieved through formal and informal education. Education, that 'essential terrain of social reproduction' (Muller 2008: 122) is used to transmit discourses on patriotism, nationalism and the citizen. In fact, 'civic education' (also called 'political education') is included in official curricula. At NURC itself the most important department is the Department of Civic Education. The aim is to create a person who 'responds to the requirements of the country', a person 'of exemplary character who participates in development and other activities related to good governance and poverty reduction' (MINAGRI 2006: 17).

In Rwanda, 'good' education (civic and state-organized) is counterposed to 'bad' education (passing on of ideologies inside families, referred to as 'intoxication' or 'contamination' of children by parents). To counteract the latter, 'they [the teachers] start very early in civic education, from nursery. Just like intoxication starts from very early age, so civic education needs to be started on early'.[61] Education or 'state tutelage' not only starts early, it almost never ends. This might be connected to the paternalism characteristic of authoritarian systems, infantilization of illiteracy and the high-powered agenda of a developmental state.

Education does not only happen in classrooms or in organized activities such as *ingando* camps or *itorero* (traditional schools). It occurs more widely through meetings, radio, television, activities, even songs and slogans on T-shirts and is best understood using the popular and ubiquitous terms of 'sensitization'.[62] In Rwanda, this word is employed daily in a variety of settings, including the NURC. The Kinyarwanda equivalents of the English 'sensitization' or French *sensibilisation* are *gushishikariza* or *kubisenzibiliza* (though these are not used as often). When asked 'How can one combat genocide ideology?' or 'What is the most important thing to build national identity?' the instant response by an RPF Headquarters employee and an employee at the National Human Rights Commission (NHRC), respectively, was 'sensitization'.

One informant explained sensitization to me broadly as 'to teach someone, to explain things'.[63] But there are nuanced and important differences between 'teach', 'sensitize' and 're-educate'. One can 'teach' English but one 'sensitizes' others to learn English. One can 'teach' about the different ways of approaching justice post-genocide, but one 'sensitizes' others to suppress ethnicity. Sensitization means urging others to adopt certain behaviours, opinions and values. When people are sensitized, they are handed 'indisputably' positive guidelines; these are not to be discussed. Sensitization of course comprises teaching too (e.g., what is HIV?). Finally, 're-education' contains a strong undertone of trying to remove 'negative' mentalities – genocide ideology, hate and divisionism – and to bring someone from the 'bad' to the 'good' path. Re-education courses, such as *ingando* for FDLR ex-combatants or released prisoners, comprise both teaching and sensitization, but are special due to the intensity of the attempted 'turnover'. Overall, sensitization remains the most widespread manner of 'passing information' to the masses (*baturage*) and is believed to be one of the most important tools in the population's transformation. In essence, sensitization is a top-down exercise connoting persuasion, if not simply instruction. Sensitization's *raison d'être* is rapid and mass diffusion or *vulgarisation* of ideas and attitudes that underpin desired behaviours.

Conclusion

In Rwanda, the state saturates lived social space. The true 'extent' of the state is sometimes hard to gauge because it reaches beyond its 'official infrastructure'. Multiple platforms, positions, even perceptions (as the intangible infrastructure of power), as well as some activities discursively separated from the state ('community' activities, 'student' activities or 'youth' initiatives) are de facto part of it, together constituting the 'state effect'. In addition, the state infrastructure itself is intensely deployed for multiple purposes as and when needed, including mobilization for public works, meetings, *gacaca*, night patrols, state-organized demonstrations, sensitization or informal military recruitment for foreign proxy wars (HRW 2012).

This is not to say that the Rwandan state is all-powerful and uncontested, all-permeating or even homogeneous in its reach. Nonetheless this observation should not detract from the powerful effects that the state does have. The state reach in today's Rwanda is not only deep and manifold with little counterweight, but it directly leads to more effective political control. Through presence and indirect control, a state of surveillance is created. This decreases open dissent and tightens the reproduction and reproducibility of the official script. The system not only creates strong governmentality due to its 'reach' – the intimate contact, the responsiveness, the readability of the social 'scape'. As the next chapter will show, it governs through its accompanying effects as well. Suspicion, distrust (strongly compounded by the genocide), fear and the resultant decreased dissention all assure that the state is better able to gather and disperse, to stage and broadcast, to attempt its desired transformations.

Overall, the findings urge a more critical scrutiny of 'local' 'participation' in 'traditional activities', of their actual meaning in the context of strong hierarchies of authority and a highly centralized political system, which has at its disposal a dense state apparatus. The analysis shows that 'grassroots' does not always mean 'free of central power', that 'local' activities bringing together scores of people do not mean power has been 'decentralized', that people have a greater stake in 'say' or power over their lives, or that the most pressing issues are in fact openly discussed. Despotism can also be decentralized (Mamdani 1996), and so can disempowerment.

Notes

1. MTN is a mobile phone provider recognized by its ubiquitous yellow logo. Personal communication with a researcher friend, 7 May 2010.
2. Historically, the abundance of land on this continent (Reid 2009; Herbst 2000) made state consolidation a question of control over populations (through construction of loyalties, use of coercion, creation of infrastructure) rather than territories.
3. Umusozi (the hill) was the basic socio-political unit in the kingdom, usually divided into several neighbourhoods. In each neighbourhood, one family head was used as its head by the hill chief, and was called umukoresha.
4. The description draws on numerous visits to my own sector offices but also those of other Kigali sectors and observation of various local administrative offices within and outside Kigali.
5. The area where I lived was still referred to as 'Nyamirambo' but in fact it fell under the Nyakabanda sector administration. Nyakabanda ambere (literally 'first') was my cell.
6. Interview with a researcher (Augustin), 25 February 2009.
7. Ibid.
8. Ibid.
9. Informal discussion with a foreign researcher, 4 April 2009.

10. Informal chat with an employee at the National Curriculum Development Centre, Kigali, 30 March 2009.
11. MINALOC website.
12. Interview with a researcher (Augustin), op. cit.
13. *Abakangurambaga* are literally 'people who wake up the masses' – they act as 'promoters' or liaisons. Interestingly, *abakangurambaga* – highlighted by NURC as one of the local and traditional 'unity and reconciliation resources' – are directly part of the bureaucracy of the state. They used to be part of state structures even pre-1994 when they were known as *animateurs*.
14. Interview with Bernard, 22 February 2009.
15. It is unclear how this process works exactly; i.e., to what extent is the election only a confirmation of pre-selected candidates.
16. Interview with Bernard, 18 March 2009.
17. Ibid.
18. Ibid.
19. Interview with Augustin, 6 April 2009.
20. For example, when the employed and 'able' in the congregation are called forth to contribute their 'one tenth' in a sealed envelope.
21. Interview with an employee at the Ombudsman's Office, 14 January 2009.
22. Interview with Bernard, 18 March 2009.
23. Interview with Augustin, 6 April 2009.
24. Interview with a Professional for Good Governance, MINALOC, 12 March 2009
25. Visit to the Muhazi *ingando* for youth ex-combatants, 28 January 2009.
26. E.g., MINALOC 2010; McConnell 2009; ERD 2009.
27. See also e.g., the 2009 European Report on Development (page 96) lauding the imihigo model.
28. Prime Minister's Office (2009: 6)
29. Informal chat with a NURC employee, Nyanza, 17 November 2008.
30. Interview with a Rwandan researcher who worked at MINALOC during imihigo inception, 21 January 2009.
31. Ibid.
32. Interview held at a research institute, Kigali, 21 January 2009.
33. Ibid.
34. Interview with Bernard, 18 March 2009.
35. Ibid.
36. Tangible (though problematic) sources include: a 2009 asylum seeker court testimony repeatedly referring to lists, and an actual 'hit list' embedded within a document entitled 'Some of the Conclusions of the Ambassadors' Meeting in Kigali', February 2010. The document contains a list of names identified as 'enemies of the country who should be fought by all means possible and if necessary by assassination' but the original source is unverified. Received from a friend (university student), who in turn received the document from a Kigali-based journalist.
37. Interview with the Muhazi camp coordinator, op. cit.
38. Interview with Bernard, 22 February 2009.
39. Interview with Augustin, 6 April 2009.

40. On 19 November 2008, when the protests reached their peak, I was travelling with NURC's Director of Civic Education to Ruhengeri.
41. Private email communication between the Reuters Rwanda correspondent and his superiors in the UK, forwarded to me on 28 January 2009.
42. Ibid.
43. Informal chat with an anthropologist who conducted long-term fieldwork around Butare a couple of years before my own fieldwork started.
44. Interview with Augustin in his office on 25 February 2009.
45. Interview with *ubudehe* coordinator at a government ministry, 30 January 2009.
46. Best among administrative levels such as districts but also among individuals.
47. Interview with Bernard, a civil servant, 30 January 2009.
48. Ibid.
49. Ibid.
50. NUR campus, Butare, 5 February 2009.
51. Interview with Bernard, 22 February 2009
52. A couple of important specifications: first, the Saturday *umuganda* might directly affect overall sales of small and big businesses as the one rule that remains well-enforced is that all shops must be closed. The same holds for other mandatory meetings, gatherings, official protests, etc. Second, there are cases of private sector and public offices closing early due to different state-organized activities (e.g., official protests over Kabuye's arrest).
53. 'Groupness' (Brubaker 2004) is the ability and degree to which a collectivity can assume a corporate dimension, be effectively communicating, mutually interacting and acting on its corporate goals.
54. People question whether there is a 'private' sector at all. Most lucrative businesses are said to de facto belong to the party (are controlled by it) (see Willum 2001: 115), and the private sector federation chairman is a political appointee.
55. This has been the case repeatedly in the asylum case I worked on in 2009.
56. E.g., maximization of wealth, provision of sufficient means of subsistence, assuring 'that the population is enabled to multiply' (ibid.) (Foucault 1991).
57. A tool for tracing people (e.g., the relatives of young ex-combatants) by putting together a map of places and landmarks that the young man remembers. Interview with the Muhazi *ingando* coordinator, op. cit.
58. A civil servant showed me a large cloth with a hand-drawn map of a village, each house being coded according to the type of structure (e.g., abandoned) and level of poverty of each household. Every village in Rwanda has such a 'social map'.
59. Officially called L'ordre de mission.
60. Tindiwensi for NTK 2009.
61. Interview with the Director of the KIST Language Centre, 10 March 2009.
62. Naturally, this term has a foreign origin and is employed everywhere where the word 'development' itself is employed intensely. In other words, it is a staple of vocabulary in places of high insertion of the development enterprise.
63. Informal discussion with a Rwandan friend, Kigali, 12 December 2008.

5

Incorporation, Disconnect

The Embodiments of Power and the Unworking of Contestation in Rwanda

That a repressive regime might create a specific structure of feeling is not a surprising proposition. But perhaps a more interesting thesis emerges, namely that feelings are part of a governance on the 'inside', and that such indirect form of domination is both vital to our understanding of the political dynamics in Rwanda, and vital more broadly in expanding our understanding of the 'affect effect' in politics (Neuman et al. 2007). Interestingly, the literature on repression avoids affect and focuses on concrete actions of terror or violation of physical integrity and the structures put in place to effect the denial of rights and surveillance (Escribà-Folch 2013; Davenport 2007a and 2007b). On the other hand, the literature on emotions in politics (Marcus 2000 and 2003; Demertzis 2013; Goodwin et al. 2001) tackles feelings directly but focuses mostly on the manner in which emotions impact political judgement and participation, rather than the ways in which a regime behaviour impacts on the citizen and consolidates non-participation. Yet it is precisely the latter directionality, or rather circularity from regime to citizen and back to the regime, that allows us to glance the last but no less potent pillar of power's operation in Rwanda – its indirect replication through affective 'embodiment'. The Rwandan political system inscribes itself into many bodies through production of feelings and social attitudes that are both collectively defeating and generate self-limiting behaviour on an individual level. The manifestations of *ubushobozi* are far from 'unfortunate externalities' of a repressive system, however. Rather, these directly help consolidate the government's hold on power through the simultaneity of incorporation (affective embodiment) and disconnect (unworking of contestation).

The goal of this chapter is then to analyse the workings of power and their concrete effects on people: What are some of the feelings that the workings of power inspire? What behavioural strategies result? What are the consequences of all this for unity as 'social togetherness'? What is 'dissent' and how does it manifest in daily life? In the context of exclusion and structural violence, what do 'resilience' (Betancourt 2010), 'bearing' or *kwihangana* (Zraly 2008) and 'resistance' (Thomson 2011 and 2013) mean? How do we productively and meaningfully speak about repression's translation and work 'through' the person and society without symbolically robbing the latter of assertiveness and control?

The present analysis centres on the political concept of contestation and power as a structuring field of possibility (Foucault 1982; Hayward 1998). To be even more precise, contestation is defined here as the ability of people to transform discontent or, more generally, demands for change into impact on government policies, plans and activities that affect their lives. The argument is that the techniques of indirect constriction of the official sphere of contestation in Rwanda result in disempowerment. The focus thus is not primarily on overt disempowerment (i.e., open political play) but on covert (political 'non-issues' and exclusion) and latent disempowerment (i.e., symbolic power). The focus lies on 'non-decision making', explained by Lukes (1974) as 'a means by which demands for change ... can be suffocated before they are even voiced; or kept covert; or killed before they gain access to the relevant decision-making arena; or, failing all these things, maimed or destroyed in the decision-implementing stage of the policy process' (ibid.).

There is no denying that Rwandan people possess 'agency'. Naturally, agency is everywhere every day as people make decisions, struggle with life (*kurwana n'ubuzima*, struggle to survive) or find ways to enjoy it, manipulate or escape the state, or as they straddle spaces and temporalities disconnected from the state altogether, such as when they are immersed in prayer, joined in song, or enjoying a good joke. Politically speaking, however, resistances, manipulations and parallel time-space do not alter the fact that the state works on unworking contestation, often through indirect ways (which are more, not less potent) that inscribe themselves on the individual and the social body and that limit people's 'fields of possibility'. This political dimension is powerfully present, needs to be understood, and cannot and should not be diminished by pointing to the inventiveness and resilience of common Rwandans who are asked to bear it.

The Styles and Strategies of Power in Rwanda

In its attempts to assure domination over society, the Rwandan government wields many forms of power, from physical coercion, threat and pressure, to inducement and co-optation, persuasion and knowledge. Power nonetheless works predominantly through indirect means and, more specifically, through two key structuring principles – the 'principle of deterrence' grounded in perceived costs of dissenting action, and the 'principle of possibility' that feeds off the uncertainty and arbitrariness of power's application. This reflects well the broader notion that power is a relational process operating at all levels of the social body (O'Farrell 2005). Power can be meaningfully approached through the Foucauldian notion of 'government' as the 'conduct of conduct', ranging from governing the self ('technologies of the self') to 'governing others' (Lemke 2000: 2). Hence while agents of power vary, what joins these instances together is the notion of power as the 'management of possibilities' (Foucault 1982: 341), 'structuring and shaping the field of possible action of subjects' (Lemke 2000: 3). As such, rather than being 'negative' or 'positive' *per se*, power is simply productive – it can either 'empower' or 'disempower'. At the same time, power is not external to subjects' wishes, beliefs and behaviours but works through these, trying to 'shape and determine' them (Lukes 1974: 27). This is the entry point for our analysis of 'disconnect through incorporation' since from this perspective, the 'polarity of subjectivity and power ceases to be plausible' (Lemke 2000: 12).

Some of the government's styles of power have already been introduced. The discursive power connotes the ability to appropriate the implicit logics that structure official narratives to achieve political or private ends. For example, the vague crimes of 'divisionism' and 'genocide ideology' can serve to attack political opposition or dissenting voices, or those who are successfully construed as such. But the discursive effect is more diffuse, and includes communication of the desirable political 'disposition' as one of consent and alignment. A related indirect style of power is 'guidance' consisting of advice and sensitization on expected norms of behaviour. Political threats or warnings, on the other hand, are a more direct form of communication – though they might come in veiled statements, they nonetheless communicate powerfully. This style of power is still indirect inasmuch as it aims to work through deterrence, and it is effective inasmuch as it avoids usage of more explicit forms of pressure. Importantly, all indirect modes of domination are backed by a coercive apparatus, which 'works' through the occasional demonstrations of its effective application (through imprisonment, disappearance or harassment).

The intricate system of administration strengthens non-contestation in a number of ways at once – we can speak of a state's infrastructural advantage in 'outflanking' (Mann 1986) resistance, and the system also offers an opportunity to co-opt multiple people to the government's ranks and to mould people's behaviour through the 'overseer' effect. Surveillance especially is a highly effective and a financially non-burdening technology of indirect control (see also Bozzini 2011 on the 'low-tech' surveillance in

Eritrea). But the power of the gaze does not only derive from 'ears and eyes' being dispersed in the external environment (whereby the very uncertainty but high probability that someone is watching produces effects), the gaze is also gradually internalized by a person who will then 'exercise this surveillance over, and against, himself' (Foucault 1980a: 155).

The role of perceived surveillance should not be underestimated. Even in countries without the remarkable state density and reach witnessed in Rwanda, including Ethiopia and Mozambique, people see the state as a 'powerful actor' able to surveil and possessing ways of 'knowing' not always apparent. The parallels are striking. In Ethiopia, people are profoundly distrustful of and sceptical about the possibility of 'anonymity' during elections. René Lefort (2010) found that local residents in Amhara state 'believed that the authorities have unknown means of tracing everybody's vote'. In Mozambique, Harry West (2007: 66–67) found that people on the Mueda plateau were reluctant to register for elections in 1994, associating registration with historical forms of surveillance and attendant monitoring, control and extraction. As a result, 'many Muedans doubted that their votes would remain secret' (ibid.). In Burundi, many people who take payment in 'vote buying' practices believe the state has ways of checking that their 'investment' was not spent 'in vain'. In Eritrea, the state has developed a system of surveillance of conscripts that 'contributes almost on a daily basis to reproducing various uncertainties, fears, beliefs and expectations that are the core of relative coercion in the National Service' (Bozzini 2011). This repeated pattern clearly suggests that in order to fully understand state power, we need to incorporate social perceptions and imaginaries into our framework. The study of physical infrastructures needs to be accompanied by our study of the more intangible infrastructures of power. From this perspective, historical memories, rumour and conspiracy connected to the state (West and Sanders 2003; Turner 2007), in addition to perceived surveillance, can all translate into self-governance from below.

Indirect power does not operate on its own. The power of the discourse and its translation (through extension of its structural logic) into selective coercions by the administration, the courts or the police or into the making of 'helpful' laws and wars, or the power of the gaze, not always clearly identified through a uniform and a body in a 'panopticon' (Foucault 1975) and thus strengthened by it being 'possibly anywhere', are important but not sufficient. More explicit styles of power such as coercion are also employed at the local level, coercion being necessary to assure attendance, compliance and contributions, and again to provide a motor to deterrence. 'If you don't go to the activities', explains one of my informants, 'you are putting yourself in a trap like a rat. Why? Because there are so many instances when you need medical insurance, travel documents, and wherever you go, whatever service you need, they will ask you, did you participate, where is your *umuganda* card? Automatically, you will not get what you want ... this is the social compulsion and social control mechanism used.'[1] This observation seems to comport well with reality (and other research, see Chemouni 2014). Refusal of administrative services and denial of access to markets are two common coercive strategies. To monitor attendance and compliance with policies, the government has also resorted to using documents such as *umuganda* and *gacaca* cards, *mutuelle de santé* cards (proving required health insurance payment) or *Umurenge Sacco* cards (required savings deposits). It has been reported that 'leaders in Kiziguro sector have pegged local authority service to residents' attendance of *umuganda* in order to attract more participants' (Ngabonziza for NTK, 12 August 2009). Coercion is often used by local officials anxious to meet *imihigo* targets. For example, the *New Times* reported how:

> Commotion erupted in Ruhengeri town on Thursday when residents with no health insurance cards were locked out of the market. Residents were shocked to find gates closed, by sector leaders with the help of local defence personnel who demanded health insurance cards as a requirement to access the market ... Jonas Nkomeze, the town cell leader who was manning the entrance said they wanted to ensure that 90 per cent of the residents have cleared health insurance dues by the end of this month ... Sensitisation campaign for the *Mutuelle de Santé* (health insurance) has been one of the highlights in the performance contracts (*imihigo*) of the district leaders. (NTK, 15 March 2007)

A government report (MINALOC, 2006: 39) mentions a similar type of coercion with regard to assuring contributions to the sector community education fund (*ikigega cy'uburezi*):

> Contributions are supposed to be voluntary depending on the means available to each resident. However, according to several focus group participants, there is an element of coercion in this process. They claim there are no open sanctions for those who do not pay, but noted that people pay especially on market days and when they want a service from the local government. One interviewee felt it was impossible to sell one's produce on market days unless the education fund had been contributed to.

At the extreme end of coercion, there are personal threats and physical harassment, imprisonment without charge or on fabricated charges, ill-treatment and degrading treatment, torture, disappearances, even assassinations (AI 2010 and 2012; US DoS 2014; HRW 2014, among others). Besides physical abuse, the experiences in detention involve and further induce humiliation and emotional abuse, and detailed testimonies speak of a Rwanda of mock and real executions, arrest lists and hit lists. Those targeted who manage to flee such escalation in state 'attention' (the term of art being persecution) rarely do so at its first instance (as refugee testimonies repeatedly demonstrate). What is key in these power dynamics, besides the stress and terror faced by the persons immediately concerned is again the 'demonstrative' effect of such exercises – the spillover and indirect effects that are put to 'work'. It is only by understanding this mechanism that we also understand why, despite small-scale resistances and a 'great deal of resentment' (Chakravarty 2014) local elites nonetheless 'comply with directions from above' as noncompliance is not perceived by these local elites as 'an option, given the coercive might of the RPF apparatus' (ibid.). Compliance is thus the result of deterrence through effective demonstration, it is the result of perceived costs of directly dissenting action. The perceived costs combine with the perceived visibility of one's actions to create an effective (and affective) indirect state of domination. Thus the broad proposition that a repressive system lives through the person should be better understood. Below the macro facts of 'dominance of the executive' and 'lack of opposition', there is a wide array of indirect styles of power that penetrate and incorporate people's lived registers not only into a form of governance through control, but really into the task of constricting contestation, and in turn, into the reproduction of the current political system.

Power Inscribed: The Landscape of Feelings, Attitudes and Relations

An important piece in the puzzle of the state's 'incorporation' is the empirical evidence recently presented by Bert Ingelaere (2014: 219) who ingenuously demonstrates 'state presence' in rural Rwandans' lives through the word frequency counts in their life histories. Interestingly, the word 'authorities' is the third most frequent word after 'land' and 'children'. This evidence not only corroborates a state 'presence' of sorts, it also demonstrates how people ostensibly 'on the margins' of the state are in fact intimately linked to it. While these findings suggest preoccupation and insinuate affective effect, we do not quite know what form these take, and how, if at all, they tie back to political power.

Naturally, the 'productiveness' of a repressive system, in terms of feelings and attitudes, has to be seen side-by-side with the lingering effects of the genocide as the two often compound each other. But while we know and even expect that 'fear and suspicion is likely to exist in post-conflict settings' (Fujii 2010: 240), that it can become a structuring force in society (Hampson 2004), we need to firmly establish the contribution of the current political regime to the production of negative emotion. We need to politicize fear, to show clearly that it is not simply an issue 'among communities' that can be resolved by 'confidence building measures' (Alusala 2005). What follows is not an ethnography of 'inner landscapes' or a structure of feeling, it is a very modest attempt to offer insight into a topic that deserves much more systematic and extensive analysis. Nonetheless its inclusion here is deliberate – power's embodiment is no ethereal issue, quite the opposite. It is also, arguably, a key aspect of power's operation in Rwanda.

The topic of fear has already emerged numerous times but deserves reiteration as it structures non-contestation most powerfully. As mentioned, the feeling of fear is not a constant emotive state and Rwanda is thus not 'engulfed in fear'. Selective acts of physical repression, threats and the communication of the 'cost' to dissent produce anxiety, carefulness and avoidant behaviour. People avoid public mention of sensitive topics or dissenting opinions for fear of imprisonment, they decide to participate in rallies and activities to avoid hassle, or they 'hide' to escape the state's eye and hence avoid the costs of punishment for non-participation. All of these derive from fear and all contribute to non-contestation. It is with this caveat in mind that we can agree that indeed 'the dominant emotional tone in public life tends to be one of fear and distrust' or that 'far from supporting the regime, most Rwandans fear it' (Hintjens 2008: 18). However, what makes fear so potent is that it is not confined to public spaces (as the quote above suggests), it is carried or enters (in the form of officials) into private spaces and daily 'ways of being' as well (see e.g,. Burnet 2012).

Other feelings and attitudes are tied to and compounded by fear, and produce similar political effects. For one, there is general distrust. 'In this country there is no one to trust',[2] suggests one of my long-term Hutu informants. 'Rwandans do not trust each other',[3] confirms another. Trust has to be built because it is never there completely. The genocide undoubtedly and profoundly heightened distrust. As a survivor explains, the genocide makes you 'forever lose a part of your trust in others'.[4] Another survivor talks of a 'doubt about everything' that settles on a person who has witnessed, and a distrust of everyone – 'strangers, colleagues, even neighbouring survivors'.[5] After the genocide, perhaps paradoxically, thousands of local *gacaca* courts and a decade of 'grassroots justice' produced further tension, distrust, even frustration based in a sense of injustice (Rettig 2008; Chakravarty 2014, among others). Distrust in turn is closely related to prevalent suspicion. 'It has developed as some sort of culture,' I was told, 'that wherever you are, you have to be suspicious.'[6] Surveillance definitely further contributes to distrust and suspicion, and ultimately fear and paranoia, especially when trying to share information challenging the official script. When suspicion reaches a sufficient scale, it can become self-enhancing.[7]

The repressive nature of the political system also pushes people to 'falsity'. Official transcript is a currency and a safeguard and sometimes it has to be used or manoeuvred around, even though this might come at some cost to personal integrity. Suppression of opposition and constant surveillance at times force people into humiliating silence. The necessity for people to agree and to support at times forces them to adopt a degrading voice. The feelings that result from reflections on such compromises are shame, frustration, anger, even guilt arising from feelings of duplicity.

But there is also the other side of the emotive spectrum, albeit pertaining to a narrower segment of the population that benefits from power (the elite's 'social base was, and remains, very narrow' (Reyntjens 2013: 253)), the ideologue minority who truly believe and those who are enchanted (whether momentarily or not) by the government's promises. There is the excitement and elation of the relatively privileged, educated young people. There is also the gratefulness of many former refugees for the opportunity to return. A journalist working for the government-leaning NTK and a returnee from Uganda remarked to me: 'Some Rwandans say that Kagame is like a gospel … he is like a miracle'.[8] There are also those who are proud of their official positions and who sincerely believe they are making a difference from within the government. But importantly, while this captiv(ated) minority by definition does not contest the centre and can derive power from its alignment with it, this does not mean that they have any real power to contest should they want to resort to contestation. As demonstrated on various occasions over the past years, even those networked into power or those who hold official positions can face repression once they break ranks with the government, turn critical of it or become perceived as a political threat.[9]

Turning the focus away from emotions that do not challenge disempowerment back to those that produce it, the aggregate of people's feelings, attitudes and behaviours detailed above produce collectively defeating social dynamics or 'public bads'. The micro or individual level, and the meso level of social relations are thus not easily separable, but rather conjoin to create the overall effect of indirect disempowerment. The asymmetries of voice have already been discussed in a previous chapter; here it is merely useful to link these explicitly to the unworking of contestation. To put it simply, if stories, histories and positions cannot be officially recounted, they cannot be promoted, or defended. Connected to this, anxieties and uncertainties arise from the controlled market for information. In a system tightly controlling voice and silence and the propagation of information through mass media, the only antidote is unverified information exchange to which people resort on a daily basis and which includes rumour, *radio trottoir* (street chat) and informal exchanges dismissed as 'bar talk'. But rumour, though headless and sourceless, remains a powerful tool as it can spread fast, reach wide and can have a concrete impact on behaviour.

For one, rumour can induce fear. The inability to verify the information contained in something 'rumoured', the resulting impossibility of ascertaining or refuting its content, in fact the broader environment of generalized carefulness (arising from suspicions or lack of trust) and uncertainty (controlled information and arbitrariness of power) leads to seeming 'overreactions' – e.g., fleeing to exile in Burundi just because the anthropologist in the community is rumoured to know what they did and to 'hand them over' to the authorities. But such a disproportionate act might in fact be no more than a calculated protection, an insurance against the possibility that what is said is true. This eventuality is worth protecting oneself against in the context of an imperfect information market.

Imperfect information thus creates negative externalities – effects that reach beyond the parties who originally exchange this type of information or who fail to communicate. For example, with regard to the Kigali expropriations, rumour created maps of fear far broader than the actual areas to be cleared. A Gitega sector official commented to me while pointing down to the valley: 'You see how Gitega is [referring to the poverty] ... expropriation, they fear it ... People are coming to see us "When will we go? When will they come to expropriate us?"'[10] People in Kicukiro were said to fear similar rumours. An urban planner at the City of Kigali, however, was surprised to hear this. Gitega was not on the master plan as a target for expropriation. 'But maybe they are scared', she suggested, 'because we visited and assessed the area some months back.'[11]

In other words, power at the micro level works on the principle of 'possibility'. Widespread surveillance and control makes it possible, even probable that you too are watched and that this moment is monitored. Arbitrary power cannot be completely predicted, but it does manifest, it is possible. Rumour works because it, too, is possible. In other words, not knowing exactly prevents us from refuting a given statement with absolute certainty. The principle of 'possibility' undermines perceived control over one's life, it undermines trust, fosters suspicion, even paranoia, and creates fear. The principle of possibility can also be used as a direct tool of suppression. Stigma or 'the blemish' (an attack on reputation) is a powerful strategy to neutralize a person. The power of the blemish does not lie in its veracity as one is tainted simply through association and tamed through the anxiety over potential impact.

The micro effects of power are also recognizable through people's self-censure, self-editing and self-silencing. 'The Kinyarwanda word *kwibwizira* [from *kuzira*, to exclude],' writes Bert Ingelaere, 'entails this idea of auto-censorship ... that people do what authorities want them to do, without the latter asking them to do so or using coercion' (2009: 526). My own research corroborates these findings. I had the opportunity to observe how my informants would switch subjects or stop talking when sensing surveillance, and how some of my researcher friends considered revising their projects after unpleasant political encounters. At a Kigali-based human rights watchdog, I inquired whether it is sufficient to mention ethnicity to get punished for it. 'No, it is not sufficient, however, people self-edit to avoid getting into trouble.'[12] The analysis of voice and silence suggests why many might not open up in the first place or produce mere echoes of the official script without someone urging them to. At a different research institution, we discussed social exclusion in Rwanda: 'This is complicated', suggested my informant. '[On the one hand] there are mechanisms put in place that exclude, and [then] there is auto-exclusion. People are self-excluding ... [they say] ah, these are Tutsi things.'[13] After learning about political sensitivities and costs of transgression, some people revisit their capabilities and possibilities, restrict their goals ('Muhima is perhaps too controversial to work in'; 'If I include this research module, can they do something?').

Overall, the analysis above gives a different shade of meaning to Bigo's concept of 'government by unease' (2002) as rule through structural anxiety and uncertainty. The system of power in Rwanda inscribes itself into bodies through feelings and attitudes and these in themselves aid the project of both governance and political closure. Power at the micro level is often hard to 'see' and measure because, rather than materializing through physical contact, it is dispersed and embodied. This is why it might be difficult to grasp repression in Rwanda. The *chicote* – the whip – a symbol of disciplining and the culture of terror under colonialism, has been replaced by more subtle forms of power. Yet it is precisely these forms that are favoured as 'indeed, power is at its most effective when least observable' (Lukes 1974: 1).

What is Dissent?

Dissent can be conceptualized more broadly as the power to defy and to reclaim meaning and control over one's life. This broader reading reaches beyond dissent as an open expression of dissatisfaction or opposition. In Rwanda, active and organized resistance is largely absent and in its stead we find more subtle forms of escape and subversion, ingenuity and manipulation, resilience and persistence. What is at issue is not whether these are forms of dissent or resistance, but rather whether they can be considered 'contestation' as we have defined it here. The government through strategies already explored not only suppresses active resistance, it literally quietens and unworks voiced opposition and dissatisfaction, and thus again the ability of people to contest prevalent politics and policies – to pressure for change.

The issue of Rwandans' compliance should be firmly delivered from the depoliticizing talk of a 'culture of obedience'. Some of my informants pointed to the absence in rural areas of 'refusal' and 'saying no':

> Especially in the countryside there is a tendency to accept what you hear ... Rwandans should learn to say 'no' to the politicians ... The government [managed] to seduce them ... Even today, the government says close all the shops, and they don't refuse. Otherwise they can go to jail. [But] with that, they will feel anger, you cannot have reconciliation.[14]

This interpretation, while accurately describing the absence of direct contestation and its potentially harmful effects, is problematic nonetheless as it shifts the interpretive locus away from structure to people's 'habits' and 'proneness to conformity'. What suppressed disquiet might reflect instead is the control over populations in the rural areas, their perceptions of the costs to dissent and their relative lack of resources. Such a model can accommodate both the almost unanimous voiced agreement that 'it is important to obey the authorities' (Rettig 2008: 41; elicited through a questionnaire in Sovu) and the occasional and ostentatious display of dissatisfaction, such as when the inhabitants of the Gishwati Forest, upon hearing of their impending eviction in May 2009, uprooted 70,000 nursery trees planted on forty acres of land (Tindiwensi for NTK 2009).

Repression and control in Rwanda explain both the relative lack of organized protests, the relative lack of public criticism and the relatively high compliance and attendance at activities and programmes. But the absence of open refusal to follow orders, and even the overt pronouncement that it is important to follow them, naturally does not mean that people accept what they hear and even what they themselves say. 'Simulated loyalty' (Thomson 2011: 453) or 'withdrawn muteness' such as 'purposeful and strategic moments of silence' (ibid.) are common coping strategies. Talking about the mandatory post-*umuganda* meetings, an acquaintance of mine has earnestly suggested that 'the most important thing is to be there'.[15] Interestingly, even the agents of state suspect a surface-level nature of 'acceptance'. A district official in Southern province confessed to a researcher (Ansoms 2009: 298): 'You talk to them [peasants] and you think they listen, but the people do nothing with the good advice you give them. They say "yes" because they are tired of you and your speeches, but they are never convinced ... They are resistant, they are really difficult.' But should this situation be read as a stand-off, a balance of forces? I would argue not – while it might spell the limits of the state's impositions, the fact remains that people are pushed to weak and unofficial contestation or else costly confrontation.

In a system set to produce and oversee suppression and containment, a lot of the outcry moves inside – the revolt is the anger that one of my informants mentions, the resistance is the refusal to believe. It is a play on words and rules and their appropriation. It is denial, lying, laughter and derision. It is 'foot-dragging', 'working the system' (Scott 1985: xv–xvi). It is the guarding and passing on of counter-narratives. Multiple strategies of dissent exist in Rwanda that, just like the power from the top, are more subtle.[16] One adaptation strategy against surveillance and compliance is ducking, hiding, evasion – the skilful disappearance from the state's eye. Street hawking, forbidden in Rwanda, is a good example. Walking the back streets of Kigali, indeed you do not find 'stalls' and goods spread on pavements. But a new alternative has developed – the 'sauntering salesmen' clad with goods, slowly passing by. The government does not give up. In order to effectively eliminate the tricking of the state, it started deploying a 'unit of police in plain clothes' (Barigye 2008). But the street vendors are not discouraged either. A woman caught selling in the street explained: 'We cannot stop working because we cannot stop eating' (ibid.).

But surveillance can be played with and used to one's own purpose, not only dodged. Thomson (2011: 452) here talks about the strategy of 'irreverent compliance' as in 'following the rules … in ways that covertly undermine the authority of local officials and other agents of the state', for example by laughing out loud at speeches or glaring. In a situation of suspected surveillance, one can also pass on messages that are not only (or at all) meant for the interlocutor but for those who are 'listening in'. They might seem ambiguous if considered in the context of the 'official' audience but take a specific and clear meaning if the agent of surveillance is incorporated into the scene. During one of our interviews, my informant and I realized that we were being listened to and observed by a man who sat at the table right next to us. My informant adjusted to the situation by lowering his tone of voice and turning to me though he still continued with his narrative (unlike at another occasion when he abruptly switched themes, choosing a 'light' topic). At one point, unexpectedly, the hushed tone was replaced with an unusually loud voice, as if making an announcement: 'Once my university professor at Dar es-Salaam University told us to bear in mind the following statement. Absolute power corrupts and absolutely collapses!'[17]

The monthly *umuganda* is another good example of a variety of dissent strategies. First, there are the tacitly 'excused' groups. Children and old people are not required to attend, but women also seem to have some leeway for either absenting or, if they do come, for sitting down and chatting together. 'Normally men go, women not so much', I was told.[18] Another officially excused group are the Adventists who have an alternative day for *umuganda*. Based on the numbers of people strolling the roads freely one *umuganda* day, I joked with a NURC employee that there seemed to be an 'awful lot of Adventists in Kigali'. But people also manipulate the talk itself: 'I am doing *umuganda* of my home', a friend tells me one Saturday. Others also said they 'participated by cleaning their living room'.[19]

The strategy of 'dodging rules' and 'pretending to work' during *umuganda* seems to be quite widespread in Kigali (again, this should not be treated as representative of the countryside). One *umuganda* Saturday, I decided to do a transect tour of Nyamirambo in order to see what happens in different parts of my neighbourhood on *umuganda* day. Shops and markets were indeed closed and locked, but street sellers operated. Buses and cars did not pass the main roads, but *motos* (motorbike taxis) offered rides through back roads and avenues without roadblocks. Multiple people could be seen just strolling and milling around Byriogo at the height of *umuganda*, or just watching the occasional group of men at work on a specific project (usually digging a ditch), or chatting seated on the stoops of houses. A loud chatter of multiple voices could be heard from a nearby *urugo* (enclosure).

In general, I saw few organized activities, and in their lieu the popular activity was 'sweeping dirt'. Already at 6am that day, I had woken up to the persistent 'swoosh swoosh' of multiple brooms (*imikubuzo*) at work. Our security guard explained that people often just clean around their houses, doing *buhabanura, gusukura* (cleaning). Another favourite activity consisted of manicuring lawns and grass patches. One woman was eagerly working on a patch of grass on a small traffic island made for a single traffic sign – 'forbidden to turn right'. Yet another skilful compromise was 'leaning over a hoe or shovel'. In the back streets of the Rwezamenyo cell, I saw a number of men standing in one position, immobile yet ready to move and demonstrate involvement if need be by digging in the dirt. On the clearing outside of our market, the gate to which was besieged by police, I asked a woman 'What do you do on the day of *umuganda*?' '*Gusukura* (cleaning),' she responded resolutely, not flinching in the least at the fact that plenty of people, in plain sight, were doing exactly nothing.

The most interesting aspect of the scene, though, was the Local Defence Force (LDF) with their red overalls, walking through the streets with no seeming effect on the co-promenaders. A tacit agreement seemed to have been struck – as long as someone is working and as long as the rules of closing business and traffic are observed, then they leave people be. This is how an enforced state activity – whether glorified by the state and some foreign observers, or condemned by those who see it as a restriction of freedom or harmful to business and subsistence – can in fact turn into a parody of official intent, a nuisance to be manoeuvred around. This should not suggest that no work is done, whether physical or symbolic (as in extraction of legitimacy through images of 'communality', discipline and 'cleanliness') or that the constrictions *umuganda* imposes are unproblematic or can be equally manoeuvred by all.

Internal 'flight' is another dissent strategy, and one that takes many forms. First, there are the duckers and deserters from activities and institutions. In the makeshift TIG labour camp in the Gikomero sector, a daily-updated blackboard announced a total of forty-four 'deserters' in a camp of 603 *abahari* (people present). Besides physical flight, there is escape in sleeping, dreaming or not paying attention. During the seven-hour-long lectures at *ingando* attended by a thousand students, many dozed off, talked to each other in hushed voices, passed each other scribbled notes or let their bored minds trail off. This happened despite the hawkish looks of the 'disciplinarian' seated by the speaker and despite the soldiers promenading through the aisles, checking notes and delivering punishments that included pouring water down the collars of the dozers. There are also many who want to escape the invasive heaviness and ever-present reminders of the genocide during *icyunamo* – the commemoration period spanning the months from April to July. Expatriates take vacations outside Rwanda, many Hutu 'close themselves in their houses' to avoid the heavy atmosphere. But even some survivors want to escape the pain that comes pouring in from all sides. One evening, when we were all seated in the kitchen, we asked Alex – a genocide orphan and former street child cared for by a housemate – about what he wanted to do during *icyunamo*: he responded in English in his soft, barely audible voice: 'Sleep ... yeah'.

Uncertainties and pretences of power are mirrored in dissent strategies, producing the unsettling sense of feigned compliance and an uncertain political friendship. The optimum strategy becomes dispersion, context-specificity and vagueness; evasiveness protects and opens possibilities, it permits one to escape the strictures and indignities of power without losing the benefits of political friendship. 'I am on no one's side', an employee of a small peace association told me after explaining identity-based conflicts in a human rights organization she used to work for. On another occasion, a discussion with a long-term informant finally delivered an answer to a sensitive question: How do you resolve the tension between working for the government and being so critical of it? My informant responded immediately: 'You cheat me [by saying] you love me, I cheat you [by saying] that you are my friend.'[20] This is a fitting simile for the broader 'bad faith economy' (Scheper-Hughes 1992: 111) operating in Rwanda where all sides pretend but might feel ill-served in the end. It is a mutual trickery, a thin friendship indeed, and yet its payoffs and burdens are not equally distributed.

Conclusions

In Rwanda, indirect styles of power – guidance, visibility and deterrence, and the resulting anxiety, distrust and self-censure – are key tools in the unworking of contestation. State power in Rwanda might not be primarily 'carnivorous' as Mbembe suggests in his 'feasting' metaphor (2001: 201), the government rather appropriates power for itself through the emotions that it cultivates. It is in this sense that we can say that the political system governs through embodiment as it unworks contestation through its own affective effect. The effects of repression on the person and social relations are thus hardly an unfortunate externality of the political system, effects that are merely 'internalized' in the lives of ordinary Rwandans. Rather, they are a key component of power's reproduction. The analytical distinction between the micro and the macro thus effectively collapses, and paradoxically, it is through the intimate incorporation of people into its mechanism that power simultaneously disconnects them. In response, people themselves distance the state by retrenching inside, showing surface-level consent while manoeuvring constraints, producing in the end a fragile social equilibrium.

This chapter has tried to demonstrate that something quite systematic is going on in the grain of everyday life in Rwanda that has, potentially, systemic importance. The unworkings of contestation certainly produce stability for the political system, in the sense that it is able to reproduce itself without a disequilibriating opposition. Continued 'stabilization' of this sort, however, might simultaneously undermine the system from within, eroding legitimacy and social cohesion, constricting responsiveness to needs and demands, producing and suppressing grievances and foreclosing institutional mechanisms that could channel discontent in a peaceful way. Stability in Rwanda is thus built on socially disintegrative, and thus potentially destabilizing, dynamics.

By way of a broader conclusion to this section, the embodiments of power are only one pillar of power affecting and potentially subverting the unity-building process. On a broader plane, the government in Rwanda has been using the appealing, seemingly non-political profile of unity and reconciliation language to consolidate non-contestation. Specifically, the discourse on unity is being used as a power instrument to silence and discourage dissent. Unity is thus not simply a technocratic or post-conflict justice term in Rwanda, rather a broader and fundamentally political notion insinuating consent, non-dissention, agreement and convergence, and painting these as morally imperative to achieve security and development. In Rwanda, the 'wording of power' through key legitimation narratives has sufficient gravity to affect the meaning of unity and the ways in which it is pursued in specific activities. Or, in another (equally valid) formulation, the sufficiently malleable notion of 'unity' can be imbued with meanings that appropriate it in the service of political goals other than the harmonious coexistence of the populace. On the side of power's infrastructure, the state possesses an unusual ability to saturate everyday life, to stage and gather and make a convincing show of its attempts at social transformation. But however localized in outlook, the exercise is top-down, from its conception to its execution. The general surveillance and the reach of the state, together with evidence suggesting that it is precisely the rural space that is a site of coercion to a disproportionate degree, put in question accepted notions of a 'periphery'. At a more intimate level yet, state-originated surveillance and repression fundamentally inscribe themselves into people's bodies through emotions such as generalized suspicion and distrust and constrict not only what people say and do, but at times also what they want or deem possible. A unity (of a kind) is thus indeed created in Rwanda, partly because it is wiser not to openly challenge such a claim.

Notes

1. Interview with Bernard, a civil servant, 22 February 2009.
2. Ibid., 12 March 2009.
3. Interview with Augustin, 6 April 2009.
4. Commentary made to Hatzfield (2000: 17).
5. Ibid.: 124.
6. Interview with Bernard, 18 March 2009.
7. Suspecting people can become suspicious. When being observed at close quarters, one tends to lower one's voice, lean over, look around, lay the head on the shoulders to create a more intimate space. The tendency to talk about certain subjects in hushed voices, leaning towards the centre with a changed, serious expression is likely to draw attention.
8. Informal discussion, 21 November 2008.
9. On dissident assassinations, see York and Rever, The Globe and Mail, 2 May 2014.
10. Interview at Gitega sector offices, 21 January 2009.
11. Informal discussion, 21 January 2009.
12. Interview, 9 January 2009.
13. Interview with Augustin, 21 January 2009.
14. Interview with an NGO communication officer, Kigali, 23 February 2009.
15. Informal discussion, 1 December 2008.
16. There are also moments of open 'voicing' and more direct confrontation. For example, a community sent a letter expressing dissatisfaction over expropriation and their insufficient compensation. In an *ingando* lecture on materialism, people openly communicated their disagreement, etc.
17. Interview with Bernard, 22 February 2009.
18. Ibid.
19. Janna Graham's online blog named 'Umva [Listen];' entry from 2 June 2008.
20. Interview with Bernard, 18 March 2009.

Part III
Making *Ubumwe*
The Imageries, Planning and Performances of Unity in Rwanda

The present section revolves around a simple question: What is being done by the government under the banner of 'unity and reconciliation'? This question assumed greater significance as my fieldwork progressed and as interesting and systematic discrepancies appeared between official descriptions and actual happenings. It became clearer that instead of asking 'Do these activities work?' we should be asking 'How do they work? What is the nature of these activities?' and, finally, 'What are their effects, whether intended or unintended?' Rather than being 'led by labels', the questions lead us to analyse labelling itself as a political force.

While the previous chapters analysed the core political dynamics in post-genocide Rwanda and the appropriation of terms such as unity and division for broader political goals, the present section seeks to offer a different 'entry point' to understanding *ubumwe*. The aim is to explore the daily deployments of unity, referring here to the actual work of nation building and the nature of the activities intended to carry out such work. There are two broad aims to this section. First, to avoid, as much as possible, any preconceived notions of unity and reconciliation and to elaborate a 'multiplicities of unity' approach. Second, to detail the politicized nature of unity and reconciliation activities, which contrasts with the usual portrayals embalmed in different forms of depoliticized language. Part of this endeavour is to uncover the 'politics of naming' (Bhatia 2005; Mamdani 2007). While Bhatia and Mamdani refer to the representation of conflict, I apply the phrase to a similar process of simplifying, decontesting and legitimating peace building.

The overarching concept of reconciliation is a vague term (Renner 2014). It escapes a single definition and seems to mean 'different things to different people.' I circumvent this problem by accepting that, indeed, not only in academia, but also across cultures and within a single society, reconciliation and unity might mean different things to different people. While the academic literature on Rwanda has usefully explored 'local' understandings of these two terms (Longman 2010; Burnet 2012; Buckley-Zistel 2008; Ingelaere 2009), there is little study of the coexistence of different 'versions' (see Burnet 2012 for an exception) and no study at all of the underlying dynamics and interaction among them. Yet it is precisely such framing that opens space for political analysis properly speaking and that allows for a dynamic, though still emplaced treatment of abstract conceptions. Multiplicity will be explored in other ways too. The section will consider 'conceptual fragmentation' that occurs when elusive notions such as *ubumwe* are refracted through technocratic tools and institutional needs. It will also outline the variety of official 'strategies of unity', challenging the predominant focus in the literature on the rewriting of history, which, while important, is only one among many strategies used.

The analysis will subsequently turn to the concrete activities meant to propagate and enact the government's idea of national unity. The focus will be on activities *in toto* and on placing these into the contexts and relations of power. As will be shown, power dynamics enter the very conceptualization of activities, and they affect performance itself. To approach relations of 'conceptualization', I look at power over meaning making through naming and narrative characterization. With regard to performance, I hope to demonstrate at least three ways in which unity and reconciliation activities are politicized – from the ways in which they perform concrete political work, to their role as stages for dissemination of development messages and finally, their 'doubling' as platforms of state presence and exaction. The last two chapters in this section focus specifically on analysis of the *ingando* camps.

The section hopes to make a number of contributions. First, by placing emphasis on the 'mundane' aspects of nation building in a post-genocide context, the book hopes to complement more macro-level political analyses of institutional mechanisms, policies and laws. Second, by bringing into focus a score of previously unstudied activities, this section hopes to expand our view of the Rwandan post-genocide 'social project'. Over the past decade, the *gacaca* courts or 'justice on the grass' have dominated academic debate and have produced voluminous literature (e.g. Oomen 2006; Waldorf 2006a and 2006b; Rettig 2008; Clark 2010; Clark and Kaufman 2009; Ingelaere 2009; Thomson and Nagy 2010, among others). The uniqueness and importance of the courts is without dispute and yet such singular focus might serve to obscure a much more wide-ranging process of post-genocide reconciliation, one defined by a true proliferation of 'neo-traditionality' and a temporal orientation both backward-looking – seeking solutions to injustice – and forward-focused – orientated towards the building of a new community and citizenship. Finally, through the exploration of 'mulitplicities of unity', the section hopes to demonstrate the plurivocality that exists in any society, the way in which states might reduce such multiplicities of interpretation in their unity-building projects, how those in power are able to manipulate meanings and capitalize on gaps of understanding, and finally, how it is possible to insert into activities agendas that are not outwardly part of them.

6

Unity's Multiplicities
Ambiguity at Work

Unity in Rwanda is far from 'one' project. Not only are there many takes on the term and strategies of pursuing it, the concreteness also begins to slip as we look closely at unity 'in the office' (*kwa biro*). Indeed, we can playfully unwork the notion of unity from the inside, from within the very institution that bears its name. The day-to-day work at the National Unity and Reconciliation Commission (NURC) offers insights into the ways in which unity and reconciliation become performed institutionally and, perhaps paradoxically, how policy planning and implementation, and the need to translate concept into action, fragment unity as a concept and an aim. However, this should not be taken to mean that unity is 'lost in translation'. Rather, it is simply found in multiplicity and fragmentation. The analysis here draws inspiration from Eisenberg's (1984) findings on the prevalence of ambiguous communication in organizations and its strategic nature. Ambiguity not only creates the potential to promote 'unified diversity' – to accommodate various, even seemingly incommensurable objectives (Contractor and Ehrlich 1993) and as such to accommodate diverse interests, audiences and 'foster deniability' (Eisenberg 1984) – it can also mask power and preserve privileged positions (Eisenberg and Goodall 1993; Eisenberg 2006).

The Fragmentation Story: Working and Planning

The present section briefly investigates what becomes of unity when it is turned into a 'working scheme'. From among the many events and exchanges that I witnessed at NURC, one occasion stands out as emblematic of the broader themes explored here. That the event proved enlightening does not mean it was out of the ordinary, quite the opposite. This was a 'meeting' (*inama*), a standard fare in the work of the commission, dragging on for hours, propelled by the inevitable progression through a technical task, the rhythm of the page-by-page and the to-and-fro of verbal exchange across the table. This was a general meeting of all commissioners with the UNDP consultant, whose role was to overview and help put into final shape NURC's 2009–2012 Strategic Plan. The meeting took place in the offices of NURC on 15 December 2008. Its sole focus was a forty-two-page document, a 'Results Based Matrix' (RBM) detailing forty-two different indicators meant to measure progress towards achieving unity and reconciliation in the country. This was a key and symbolic object – a schematized model of the 'what' and 'how' of this work. 'RBMs' more broadly have of course by this time attained the status of a standard and commonplace institutional 'imaginary,' often of vast, and not easily graspable, social change.

If this moment in the conference room were your first encounter with the notions of unity and reconciliation, you might be excused for feeling deeply uncertain about their meaning but you would also make a number of interesting observations. First, you would be struck by the overarching desire to measure these categories, whatever their meaning, to quantify them, to show steady 'growth'. 'Indicators that can be measured are good,' suggests Sammy the UNDP consultant, 'find them and these should be ones on which to report'. You would note how, as a result of this need to measure, broad terms are broken down into measurable units, divided and sub-divided further into discrete packages of activity. 'I want you to focus on purpose and outcome,' continues the consultant. 'The UNDP will want you to report on outputs as well. I do not agree, but they are the ones giving you the money.' The consultant then expresses concern about the overall number of indicators, but when Felix quickly sketches a new, slimmer scheme on a piece of paper, the consultant intercedes, 'I don't want you to cut though if things came up as important'. Now Felix looks like he merely wanted to please.

Looking at the performance indicators, you would notice that success is both the volume of activity produced by actors in this enterprise and, to a lesser extent, the purported social transformation occurring in society. For example, the first indicator in the matrix is the number of NURC recommendations taken up by other policy makers. The third indicator is the proportion of actors who have mainstreamed unity and reconciliation in their programmes. Another indicator similarly measures the number of associations participating in unity and reconciliation initiatives. And the volume, you would note, surely is impressive. In 2009, NURC counted 986 'initiators' of unity and reconciliation. This included 625 community associations that indicate at least some involvement in unity and reconciliation and 361 clubs called Student Clubs for Unity and Reconciliation (SCUR).

Additionally, you would notice that a measure of 'progress' is the increase in the volume of participants at activities such as the *ingando* 'solidarity camps', or *itorero* schools, or cases referred to the *abunzi* mediators, or capacity building and seminars of different kinds. Another progress indicator measures the number of organs successfully sensitized on the 2007 National Unity and Reconciliation Strategy. In fact, you would note that only three of the indicators in the matrix refer to transformation. One of the three mentions measures of trust, another the percentage of citizens who feel there is change in social cohesion and the last one the proportion of citizens who feel that NURC interventions lead to reduction in conflicts. As measures of perception, and especially ones solicited by the government, these are surely problematic yardsticks of change.

Across the document then, a particular image of success arises – as growth of an enterprise, as voluminousness many times reflected, in institutions, activities, members and participants, and in words confirming this. This is a complex proxy, and precisely one that the government can so successfully manipulate through social control – through its ability to congregate, mobilize, align and restrain.

All in all, as an observer you would be disappointed to learn that the matrix shows little about the conceptualization of unity, about how the transformation is envisioned, or in fact about what actually goes on, and why. Why, for instance, is the central department at NURC called 'Department of Civic Education'? Or why are *ingando* camps a key, 'flagship' activity of NURC? Why the proliferation of traditionality and the production of official ceremoniousness in multiple activities at the local level? The conceptual slippage would naturally not obstruct a serious and detailed back-and-forth across the conference table or the subtle but palpable tension of a power play referencing the seriousness of this business. The matrix does reflect one concrete dimension though – the vast energies spent in coordination, alignment, spreading the message, confirming success and acting as a censor and gatekeeper. This in itself is telling of what unity, not only unity building is about, and again it echoes the analysis of unity as a particular political force.

The meeting with the consultant not only demonstrated the curious life of unity as an operationalized category, made 'implementable' in a particular way, it also demonstrated the tensions with regards to ownership. The outside sponsorship of the commission, together with the development consultancy and its standard 'ways of doing', certainly imposed the necessity for a proper, donor-pleasing language of complex schematization and tokens of advancement. On the other hand, naming proved a site of strategic play for the local actors. It was quite striking just how little the consultant knew about the activities in the RBM matrix. '*Itorero*', he commented jovially, mulling the word over in his mouth for the first time, 'it sounds like an Italian word, you know, like itooorero contoore otoore'. Later, as we started to talk about another activity, he interrupted with a confused look: 'Maybe I did not understand *abunzi* ... is it the same as *gacaca*?'[1] This interaction lent rich insight into how (easily) the dynamics of gaps between text and its referents could be maintained, and by extension how and why alternative agendas might be inserted into the unity and reconciliation process.

The encounter also reflected other things about the project as it is performed institutionally. It showed that while activities are carried out, work is done, surveys undertaken and success shown, at its core unity is a fuzzy and fragmented concept, dismembered through technocratic imaginaries[2] and dislocated by strategic characterizations and re-characterizations, such as when official documents alternatively refer to *ingando* as 'solidarity camps', 'leadership seminars' or even 'vacation camps' depending on audience or context. At the same time, the fact that unity can be many things is useful. What some see as vagueness others use for its ability to accommodate diverse needs. It is precisely the vagueness that invites creative play and strategic dissimulation on behalf of state actors. It also shows that it is not only 'those below' the state that rework and appropriate, but rather that at every level, social actors creatively appropriate language, as any other structure, to serve the aims they choose to or come to serve. As such, the focus on vagueness and multiplicity helps to complicate the simplistic binaries of power versus counter-power ('dissent and subversion'). Government officials 'work' those more powerful, the uncertainties of meaning and believable 'versionality' allowing them to press forth with their project, and equally they resist resistance on the ground in what is a mutually creative play of disarming.

The meeting with the consultant ended after many hours, and by that point the tension and frustration in the room was palpable. Someone read out Article 178 of the Rwandan Constitution, outlining the mandate of NURC:

> The National Unity and Reconciliation Commission is an independent national institution. Its responsibilities include particularly the following: 1° preparing and coordinating the national programme for the promotion of national unity and reconciliation; 2° putting in place and developing ways and means to restore and consolidate unity and reconciliation among Rwandans; 3° educating and mobilizing the population on matters relating to national unity and reconciliation.

'These are our responsibilities', emphasized Fatuma Ndangiza to the consultant. 'Not very smart', replied the consultant, 'these are merely activities, your goal is peace among Rwandans'. 'But they evaluate us on the basis of these responsibilities ... you know, Sammy, when this [constitution] was written, we were not consulted.' People slipped into Kinyarwanda again, until Fatuma reined them in: 'Please discuss in English or French!' Sammy seemed irrevocably irked. He was now keen to end the meeting: 'Actually, I don't think you will have to do more work on this, I will make the suggested corrections and send it back.' In the complex clash of law, technical discourse, roles and layers of inside and outside that made up this situation, pressing but unanswered questions arose of moral right, who indeed should pursue unity in Rwanda and how. The poignant point of 'doability' would also impress itself on a watchful observer, in fact how the need for the 'doable' and the doing itself created a very concrete unity – this time the assemblage of all words and things created in its name.

The situation just described serves as a useful entry point into a broader discussion on 'unity's multiplicities', which challenge the project of building a social whole from without as well as within. It is the 'within' that is explored in this chapter, rather than the 'without' – the project of unity as a particular type of 'levelling' identity politics that confronts a context of complex and multiplying difference and division on the ground.[3] A key 'external challenge' is also tied to the nature of the project, which is essentially a top-down imposed imagining of a social togetherness even as it proliferates notions of tradition, authenticity and connection to the local. As analysed earlier, the problem of the outside on the very inside of the project is also manifested within the 'unifier' itself – the commission serves as a microcosm of the tensions and challenges that this project faces 'on the outside'.

The phrase 'unity's multiplicities' is thus a purposeful play on words meant to help unwork the idea from within. By looking at the project's aims, policies and translations into practice, the word's allusions to coherence, cohesion and uniformity are instantly challenged. Unity as a performed project is many things – a multi-referential idea that is deployed and redeployed by various actors, a policy that fragments the concept in its attempt to make it operational, a strategy that is in fact many strategies, a collection of symbolic enactments in multiple activities.

In what follows, the chapter offers two additional looks at ambiguity, complementing the story of technocratic fragmentation with the discussion of conceptual 'versionality' and 'unified diversity'. The chapter first demonstrates the coexistence of different notions of unity in Rwanda (marking it as a 'plural' concept), the 'nationalist' conception being one among others. The versions are not separate, however, as the government clearly borrows from broader cultural understandings, appropriating certain aspects and modifying others according to need. But even when it comes specifically to 'national unity', the government uses the broad and vague scope of the term unity to multiply its strategies. Multiplicity is nonetheless only half of the story. We have to push these points on unity's 'essential heterogeneity' further and ask how it is possible that despite the fraying and versionality, reworking and resistance, a very particular social project nonetheless results. In what follows, I hope to offer at least a partial insight into this process by looking at the ways in which particular notions are 'empowered' to enter the public sphere and subsequently (in later chapters) by looking at a more symbolic level of performance and how a particular type of unity is enacted in the space of the *ingando* camp. Thus while no dictate of the 'one' exists in Rwanda, particular versions of unity emerge as publicly desired, together reinforcing a unique relation to the state and the status quo of power.

The Story of Interaction: Conceptual Versions

When donors or the government talk about 'unity' or 'reconciliation', whose notions are they using? In order to avoid introducing conceptualizations of these terms that bear little resemblance to how people on the ground understand and treat them, we need to look more closely at the contemporary notions of 'unity' (*ubumwe*) and 'reconciliation' (*ubwiyunge*). The aim is not to reach an 'originary' and unchanging meaning, but the current understanding, which is not completely unaffected by politics, contexts, respondents' agendas or persons to whom it is entrusted.

The analysis below draws on a variety of sources[4] but two in particular need to be highlighted. In the Mutobo *ingando* for ex-combatants[5] and the TIG[6] *ingando* for released prisoners, I administered a questionnaire to participants, which included two questions not explicitly related to life in the camp: 'According to you, what is "unity"?' and 'According to you, what is "reconciliation"?' In this way, I was able to collect seventy-three written interpretations of the two terms in Kinyarwanda.[7] It is important to engage Hutu ex-prisoners or former members of armed groups in conceptualizations of notions such as 'unity' or 'reconciliation' because these groups are a fundamental link in the Rwandan 'experiment' in coexistence. The two respondent groups were in fact quite distinct – ex-combatants were abroad for many years, while TIGists spent years in Rwandan prisons – but there seems to be no systematic difference between their responses, such as one collection being more homogenous, or collections using different types of phrasing. In the controlled setting of a re-education and reintegration camp or a work camp, one would expect similarly 'controlled' responses to sensitive questions. Indeed, sensitive questions such as 'Can *ingando* change a person? How?' or 'What have you learnt about pre-colonial history?' invariably received the expected response. The two questions on unity and reconciliation, however, produced a rich variety of responses, though nonetheless with discernible key themes. Most likely, this is because the questions were broadly phrased and did not invoke any judgements (i.e., 'Is reconciliation possible?' or 'Can unity be achieved?').

Overall, it is clear that both terms – unity and reconciliation – invoke social interaction. Starting with unity or *ubumwe*, being 'one' and being 'together' are linguistically related. *Mwe* is the root for both concepts – *u-mwe* meaning one, *ha-mwe* meaning together (literally, it means 'in one place', where *ha* indicates a place), and *ku-mwe* combining both meanings by referring to being 'together, as one'. The *ingando* descriptions also suggest that being one is really being together and to be together is to be unified. Besides two rather infrequent themes focused on equality and lack of discrimination,[8] and discovering or seeing basic connections among people,[9] most interpretations focused on 'social togetherness', on mutualism, exchange, sharing, dependence, coexistence and occasionally the requirements for this such as respect (*kubahana*), lack of fear (*kutashishanya*) or love (*urukundo, gukundana*).

A large proportion of respondents equated unity with coexistence. They used the phrase *kubana nabandi* or living together with others, appending to it 'in peace' (*mu mahoro*), 'without problems' (*ntawe ubogamiye*) or 'without creating divisions' (*tutiremamo ibice*). Even more responses highlighted an element of coming together, putting together forces and acting together towards a common goal. They have either explicitly mentioned 'working together' (*gukorera hamwe*), or more often expressed the idea with *ugushyira hamwe*, which means acting together, putting together resources and force, or with the verb *guhuza*, which also suggests bringing or gathering something together, for example putting together strength (*guhuza imbaraga*). Respondents often used the idiomatic expression *gutahiriza umugozi umwe* translated to me as 'to be together and to be together' (also explained as 'synergy'). Other responses highlighted sharing and gathering together to share, using expressions such as sharing everything (*basangira bimwe*), sharing good and bad things (*gusangira ibyiza nibibi*) or enjoying together (*gusabana*). Many responses also highlighted elements of mutual dependence, suggesting unity means helping each other (*ugufatanye, bafashanya*), supporting each other (*guterana inkunga*), completing each other (*kwuzuzanya*).

The last theme, and perhaps the most interesting, was mutual understanding. Rather than echoing the notion of empathy (of being able to comprehend the motives, thoughts and feelings of another, expressed as *ubworoherane* or tolerance), the notion of mutual understanding (*kunvikana*) emerging from the responses was one of 'meeting in the middle', of arriving at or adopting a consensus, of having the 'same understanding'. Even here then, the dominant theme of 'meeting' together and 'being together' in thought and feeling was reproduced. The verb *guhuza* was used again in phrases such as 'meeting each other in everything' (*buhuriza hamwe muri byose*) or 'meeting in thoughts' (*guhuza mu bitekerezo*, translated as 'understanding the same way'). Another verb used was *guhura*, which also means 'to meet', in phrases such as *kuba muhuje* (to be meeting each other) or *muhurije ku kintu kimwe* (meeting on the same thing). Understanding each other in the sense of 'understanding in the same way' was also expressed through phrases such as 'to speak the same' (*kuvuga rumwe*), having one understanding (*tukagira imyumvire imwe*) or 'my step is that of my fellow' (*igikonera cyanje ari cya cyo mugenzi wanjye*). Interestingly, this 'meeting in understanding' was often highlighted in other contexts as well, notably by university students who repeatedly suggested that people need to have the 'same understanding' on certain issues.

The notion that convergence is important for social cohesion is notable and of course can become politically expedient. It echoes the official political line highlighting consensus and painting the divergence of opinion as divisive and thus dangerous. Though clear themes emerge from the interpretations of 'unity', what should also strike the reader is the diversity of descriptions within these themes, the pluralities of 'unity'. The story here is not one of a government purposefully glancing over such pluralities. Rather, the story is one of a government accommodating and modulating those aspects (and 'stock phrases') that best fit its top-down systems of power and its social transformation goals.

The simple fact of diversity in responses naturally does not render interpretation straightforward. To begin with, it is hard to presume that an 'a priori' or 'neutral' cultural space exists from which these interpretations emanate. In highly politicized settings with a long history of conquest and state penetration, perceived oppression and political violence, and with marginalized populations in fraught spaces of 'voice', such a proposition is indeed difficult to substantiate. The diversity is noteworthy (when compared with most other responses) but does not assure that no censure happened, occluding some and underplaying other interpretive options, or that indeed the category is not considered a priori ideological, being a 'government' term, or one that a restricts meaning in particular ways. Here it is noteworthy that both *ubumwe* and *ubwiyunge* are largely congruent with the notion of coexistence, rather than the more politically incisive notion of equality or the deep work of emotion.

The concept of *ubwiyunge* (reconciliation) is not too far removed from the socially interactive conceptualization of unity. *Ubwiyunge* means merging, coming together or joining together.[10] Some respondents even suggested to me that unity and reconciliation 'mean' the same. After all, the phrase *kunga ubumwe* (meaning 'to be united') combines the roots of both words. Indeed, these two terms are not easily separable, instead they form part of a broader conceptualization of a cohesive society. First, both words refer to forms of 'being together'. Second, the words *hamwe* and *umwe* often appear in descriptions of both terms. Third, aspects of descriptions often overlap, with *kwishyira hamwe, ugushyira hamwe, ukuvuga umwe* and many other phrases being present in both interpretations. But whereas unity applies to every person, people, you and your fellow (*umuntu wese, abantu* or *wowe numugenzi wawe*), reconciliation applies to victim and perpetrator (*wahemukiye* and *uwakoze icyaha*).

Reconciliation was most often described as composed of a specific social interaction – *kubabarirana* or forgiving each other, which then allows for the 'refreshing' (*gukongera*) of social relations.[11] Reconciliation was depicted as the process of returning to unity, as the basis on which unity can be built.[12] The phrase *kunga ubumwe* (to unite) mirrors this relationship. The two terms are connected and not separable, and *kunga* precedes *ubumwe*. The process of *kubabarirana* or mutual forgiveness was described by Hutu ex-combatants and ex-prisoners in a highly scripted way, almost as if it referenced a ceremony, a rite of at least partial, surface-level passage. 'First, you sit down together, the offender asks for pardon, the victim grants it, then you become one as before.' The process as described did not invoke feelings, but instead phrases to be passed between and 'granted' by the victim and the perpetrator, almost as if a partial (even if surface-level) agreement of coexistence was thus being sealed. The business of *kubabarirana* appeared to be a concrete and officially sanctioned social ceremony – indeed the government explicitly encourages such exchanges through national policy (NURC 2007). Survivors dismiss them as 'theatre, performance' to please the state (Ingelaere 2010).

Interestingly, field research conducted by Uvin and Nee (2009) in neighbouring Burundi resonates with findings on unity and reconciliation as 'social togetherness'. Uvin and Nee wanted to 'solicit ordinary community members' desires and beliefs regarding justice and reconciliation' (2009: 146) and to contrast these with the broad discourses and aims of the transitional justice regime. They found that 'Burundians prefer efforts that help them find ways to live together again [on a community level], rather than seeking to establish root causes or apportioning blame [at the level of the state]' (ibid.: 161). The organizing theme was that of *entente* – 'getting along, living without friction, cohabitation or coexistence' (ibid.: 162). 'Burundians themselves talk about *flexibility* when they describe how this [coexistence in a divided society] happens. What they mean by this is that they value the capacity to compromise, to go with the flow, to hide their true feelings, to move on' (ibid.: 166). In Rwanda, Buckley-Zistel (2008: 137) finds a similar 'necessity of pretence': 'The Kinyarwanda phrases *kwishyira mu mutuzo* or *kwiha amahoro* mean "pretending peace" and signify a coping mechanism by which all antagonism is silenced to maintain the social equilibrium'.

Just as in Burundi, in Rwanda living 'side by side' is not an option and coexistence becomes both a 'necessity' and an ideological and normative status quo. The government's soft appeals to *kubana neza* (coexist nicely) euphemize this political reality. This certainly precludes a 'neutral' or exclusively 'cultural' reading of *entente* and coexistence, and raises again the question of priority and alternatives (i.e., Is this a genuine 'preference' or a politically safe double, or the best of alternatives under current conditions?). The community mechanisms of compromise and mutuality are certainly elaborated and accentuated by the Rwandan state for its own purposes, and they are used in the wider calls for flexibility and containment.

The analysis here naturally cannot capture all the nuances of interpretation on the ground. For one, in the religious and psycho-social healing community, and to many individuals, including some government employees, the concept of reconciliation (or 'genuine' reconciliation) is understood differently. It applies to all people (*tous les Rwandais, nous sommes malades ... tous sont rescapés de la guerre*,[13] or 'every Rwandan has their own wounds, we are all victims of our past'[14]) and involves the long and individual process of freeing and transformation of feelings. Notwithstanding the divergence of opinion on 'genuine' reconciliation (e.g., meeting of feelings rather than just bodies and words), and fully recognizing the work of churches and small associations in the 'deep work' of emotion, reflection and dialogue, the fact remains that it is the above-described ceremonies (and ceremoniousness more generally) focused on re-establishing a minimalist social equilibrium on the hills that are the hallmark of the government approach. Survivors are urged to grant verbal forgiveness and to live with former perpetrators, and the latter are urged to divulge their acts and ask for forgiveness in exchange for release. But the active promotion of forgiveness places further strain on the inner resources of survivors. This rough and enforced process can be opposed only by keeping the resultant publicly undesirable feelings, images and narratives out of view, kept as a hidden and carefully disclosed store of counter-memory.

On a broader cultural landscape, the notion of 'restoration' appears. The churches are at the forefront of the initiative. The Restoration of Hearts church headquartered in Kimisagara, Kigali, attracts an immense congregation. The born-again movement also works with the idea of cleansing and offering a fresh start. But the notion reaches beyond religious groups and permeates the nationalist narrative. One of my informants, a linguist, spoke boldly of organizing a national 'rebirth': 'Rwandans themselves need to recreate the Rwanda of pre-colonial ages. The nation that existed by itself, it will re-exist by itself.'[15] But to achieve this, he continued, people need to regain their 'sense of civism', which they lost 'through this dark history ... some through the influence of the killers, intoxication, others through the loss of relatives in a brutal way, others as a result of this big anger which grew up at the sight of what had really happened' (ibid.). It is in this context, he concluded, that 'cleansing of people's minds' is needed in order to remove these different kinds of emotional 'dirt' (ibid.). Another man gave a more extreme reading of restoration. On a bus to Rwamagana, this fellow passenger spoke of perpetrators' 'lost humanity': 'People think that only the victims need counselling, but this is not true, those who killed need it too. It takes a lot of counselling to make a person human again.'[16] Even in less extreme readings, however, restoration can become a powerful political idiom underwriting symbolic and actual social domination through the appeals to necessity, profundity and possibility of change.

In addition to the above, idioms of intoxication, contamination and dirt are also commonly used in Rwanda, as well as the corresponding notions of cleaning, cleansing and medicine. Bad ideas of the past come out or are let out from inside (*bimuvamo*), they are removed (*bikamushiramo*). Restoration is also spoken about as something that brings people to the 'good path' (*inzira nziza*), the unblemished path (*inzira nde de,* literally whiter than white), the true path (*inzira y'ukuri*). The metaphor of uprooting (*kurandura*) and burning the roots is often used in the official political discourse with regard to genocide and genocide ideology. At an *ingando* camp at Nkumba, the rallying call '*jenoside!*' (genocide!) brings the assembled *banakosi* to cry out in response: 'We avoid it, we pull it out, and we put its roots on fire!' (*Tuyamagane, tuyirandure n'imizi yayo tuyitwike!*). Along the winding road from Kigali to Ruhengeri in the Northern province, a similar political slogan is painted on most houses. The slogan disappears and reappears a hundred times: 'Pull out genocide ideology by its roots!'[17] The fact that both of these exhortations 'take place' in the Northern region is not incidental. From the viewpoint of the government, this is the 'problem' area, once the stronghold of the *akazu*, it was also the last region to be annexed before independence and the last region to be pacified after the genocide.

The Story of Alternatives: Strategies and Paths of Unity

Interestingly, nationalist conceptions of unity as an imagined community of all Rwandans have not figured prominently in the responses I gathered. Most interpretations of unity and reconciliation revolved around very tangible 'being together' and interaction with concrete others. Only a couple of respondents suggested that unity or reconciliation occurs when 'all feel that they are Rwandan' (*bakunvako bose ara banyarwanda*) or that unity means 'to be Rwandans with the same language and culture' (*kuba turi abanyarwanda duhuje umurimi rumwe, umuco*). Nonetheless, it is precisely the nationalist interpretation that animates government action. Unity building is largely nation building, and only the machinery of the state can set out to 'make' such a large imagined community. Differences in Rwanda are not only considered as potentially politically divisive but also as counterproductive to the levelling necessary for a uniform and cohesive nation-state. Besides the rewriting of history to 'find' an undivided pre-colonial nation, the official strategies of unity are multiple, even if interconnected.

The cultivation of 'Rwandanness' represents the first (but far from only) unity strategy. Being Rwandan is meant to serve as the 'greater us' and as primary loyalty. Embracing this imagined abstract community is to turn attention away from any divisions at lower orders. A 'fresh identity has been created', extols Grace Kwinjeh with reference to the introduction of a new Rwandan ID card (Kwinjeh for NTK, 26 July 2008), commenting on the powerful symbolism of a Rwandan national document without ethnic classification. In order to construe 'Rwandanness' and 'Rwanda' as real, they are personalized, taking on anthropomorphic qualities. 'Rwanda' comes alive. Whereas identities such as Tutsi and Hutu are said to have been constructed and imposed by the colonizer, representing false consciousness, 'Rwanda' becomes essentialized and everlasting. 'Our beautiful Rwanda will live forever' (*Rwanda yacu nziza uragahoraho!*), a long sweet tone echoes from the speakers at a wedding ceremony. The aim of seminars such as *ingando*, an informant explains, is to give all youth 'the opportunity to see the beauty of Rwanda, which has *survived* catastrophes' [emphasis added].[18]

In the official discourse, Rwanda is not a collection of concrete people struggling to live together but rather an autonomous and indestructible realm, which can be accessed within and restored, an alterity to strive for: '[Due to all that has happened] Rwandanness was losing sense', tells me a woman parliamentarian, 'so it had to be restored. Of course it is a struggle, a process, but it is coming'.[19] More precisely, the attempt is to restore the 'good' core – the golden ages of Rwandan history construed through historical rereadings as a time of harmonious pre-colonial unity, constructive cultural values (*indangagaciro z'umuco*), pride (*ishema*) and dignity (*agaciro*). The founder of the RPF and former Ombudsman of Rwanda offers the short version of the new official narrative: 'Before the coming of Europeans, there was unity, there were no divisions Hutu, Tutsi, Twa.'[20] 'People lived in harmony and symbiosis,' adds a ULK student in his thesis (Gashanana 2005: 20), 'conscious of being unified peoples known in Kinyarwanda as *imbaga y'u Rwanda*'. A talkative bus passenger adds the chapter on genocide: 'Genocide, it is not Rwandan, it was imported from France, it is the French who brought it here ... this kind of killing, it is not African, it is not indigenous to this place.'[21]

The official historical narrative was tightly reproduced in the questionnaires and interviews I conducted with *ingando* participants.[22] Only very few respondents diverged from the official line. At the Nkumba *ingando*, a student from NUR reflected on the history lessons:

> They told us how people arrive to post-colonialism ... We start from pre-colonial [times], how we lived peacefully ... [Then] colonials began dividing our people, they told [us] we have three ethnic[ities] ... [they] started telling [us] if you have money, cows, you are now Tutsi! ... if you are agricultural man, you are a Hutu, if you hunt animals in the forest, you are a Twa.

An *ingando* participant from Mutobo wrote:

> We have studied that the bad events that happened in this country were under the sole reason of colonialists. Rwanda did not have 3 ethnic[ities] before, they had 18 [uses *amoko* for both, which means 'type;' the second use referring to clans]. Then the whites, seeing that Rwandans were unified, they started dividing [*guca*, literally 'cutting'] them into three parts, those of Hutu, Twa, Tutsi. Then, there used to be *kiboko* [transl. slave work], *uburetwa* [forced labour].

Another Mutobo participant suggested: 'Before colonialism, Rwandans used to coexist nicely [*bari babanye neza*] but when white men [*bazungu*] came, they brought sectarianism. The message I took is that we cannot follow people with bad ideas, because here the white men's ideas have caused genocide to occur.' Shorter descriptions came from TIG: 'Before colonialism, we were one. Colonialists came and divided us', or 'the colonialists troubled the Rwandan society by dividing it into ethnics, which has ultimately resulted in genocide'.

The historical narrative has to be understood against the post-genocide social context and the political forces and logics that propel it. At its core, this is meant as a 'redemptive history', a narrative displacing the 'ultimate blame' for genocide and, in that way, opening a space for unity. After the genocide, the government (GNU) was faced with an aggrieved society, a mass of perpetrators, and a majority who distrusted, feared or in some cases despised the new government. The official history thus had to be in some form a 'restorative' history, a 'usable' historical narrative that would offer the possibility of a life together. The possibility of restoring pride or dignity (*agaciro*) for all had to be part of the narrative, and it was offered through the process of cleaning, reforming and refilling. The metaphors and idioms of transformation and restoration post-genocide revolve around 'purging' – purging the sedimented 'dirt' (divisionism, genocide ideology, etc.) and embracing the good core (the cultural values of Rwandanness). The activity most closely exemplifying this attempted process of return, redemption and restoration is precisely the liminal space of the *ingando* camp, discussed in the coming chapters. The narrative undercurrent of redemption accompanies, rather than counters, the actual as well as symbolic recognition of guilt, even, potentially, collective guilt (Reyntjens 2013; Straus and Waldorf 2011; Thomson 2013). Redemption and guilt work together, legitimizing a particular government approach to transformation.

Rwandanness is present and acknowledged in diverse ways on a daily basis. In a news article, Kagire (2009) capitalizes the words Nation and National Unity, performing a symbolic 'inflation'. Official activities often open and close with the national anthem, and songs about 'Rwanda' and 'Rwandanness' are sung. The mounting of the new flag of unity, introduced in October 2001, can be an event in itself. The staged fervour and constant presence of Rwandanness are a reflection of the fact that 'Rwanda' is still being built and is not simply 'inherited' – it needs to be actively embraced, repeatedly 'made real'. In the most symbolic show of its importance, Rwandanness enters the ceremonies of the oldest of institutions – the family: 'Government officials presiding over wedding ceremonies generally required couples to take an oath while touching the national flag' (US DoS 2009: 14).

Rwandanness also requires the cultivation of 'patriotism' (*l'amour de patrie* or *rukundo rw'gihugu* in Kinyarwanda) and 'heroism'. This implies respect, but also pride and love for Rwanda, the willingness to sacrifice oneself for it. At the TIG *ingando* for released prisoners, an administrator tells me that the participants learn about 'how to love the country, why to love it ... that we all are Rwandan, there is no ethnie, that we are one'.[23] The RPF website mentions patriotism as one of the main points of its political programme: 'The RPF will continue to coach Rwandans to love their Country, to be proud to be Rwandan, to build it and to give ourselves to it/self-surrender to it'.[24]

The government has also recently been elaborating the cult of the 'National Hero' (*Intwari z'u Rwanda*). On 'Hero's Day' – the annual celebration held on 1st of February – people are called to assemble at the Amahoro stadium in Kigali or in their sectors to listen to pronouncements on heroism and how to be a 'living hero'. Universities organize 'Heroes' Clubs' and the recently established 'National Chancellery on Heroes and Medals' teaches values connected to heroism, declares heroes and awards recognitions. Official characteristics of a hero comprise a long ten-point list.[25] The National Heroes' Mausoleum in Remera, Kigali spatially reflects the strict hierarchy into which heroes fall. At the top lie the *Imanzi*, a category of 'supreme heroes' that comprises only Fred Gisa Rwigema and the Unknown Soldier. Then follow the *Imena* heroes such as King Rudahigwa who opposed the Belgians – these are men and women reputed for the 'extraordinary acts' delivered for their country. Finally, the *Ingenzi* are living heroes – an open category with no one yet declared.[26]

'Rwandanness' – identifying first and foremost as Rwandan, and the loyalties and attachments that come with it – is meant to be filled with 'Rwandanicity' – the specific nature of 'being Rwandan' (also called *la Rwandité* or *Ubunyarwanda*). The second strategy of unity thus focuses on highlighting and teaching the 'one culture' of Rwanda. 'There is no Hutu or Tutsi culture,' I am told at the Ministry of Sports and Culture, 'it is Rwandan culture ... when one sings, one sings in a Rwandan way, when one dances, one dances in a Rwandan way'.[27] There is not only said to be one culture, 'culture is what defines us, rather than ethnicity or region'. Such encompassing and defining heritage is again said to have flourished in pre-colonial times: 'You see, colonialism destroyed a lot of these cultural traditions', a returnee and NURC employee tells me, 'so now we have to go back to recover them through activities such as *ingando* or *itorero*.'[28]

Rwandanicity comprises a set of cultural values (*indangagaciro z'umuco*) that 'defined what people of Rwanda understood themselves to be, what they knew about themselves and how they defined their country' (PRI 2004: 111). It specifies not only what makes a 'true' Rwandan but also a 'good' one – it is not simply purity but moral purity that is being invoked. The most important value is said to be *ubupfura*, a complex model behaviour,[29] a composite of many virtues. An employee at the Ministry of Sports and Culture lists these for me: '[being] correct, polite, convivial, respected, patriotic, influential socially ... being honest, dignified, having culture (*kugira umuco*)'.[30]

The reinvention of Rwandanicity, however, does not depend on the past alone. The social transformation goals of the current government as well as the pragmatic needs at lower administrative levels determine what gets presented as 'Rwandan values'. 'We are cultivating many new values', reveals an employee at the Rwandan Academy of Language and Culture.[31] Indeed, a number of new values were literally 'announced' in early 2009. 'The government has decided to promote and instil cultural values in the Rwandan tradition to help speed up development goals' (Kwibuka, 26 January 2009). Soon after, every door in the the corridors of government buildings was adorned with a single sheet of paper with the following list of values to internalize in the name of development: 1) speed and respect for time: a country in a hurry (*igihugu cyihuta*); 2) customer service mentality; 3) quality of delivery; 4) completion – towards results; and 5) national pride.[32] At the district level, meanings could be slightly tweaked to fit local administrative needs, principally a more effective accomplishment of *imihigo* goals. For example, Gisagara district website in its detailing of the new values expanded 'hurry' (*kwihuta*) to 'speed in what you do, having determination/zeal' (*kugira umurava*). The focus on results was interpreted explicitly as 'striving for the fulfilment of *imihigo* contracts' (*guharanira kwesa imihigo*).

Rwandanicity as a 'reinvention-in-progress' is meant to fulfil many objectives. At the official level, the attempt is restorative and transformative, to show Rwandans 'an example' in their own past, one they should thus 'naturally' connect with and embrace. As Ndekezi (2006: 12) explains, 'in the same way that *ubuntu* is an antithesis to apartheid, Rwandanicity is the antithesis to genocide ideology'. Rusagara (in Bergman 2004: 8) mentions *ingando* participants 'are reconstructed using [this] ideology'. Others highlight transformation: 'After genocide, there was a crisis of values', suggests Fatuma Ndangiza of NURC, 'but we need these [positive] values as a way of transforming our nation'.[33] Naturally, the discourse needs to be read critically. The widespread references to culture and tradition are used to rubberstamp multiple state-organized activities. Such 'cultural sanctioning' is at once depoliticizing and deeply politically involved.

The strategies of unity do not stop at reinventing and forging Rwandanness and Rwandanicity. An additional strategy is that of 'oppositional constitution' – contending with a greater 'other' (a challenger, an enemy) can also contribute to creating a greater 'us'. A fight against a threat whether real or imagined has always been an effective tool to consolidate forces and identities on the inside (out-groups help define in-groups). The threats can emanate from outside the country (FDLR, genocide deniers and political opponents in the diaspora, certain foreign countries) or from the inside. It is not a coincidence that a key Rwandan military operation against the FDLR in the DRC (January–February 2008) was called *Umoja Wetu* – Swahili for 'Our Unity'. In another example, the shifting of blame for a past of violence on the other can also be used in efforts at exculpating the self. As mentioned previously, the official historical re-readings work on the premise that divisions were created by outsiders and that genocide ideology was imported by the colonizer. On our trip north to Gakenke, a NURC employee pointed to the 'countryside ambulance' (the *ingobyi* stretcher): 'Our culture is so nice, I really do not know why that genocide. It must have been brought from the outside ... the genocide was brought from Europe'.[34] A Rwandan researcher was critical of such interpretation but saw its functionality. 'It is biased history, the responsibility for conflict is on the white colonizer. I guess [it is meant] to create this national unity, you have to blame it always on someone else.'[35] This other-against-us discourse gained sharp salience when Rose Kabuye, a high-ranked ex-RPF official and the president's Head of Protocol, was arrested in Germany on a France-issued arrest warrant in November 2008. The arrest triggered large-scale state-organized protests in Kigali and the provinces, and these served the nationalist agenda well. A radio slogan immediately proclaimed 'Rwanda under Attack'. The arrest was painted as an unjust act by the once-colonizer ('Europe') against 'one of our own' – *Roza wacu* (our Rose). The song of the same name authored by the famous 'Dokta Claude' was played ceaselessly on the radio and many other tailor-made songs for Roza and against certain European countries flooded the airwaves.

Yet another official strategy of unity is the 'common vision' or 'common project' of development, symbolized by the 'Vision 2020' document (MINECOFIN 2000). Development can only be achieved by a joint effort that, in turn, will benefit all. It requires unity and it will strengthen unity once achieved. People in Rwanda are constantly reminded to put aside their problems and sorrows and to focus on the development goals, the brighter future that can only be achieved by working together. The message is tailored and places special weight on the survivors (don't languish in the past, look towards the future) and those 'repenting their sins' and being re-educated in TIG labour camps. In fact, many of the TIG *ingando* participants included the phrase *kubaka igihugu* (building the country) when describing their work in the camp. The general implicit dictum is 'sacrifice today for a better tomorrow', 'like the Unknown Soldier', urges Paul Kagame (Kagire for NTK, 1 February 2009). For the TIGistes, the key unvoiced maxim is 'working together to rebuild the country that you have helped to destroy'.[36]

Last but not least, there are the 'performative' strategies of unity – the diverse activities of unity and reconciliation meant to encourage mixing and mingling, spending time together, 'being together', and thus relate most closely to the notions of unity discussed in the previous section. The attempt is to bring together people from across the social divides (perpetrators and other *abaturage* – people in the villages) with the aim of 'making them understand one another through social gathering and discussion'.[37] An aid worker participating in the obligatory *umuganda* works wrote on his blog: 'It was remarkable. The whole purpose of *umuganda* was not just social action, but also to bring people together – to unify.'[38] But what are these activities, what happens in them, and what are the effects? Do these platforms of 'being together' build what was described to me so often by people – mutuality, reciprocation, sharing? The following chapter will try and tackle these important questions. Though the focus will now shift to state-orchestrated activities of 'being together', it needs to be noted that all of the above-mentioned strategies of unity make their appearance within that space. The official historical narrative, calls to heroism and embracing of Rwandanicity, references to development and Vision 2020 – all of these discourses are interwoven, point to each other and make their appearance on the stage.

To conclude, ambiguity when put to work multiplies, fragments, puts out of focus, puts in tension and conversation, creates options and alternatives. The latitude and uncertainty characteristic of ambiguity offer an advantage as they widen the scope of operation and manoeuvre. The chapter offered three different glimpses of the politics of ambiguity in Rwanda. The 'work' of unity in the office showed how fragmented and uncertain meanings can still (re)produce very concrete interests, specifically through the cultivation of political dispositions and demonstration of tokens of success. The discussion on conceptual versions of unity pointed to the versatility that ambiguity creates. It highlighted the process of dialogue, accommodation and manipulation that ambiguity invites, as well as the ability to better camouflage a very particular reading of unity as convergence and suppression of discord through such resourceful borrowing from a wider cultural register. Finally, the dominant nationalist reading of unity emerged in its particularity (despite the common universal currency that it has become). As we have seen, even the nationalist vision uses ambiguity to multiply its strategic avenues, appealing to loyalties, culture, values, threats and promises of betterment. Altogether, the chapter hoped to offer three different ways of understanding the meaning of 'unified diversity' – diversity tied together under a common theme, interest and particular structuring, and to make the vague assertion of 'power's assertion in ambiguity' more concrete. The government manoeuvres a complex social landscape and ambiguity suits its tasks well.

Notes

1. Meeting at NURC offices, Kigali, 15 December 2008.
2. Imaginary is here understood as the system of meanings that govern a given social structure.

3. National unity is often read against the simplified background of ethnic relations but any deeper study of Rwanda clearly shows the complexities of difference that reach beyond ethnic identification.
4. The analysis that follows is the combined product of gradually discovering cultural themes over months of observation and interviews, and the more explicit collection of interpretations of these terms through questionnaires.
5. This *ingando* camp in the Northern Province is meant as a transition and re-education camp for repatriated Rwandan ex-combatants, mainly from the DRC.
6. 'TIG' stands for Travaux d'Intérêt Général (Public Interest Works) and is an 'alternative' punitive system of labour camps for released prisoners who have admitted their crimes and participated in *gacaca* courts.
7. Normally, in Rwanda I communicated in English or French and had to elicit Kinyarwanda terms. Gathering responses directly in Kinyarwanda allowed me to access a richer register of descriptions.
8. E.g., *bakumva ko bafite uruhare rungana ku gihugu cyabo* meaning 'they feel they have the same share in their country'.
9. E.g., *kumenyako muhuriye...* – 'knowing that you meet in...', meaning 'to have things in common' such as *ubumuntu* or 'humanity', *igihugu kimwe* or 'one country', *umuco umwe* or 'one culture'.
10. *Kwiyunga* – 'to reconcile/unite' (assumes previous separation) – comes from the verb *kuunga* meaning 'to join' or 'merge'.
11. *Gukongera* is 'to refresh/do again/return to doing' (e.g., *mukongera kuba umwe mu mibereho yanyu*, 'return to being one in your daily life').
12. Translated from *ubwiyunge ni kibanzo abanyarwa bubakiroho umubano wabo.*
13. Interview with an employee at Justice, Paix, Action, Nyamirambo, Kigali, 13 January 2009.
14. Interview with a World Vision workshop facilitator, Kacyiru, Kigali, 31 October 2008.
15. Interview with an employee at KIST University, Kigali, 10 March 2009.
16. Informal talk with a Tutsi man living in Uganda, 6 March 2009.
17. The initiative dates to the era of governor Boniface Rucagu, an aggrieved Hutu appointed by Kagame to pacify and 'win over' the North.
18. Interview with an employee at KIST, op. cit.
19. Interview with Connie Bwiza of the Chamber of Deputies, Parliament of Rwanda, 23 March 2009.
20. Interview with Tito Rutaremara, Kigali, 14 January 2009.
21. Informal talk with a Tutsi man living in Uganda, op. cit. See Purdeková 2008a and 2008b for further exposition and analysis of this historical narrative.
22. Interviews were held with forty students at the National University of Rwanda in Butare. Questionnaires were administered to thirty-five ex-combatants at Mutobo and forty TIGists at Gasabo.
23. Interview with an administrator at 'Ingando wa TIG', Gasabo, Gikomero sector, 4 March 2009.
24. Translated from Kinyarwanda: *Umuryango RPF- Inkotanyi uzakomeza gutoza Abanyarwanda gukunda Igihugu, kuba ishema ryo kuba Umunyarwanda no kubaka u Rwanda ndetse no kurwitangira.*

25. Ministry of Sports and Culture, 2004: 11–13.
26. Interview (and cemetery visit) with an employee at the Rwandan Academy of Language and Culture, Ministry of Sports and Culture, Kigali, 10 February 2009.
27. Ibid.
28. Informal interaction with a returnee from the DRC (NURC employee), 17 January 2009.
29. The word Infura refers to the first born in the family, who needed to be a positive role model, exemplary in all respects (PRI 2004).
30. Interview with an employee at the Rwandan Academy of Language and Culture, op. cit.
31. Ibid.
32. For an example of the print-out, see MINALOC (2009).
33. Fatuma Ndangiza addressing participants at the 'NURC Meeting with Partners', Hotel Novotel, 26 March 2009.
34. Informal discussion on the way to Gakenke, Northern region, 11 November 2008.
35. Interview with the communications and public relations officer at a research institute, Kigali, 3 November 2008.
36. In fact, two respondents in TIG do directly mention this 'maxim' in their answers.
37. Interview with a MINALOC employee, Kigali, 30 January 2009.
38. For the blog entry, see Halfon (2008).

7

Performances and Platforms
Activities of Unity and Reconciliation in the Contexts of Power

In the last two decades, Rwanda has seen a profusion of reinvented 'traditional' institutions and a multitude of government-organized 'unity and reconciliation' activities, many of which also appeal to tradition. Why such an explosion of activity? What are these activities and what joins them together? Besides the *ingando* camps and *itorero* schools, there are *abunzi* mediators, *ubusabane* festivals, theatre and music performances, *ubudehe* work schemes, football games, speeches, conferences, visits to memorial sites, student clubs for unity and reconciliation, a thousands-strong network of community volunteers in unity and reconciliation and more. Some of these activities and actors are organized or were created by NURC, though not all.[1] Not all activities have been 'written down'.[2]

Facing this long list, one might doubt its overarching identity. The myriad activities might seem only ambiguously connected. After all, the label of 'unity and reconciliation' has been applied even to activities such as the monthly *umuganda*[3] community work or the work of cooperatives (*amakoperative, amashyirahamwe*). The general underlying rule seems to be that all that 'brings people together', from across the different social divides, can be designated as 'unity and reconciliation'. In this reading, *umuganda* public works bring all locals from across the social divides together in improving their neighbourhood. Yet the most important thing, one soon realizes, is not to prove or disprove that all of these activities indeed are, at some level, what they claim to be. A much more revealing exercise is to try and uncover the rules that guide the creation and shifting of 'assigned' identities (i.e., categorization). Beyond asking 'What is in a name?' and uncovering discrepancies, we need to ask 'How are things named?' and 'What is the power of a name?' In what follows, I first consider the political dimensions of labelling, before turning to study the actual platforms and performances of unity and their effects.

In a sense then, the present chapter deals with the politics of identity, but not individual or group identity, rather the identity of 'things crafted' – it investigates why and how specific activities are identified through labelling and the real political effects of such seemingly abstract and surface-level acts. The very practices of inclusion and exclusion from a set can be revealing in themselves. Official categorization and representation create political effects both through their 'sanctioning' power and the power to conceal. The depoliticized identities of unity and reconciliation activities will be contrasted with an alternative reading that incorporates the contexts of power. In this manner, the chapter thus hopes to offer two additional glances at 'unity' in Rwanda – one revealed through the narrative threads that 'unify' disparate actors and stages under a common label, and yet another that arises from the actual assemblage of performances staged in its name.

The Political Economy of Naming and Characterization

In the context of careful image management and in view of tangible payoffs to 'wording' itself, it is perhaps not so surprising that labelling and characterization of activities become a political task. Appropriating the plural notion of 'being together' and using its widest interpretation – people gathered together in the same activity – to 'characterize' the nature of activities can be politically expedient, such as when calling *umuganda* 'unity building' or 'a patriotic act to achieve a dirt-free Rwanda' rather than 'compulsory community works' or 'tax on time and labour'.[4] In general, the unity and reconciliation front is soothing, it tends to be seen as unambiguously positive and as something required and expected in a post-conflict society. The result is depoliticization that simultaneously opens space for political manoeuvre. This is not to suggest that the government has total control over naming and categorization or that all things in Rwanda wear a mask, but that indeed the process is manipulable and subtly manipulated.

The other important dynamic at play in naming has more to do with the political economy of fundraising in a developing country dependent on donor funds. Maintaining appropriate and sometimes varied 'character fronts' for activities becomes fundamental to maximize funding. In a post-genocide society, the unity and reconciliation label is more likely to garner external legitimacy and funding, and this might explain why it is stretched to maximum ambiguity. Having either multiple 'character fronts' or malleable identities can also be useful in attracting fragmented resources from donors.

This might explain otherwise perplexing occurrences such as when the logical framework matrix of the Ministry of Trade and Industry (MINICOM) includes *ingando* camps as an important activity to 'foster private sector development'.[5] These dynamics, together with most big donors' shallow grasp of the local language, cultural norms, political dynamics and their infrequent visits to activities explain the (often) large discrepancy between activities as presented in official memos and reports (the official and 'fixed' voice) and activities that actually take place.

The primary focus of this book lies on government-organized 'unity and reconciliation' activities and this is both a purposeful and a necessary limitation. NURC's 'Databank of Unity and Reconciliation Organizations' counts more than six hundred organizations – some directly, others only marginally involved in issues of unity and reconciliation – and this is not an exhaustive list. *Abiyunze* (Those Reconciled), *Ntibizongere* (Never Again), *Abunzubumwe* (United People), *Duharanire Ubumwe* (Striving for Unity), *Ubumwerusange* (Common Unity), *Intango y'ubumwe* (The Base of Unity), *Nkunda Amahoro* (I Love Peace) are just some of the small, very local organizations whose names appeal to ideas of unity, reconciliation, coexistence and peace. But drawing a fast and clear distinction between official and non-governmental activities might overshadow the interaction between these two spheres, and misleadingly suggest the independence of the latter sphere from the former, a freedom from control and from pressures for alignment, in short insulation from the dynamics of power.

Only about twenty or thirty of these six hundred plus organizations are official partners of NURC. At the time of fieldwork, an active discussion within the commission was concerned with how to 'reach' the rest in order to assure that they, too, follow the National Policy of Unity and Reconciliation (NURC 2007). Facing such a plethora of community organizations, NURC's Executive Secretary suggested that 'mainstreaming is needed ... a way of coordinating all of these actors ... to build their capacity and monitor what they are doing'.[6] The Director of Civic Education, on the other hand, proposed that 'we don't need coordination, rather evaluation. Are they in line with the unity and reconciliation policy?'[7] But even without an effective national mainstreaming and control mechanism, it is important that NGOs and civic organizations are already directly constrained in what they can and cannot do. Debating ethnicity or campaigning for recognition of Hutu victims of RPF violence, for example, are some of the constraints. Though notionally outside the state, these actors are always already part and parcel of the politics (if not yet policy) of unity and reconciliation. One of the aspects of this politics is the management by the state of the diversity of notions and opinions on unity or reconciliation, and the promotion of its own vision.

Turning away from issues of inclusion and towards characterization, the official activities under review are discursively depoliticized and we need to break through such constitution of their character. In what follows, I consider two forms of depoliticization specifically relevant to objects emerging in fields of power at the interstices of developmental and transitional justice discourse. To begin with, the problematic of development uses universalist language suspended above local understandings of social reality, fragments the socio-political field (e.g., 'good governance', 'rural extension') and wraps its subjects in a technocratic, 'problem-solving' discourse.[8] Together, these dynamics obscure the insertions of the political apparatus and make political analysis difficult. The standardized language of development can also produce the 'black box effect' whereby outside actors do not actually know what is in a name unless they observe the thing itself, the wider socio-political process, and learn about the process of naming itself. This is not to suggest that the issue of 'technocratizing' of unity building, state building and peace building is unusual, that it does not occur in other conflict-affected states. But if anything, such wider entrenchment surely makes the dynamic more, not less worrying. As already discussed, in Rwanda technocratizing of unity involves its transformation into a measurable entity that can be assessed through a multiplicity of discrete activities, policies and indicators, outputs and outcomes. The concrete productions and accent on quantification can in themselves create a mirage of substance – the sense of work done, effort expended and progress made.

The discourse of 'traditionality' is even more directly relevant as it draws its power from the recent embrace of 'home grown' solutions in post-conflict transitional justice. Many unity and reconciliation activities, *gacaca* notwithstanding, are presented as a 'Rwandan tradition', as 'looking for answers to our problems in the past'.[9] As mentioned, there has been a profusion of such activities after the genocide. *Itorero* are 'traditional schools'. *Umuganda* is a 'traditional practice of collective work' (MINALOC 2006: 61).[10] The reaching to the past for inspiration arises from the 'tiredness with these Western approaches'.[11] While it is true that 'all is made in Rwanda',[12] that these are 'home-grown' ideas, what goes on upon closer look is a skilful government-led reinvention, and often plain experimentation rather than a recovery of activities from the popular pre-colonial past or a reapplication of 'classical approaches'. What used to be localized activities of communal mutuality (*umuganda*), conflict resolution (*gacaca*) or mediation (*abunzi*) are now government tools of large-scale social transformation. Some activities seem to be only tenuously connected to the claimed precedent (e.g., *ingando*). But tracing the transitions of activities' 'identity' is not the key aim here. Instead, I want to highlight the discursive effects that result from labelling activities as 'traditional'.

The traditionality discourse obscures both the political aspects of activities it comes to 'define' and the politics of its own conferral. The main outcomes of the traditionality discourse are the bestowal of authenticity and subsequent legitimization – activities come to hold an unvoiced 'traditional authority'. The tyranny of the authentic lies in its tautological claim on the person – it pre-emptively breaks protest because, after all, you have to be 'it' as this thing is you. The traditionality label also depoliticizes, increasing the sphere of the traditional as arbitrary (what Mamdani 1996 discusses with reference to the 'customary' sphere). Traditionality, broadly understood as appeals to invariance and essence, creates a boundary, the content of which is then sanctioned by the label. In this manner, contours and spheres of the arbitrary are created within which unfreedoms, political manipulation or even economic exploitation can pass unnamed. As Phillip Verwimp noted in his work on pre-genocide Rwandan peasantry (2000: 345) 'it is common practice for Habyarimana, as for other dictators, to use cultural arguments to justify economic exploitation.[13] Working for the collective good, as *umuganda* was called, is a prime example of this'.

In the realm of traditionality, culture and politics are also discursively separated. An impact assessment of NURC, carried out by the Institute for Justice and Reconciliation (IJR), suggested that 'ordinary people are more in contact with cultural institutions than political ones' (2005: 44). This is indeed true, but not because an apolitical sphere in fact exists or because 'ordinary people' are naturally part of a cultural, non-political world, but largely because they are relegated to such an arena. In this way, the rural space and its inhabitants (*baturage*) are depoliticized and yet effectively permeated for purposes of social, political and economic engineering, the extraction of local labour contributions (spoken of as 'the culture of volunteerism', MINALOC 2012) and legitimacy.

What is in a Name? Power and Performance

The portrayal of unity and reconciliation activities as 'local', 'traditional', 'participatory', even as 'unity and reconciliation', needs to be contested and ultimately resignificated. On the basis of previous analysis, we can already start contesting the meanings these terms invoke – ownership, authenticity, legitimacy, thematic content. To begin with, rather than reflecting some unchanging forms of culture, these activities are contemporary and creative tools in the hands of the government. Importantly, as will be shown, the activities become platforms both of direct politicization – additional means to achieve concrete political objectives, wider governmentality needs and social transformation goals – and indirect politicization – reproducing wider dynamics of power and etatization. This means both that official goals of unity might be undermined, and that other unofficial objectives might be served.

On our way to 'sensitize' the Gakenke Mayor on the upcoming Unity and Reconciliation Week, I queried my NURC companion on the source of the many new unity and reconciliation activities. 'Oh, it is people, they demand them!' she exclaimed resolutely. A few hours later though she explained that the NURC staff visits all mayors because 'you have to work with the political actors since they are the owners of this work, we just coordinate'.[14] The planning of the *Icyumweru y'U&U* (Unity and Reconciliation Week) revealed something else altogether about ownership. Rather than the people or their political representatives, it is the higher-level executive that seems to provide the creative muscle. The Commission prepared a concept note including the aims, strategies and possible activities, then 'sensitized' the mayors, going through the document with them point by point. The mayors were subsequently responsible for passing the message to the lower authorities. At the cell level, meetings were to be held to decide each cell's contribution. At a lower level yet, a 'traditional' institution known as *abakangurambaga* ('those who wake up the crowd', also often labelled as a 'unity and reconciliation' activity) is called upon to mobilize and organize people. According to Rwanda's Centre for Conflict Management, this 'network of 3,720 voluntary unity and reconciliation mobilizers active at the level of communities … [is] a sign of ownership of the process of reconciliation by grassroots communities' (Ndangiza and Mugabo 2008: 14–15). This assertion however completely obscures a long history of *abakangurambaga* as the right hand of the state, as *animateurs politiques* (Mironko 2006: 199) used already before the genocide to increase awareness, acceptance and ultimately success of specific government projects (see e.g., McNamara et al. 1992; Ndaruhuye et al. 2009). While such figures are certainly 'in' the local community and even 'of' the community and might be pressured and/or co-opted into their positions, this sort of 'political intimacy' and 'local presence' should certainly not be conflated with 'ownership'.

'Participatory' is another difficult and ambiguous term, as is the term 'local'. People might gather in large numbers but attendance at activities is required. The government closes shops, for example, to assure greater involvement in *umuganda* work or *gacaca* courts. People might speak up but not everything can be discussed. Most unity and reconciliation activities are far from 'informal' happenings; they involve authorities of the state. 'Giving people voice' in such contexts can thus, paradoxically, further entrench voicelessness on key issues.

Similarly, 'grassroots' and 'local' activities might not be what their names suggest. The trope of localization appeals to physical and conceptual 'closeness' to the people, and yet such proximity might have counter-intuitive political effects. Earlier chapters have demonstrated how 'local' does not always mean 'free of central power' and that, in fact, rather than decentralization of power, what we see is dispatching or broadcasting of central power with the effect of making it more pervasive. The organization of unity and reconciliation activities only further entrenches this system of power's propagation.

The terms 'unity and reconciliation' also require critical assessment. The official activities do not revolve exclusively around discussions of nation building, patriotism, or 'being together' as mutuality, exchange and sharing, or any other topics typically associated with these terms. The activities often comprise messages that are much more varied and include calls to follow the Vision 2020 or to participate in state-sponsored demonstrations. This begins to intimate that unity and reconciliation activities are part and parcel of a bigger project in governmentality. The aim in the remainder of the chapter is to demonstrate this in detail, and discuss the effects.

The Theatre of 'Unity and Reconciliation'

An element of staging and performance permeates many official activities of unity and reconciliation. Often, activities involve performances 'by and for', with a clearly demarcated stage and a space for the audience. The best way to demonstrate the stage(d) dynamics is perhaps to offer an abridged description of three events – a local *ubusabane* festival organized at the opening of the 2008 Unity and Reconciliation Week, an *ingando* camp closing graduation ceremony and a football match between the TIGistes and the 'local population'.

An *ubusabane* at the Launch of the Unity and Reconciliation Week, Nyanza, 17 November 2008

I follow Aloys to the neat rows of plastic chairs under the 'guest tent'. I ask where I can sit and he says he needs to ask 'the lady organizers', he does not want to upset the protocol. I am seated in the first row, next to me is a military representative (a captain) dressed in his khaki outfit. Next to him sits a police representative in dark blue, in the centre the mayor, then Fatuma Ndangiza and then more people I do not recognize. A small cap sits on the head of the military representative, and tucked in one of his black leather boots is a short wooden stick; he plays with it at times.

The two 'visitor tents' form an 'L' with a grass clearing in front where the performances and speeches will take place. Many people – the 'local population' – are already assembled, they stand around the stage, completing its invisible contours. They sing and clap. Other people, also singing, are slowly trickling in. A number of people help prop up a large paper sign 'Cooperative [xxx] supports unity and reconciliation'. On the clearing, there is a microphone and a tall, wooden pole where three men are at work mounting the flag. We listen to the anthem twice, at the beginning and then again at the close of the event.

What we are witnessing is an *ubusabane*, explained to me as a 'community festival' meant to 'bring people together', comprising dancing, singing, theatre and feasting. People are slowly trickling in; they form a tight, colourful and rather silent mass. Women and children, old men and old women leaning against their long *inkoni* sticks. They are just observing silently, there is no talking, and almost no movement. A couple of Local Defence (LDF) officers dressed in their dark red overalls and fitted with guns stand in front of the line of people. We watch the music troupe (*itorero*) perform for a long time, they are always facing our guest tent. The show then continues with a short theatre sketch about the asking for and granting of forgiveness. The mayor and Fatuma Ndangiza give speeches. Tree-planting ceremonies take place. Towards the end of the *ubusabane*, the *itorero* troop members call us (the first row visitors) to join them in dancing while the rest sing and clap, people clearly enjoy this and start cheering. The visitors leave after the official activities end; some are giving interviews under the trees. 'Feasting' for important visitors takes place apart, in a small restaurant in town.

Ingando Graduation Ceremony, Nkumba, Lake Ruhondo, 22 November 2008

We walk straight to the large clearing where everything is set up, our backs to the Muhabura volcano, Lake Ruhondo unfolds in front. We sit in the back row of the tent on plastic chairs, the first row is reserved for VIPs seated on office chairs covered in leather – the president and executive secretary of NURC, the head of the Demobilization and Reintegration Commission (RDRC), the Minister of Cabinet Affairs, representatives of the military and police. On the clearing, a thousand *banakosi* (*ingando* participants) stand in perfect formation. The VIPs stand up one by one, get introduced, some try the call-and-reply: *Amahoro!* (Peace!), they exclaim, or *Jenoside!* (Genocide!) and the students respond in unison with the learned response. The national anthem plays.

The graduates are meticulously organized in military units (platoons) in front of us, with the leader standing slightly in front of his unit. The *banakosi* are wearing their gumboots, khaki trousers and – especially for this occasion – a white T-shirt given to them by NURC. All are facing us, and each student is holding a piece of bamboo to serve as a gun. The overall leader standing in front cries out instructions. A military routine follows – all move in unison, perfectly coordinated. Gun placed at the foot, then lifted again, turn right, then turn again ... Then the march starts. Platoon after platoon break off from the central formation and march in a circle, in front of the guest tent and then back to the centre. The leader in front cries out, the rest of the group replies. As each platoon finishes the military promenade, it rejoins the initial formation. The overall leader cries out: 'Rwanda viva!' All cry back: 'Viva!' raising their bamboo sticks. A thousand new participants who have arrived just hours ago sit together on the grass, silently observing the ceremony. They are still in their 'civilian clothes'. As soon as the ceremony ends, they will be given uniforms.

A cultural show is next up on the programme. The *kos* move closer to the visitors' tent and sit down. The *itorero* troupe puts on dances, and warrior and patriotic songs are sung, interspersed by the call-and-reply: 'One, two, three' cries out a student, the reply from the *kos* follows: [hands clapping] 'clap, clap clap ... clap clap clap' '*kos!*' One student recites a poem (*poème de pays*). A number of long speeches follow. There is dancing again, and the 'first row' VIPs are taken by the *itorero* to join them in dance. Most stay only for a brief while, some only seconds, then they return to their seat. The five best *ingando* performers receive their certificate from the minister himself. Their name is called and they march forward, stomping to a halt in front of him. At the very end, the *kos* are allowed to relax to music, they start jumping and screaming. After a short while, they are allowed to leave and, still screaming, they rush headlong across the field to their dormitories to pack their bags.

'TIGistes Enjoy Together with Other Locals, Here and There in the Country' (*Abatijiste Basabanye n'Abandi Baturage, Hirya no Hino mu Gihugu*). Documentary video, 28 minutes, October 2008, NURC

A popular activity attempting to 'bring together' people from across the genocide divide (and hence also a sort of *ubusabane*) is a local football match between the *batijiste* (released prisoners serving 'alternative sentences' in TIG labour camps) and the rest of the population in a given district. What we see is most plainly a performance. This is an actual spectator game. The familiar spatial division reappears. There is the 'visitor's tent' with VIPs seated in the first row. The visitors are separated from the *abaturage* who are just pro-forma intermingled with the TIG. The *tigistes* are generally huddled in a dusty, blue-violet uniform mass apart from the rest.

The two teams begin to play – a TIG team and a team composed of the local population. Everyone else sits motionless and watches. People sip their Fantas but do not really interact, most of them sit and watch apparently spiritlessly, except when the *itorero* plays, then people start to sing and dance. At the end, the bestowal of the trophy turns into an over-elaborate ceremony. TIGistes shake hands with the VIP row visitors, passing them one by one at the tent. Then later it is the government officials who pass the broader football delegation, passing its members one by one and shaking their hands. Then they all hold the trophy up together. There are many official speeches. Fatuma Ndangiza speaks at length, but there is also a speech by a TIG representative, the TIG administrator and other members of NURC.

A number of themes come out from the observation of unity and reconciliation activities such as *ubusabane, ingando* and *itorero* graduation ceremonies, community games, NURC visits to prisons, but also speeches or presentations. First, the space is always carefully divided, with hierarchies fastly defined and boundaries between people thus apparent, whether these are planned or arise through 'protocol' (visitors and *baturage*) or emerge informally (between *baturage* and *batigiste*). Second, the activities are hardly participatory since most people come (often grudgingly) to 'watch a performance'. The performance is literally oriented to the visitors, specifically the elite. The acts are put up to honour and certainly please the 'big people'. The presence of *les grandes personalités* – either high-up government dignitaries or within NURC Fatuma Ndangiza, are seen as giving a proper weight to the occasion.

The official goal of activities such as *ubusabane* is to 'bring people together', to make them 'mix' with each other, share food and drink, join in dance, song and discussion.[15] But there seems to be a profound gap between the government-sponsored ceremonies creating physical proximity and the hoped-for genuine community interaction. As mentioned, the design is top-down and attendance is required. Reporting on the 'U&R Week', a NURC employee commented that in Ngoma district 'only very few people came, coming in slowly because they were tending their fields'.[16] In Nyanza, people were also coming in slowly and no more than a couple of hundred attended. My own observations and those of others suggest that people employ multiple strategies to evade participation, though again this might be harder in the countryside, and for those who need a government service (e.g., to get official documents) and thus need to stay in favour with the local administration.

The carefully hierarchized space that is a general feature of all official activities in Rwanda is naturally completely at odds with the notion of 'mixing'. The tightly observed boundaries – the official hierarchies and unofficial divides separating people spatially – point to a lack of communication across these lines. Such dynamics do not resemble the wished-for mingling and mixing that would transform relations in communities through the 'time spent together'. *Umuganda*, meant to bring all people from a neighbourhood together, in fact reflects similar dynamics. People with formal employment go to *umuganda* organized by their employer and thus rarely mingle with their 'community'. TIGistes might be present in these settings, but there is little interaction with them. *Umuganda* is also mainly about work rather than 'mixing', and those who evade it *in situ* usually chat with their friends. The post-*umuganda ubusabane* is generally a sensitization session with 'fanta' (soft drinks) and any unity might consist of 'being together' at the receiving end of lengthy speeches. This is not completely lost on the commission however: 'Unity and reconciliation is very good if it is done by the people themselves, taking the initiative, making it theirs', comments one employee to the full NURC assembly. 'If they receive it from the top, from the commission, the impact is very low.'[17] But the problem reaches beyond the ineffectiveness of 'top-down' measures. Staged initiatives of the kind I have described above might directly undermine bottom-up togetherness by reproducing, symbolically, the rules and relations of power and a separated and ranked social order, thus further unworking trust, confidence, communication and exchange.

Governmentality Needs: Making Dutiful and Responsive Citizens

Not only do unity and reconciliation activities become ceremonial platforms of desired display and limited interaction, they also fall prey to more explicit political agendas. Such agendas are not hidden from view. It is only in official written and spoken discourse that they might be covered up, and even then imperfectly. The official line is that unity and reconciliation activities are meant for people to understand and feel that 'the ethnic cliché surely has no basis'[18] and that 'we all, we are Rwandan, we live in the same country, we speak the same language'.[19] Upon a closer look though, other narratives and other key goals besides 'unity' emerge.

At the planning meeting between NURC and district-level youth coordinators, a bottle of water and a blue booklet awaited the participants. The booklet contained the 'National Policy of Unity and Reconciliation' (NURC 2007) printed only recently. One of the participants explained that the meeting and the booklet were to be a *ligne de guide* – a guideline. In fact, all actors in the field of unity and reconciliation are expected to abide by it. Sensitization on the policy or imparting of its messages, often in a very formulaic form, is in fact the most important component of speeches in unity and reconciliation activities. Confirmation of its main points is what leaders look for in official performances. Rwandans are to make this policy 'their own' (*bakayigira iyabo*).

A telling insight into the significance of 'passing the message', and the corresponding importance of who delivers it and how, was a NURC employee's evaluation of the opening ceremony for the Unity and Reconciliation Week in the district of Ngoma: 'Police and military authorities were all present. Minister made a speech [*ijambo*]. Both the Mayor and also the Executive were present. The Concept Note was read well by the Minister and the message was clear to all the participants'.[20] On a different occasion, another NURC employee explained that music concerts by famous artists can be a very good unity and reconciliation activity because 'many people will come to hear them and then we can pass on the message'.

The content of the policy, however, is vague. The preamble states that 'this National Policy will particularly help to define the duties of every Rwandan at all levels'. One learns that people should 'beg for forgiveness and give pardon', tell the truth (ibid. 2007: 7), and that parents should be sensitized on 'not giving their children names which refer to hatred and violence'. Concrete prescriptions such as these, however, are drowned out by generic statements. The main duty seems to be 'to be dutiful'. The message is to comply, abide by, and harmonize in accordance with already-settled meanings, wider policies and instructions. Under the heading 'Grassroots Structures', the first goal highlighted is 'to make known the National Policy of Unity and Reconciliation among the population in such a way that every Rwandan understands it as his/hers and abides by it'. The section on 'mass mobilization' (2007: 9–10) sets as one of the goals 'mobilizing Rwandans into responding positively to Government programmes'.

The overarching goal seems to be alignment. The policy document prescribes NURC to 'attempt harmonizing the same understanding of the concept of unity and reconciliation' (2007: 16). NURC is also seen as a safeguard and disseminator of the official history. As the policy document points out, one of the obstacles to unity and reconciliation is 'various interpretations of the history of Rwanda' (ibid.: 6). At the time of research, NURC was also responsible for putting together new higher education history curricula (contracting out this task mostly to select NUR professors) and vowed to 'do research ... so that Rwandans could know their true history'.

Party Agendas: Helpful Partners and Useful Stages

Since unity and reconciliation have always been considered a delicate subject matter by the government, it is difficult for NURC to escape political considerations and at times direct political work. The commission's institutional history and set-up reflect this fact most clearly. Since its inception, NURC has undergone special scrutiny. 'NURC was the only national commission made to report by law to the Office of the President', explained a parliamentarian. 'Due to the sensitivity of what was expected to be done ... they initially reported every day to the President.'[21] Only such close linkage could assure 'thorough review, evaluation, checking, due powers to perform, review ... because it had to be seen how the commission was giving [reconciliation and unity]'.[22] But how does a commission get embroiled in more explicit political work? Interestingly, it achieves this most effectively through indirect support and control of its 'partners'. The case study of a NURC affiliate – the student *skari* clubs – perhaps best demonstrates the imbrications of unity and reconciliation actors in political work on behalf of the government. In what follows, I show how *skari* become the government's helpful partners in more than just 'u&r' work.

The first Student Club on Unity and Reconciliation (SCUR or *skari* for short) was started in 1999 at the National University of Rwanda in Butare to 'continue the work of student *ingando* [camps]'.[23] The president of the national SCUR forum (and the highest authority within the organization) once took me to his small one-room office with walls fully covered in photos of the forum's activities – visits to memorial sites, special *umuganda* community works, student discussions, visits to genocide orphans and widows' houses, talks at TIG camps, *ubusabane*, and visits to *ingando* camps. This was the familiar, standard 'u&r' fare and SCUR was certainly becoming a significant partner to the thirty-five-strong national commission in promoting and proliferating these stock activities. As of 2009, NURC counted more than five hundred *skari* clubs across universities and secondary schools in Rwanda. The clubs originated at the university level and gradually expanded to lower branches of the education system. During my fieldwork, the plan was to finish establishing clubs at the secondary level, and then target primary schools.[24]

Far from being an independent student organization, SCUR was clearly aligned with and promoted the official unity and reconciliation policy. One photo at the SCUR Forum headquarters was especially arresting – it showed a couple of student SCUR members giving a speech to hundreds of men in a TIG labour camp. The president explained: 'We go there to talk to TIGists about what one should do to help reconstruct the country, about all the changes that have occurred while they were [imprisoned] ... and also to show to the kids [students in the club] the consequences of this [genocide] ideology, of what they [the *tigistes*] have done'. What was striking was not only the parallel the situation bore to government 'sensitization', both in image and message, but also the asymmetry of power being played out in the image between the student speakers and their seated audience. I was told that SCUR members also engage in *formation* (capacity-building) of their own members, so that they can 'better transmit the message', and they even sensitize the local authorities because these are 'with the population day to day, and they should promote the policy of unity and reconciliation'. Further down the wall was another photo of a classroom filled with local authorities and two SCUR students speaking in front of them. Then we turned to the photo albums filled with images of football games ('sport is very popular and so is good for transmitting the message'), *ingando* visits (the participants are 'our future members'), the 'memos' (guardians of memorials), the walks to memorials ('even slogans on shirts are sensitization'), the solemn swearing-in ceremonies of the members of the SCUR 'national committee' (taking an oath that they will 'work in the best interest of the nation').

Besides the fact that this burgeoning youth body was directly networked into the national commission, itself under the scrutiny of the Office of the President, and that it helped mainstream the messages set above, some SCUR activities counted as more direct 'political work'. On 26 January 2009, NURC met university SCUR presidents for '2008 Review and 2009 Planning'. Altogether, sixteen presidents attended and presented on their club's work. Interestingly, at least[25] three presenters mentioned that their SCUR helped sensitize students to attend *ingando*, and at least two mentioned 'sensitization for people to participate in community works [*umuganda*]'. One mentioned that their SCUR organized a protest 'against the people who try to minimize the genocide like Jean Luis Brugière'. At least three mentioned sensitization 'to get new members of SCUR'. Political enmeshment was apparent as these activities tried to increase responsiveness to government policies. More surprisingly though, at least five presenters explicitly mentioned that their SCUR 'helped' or 'participated' in parliamentary elections (held in September 2008). One SCUR president talked of 'participation in the sensitization during parliamentary elections, to teach the population, to tell them to participate'. But SCUR is not the only 'unity and reconciliation' platform used for political campaigning. Campaigning makes its inroads into other platforms as well. At a 2009 *itorero* graduation ceremony 'it was announced that the group [of graduates numbering 42,000] nicknamed *Imbagukiragutabara* intends to back President Kagame if he contests in the 2010 Presidential elections' (Kagire for NTK, 3 August 2009).

The *skari* are also a good example of the indirect way in which actors are co-opted into the work of the government. Youth is a great asset: enthusiastic, seen as still capable of change, unpaid but offered incentives such as the ability to learn leadership skills, manage resources and organize events, network with 'big people' and potentially get a secure job in the government. Through the SCUR networks, which are to span multiple secondary and primary schools, the work of 'unity and reconciliation' will be greatly extended, 'mainstreaming' made easier and control made more pervasive.

Transforming Subjects: Interpenetration of Themes and the All-Purpose Mainstreaming Fora

Unity and reconciliation might indeed be 'cross-cutting issues',[26] relevant to discussions across thematic divides. At the same time, multiple topics of sensitization cut into their own sphere. In almost every activity that I observed, messages other than those on unity and reconciliation were transmitted; this holds true even when we exclude activities with a more tenuous relation to unity and reconciliation such as *umuganda* and *ubudehe*. Any observer of unity and reconciliation activities will notice such thematic 'interpenetration' – a situation whereby fields of activity that are officially discursively separated (such as family planning, education, unity and reconciliation) are blurred in practice.

Besides expressly political messages, unity and reconciliation platforms regularly circulate messages on economic development (mentioning Vision 2020), as well as other aspects related to the country's 'progress' – participation in the health insurance scheme, saving schemes, the importance of sending children to school. At an *ubusabane*, the mayor mentioned Vision 2020[27] and also urged attendees to participate in the government-organized demonstrations. The guest speaker at the *ingando* graduation ceremony in Nkumba referred a number of times to *vision venti venti* (Vision 2020), also mentioning the importance of 'ICT' and 'knowledge-based economy'. In my sector, an administrator explained *ubusabane* festivals to me by saying that people often talk about 'development at the village and cell level, about what can be done'.[28] *Ingando* camps show interpenetration best. Student *ingando*, for example, combines 'being together' with (re)learning/practising Rwandan folklore, military drills and long lectures on themes ranging from history all the way to the economic needs of the country.

Though development messages might not be explicitly political, such sensitization does nonetheless have a broader governmentality goal – the transformation of people into 'ideal development subjects' (discussed in greater depth in Chapter Ten). A wider dynamic emerges, one reaching beyond unity and reconciliation activities, and namely the appropriation of all stages to carry out this ultimate social transformation goal. In this project, 'unity' is an especially useful narrative device for it accommodates various political goals at once – it can insinuate non-dissidence and convergence, the importance of 'following policies' and it can narrate development as a future that will benefit all. Unity can be stretched into and does become all of these connotations. Talking about 'Vision 2020' is thus not 'out of place', it simply becomes part of unity's narrative whole.

(While Inside…)

Naturally, there are limits to the above-described performative display. Even the government itself underscores the difficulty of accessing the 'inside' – the closed-off domain of feelings, opinions and attitudes that exist off-stage. This domain is problematic vis-à-vis governmentality objectives as it might diverge from performance but is undisclosed and hard to reach. But in fact people of all backgrounds return to this theme, regardless of ethnicity, age, gender or type of employment. The strong closing off by people seems to be a mix of cultural aspects (*gukomera* – 'be strong', *hagarara kigabo* – 'stand firm like a man', *kwihangana* – 'or bear with it, endure, have patience'), political dynamics (management of voice and silence, the push to align and sacrifice for the 'greater good') and the social impacts of mass violence (losing trust in others).

Suffering is hidden: 'In Rwandan culture, normally you do not show pain,'[29] a coordinator working in psycho-social healing tells me, 'the suffering is inside'. According to Bagilishya (2000: 347), 'a strict code of behaviour [guides people] when confronted with great sorrow', one that stresses self-control and discretion over painful emotions at all costs. A Rwandan name that best reflects the emotional containment and maintenance of the composed public persona, suggest an ex-minister in a private discussion, is '*Nsekambabaye*' – I laugh while inside I suffer.[30] According to a young returnee from Congo, 'Rwandan people are so silent, so quiet, so to themselves ... In Congo, if someone is weeping, the whole town knows, here it can be your neighbour weeping and you don't know and they don't want you to know.'[31]

Personal opinion is not shared: 'Rwandese have a culture of not sharing what they think,' NURC's Fatuma Ndangiza tells the assembled youth leaders. 'We should change that culture.'[32] What is at issue is not only veracity, but also the distrust created by perceived duplicity. 'In Rwanda ... you can have a problem with me but you smile,' confides a low-level university employee. 'If he [the Rwandan] hates you, you don't even know, he can even smile.'[33] A young genocide survivor expresses a similar thought: '[Another problem is the lack of] culture of speaking the truth ... [me:] You mean after the genocide? ... [Protais:] No, even before, that is why I say culture ... people can smile, but inside the heart, they can even kill you, [though] of course I don't want to generalize.'[34]

The outside façade might be one of calm and careful coexistence, but the inside space of contradictory opinion and suppressed feelings does come out at times. A NURC employee reported that the opening of the unity and reconciliation week in Rutsiro was accompanied by a 'big problem': 'The TIGists were supposed to maintain the banana gardens, but instead they destroyed those gardens that belonged to the Tutsi. They were asked to ask for forgiveness but they refused.'[35] The feelings come out especially during the commemoration months.[36] 'One says that during those three months, there is no unity among Rwandans', suggests the 'ES' (the executive secretary) of NURC.[37] This period is 'the serious case', tells me a young survivor 'there are many conflicts in this period, many fears [come up] ... It is not a good period. Some people think "*abatutsi ... abahutu*" and survivors don't want to talk to the *abahutu* even if these did not kill. I am never angry, but in that period, I get angry'.[38] Many survivors 'collapse' in official ceremonies[39] during the commemoration period known as *icyunamo*, letting out screams while reliving scenes of horror.

It is during ruptures like these that the bad faith economy, based on mere surface consent to coexist and enacted through ceremonies of 'asking for' and 'granting of' forgiveness, really comes to light. Perpetrators cannot be certain that the survivors really grant forgiveness instead of simply accepting in order to be left alone and to please the authorities. The survivors, on the other hand, cannot shrug off the idea that perpetrators do not really repent and use the surface contract to get to freedom. 'All they want is to get out' says a NURC intern bitterly after a prison visit. The unity and reconciliation discourse, after all, is not only manipulable by the government itself. After the Director of Civic Education at NURC delivered her speech at the packed courtyard of the Ruhengeri prison, she opened the floor to comments. One man who escaped TIG suggested he wanted reconciliation and to get back out of prison. Another suggested earnestly that 'they [prisoners] want to participate in unity and reconciliation but it would be much easier outside the prison'.[40]

What does all this suggest? Does the theatricity and ceremoniality lead us to proclaim that these activities 'fail'? Interestingly, even some people within the government acknowledge that these are mere surface-level enactments of unity and reconciliation: 'Unity and reconciliation can be done but cosmetically [only]' suggests a member of the Rwandan parliament, 'we cannot assume we can come to reconciliation, but rather unity without reconciliation'.[41] In that case, we have to ask what concept of unity is it that emerges from such performance?

Claimed and Actual Effects

Unity and Reconciliation 'Found': Measuring Desired Impacts

Unity and reconciliation activities are supposed to produce 'unity and reconciliation' and certainly this is being affirmed through official discourse and 'found' through government-sponsored research. 'On the national level, the NURC has achieved tremendous success. As Habyarimana [President of NURC] puts it, "currently the success of unity and reconciliation can be measured at 90%"' (Ruburika for NTK, 13 December 2009). 'Unity and reconciliation are advancing well',[42] a Nyakabanda sector officer confirmed to me. At the RPF headquarters, an employee emphasized that the government can boast about 'many achievements, [one of them being] that Rwandans live in peace, together'.[43] Notwithstanding more nuanced takes that emerge through interviews, there is a prevalent official narrative that highlights steady and impressive improvements on this front.

Research conducted by NURC itself suggests that activities are effective and improvements visible, claims supported mainly through various opinion surveys (*sondage d'opinion*). These results get uncritically reproduced in important international reports. As an example, the US Department of State Human Rights Report on Rwanda (2009: 9) informs us that 'during the year NURC released the results of a survey on *gacaca* process and national unity and reconciliation. The overwhelming majority (99 per cent of the general population and 92 per cent of survivors) expressed the belief that the *gacaca* process "is an essential step towards peace and reconciliation in Rwanda"'.

The basic problem with opinion surveys, highlighted by Rettig (2008) but even the Executive Secretary of NURC herself, is that 'Rwandese have a culture of not sharing of what they think', that they 'tend to guard their true opinions and to adjust their responses according to what they think the interviewer wants to hear' (Rettig 2008: 2). In settings fraught with power imbalances, such a dynamic should not be unexpected. Since the interlocutor in this particular case is the government, the 'safe response' bias will be especially prominent. Besides the politics of voice, some of the research instruments pose questions of internal validity. Often, we simply do not know what has been measured.[44]

If we leave surveys aside and focus on proxies such as the number of activities, the number in attendance or compliance with policies, we come across other problematic dynamics. Most prominently, the local authorities' attempt not to disappoint those higher up leads to a false idea of achievements in unity and reconciliation (and more broadly) through two mechanisms – the extraction of compliance through deployment of coercion, and the hushing-up of problems that occur (i.e., not reporting on TIG destroying Tutsi banana gardens during 2008 Unity and Reconciliation Week).

On yet another level, it is difficult to assess what should we be measuring 'improvements' against. Bierschenk and Olivier de Sardan remind us that 'face-to-face societies' in general (villages or other small-scale settlements), which might be perceived as harmonious and homogenous by the short-term visitor, are 'like any other groups, pervaded by conflicts', which explains why some prefer the term 'back-to-back societies' (2003: 160). 'Bottling up' is a wider strategy of equilibriation. Cooperation and mutual dependence coexist with rumour, suspicions and accusation (ibid.: 161). Yet most acclamations of progress made in Rwanda (and even by outside actors) focus precisely on coexistence. We hear that Rwandans used to coexist before the genocide (*bari babanye neza mbere y'ubukoloni*) and that a form of such coexistence has been re-established. Yet instead of a level of success, what we should be reading from the data is the insufficiency of coexistence mechanisms in averting violent conflict. More importantly yet, the community-centred approach of *kubana neza* or 'good/nice coexistence' fundamentally obscures the role of political exclusion, repression and the state in structuring those very community dynamics from which bodies like NURC read their success.

Actual Effects: From 'Effectiveness' to 'Productiveness'

Not only is the subject of 'effectiveness' made problematic due to fraught methods of its measurement, there is also a strong sense that some activities put forward to create a unified community in Rwanda might actually perform negative work. *Gacaca* courts have been said to build negative social capital, lower inter-ethnic trust, contribute to a rise in community conflicts and produce a more salient sense of injustice (Rettig 2008; Chakravarty 2014). Certainly, more has been at stake in *gacaca* than in the other activities I have overviewed, and these, when looked at through the lens of effectiveness might simply be proclaimed as unable to bring about change (e.g., increased trust and interaction, a strengthened sense of national belonging). But my focus here is slightly different. Rather than asking 'Are these activities achieving what they say they want to achieve?' I ask 'What are the different effects that are actually produced?' In other words, my focus is on 'productiveness' of social events, rather than their effectiveness.

Many unity and reconciliation activities may well be repeated surface enactments where unity and 'being together' seems to consist primarily of attending together, hearing the same, behaving alike. The displays of activity, volume and presence are not 'empty', however – while these might hold only tenuous links to actual claimed transformations, they do become productive politically in other ways. For one, these platforms serve to communicate desired attitudes and behaviours and in this way they facilitate the reproduction of official scripts. On another level, the success of staging itself and projection of a desired image are a form of symbolic power. Third, the activities' ceremoniousness speaks of a fragile social contract that needs to be repeatedly re-enacted and procedurally outlined. Official ceremonies of 'being together' represent such a continual effort to affirm. From this perspective, seemingly shallow and cosmetic activity becomes a fundamental governance tool in a post-genocide society based on the maxim of 'nice coexistence'.

The official emphasis on nice, peaceful, 'unproblematic' coexistence in turn explains the government's accent on the ceremonies of asking for and granting of pardon. This social 'exchange', almost schematically described in *ingando* questionnaires, is important even if not genuine or deeply felt. Ceremonies everywhere are meant to affirm, to make real, to catalyse desired change through acts ranging from swearing in, making a pledge, to granting forgiveness; from pronouncing a script to simply showing up, being there, taking part. Just like wedding vows, these ceremonies do not necessarily produce a happy or lasting marriage. Far from 'empty' then, unity and reconciliation ceremonies get one 'involved', not only in a symbolic service to powers that be, in upholding the façade, but also in bearing further containment as a result of the imposition.

The Kinyarwanda word used today to refer to 'participation' in public activities is *ubwitabire*. It derives from the verb 'kwitaba', meaning literally 'answer when called' (e.g., *kwitaba imana* means 'to die', literally 'to answer the call of God'). There is a rhythm and symmetry to the notion underlying *kwitaba*, which reflects the relations in the public sphere quite well. Someone calls out and you respond to the rallying call, and you respond to the propaganda in its own language too. People show the expected face, keeping the rest inside. As long as people respect the call, you might temporarily lull each other into believing in the genuineness of the act. Participation in government programmes (unity and reconciliation activities notwithstanding) should be read against the connotations that the word *ubwitabire* invokes – those of a duty, an obligation to answer the call coming from above. Today it is invoked when calling people 'to participate in *gacaca* courts' (*kwitaba inkiko gacaca*) or to 'participate in elections' (*kwitabira amatora*), to participate in 'works' (*kwitabira umurimo*), to participate in *umuganda* (*kwitabira umuganda*), and in a more overarching way – to participate in the 'programme/agenda of the government' (*kwitabira gahunda za leta*) (e.g., NURC 2007: 14). All of these expressions invoke a responsibility to share in a common activity, to partake in a public and collective 'good' (*gacaca* – justice; *umuganda* and other government programmes – development). The concept of *kwitaba* as a duty to respond thus connects to notions of contribution (*umusanzu*) and 'taking part in' (*kugira uruhare*), both evoking individual roles in a collective duty.

At this point, the claim that activities of unity and reconciliation are insertion points for political power should be better understood. The many activities created by the government are at once a type of tax on people's time and energy and additional platforms of governance. Besides the explicit political messages and instrumentalizations that at times characterize unity and reconciliation activities, it is the governmentality effects that are most pronounced. Activities become fora for sensitization ('passing of messages') but also for making people more 'sensitizable' (e.g., urging them to respond to government programmes). More specifically, they become platforms for the mainstreaming and dissemination of knowledge, attitudes and behaviours seen as necessary for the project of transforming people into catalysts of development. Containment and 'bearing' in the name of promises of future development has become a peculiar form of healing at the national level.

Overall, the chapter has tried to show how labelling, staging and ceremoniousness create political utility. The 'production' itself, the mirage of presence and the tokens of effect, produces a symbolic form of power, alongside which, within the same spaces, operates a power of a more tangible kind – one of containment, ordering and control, one that publicly appropriates and overwrites. Labels not only have the power to foreground and obscure, they have the power to sanction, and the platforms created in their name can become the staging grounds of power.

Notes

1. In fact, the Minister of Local Development (MINALOC), Musoni Protais, is behind multiple current policies and unity and reconciliation activities (he is the 'father of decentralization', land consolidation, *imihigo*, *umudugudu*, *itorero*, *ubudehe*, Vision Umurenge 2020, etc.). Interview with a Rwandan researcher, 25 February 2009.
2. An address to SCUR Presidents by Fatuma Ndangiza in Kacyiru, Kigali, 26 January 2009.
3. *Umuganda* 'is meant to forge unity, reconciliation among Rwandans, and reduce government expenditure on public services' (Kakimba for NTK, 29 September 2006). Fatuma Ndangiza of NURC: 'It is a civic duty to participate

in Umuganda to ensure that all participate in reconciliation and development'. (IRIN, 26 August 2008). Most recently, NTK published an article entitled 'Umuganda is a healing tool' (6 August 2010).
4. Interestingly, *umuganda* was criticized by the RPF during the 1990–1994 civil war, drawing precisely on such alternative and incisive language of labour and exploitation.
5. A GTZ-Rwanda employee has overviewed the above-mentioned document for work and noted this to me in person in an informal discussion on 20 January 2009.
6. NURC meeting to overview the 2009–2012 Strategic Plan, 15 December 2008.
7. Ibid.
8. The discourse reduces the problem to a technical issue that requires a technical (as opposed to political) solution (Ferguson 1994: 256).
9. Interview with an employee at the Conseil National de la Jeunesse du Rwanda, Kigali, 13 January 2009.
10. *Umuganda* is 'the tradition of work on public projects', *ubudehe* 'the tradition of mutual assistance', *gacaca* 'the tradition of communal resolution of disputes', *umusanzu* 'the tradition of support for the needy and contribution to the achievement of a common goal' (Musoni 2003: 10).
11. Informal discussion with NURC's Director of Civic Education, 11 November 2008.
12. See for example, review of Kagame's closing speech at the Seventh National Dialogue (Kagire for NTK, 8 February 2010). In Kinyarwanda, he said, 'Gacaca, Ubudehe, Umuganda, Ubumwe n'Ubwiyunge, byose ni made in Rwanda' [all of these are 'made in Rwanda']. The word 'home-grown' is used quite often to describe unity and reconciliation activities.
13. The use of the term 'exploitation' might be too strong here. As Pottier (1993) but also Jefremovas (2002) show, a substantial deterioration in conditions occurred only in 1989 when peasantry was really let down by Habyarimana. OPROVIA, Rwanda's parastatal agent dedicated to managing food reserves and smoothing price fluctuations was bailed out almost every year by the Habyarimana-led government. It was in 1989 when the government failed to underwrite OPROVIA's debts. At the same time, the government stopped its support to the peasant Cooperative Movement.
14. Gakenke District, Northern region, 11 November 2008.
15. 'On mange et chante ensemble; On cherche des bières, des fantas et organize une fête, une reception ... les gens se mettent ensemble.' Interview with Nyakabanda sector officer, Kigali, 19 January 2009.
16. NURC meeting to evaluate the Unity and Reconciliation Week, 27 November 2008.
17. Ibid.
18. Interview with an employee at the Diaspora Department at RPF Headquarters, 23 January 2009.
19. Translated from French. Interview with a researcher at the Ombudsman's Office, previously President of the National SCUR Forum. Kigali, 14 January 2009.
20. NURC meeting to evaluate the Unity and Reconciliation Week, op. cit.

21. Interview with Connie Bwiza of the Chamber of Deputies, a Ugandan returnee, op. cit.
22. Ibid.
23. Interview with the President of the SCUR National Forum, Kigali, 9 January 2009.
24. Discussion with the President and Vice-President of a university SCUR club, 2 February 2009.
25. I mention 'at least' because of occasional gaps in translation.
26. Reference made by a representative of the Ministry of Youth explaining his presence at the January 26 2009 NURC meeting with SCUR presidents. On another occasion, the Nyagatare district took creative license during the U&R week and, as a NURC employee reported, imparted messages of 'unity and reconciliation' in all weddings.
27. The 'Vision 2020' – a key policy document detailing where Rwanda wants to find itself in the near future. This must be one of the most intensely disseminated documents – most people if not all know it by name.
28. Interview with a Nyakabanda sector officer, op. cit.
29. Interview, Kigali, 31 October 2008.
30. Informal talk, Kigali, 25 March 2009.
31. Informal talk with an employee at 'Ulka' – Kigali Independent University (ULK), Kigali, 11 March 2009.
32. Fatuma Ndangiza at the NURC meeting with SCUR presidents, 26 January 2009.
33. Informal talk with a ULK employee, op. cit.
34. Informal chat with an *ingando* administrator, Rwamagana, 16 March 2009.
35. NURC meeting to evaluate the Unity and Reconciliation Week, op. cit.
36. The trauma comes out in smaller doses before and after the official commemoration. Sometimes a scream can be heard in the neighbourhood but it is usually enclosed at home. Those who killed can also suffer from trauma.
37. Ndangiza at the NURC meeting with SCUR presidents, 26 January 2009.
38. Informal discussion with an *ingando* employee, Rwamagana, 16 March 2009.
39. *Ikiriyo* is a traditional wake, a gathering of people to support those in grief. During the official commemoration week, large official ibiriyo of sorts are organized in Rwanda.
40. Visit to the Ruhengeri prison, 19 November 2008.
41. Interview with a female parliamentarian, a returnee from Uganda, op. cit.
42. Interview with a Nyakabanda sector officer, op. cit.
43. Interview with the Head of the Diaspora Department, RPF Headquarters, op. cit.
44. In an effort to evaluate the 'impacts' of NURC (IJR 2005), three broad questions were included in verbally administered surveys: Do you know about the NURC? (meant to measure 'general knowledge'); What does reconciliation mean to you? (meant to measure 'ownership'); and Do you feel that things have changed in Rwanda since 1994? (meant to measure 'impacts'). Not only are these questions extremely vague and the link between measure and what it aims to measure tenuous, it is also the interviewers who circle categories such as 'excellent', 'good' or 'poor' (knowledge) based on 'give me detail' probes.

8

Ingando Camps
Nation Building as Consent Building

The Nkumba *ingando* camp lies in striking surroundings. In front of it spreads Lake Burera hemmed by layers of terraced hills, behind it rise the slopes of the Muhabura volcano. Banana groves stretch as far as the eye can see, a gently moving sea of dishevelled fronds. The ground in these parts is strewn with black volcanic rock. A typical day at the camp starts well before the dawn can draw these outlines.[1] The participants – *kos* or *wanakosi* in full – wake up very early, at 4–5 A.M. when it is 'very very cold, it is night'. The daily routine starts with *mucakamucaka*, or running. Then come the military exercises – stretching, push-ups, parades – 'the walk of the military'. We learn how to hold and shoot *imbunda* (guns), the *kos* tell me, how to dismantle a gun and put it back together, how to clean it. Then as first light reveals and then clears the mists, we eat some sorghum porridge – *masaka* – or some corn and beans.

After breakfast, at 7:30–8 A.M., the lecture starts in the large pentagon-shaped building in the centre of the premises. The *wanakosi* learn different things on different days, according to a set schedule. Every lecture is delivered by a different government representative. The guest lecturers speak about history, philosophy (idealism versus materialism), unity and reconciliation, genocide ideology and ways of avoiding it, military operations (different systems of combat), 'how politics was in the past and now', and 'the programme of our state' – the 'policy of Rwanda in each domain', in economics (Vision 2020), environment, even health (family planning, methods of contraception, HIV etc.). We also learn about patriotism – 'the culture of liking our country' – and about *ubutwari* – heroism and 'how our ancestors were heroes'. Classes can take up to eight hours each day.

Lunch is always beans and maize, with extra rice or sweet potato added for supper. After lunch, either the lecture continues until the evening or battle drills take place on the large clearing. In the evening, from eight until ten or eleven, us *kos* gather together for *gitaramo* or *igitamaduni*. We sit on the ground and sing songs, some people dance in the front. Sometimes there are war or heroic poems – we say *kwivuga* or *icyivugo* – it is a poetic form recounting good achievements, usually delivered without pause for breath. There are traditional tales, even jokes. Then we go to sleep. It is the same every day.

The description of a typical day at a student *ingando* has been pieced together from multiple personal recollections. But besides students, many other Rwandans of very different walks of life have undergone routines like this. Since shortly after the genocide, hundreds of people at a time have been gathered in remote camps where they have stayed for weeks or months, isolated from their communities and families, learning about the history of Rwanda, the 'work of the government', singing and dancing, doing community work and military exercises together. In the tense atmosphere of the late 1990s, when distrust ran high and social relations were severely strained, and when hundreds of thousands returned to Rwanda from various countries in the diaspora, many seeing the country for the first time, *ingando* camps were proposed by the new government as a key tool of nation building. Not only have *ingando* camps continued to this day, camping in the service of nationalist goals has become much more widespread through the introduction of a country-wide *itorero ry'igihugu* programme in 2009 – a 'decentralized' and 'advanced' *ingando* – through which hundreds of thousands of Rwandans have already passed.

But what exactly is *ingando*? The question is simple, and yet so sensitive. It drills down to key dynamics introduced at the outset – the politics of characterization, the value of certain labels and the danger of others, the dynamics of gaps between official documents and what unfolds on the ground. The little that has been written labels *ingando* in broad strokes, as brainwashing or re-education. Indeed, *ingando* is about re-education as it is about governmentality and social engineering. But rather than quickly dismissing *ingando* or unquestioningly accepting programmatic descriptions of the government, we need to pause and afford these retreats more detailed attention. As a concentrated interpretive space where wider social dynamics converge, *ingando* is a unique window to understand the social transformation project of the Rwandan government.

The fact that camps – an activity defined by transience and liminality – are explicitly chosen to underpin a project of nationalist rooting and fixing reflects the perhaps paradoxical importance of movement to both the expansion and consolidation of a collective imaginary (Malkki 1995). It demonstrates how rites of passage and acts of transition to a new and settled 'imagined community' (Anderson 1981) are often attempted through physical, symbolic and ideational *movement*. What we witness in camps such as *ingando* is then an interesting interplay between the uses of transience, movement, liminality and dislodging in order to anchor, to locate, to fix in form a specific sense of 'Rwandanness' and a specific sense of place in a new political order of things. Uniquely, *ingando* erases the line between staying and going and is indeed best described as both a 'stopping place' and a 'passage'. As such, *ingando* also emphasizes the tension between containment and movement in Rwanda's state building. On the one hand, movement has shaped Rwandan society to an extraordinary degree (Purdeková 2008b), its recent history being marked both by a returnee capture of power and mass displacements resulting in transitory and transnational experiences and identities. On the other hand, the current governmentality drive is squarely centred on containment in the name of social control (Purdeková 2013). In *ingando*, movement is meant to achieve precisely the opposite of past out-migration – it is meant to converge and create 'the same experience', a common understanding, and a clear location and orientation in the post-genocide order.

Despite being relevant and revelatory spaces, encamped experiences in the service of nation building (or 'community building' more broadly, whether the community is a corporate 'team' or a community of ideology) have received hardly any academic attention. Yet as spaces meant for intensified transformation, camps offer potentially key insights into the massive social re-engineering exercise underway in post-genocide Rwanda. The fact that NURC's key department is one of 'civic education' only further highlights that, even in the sphere of unity and reconciliation, the primary task is to shape the citizen. Tellingly, *ingando* is not only organized under the civic education rubric, it is also highlighted as the commission's 'flagship' activity. These are just some cues to what the book aims to show much more directly, and namely that *ingando*'s spatial, symbolic and performative nature, in addition to specific texts being disseminated, make it an example par excellence of the government's unity-building project.

The 'dynamics of gaps' between official descriptions and what unfolds on the ground is also perhaps greatest in the case of *ingando*. For one, the descriptions are vague and multiple and the research scant, so it is hard to make sense of something variably referred to as 'solidarity camps', 're-education camps', 'civic education camps', 'political awareness camps', 'reorientation camps' or 'reintegration courses'. One NGO even described *ingando* as *camps de vacances* (holiday camps). Various rumours constitute *ingando* either as 'military training', 'making everyone Tutsi', or a 'boring succession of lessons'. The interpenetration of different themes in *ingando*'s classroom, on the other hand, allows a variety of organizations and ministries to put the camps into their logical matrices ('logframes'), highlighting different aspects of *ingando*, claiming they foster private sector development or are an aid in HIV/AIDS education.

Notably, *ingando* grapples with a powerful contradiction. Highlighted as camps building unity and reconciliation among Rwandans,[2] certain *ingando* are run like military camps and comprise military training. The cohorts from the latest iteration of the camps (*itorero*) have even been incitingly called 'a newly created RPF militia'.[3] The military nature of the camps, however, is not acknowledged in any official descriptions. *Ingando* is thus without doubt a sensitive topic – for the government but especially for the donors. The official descriptions mentioning 'peace and leadership camps' (the official name of the Nkumba site is 'Peace and Leadership Academy') completely obscure the military aspect. The surface veneer might be thin but it is still important. It shields the camps from critique from the international community, which officially associates peace building with demilitarization rather than the opposite. Any attempts at academic 'interpretation' will hence be met by evasiveness if not silence from the local donor staff.

The UNDP is one of the principal donors of NURC and has sponsored the camps directly under its 'Programme for Strengthening Good Governance' (PSGG). After much insistence and repeated knocking on doors, a young UNDP employee – a recent returnee from Canada – granted me a brief audience where she promised to email me a document describing the NURC activities supported by UNDP funding (UNDP 2008). The one-page document used highly sanitized language – the word *ingando* was not mentioned and instead the document spoke of 'seminars' and 'workshops on unity and reconciliation' aimed at 'engaging [a given section of the population] about the prevailing genocide ideology'. As will be shown below, *ingando* is not only much more than these descriptions suggest, it might be something else altogether.

The exploration of the camps is structured around the following core questions: Is *ingando* a 'unity-building tool' – exclusively, primarily, partially? If so, what type of unity is being enacted through it? Could *ingando* also be considered a 'technology of power' (Foucault 1980: 135) just as one university student proposed to me when saying that 'it was difficult for the government to manage society after the genocide, so they created *ingando*'? In my attempt to understand the 'what' of *ingando*, I approached the camp from different analytical angles – its history and evolution, its different contemporary variants, its selective targeting, and finally the different components of *ingando*, the actual 'goings-on' and the way in which they are interpreted by *ingando* participants. *Ingando* affords multiple angles of learning not only about the immediate happenings inside the camp but also about the project of 'unity' more broadly. The tracing of the camps' wider contexts brings us from the RPF's military past to its developmentalist visions of the future. As will be shown, unity as political friendship and unity as nationalist loyalty find full confluence in the space of the camp, the result being a distinct form of nation building as consent building.

Political Education from Wartime to Peacetime: Evolutions and Inspirations of a 'Tradition'

Like many other activities of unity and reconciliation, *ingando* is highlighted as a Rwandan 'tradition'. My research on *ingando*'s precedents and claimed inspirations reveals something much more intriguing: *ingando* camps are complicated composites of a military and political past that reaches far beyond Rwanda. Nonetheless, the official narrative is a useful starting point. The National Unity and Reconciliation Commission traces today's camps to the pre-colonial military custom of 'halting normal activities to reflect on, and find solutions to national challenges'.[4] An organizer of the first post-genocide *ingando* suggests that the name originates from the word *kugandika* – to camp or stay somewhere together. It is an allusion to 'military guard duty on the border in the past, you go there and camp'.[5] According to members of *Inteko Izirikana*,[6] the concept was used in the military domain to signify either a space where troops readied for combat, or a temporary resting place for the soldiers in their military expeditions, or finally a temporary accommodation for the king and his entourage during their rounds. In a related interpretation, *ingando* used to be military encampments where soldiers reflected on the campaign strategy and received their final briefing before combat.[7] The salient characteristics of pre-colonial *ingando* are its encamped and transient nature, the military character of the space and the accent on message and reflection. Whether or not these depictions are imagined, reinvented or crafted and sifted through the lens of present-day goals, they do capture core aspects of today's *ingando*.

Nonetheless, there is no clear temporal continuum to *ingando* in Rwanda. *Ingando* as military retreats stopped along with the days of grand military exploits of the Rwandan *abami* (kings). As Shyaka (2007) explains, '*ingando* lost its relevance in the colonial era, together with other monarchic institutions and practices'. The current version shows only a tenuous link to the *ingando* of yesteryear; the shared aspects (i.e., the military component) are precisely those that the government does not prefer to highlight. The fundamentally military gatherings of old are today expeditiously reinterpreted as nation-building tools first and foremost: 'In [today's] *ingando*,' suggests general Rusagara, 'individuals are reminded to subject their interests to the national ideal and give Rwanda their all' (Rusagara quoted in PRI 2004: 111).

In conversation, a number of people both outside and inside the government suggested that today's *ingando* is in fact a relatively recent occurrence, dating to a number of identifiable predecessors and influences in the diaspora. My informants traced *ingando* to the politicization campaigns of 'raising awareness' conducted by the RPF first in exile and later within Rwanda as they kept capturing territory during the 1990–1994 war. One camp coordinator explained to me that 'before 1994, there was no *ingando*, it was inspired in the diaspora.

After the [current] government was installed, it started putting this in place'.[8] Tito Rutaremara, the founder of the RPF and a veteran of Rwandan politics confirmed this in our interview: 'First we were doing them, the RPF, during and before the struggle ... It started within the RPF and then was adopted by others. NURC [later] used this instrument for all people'.[9]

The need to mobilize support for RPF in the diaspora seems to be the main reason for organizing or supporting clandestine meetings and retreats that became the predecessors of today's *ingando* (Mgbako 2005; Reed 1995). According to Rutaremara, the aim was 'to bring people together and share the ideals of the RPF. There were three purposes – to politicize people, to bring people to discuss problems, to remember Rwanda [and] to bring people to help the needy'.[10] A historian of the RPF suggested that '[*ingando*] was a tool of mobilizing members from all over' but while in pre-colonial Rwanda it was exclusively a thing of the military, 'in the RPF context [in the diaspora], it became a mix [of different aspects]'.[11] Camps or retreats served three main objectives for *banyarwanda* populations in exile. Initially, they were used to raise awareness of being Rwandan, and promote 'solidarity' or self-help. Gradually, politicization of diaspora members and provision of military training were added. Most inspiration allegedly drew on camps organized by Rwandan refugee youth in Burundi.[12] Importantly, the camps did not start as a RPF mobilization platform (rather for self-help and raising of cultural awareness) but had to be made into one: 'In Burundi, there was a youth organization that was very strong. When RPF reached Burundi, they transformed this youth organization into RPF youth. But they already had many activities – to meet in some place and help the community – [that were] practiced much before the RPF.'[13]

The increased politicization of *banyarwanda* refugees can be traced to 1980s Uganda. It was after the victory of Museveni's National Resistance Movement (NRM) in 1986 that the Uganda-based Rwanda Alliance for National Unity (RANU) decided to increase its support base by changing its political programme and its name to Rwanda Patriotic Front (RPF). The party also started organizing 'political/military schools' in Uganda and Tanzania where 'cadres learned about the goals of the RPF and received military training, though without weapons' (Reed 1995: 51). A number of my interviewees traced *ingando* to these semi-clandestine political retreats in exile. Commenting on his experience in Uganda, a returnee recounted how 'people would meet for a month, they could take [over] a home of someone, even in Kampala, and meet there. There were many strategies so that the security and police would not know. "Just a family visit", [we would pretend]. There were strict communication rules. But this was just political and cultural, not military, the noise [of military training] could attract some curiosity'.[14]

During the 1990–1994 civil war, political schools were organized within Rwanda itself with the help of RPF cells based there (Reed 1996: 496). 'From

1990 to 1993, the RPF installed participants in *ingando* or "RPF schools" for three weeks, after which participants would be expected to return to their villages and disseminate pro-RPF ideology' (Mgbako 2005: 208). In the words of one of my informants:

> At the beginning of the 1990s, 1991/92, the RPF had [captured] a piece of land in the north [of Rwanda] and then organized *ingando* with military aspects there, but even for civilian cadres [they offered] military and political training. If they could, they would train everyone militarily, to demystify weapons, so that people would not be afraid of soldiers ... If we could train the whole population [we would], it is a way to upgrade their minds to this mystification of army and soldiers. [Me: And political education?] Political education was most important, there was a message to deliver.[15]

The parallels and inspirations, however, have a deeper history and can be traced to earlier rebel movements. The overall RPF strategy of consolidating and politicizing its support base through special seminars and retreats draws directly on Yoweri Museveni's own guerrilla strategy during the years of the NRA insurgency (1981–1986) and before. This connection should not be surprising – many prominent members of the Rwandan RPF fought with the NRM and were 'socialized' into its approach that embraced political education in a most direct way. In fact, 'as early as 1971, Yoweri Museveni instituted political education as one of the main training components of the Front for National Salvation (FRONESA)' that he was leading at the time (HRW 1999). The National Resistance Movement (NRM), initiated in 1979, was inspired by Maoist principles and had a 'political commissar' in every unit and organized political education classes in which 'African history and politics were taught from a revolutionary perspective' (Kinzer 2008: 44). Museveni viewed his army as a 'people's army' and his soldiers as 'politicians in uniform' (HRW 1999). RPA/RPF under the leadership of Rwigema and Kagame followed this approach. In a sense, the campaign of 'winning the hearts and minds' has not finished with the end of the genocide. The northern and western parts of Rwanda were not pacified until the late 1990s and the enemy perseveres today in the disguise of 'divisionism' and 'genocide ideology'. For Kagame, political conversion is part of the struggle and it is in reality 'the tricky part' [the real challenge].[16]

But Uganda also offered a more concrete inspiration to *ingando*. Long before the RPF took power in Rwanda, the victorious NRM in Uganda had translated its own wartime politicization agenda into political schools in peacetime. The NRM's wartime 'mobile schools' of political education were transformed upon victory into a permanent institution – The National School of Political Education. During my interviews with Nkumba *ingando* participants, I repeatedly heard them refer to their morning exercise and march as *mucaka* or *mucakamucaka*. I learned this was Swahili military jargon

– *chaka mchaka* is an onomatopoeic expression mimicking the 'sound made by military boots during marches' (HRW 1999). This is also the name of NRM political and military education camps described by Human Rights Watch (1999: 66) as 'one of the tools used by the NRM government to increase its political control, targeted particularly at civil servants and graduating students ... [It includes] demystification of the gun and political education, which included the history of Uganda according to the NRM – a crude form of historical materialism placing blame for Uganda's past woes on the political parties.'

The descriptions of a typical day at the Ugandan *Chaka-Mchaka* retreat correspond very closely to the structure of the elite Nkumba *ingando* in Rwanda. Similarly to *ingando*, 'in the morning, you start with *chaka-mchaka* at 6 A.M. At 10 A.M. the political lectures begin' (HRW 1999). The NRM as Uganda's governing party also organizes camps called *Kyankwanzi*, run by the military. In a close parallel with the Nkumba camp in northern Rwanda, the facility in Kiboga is called the 'National Leadership Institute' and the training is meant to be 'part of preparation for the implementation of the *Bonna Bagaggawale* (prosperity for all) programme'.[17] Similarly to Rwanda, the camp is tailored to different groups (occupational, or 'age-grade' such as university entrants) and comprises political education and military training. Most recently, '29 newly recruited Grade one Magistrates have pitched camp at the National Leadership Institute'.[18] One commentator called the camps 'Museveni's fighting zone': 'Historically, the Kyankwanzi retreats are where Museveni fights and wins his wars within the party'.[19]

After the RPF takeover in July 1994, *ingando* transformed from a wartime and exile political institution to a government-employed strategy of social re-engineering on a large scale. There are very few documents detailing this transition. Shyaka (2007) mentions that the Rwandan Patriotic Army (RPA) 'revived' *ingando* 'after the 1994 genocide' to initially integrate the ex-FAR combatants into the new army. Mgbako (2005: 209) suggests the first large-scale *ingando* were organized in 1996 for Tutsi returnees. The organizer of the first youth *ingando* speaks of three initial target groups – the youth, Hutu returnees, and Tutsi returnees. A 2006 NURC impact assessment of *ingando* confirms this chronology and targeting. The first camp at Karangazi was held in May 1996 for youth from Umutara and Byumba prefectures. These were young people of 'different backgrounds and visions including those who were coming from the Diasporas and those who survived the genocide or who were presumably guilty of genocide crimes. All those people did not similarly perceive and face the national realities' (2006: 16). Soon after the first *ingando* at Karangazi, the *ingando* 'model' was properly consolidated when hundreds of thousands of Hutu returned from refugee camps in the DRC (Mugunga, Katale, Tingi-Tingi). At this time, in late 1996, 'the Government of Rwanda decided to put in place a National Programme of the Newly Repatriated

Refugees (NPNRR), based on the *Ingando* model' (ibid.: 17). For the Hutu returnees, *ingando* was meant to serve as '"reorientation", the main aim was to tell them about the programme of the government and to go against what they were told in the refugee camps [by the previous authorities]'.[20]

The first *ingando* for youth were organized by the Ministry of Youth and Associative Movement (MIJEUMA) 'with the [financial] support of UNICEF'.[21] In fact, UNHCR and WHO also supported the large tented camps of Gishari in the Eastern Province, holding up to 2,000 students, as well as camps elsewhere in the country. But the full list of early donors is long, comprising all major humanitarian agencies – 'HCR, PAM, UNDP, UNICEF, USAID, LWF, Belgian Red Cross, GTZ, MSF, World Relief, Save the Children, Italian Cooperation, Canadian Cooperation, Netherlands Cooperation, IRC' among others (NURC 2006: 17). In 1999, NURC took over the camps for college entrants, while other ministries and institutions started organizing *ingando* for other segments of the population.

Ingando started as tented camps, and permanent sites and structures like those in Nkumba in the northern region were developed only gradually. 'It really started like scout jamborees, conversations by the fire, and later activities were added such as constructions of houses for widows and orphans.'[22] Organizing retreats of this kind posed significant challenges in the post-genocide Rwanda filled with suspicion and distrust:

> But going on field trips? People ran from the government, they were afraid of them [why?] Because they were made to be afraid, people were told 'you would be killed'. We are an oral society, news travel through the tongue ... In one of the past camps, in what used to be Mutara district, the parents that were sending their children expressed the view, the rumour, that their kids would be killed. 'We will not see them anymore', they were saying ... As a result [to deal with this], we played the voices of the children over the radio. It was that much frightening! After some days in the camps, people started to talk, that is in fact how we found out about the rumour.[23]

Many years later, during the first wave of prisoner releases in 2003, the prisoners themselves expressed fear of attending *ingando*: 'At the beginning of the training, there were also rumours saying that we were going to be killed' (PRI 2004: 56). Even during my fieldwork, after more than a decade of *ingando*, university students spoke of initial anxieties, now mainly related to the 'hardships' of physical drills and discipline. 'To baptise us, we go crawling in the mud, singing', reminisces a student. The 'baptism' instilled fear: 'On the first day, I was very afraid of seeing soldiers, guns, and the way they directed us. I was afraid we might die there, the way they beat some of our students, the first day was fear.' Or: 'The first day, they try to terrify us ... already as you leave the bus, you already start physical exercise, you carry your bag on your shoulders, you kneel and go ... you cannot say any word because you feel fear.' Another student expressed the same: 'The first impressions, you are afraid ... because there are people who say that "you will do forced labour, military exercises"'.

Most political figures and camp organizers stress that the main idea of *ingando,* especially in the early stages and for returnees, was to 'open the reality of the country', build confidence among people, and most importantly, build a sense of national unity. The idea comes up repeatedly. A NURC programme officer explained that *ingando* camps were meant to:

> foster a sense of nationalism among the returnee populations from Congo, Burundi, Uganda and Europe, and elsewhere ... We thought that if we could remove these people from their daily lives and bring them together to share from a common dish – to eat and sleep together – this would build confidence in the diverse populations of repatriated Rwandans, confidence that we could indeed live together. (Mgbako 2005: 8)

The director of the National Youth Council, involved in organizing some of the first *ingando* highlighted the same aspect: 'You were frightened of one another [the different returnee groups], there were different cultural attitudes, speaking different languages, the camps were to show that we were all *Banyarwanda*'. Finally, an RPF adviser suggested that *ingando* 'shows the most important elements that are common to all, the bases of the nation, what makes the unity of Rwandans, what is the role of ethnicity ... how to construct the nation, that is *ingando*'.

In what follows, I submit the narrative of *ingando-*as-nation building to closer scrutiny. What type of unity is to be built and how? Is national unity the main purpose and outcome? If there are others, what are they and what is their significance? How do military exercises, lengthy courses and cultural performances 'fit' into the nation-building plan? *Ingando* engineers and administrators themselves suggest that something altogether different than building unity based on cultural learning, confidence building and enactions of 'life together' is at play, and namely the 'cleansing' of people's minds and fostering of 'one way of looking' at things. On one occasion, I was told that '*ingando* was made to address these various backgrounds which prevented people to really work together as before, as it had been for centuries, so one way of addressing [this] was some kind of cleansing of people's minds from this dirt accumulated by situations and recent history'.[24] On another occasion, an *ingando* camp administrator suggested that:

> *Ingando* [helps] bring together the vision of the country, the policies of the government, it becomes easier for many people to know many things [when they are] in the same place ... Before university, students go to Nkumba [*ingando*] to install a sense of patriotism, to equip them with ... they must have one way of looking at things, especially government policy.[25]

At the RPF Headquarters, I was told with reference to *ingando* that 'we [Rwandans] have opposed memories about the history of Rwanda. [But] one needs a consensus to make a nation'.[26]

Ingando's history might help to explain why consensus building and nation building smoothly interlace in the official narrative of the camps. *Ingando* draws on left-inspired, guerrilla politicization strategies traceable to a number of military movements in the region, from Mozambique to Uganda. Similarly to these movements, RPF's *ingando* represents a translation of political education from the needs of war to those of peace. Though *ingando* is clearly an adaptation to the challenges of a post-genocide society as the government saw them, the camps in Nkumba or Gako remind us clearly of their predecessors. They are run in a military style and involve, among other things, gun demystification, an accent on discipline, physical exercise and military training. Politicization also remains key, with lessons on government vision and policy being a central part of the curriculum. The unity building reproduced in *ingando* is thus one with which the RPF has the most direct experience. The success of the RPF armed movement was based on rallying the previously fragmented diaspora around a particular political platform (its own), it was about maintaining strong internal coherence and a 'unified vision'. With regard to youth specifically, we could certainly draw a contemporary parallel with the RPF 'capture' of the Burundi refugee youth in the 1980s. Through initiatives such as SCUR and *ingando*, the Rwandan state is actively involved in producing an 'RPF youth' in all but name, a youthful vanguard set to spread the consensus. As is the case with all regimes aspiring to ideological domination and preoccupied with self-reproduction, the RPF-led government takes care of its incoming elites.

Unity understood specifically as 'nation building' is also part of *ingando* as it has been in exile. The RPF political schools in exile were meant as a reminder of 'where you come from' and a manner of maintaining links with a cultural past (and by extension a political and nationalist project). In post-genocide Rwanda, the project transformed into an attempt to teach a divided population that 'being Rwandan' matters above all else and to teach them what being Rwandan in the new Rwanda means. This construction of a new citizen role in *ingando* is attempted through multiple avenues. In fact, all of the official unity-building strategies coalesce in *ingando*: the fostering of Rwandanness and revival of Rwandanicity, the calls to rally around a 'common vision', the cultivation of the 'greater us' through military performance, even in some cases the simulated 'being together' across divides. But of course the fostering of a new citizen role is inseparable from the cultivation of a new relation to the state. *Ingando* thus powerfully demonstrates how unity building and state building, the making of an imagined collectivity and the reproduction of power, are intimately linked in contemporary Rwanda.

Ingando as a Social Situation in Contemporary Rwanda

Since their introduction in the latter half of the 1990s, *ingando* camps have targeted a wide array of people. Participant groups have included 'old-caseload' Tutsi returnees and 'new-caseload' Hutu returnees, ex-FAR soldiers and demobilized rebels (adult and youth ex-combatants), provisionally-released prisoners and those serving 'alternative sentences' (the TIG programme incorporates some aspects of *ingando*), prison-born children, public and private university entrants, groups of uneducated youth, university students in the diaspora, head teachers of primary and secondary schools and district education officers, civil servants, the *inyangamugayo* (*gacaca* judges), church reverends, various associations (ATRACO bus drivers, tea growers, masons), sex workers, 'informal sector workers' (hawkers, cash changers) and street children.

While some *ingando* operate periodically (e.g., for university entrants), others have been one-time occasions (e.g., for teachers and head teachers). *Ingando* can take anywhere from days to (more likely) weeks and months. *Ingando* for students used to be three months long but this gradually decreased to two months, one month, and finally three weeks. Teachers spent three months in *ingando* (between 1 June–August 2005). All returnees from Congo attended for one month.[27] Youth ex-combatants, on the other hand, spend as long in *ingando* as it takes to find family members they can 'return' to. This can mean months, and in extreme cases, years spent in the confined space of the camp. Attendance rates have never been published and only very partial counts can be gleaned from official documents or the press.[28] *Ingando* have been organized in all parts of the country. Though they normally target adults, NURC's executive secretary suggested that 'given their impact on society, children should be no exception in these important trainings that instil a culture of togetherness' (Nkurunziza for NTK, 8 May 2009). Besides NURC (and its collaborating institutions[29]), other government commissions, departments and administrative organs (e.g., the City of Kigali) also organize the camps. The Adventist church organizes its own *ingando* for local youth.

Ingando is a form of social gathering and its different versions are tied together through a system of family resemblance. *Ingando* share important spatial, temporal, symbolic and performative aspects. All *ingando* are transitory experiences, taking place in an unfamiliar setting. They involve large groups of people (in the hundreds) going through the same experience. Many *ingando* are located in remote, secluded areas. The sense of distance and separation is intensified by the complete lack of communication with the outside – the use of mobile phones is not allowed. Separation is further enhanced by the change of attire – in some *ingando*, people put on uniforms or get new clothes immediately upon arrival. There is no movement in and out of the camp, with the exception of nearby work sites such as in the TIG camps or the Adventist *ingando*.

Attendance at all *ingando* is mandatory.[30] Time is highly structured. Hierarchies are elaborated – the participants are usually divided according to a military hierarchy or, less commonly, into sectors. There is accent on discipline and respect for authority. The space is also similarly structured and reflects wider hierarchies, especially between participants and staff. In contrast to the past when *ingando* were short-term campgrounds with tents made of wood and plastic sheeting, most *ingando* today take place in permanent or semi-permanent structures. The exception again is the Adventist *ingando* (and presumably other church-organized *ingando*), which take form of ad-hoc tented camps. TIG camps are semi-permanent – they can stay in place for years, until tasks are finished. The TIG camp in Gikomero sector, for example, was made with tree branches and plastic sheeting.

In terms of contents, out of the four general categories of activity – military training, manual labour, lectures and cultural activities – all *ingando* comprise the latter two. Lectures are the most important shared aspect and a salient feature of all *ingando*.[31] All *ingando* also comprise *igitaramo* or *igitamaduni* – an evening gathering of song and dance. Singing and dancing might be interspersed throughout the day too, for example during breaks between lectures. Military training is not a universal component and, predictably, is not a feature in *ingando* for ex-combatants or released prisoners. The *ingando* for returnees from the DRC did not feature military training either and instead the focus lay on 'reconciliation and what we used to call Marxism-Leninism'.[32] However, physical exercise is present in all *ingando* and so is the emphasis on discipline. All *ingando* also involve call-and-reply commands interspersed throughout the day.

As regards manual work, this is the main component of TIG. Where others spend seven hours a day in an *ingando* class, TIGistes perform hard physical labour, with shorter and more spaced-out classes (after all they are in TIG for years), which take place in the evenings and are combined with *utemaduni*. But even the two-week long *ingando* for the Adventist youth had a work task to accomplish – the goal was to build a hundred houses for Rwandan returnees from Tanzania in the historically uninhabited area of the Akagera Park.

The close and more distant relatives of *ingando* might provide a useful contrast. Other camp spaces in Rwanda include refugee camps, transit camps, training camps (for police, intelligence officers), scout jamborees and retreats. The annual high-level government retreats called *umwiherero y' abayobozi* bear a close parallel to *ingando*. The *umwiherero* retreat is a 'week away' meant for planning and strategy. *Umwiherero* means 'to go somewhere where there are no distractions, no communication with the outside world, to think about strategy'.[33]

Refugee camps, on the other hand, provide a powerful contrasting liminality. Whereas *ingando* are meant to be transition spaces to the 'New Rwanda' and social laboratories of the 'new citizen', refugee camps provide no transition and no integration. They are places of containment symbolizing exclusion from citizenship. Perhaps the most powerful show of this is the Gihembe refugee camp, home to 14,500 'Congolese' refugees (as of 2014). This compact settlement hugging a hilltop sits right next to the sprawling city of Byumba. The proximity-yet-separateness is so stark that even to the naked eye of a casual observer, this becomes a potent show of the 'exclusionary' double, the city of non-citizens.

Scout jamborees are another relative. Before the civil war and the genocide, scout camps were organized in Rwanda by the churches – the J.O.C. (*Jeunesse Ouvriere Catholique*) and the *Xaveriens* (Gashanana 2005: 9). These groups met regularly in a given place and had a set work goal (hence sometimes referred to as 'work camps'; ibid.). The scouts also worked on their physical skills, moral character and received training regarding 'beneficial practices in daily life' (ibid.). Contemporary *ingando* that most resembles a jamboree is the Adventist youth camp at the border with Tanzania. Although the Adventist church differentiates its retreats from those of the government,[34] its camps (organized three times a year) have, for a number of reasons, become more like an *ingando* than a jamboree. On the one hand, there is no military training and there is always a work objective, usually the construction of houses. On the other hand, already during the first moments inside the camp, one notices the spatial hierarchies and the accent on discipline that define all *ingando*. The evening *igitaramo* are interspersed with lectures. But there are also much more direct linkages with the government. An organizer inside the camp told me that it was the government who 'requested them' to put together an *ingando* and construct houses for the returnees. In fact, during the night I visited, I came with a NURC employee who was to deliver a lecture on unity and reconciliation.[35]

But the closest relative of *ingando* is undoubtedly the *Itorero ry'Igihugu* programme ('The National Academy'). Interestingly, *itorero* retreats were themselves a product of a retreat – the *umwiherero* of high-level government functionaries at the Kagera Game Lodge in February 2007. Despite being a relatively recent occurrence, *itorero* has grand aims of reaching every person in Rwanda. The government sees the main goal of *itorero* to be unequivocably 'mindset change' (NURC 2009b: 4), in fact the acceleration of mindset change through a new, decentralized structure of civic education. *Itorero* profoundly changes the nature of civic education by making it more embedded at the local level. The first *itorero* graduates (*intore*) are 'cadres' helping to organize *ingando* in all districts and, ultimately, at the lowest administrative level – the village (Kabeera for NTK, 21 January 2011). In the few years since its inception in 2007, about 241,000 people have passed through *itorero* (by December 2012; see NURC 2012). With the structure embedded at administrative levels (and ever lower ones), these numbers could certainly multiply. Last but not least, *itorero* reaches beyond the country to the Rwandan diaspora. In 2010, '350 students underwent the programme in Belgium while over 4,000 are expected to be trained in India this year [2011]' (ibid.).

Itorero schools are often referred to as 'advanced *ingando*' and also involve a stay in training camps. Similarly to *ingando*, *itorero* is highlighted as Rwandan 'tradition'. The contemporary variant is said to relate to the *amatorero* (military regiments) of the pre-colonial period where 'both young men and women would be given lessons in history and culture, trying to instil a common identity' (PRI 2004: 111). From interviews and other accounts, it is apparent that *itorero* resembles *ingando*. It includes political education, military training, lessons on patriotism, family planning, fighting of genocide ideology, as well as cultural education ('they rwandize you in the traditional sense'[36]). The difference is that *itorero* is closely linked to the system of *imihigo* performance contracts whereby each cohort pledges to continue working towards concrete goals outside of the *itorero* setting. 'Each group has its own name or *icyivugo*', an employee at the National Youth Council tells me. 'They call you by your name, you share the identity of your group, your generation, you feel challenged to carry on with your group's values, with your group, and there is competitiveness among the groups for who is better.'[37]

Selective Targeting and the Meanings it Unlocks

Ideally, all Rwandans should pass through *ingando* once in their lifetime and the official plan has been for every Rwandan go through *ingando* by 2020.[38] Limited resources, however, have not allowed this. Only select groups deemed to be 'most in need' have undergone the camp experience. In what follows, I want to show that selective targeting, in itself, can help us interpret the camps. Selectivity helps to reveal the viewpoint of the organizers and helps us understand the specific social engineering goals of the camps. Based on my analysis, the government constituted three broad categories of people as being in special need of re-education after the genocide: the groups perceived as most at disconnect or opposition to the official discourse and the rules of the 'New Rwanda', the groups that needed to be most in line with it and finally, those perceived to be in need of 'proper' socialization.

The first group comprises new- and old-caseload returnees, adult and child ex-combatants and provisionally released prisoners or prisoners serving alternative sentences in TIG. For these populations, *ingando* represents both a physical transitory space – from the outside to the inside of their communities, and a figurative one as well – from the outside to the inside of the new ideology. The transmission of official scripts is especially important in *ingando* organized for these populations because they are perceived either to be most at disconnect with the discourse, having lived abroad for an extended period or their whole life, and/or most in opposition to it, meaning potentially harbouring divisionism or genocide ideology (released prisoners, some Hutu returnees and ex-combatants). The camps serve as 'foyers of return', whether from exile or prison, and aim to 'close the gap' before actual return to daily life (*buzima busanzwe*) and 'full' entry into Rwanda. As a camp coordinator explained to me: 'Take for example the prisoners, they cannot go from the prison [straight] to the community. They have to go to *ingando* as transition, so that they are prepared before they enter the system'.[39]

Ingando for these populations is really an integration exercise outfitted not only with political education and history lessons, but also more practical lessons on government policies and programmes, lessons concerning health or literacy education. For a large subset of these groups, this is also a 'reorientation' exercise. While for the old-caseload Tutsi returnees the primary attempt was to foster a sense of unity, for the new-caseload Hutu *ingando* was equally an attempt to override divisionism. The camps were meant to 'promote ideas of nationalism, erase ethnically-charged lessons of the previous government and spur loyalty to the RPF' (HRW 2000: 3).

On 24 May 1997 President Pasteur Bizimungu officially launched a programme for 'national political awareness' for the returning Hutu. In his address, he talked about a recently-instituted youth camp: 'This camp, like many others which will take place countrywide are aimed at integrating the youth that have just returned from exile in the current social and political life' (BBC, 25 May 1997). The camps were instituted because the government felt such repatriated people needed 'disintoxication' (AFP 19 November 1997), 'clearing of minds' (Xinhua 18 February 1998) after exposure to Hutu extremist brainwashing in the refugee camps. The total number of participants, either 'old-caseload' or 'new-caseload' returnees, is not known and only estimates can be made.[40]

To ease prison overcrowding, in 2003 President Kagame issued a decree allowing for the provisional and phased release of genocide suspects who had confessed and were either elderly, terminally ill or ran the risk of being in prison longer than the sentences they were expected to incur. Often in prison since the end of the genocide, these Rwandans have been in a sense themselves newcomers to Rwanda. Their 're-education' in *ingando* was thus as important as for the returnees and perhaps more so as they were seen to be the prime harbingers of divisionism. A prisoner at Nsinda confessed that 'I never thought I would see this country again, I have been living in this country without seeing it. I am sure many things have changed' (Internews 31 January 2003). Jomba Gakumba instructed the *ingando* participants:

'You have been in prison for long and I want to tell you that Rwanda is no longer the same' (Sabiiti for NTK, 28 February 2007). From 2003 when the releases commenced until 2007, approximately 56,000 released prisoners participated in *ingando*.

'Erasing of old beliefs', 'erasing of political ideologies of previous regime', 'reorientation', 'reorienting of minds' and 'sensitization' were frequently deployed descriptions by a variety of reporters. *Ingando* was further described as teaching the participants how to be 'good citizens' (Hirondelle 6 May 2003), aiding their 'harmonious integration into society' (AFP 27 January 2003) or 'rehabilitation into society' (Internews 26 February 2003), helping them 'learn how to lead a normal life again' (Xinhua 23 April 2004), 'how to better associate with members of their own communities' (Ntambara for NTK, 28 February 2007). 'After being out of touch with the ordinary people,' a reporter explains to his audience, 'there is a need for them to be taught about what the new Rwanda needs. It is not division but unity' (ibid.). A participant at Kucikiro camp says that 'we learn that there are no Hutu, Tutsi or Twa, we are all and only Rwandans' (AFP 12 August 2005).

The second group of participants comprises those who need to be most in line with the official discourses and rules. On the whole, these are not recent returnees to their communities; their transition is not physical but instead symbolic, the attempt is to consolidate desired ideologies. This group comprises the educated elite, mainly university entrants in Rwanda and Rwandans studying abroad, teachers and education officers, government officials, but it also includes the less educated or uneducated youth. Educated youth is 'especially important' because they are 'the future leaders, the future elite'.[41] The participants realize this: 'They [the government] know we will become valuable, we will work for the country, so we are here to be well prepared'.[42] Another student also suggested that '*ingando* is to give information to the intellectuals, the *abanyabwenge*'.[43] Educated youth are in fact constituted both as hope and as potential danger – it was the elite that planned the genocide, after all. The uneducated youth are simply construed as the potential danger – it was the uneducated youth who carried out the genocide. NURC focuses exclusively on 'future elites' while non-governmental organizations (different churches) organize *ingando* for the rest.

Finally, the third category comprises groups perceived as under-socialized, unsocialized, or as social deviants (deviating not only from laws but social norms). The groups targeted include sex workers, street sellers,[44] children born in prisons and street children. Prison-born children growing up in foster families (from the age of three) are sent to 're-education centres' at around age fourteen. There they gain 'an understanding of politics', and are shown 'how one lives in good harmony with other members in the society'.[45] After my comment that 'these children have not done anything', one of my three interlocutors explained that it is community perceptions and anxieties that are targeted: 'Yes it is true [they are innocent], and it is precisely to allay the fears of the community why they are sent there. It is to show that these children have not participated, and they are sensitized to co-exist with others. It is to show the population that this is not their fault, it is the fault of the adults'.[46] The logic here of course deserves scrutiny. Arguably, anxieties are as much constituted as they are (allegedly) allayed through such targeting. It is also unclear whether it is indeed the 'community' as claimed, or rather the government, that is doing the perceiving.

In this last category, I am most familiar with the *ingando* for street children. The re-education of street children (*abana bo muhanda*, informally *mayibobo*) includes many lessons that can be found in other *ingando* – lessons on the history of Rwanda, the genocide, the fight against genocide ideology, Vision 2020 – but it takes place in a unique setting. While most *ingando* camps are simple structures in remote areas, some purposefully trying to demonstrate the 'hardships of life' to their participants, for street children the strategy is reversed – they have to be given an incentive to stay. 'If you put them [say] in the Gishari [camp], they will run away, all of them. [So instead] they live in a guest house [at the outskirts of Rwamagana], they eat well, they get enough food, they drink soda.'[47]

When I first entered the spacious *ingando* classroom, I was immediately overwhelmed by a restless and unconstrained energy, limbs flying everywhere, there was curiosity, laughter and loud talk. The movement and excitement contrasted strongly with the more contained energy in the other *ingando* camps. I was told that the *abajene* (an appellation for the group formed from the French word *jeune* or 'young') require 'intervention' because their way of life is associated with 'social evils'. The Street Children Unit Coordinator at MIGEPROF explained: 'Some of them spend long time in the streets, some [are] already using drugs, [there is] no discipline, [they] become thieves, stealing, fighting between them causing insecurity'.[48] Street children are seen to lie 'outside' of the social order of society but this has to change: they need to learn 'the love of work, they have to fight like the other children, like the other Rwandese'.[49] The *abajene* need to find their place in the national development programme too. As one of the *ingando* teachers emphasized to me, 'there is the Vision 2020 and they should know where they fit in achieving it'.[50]

Interpretations and Analysis of Components

Moving away from targeting, the present section considers *ingando*'s contents, specifically its three key components of military training, lectures and cultural activities. The aim is to understand what happens in these activities, how the participants interpret them, as well as how they interpret the 'main objective' of *ingando* – what *ingando* is 'all about'. The section draws on a variety of sources[51] but special accent will be placed on the Nkumba *ingando* for university entrants. This is the 'flagship' *ingando* organized by NURC, which is meant to 'bring together' young people from different backgrounds – Hutu and Tutsi, survivors and returnees. As such, it is meant to (in addition to other aspects) 'enact coexistence'. There is also an aspect of a rite of transition into adulthood and age-grade formation in this particular *ingando*.

Nkumba is 'like a military camp, we behave like an army', a participant tells me. Indeed, the camp is run by soldiers and all participants change into khaki uniforms and gumboots upon arrival. Civilian clothes are allowed only when students wash their uniforms. The participants are addressed by the group appellation *wanakosi* or *kos* in short, a military jargon of the RPF/RPA dating to the 1990–1994 war and designating 'military recruits'. The *kos* are divided into brigades, platoons and sections, each with its own leader. Each student has a paper card with their name, company, platoon and section number stapled to the uniform. 'RDF' (Rwanda Defence Forces) is sewn on the pocket flap just above the heart. The TIG camps for ex-prisoners are organized in the same way though there are no military drills or military clothing. But while physical and military exercises are unique to camps such as Nkumba and Gako, the military accent on discipline and uniformity characterizes all *ingando*. Commands with set replies intersperse lectures as well as the evening gatherings of song and dance: '*Morali!*' (morale!) calls out a soldier walking between the rows of students gathered for the evening *utemaduni*. '*Mizuri!*' (good!) they call back. This type of call-and-reply can be found in other *ingando* as well: '*Kos!*' shouts an organizer at Mutobo *ingando* for adult ex-combatants, '*Umoja!*' (unity!) all reply in unison. '*Abajene!*' calls out the coordinator at the *ingando* for street children, '*Imbaraga z'igihugu*' (the strength of the country) the crowd shouts back. 'TIG!' calls out the disciplinarian/animator in the labour camp, '*Ubumwe n'ubwiyunge na duterimbere!*' (unity, reconciliation and progress!), the *tigistes* call back.

How do Nkumba participants interpret the inclusion of military training? Why is it such a pronounced aspect of camps organized by a commission of 'National Unity and Reconciliation'? There are three main classes of response. Some suggest that military training changes non-desirable social attitudes, others suggest it builds desired personal attributes and a number of others conjecture that it serves for actual physical defence. Some respondents mentioned that military training is included to demystify the gun, to bring people to stop fearing soldiers and 'military matters', and make them rise in respect by gaining valued skills. Many students believe that military training is included to build desired personal attributes. The training is included 'to change our mentality'. Participants acquire the 'spirit of the soldier' (morale or *esprit de corps*), they become more disciplined and patriotic, they learn how 'not to be lazy, to be active'. Many students also relay that military training is included 'to defend your nation in any way' or for self-defence. 'The objective is basic self-defence when necessary', explained a young girl, a student of social work. 'They give you an AK47 and you shoot it', reminisces a future agricultural engineer. 'There are some cases, some girls don't want to do it. [But the idea is] that everyone can defend themselves, during genocide [people] could not be rescued because they had no military training.'

All of these aspects speak to the functions of militariness in the camps but they leave out an important integrative effect – the impact of militariness on the type of learning and unity that 'happen' in the camp. As the students themselves often recounted to me, while at the beginning they feared that the organizers wanted to make soldiers out of them, they quickly realized that this was not the case. *Ingando* is not a proper 'military service', which is not to say that the compulsory military component is negligible or unproblematic. But besides the specific exercises, there is also the military format of the camp that is essential. A military camp is a unique space where the military worldview is put into practice. Militariness is meant to create order and 'open up the mind for learning'.[52] A military context is also where three very specific unities are enacted and reinforced. First, there is solidification of in-group identity – the creation of a 'greater us' against the 'other' that threatens and that we prepare to fight. Second, there is homogenization and uniformity – all are dressed and treated the same, all respond not only instantly but equally. Finally, there is coherence – everyone is an inseparable part of a broader project to which they have to submit themselves, they act in unison and in a coordinated way. One student emphasized this dynamic explicitly: 'When they impose those disciplines, you feel the same people, you are one person'.

The context in which classes take place is also revelatory of the type of learning that happens. The lecture theatre is always a single spacious room made to accommodate hundreds of people. This is one reason why *ingando* lectures resemble large sensitization sessions, where incantation crowds out critical thinking. Though in Nkumba two half-hour question and answer sessions are included in each day-long lecture, it is simply not possible to create an in-depth discussion. The aim of *ingando* is to get to many people fast. In Butare, a professor at the National University of Rwanda confessed:

> Me, I was invited [to Nkumba *ingando*], but we professors, we are not comfortable in that space, [there is] no time for debate ... I went there once, there were 800 people, it is too many people, they cannot discuss enough. So I say 'no' [now] but don't tell Fatuma! [he smiles]. They are politicians, they are doing their business.[53]

In Nkumba, lengthy critical reflection is in direct clash not only with the mass nature of the education but with the military accent on immediate, unquestioning and coordinated response. Response of this kind directly enters the classroom in the form of interspersed call-and-reply slogans, which are meant to refocus attention.

The disciplining is not always successful and there is enough of both direct and indirect 'exit' as students sneak out of the classroom, doze off, wander off in their thoughts or chat with those sitting next to them. Neither the eagle eyes of the disciplinarian seated in front, nor the soldiers passing through the rows can completely prevent this, never mind the calls and the punishments. Neither does the constant disciplining avert open disagreement when sensitive topics such as religion are touched. In one particular lecture discussing materialism and idealism (described in detail in Chapter Ten), murmurs, critical commentaries and songs of protest directly entered the *ingando* classroom. In such rare situations of collective upheaval, students use the word 'brainwashing' indignantly and against the government. After that particular class, a young girl stopped me: 'Do you also think there is no god? I cannot accept this!' Another student suggested that through lectures such as these, *ingando* does negative work: 'In the philosophy [lesson], they were telling us that god does not exist ... they are somehow teaching us to kill each other! They should teach that god loves all of us, Hutu, Tutsi, Twa, that we are all children of god.'

The diverse lessons taught in *ingando* fall under the common rubric of 'civic education'. The analysis of educational content again shows that topics beyond strictly unity and reconciliation are being taught. In Nkumba, classes span from philosophy (materialism versus idealism) to state economic policies (Vision 2020 and poverty reduction policies), family planning, the fight against divisionism and genocide ideology, the role of police forces and security forces in 'social integration and national reconciliation', among others. History classes are part of every *ingando*. Lake Muhazi and Mutobo *ingando* for former ex-combatants also include classes on various state policies so that the participants get a 'clear picture of their country'.[54] The official class list at Mutobo includes thirty-five different classes, among them patriotism, personal and community hygiene, decentralization or the role of youth in development. The Muhazi camp for child ex-combatants includes twenty-four different lessons in 'civic education', including again various history classes, classes on STDs and HIV sensitization, classes on prevention of malaria, patriotism, the role of police and community policing. The *ingando* for child ex-combatants also include basic literacy and numeracy programmes, 're-socializing activities' (e.g., learning 'household tasks' such as sweeping and carrying water) and psycho-social support. A similar list applies to TIG camps though there accent also lies on 'how to live with others, the survivors'.[55] The street children's *ingando* also includes a variety of lessons, including lessons on history, 'the love of work', Vision 2020, or hygiene and health.

As with other unity and reconciliation activities, what we witness is the interpenetration of themes with the overarching goal of achieving the desired transformation of the participants into citizens fit for the new Rwanda. The vocabulary of transformation permeates the student responses. *Ingando* 'brings them [the students] together to shape their mind'. The aim is to 'reform the young people', 'civilize them', 'open them', 'to prepare them in mind', 'to change their mentality', 'change their mental comportment'. 'The main intention', a history student tells me, 'is to rebuild the youth, [to bring] mindset change.' Another student in clinical psychology suggests that '[the aim of *ingando*] is for that culture of divisionism, that culture of not having patriotism, that culture of genocide, to eradicate them in us'.

The key place of transformation is also overwhelmingly affirmed in the Mutobo responses. An ex-combatant from Muringa proposed that *ingando*'s aim is for 'those who were in the forest [in the DRC] to remove their outside opinions'. Another man from Rurimba suggested that the goal is 'to remove from our heads ideas that are not up to date'. A number of other respondents claimed that *ingando* changes a person 'in removing bad ideas and replacing these with good ideas', 'in eradicating bad understanding (*imyumvire*)', 'in giving good constructive ideology (*ingengabitekerezo*) and removing destructive ideology', 'in removing the ideology of the forest'.

The TIG responses also highlight transformation, again using phrases such as 'good ideas' replacing 'bad ideas', 'changing bad understanding', 'removing past ideas' or 'removing all things of the past' (*ibitekerezo bya kera bimuvamo*). A young man who has spent nine months in the camp suggested that the courses are intended to 'help us leave our past ideas behind' – *kuva maricuraburindi* – literally, to come out of darkness. Another man suggested that '*ingando* can change a person because you get many courses on distinguishing the good things from the bad things (*kuvangura ibyiza mu bibi*)'. Because of the 'courses given', suggested another, elderly man with two years of TIG as his reduced sentence, '*ingando* can change a person who was bad to be good, even in his heart'. Finally, a man with a rather lengthy, six-year sentence mentioned that *ingando*'s goal is 'to bring in a good way a perpetrator' – the word *gugorora* that he used, my translator explained to me, means literally to 'straighten', just like one straightens a young tree so that it grows in the right direction.

Besides transformation, alignment comes out as key. 'The aim of *ingando* is to be told the truth', a girl studying science explained to me, 'to learn about the country and to have the same view'. The theme of unity building as consensus building thus re-emerges: 'Hutu and Tutsi used to have different ideas,' a girl chemistry student suggested, 'but after the genocide, in *ingando*, *on les met en unité* [we unify them]'. 'Before *ingando*, people know many things that make them different,' told a young man studying applied mathematics as we were seated in an empty classroom. 'After *ingando*, they know the truth, they know the things in the same manner ... they know one [a given] thing in the same sense.' Responses from ex-combatants also highlight convergence: 'The main purpose of *ingando* is to allow me to walk the same line (*kugendana mumurongo umwe*) as other Rwandans,' suggested one. Another proposed that the key is 'to know well the *umurongo* ["line, verse", translates as "line of conduct"] of our country of Rwanda that should be followed (*kwigenderaho*)'. In yet another formulation, *ingando* 'puts someone on the country's line of ideas/conduct'. In a very different context, the head of Rwanda's Centre for Conflict Management confessed that he had some sympathy for the alignment agenda: 'I prefer them [the *ingando* students] to be united rather than different, even if they are [thus] not specialized in scientific debate.'[56] In this rendering, collective acceptance at the cost of free expression and diversity of opinion is construed as a more desirable trade-off than individual critical thought at the possible cost of social division.

The camp curriculum also includes lectures that are more directly related to unity building as nation building. This includes the pre-colonial historical narrative that is compactly reproduced in all *ingando*, as well as the lessons on citizenship. In the TIG camp, as the administrator enumerated the different classes taught, I asked whether history was part of the curriculum. 'Of course, that falls under unity and reconciliation!' Indeed, history is construed as central to both reconciliation and unity. As already mentioned, this is meant to be a restorative history, opening the possibility of a life together by shifting the 'ultimate blame'. Inter-ethnic unity is of course central to the narrative itself.

Responses to the question 'What did you learn about pre-colonial history?' both within a given *ingando* and across *ingando* reproduced the standard narrative without fail. I include only one longer 'panel' (Malkki 1995) pieced together from multiple recollections:

> In pre-colonial times, there was unity among us [*bari umwe*]. Rwandans were together, they intermarried, they loved each other, they completed each other, they shared and they helped each other in everything. The kings ruled well, though nothing is pristine white/without blemish [*nta byera ngo de!*]. We were fighting together attacking our enemies. Our ancestors were heroes, willing even to die for the country. But the whites [*abazungu*] tried to make a separation, they brought sectarianism so that they could rule us. Colonialists divided our people, telling us we have three ethnies – Hutu, Tutsi and Twa. Before colonialism, there were no ethnics, only economic stratification, and things like families, like lineages, like clans, *abagesera, abatsobe, abega, abazigaba, abasinga*... Tutsi [comes] from *gutunga* – to possess – [that is the] origin of the word. [Tutsi was] *umutunzi* – rich, had cows, it was a social class. Hutu [was] someone who does not have cows, only a cultivator. Hutu [were] sometimes given cows, one, two cows ... when you arrive at ten, you leave that social class, and then you become *umutunzi, umukire,* that is to say a rich man. [Then] came the Belgians. [They] said Hutu are the short people with big noses, Tutsi are so tall, thin.

Throughout my stay, I repeatedly asked *ingando* participants what they perceived to be the 'main message' of the history course. A TIGist replied: 'To avoid the culture of ethnics. We are all one (*umoja*).' '[The message] is to leave the things of ethnicism (*ibyamoko*) that they lied to us about (*batubeshye*)', suggested another. 'The message is that all people are equal,' proposed a farmer serving a two-year sentence in TIG. 'They all have the same blood, so they must share the best of the country without discrimination (*ntawe uhenze undi* – literally "without any more extortion, deception").' Yet another man from the same camp echoed these ideas: 'The message is that we shouldn't be guided by sectarianism based on ethnics or place of origin and to know that we are all Rwandans.' Overall, the focus lay exclusively on narrating de-ethnicization even though, as an increasing number of studies show, ethnicity was not a primary motive for participation in genocide (Straus 2006; Fujii 2009) and neither is ethnic ideology the basis of conflict today.

Other important messages relating to the official *inzira y'ubumwe* (the ways of unity) are those concerning Rwandanness and Rwandanicity. All *ingando* curricula include lectures on patriotism: 'In *ingando*, we learn how to like our country in our hearts', a biology student from Ngoma tells me. We learn 'the culture of liking our country', explains another student, 'how you have to do everything good for your country'. More responses echo these points: 'Patriotism means the love of your country,' explained a physics student from Byumba. 'For example if someone attacks, [we] are ready to combat.' A talkative history student concurred: 'We are there to be taught a sense of patriotism, to defend the country if possible ... that is why a little military practice [is included].' The administrator of the Muhazi camp also confirmed these readings: 'That is the essence of military training... military training instils patriotism in people'.[57] *Ingando* songs reflect this patriotic zeal. Consider the lyrics of a popular song at Nkumba called 'I will protect your frontier Rwanda':

> What will I do to protect?
> I will stand on your frontier Rwanda
> I will watch all the people that come towards you
> I will let in those who carry a peace basket of unity and reconciliation
> I will prevent from coming those who carry anything else till I convince them
> Rwanda I love you

All *ingando* also include an evening gathering of song and dance called *igitaramo* or *igitamaduni*. When the Nkumba *igitaramo* starts, it is already dark. Hundreds of students are seated in neat rows on a grass clearing in front of the canteen, girls on the left and boys on the right. Everyone is singing and clapping to the fast rhythm of the song. The soldiers who run the camp are walking in between the long rows holding a wooden stick, they are singing along. One of the participants, an *animateur*, is running in half-squat along the front rows, urging everyone with his outstretched hands and high-pitched ululations to step up the energy of the song. The more intense the song gets, the more ululations emanate from the crowd. Up front, there is a small group of drummers and dancers. Two boys are dancing up front, with whistles in their mouth and hands outstretched wide above their head imitating the horns of the Ankole cattle. At some points there is tugging at the jackets to symbolize the milking of a cow. The traditional 'cow dance' is called *guhamiriza* for boys and *gushayaya* for girls.

Clearly, the more salient purpose of including *igitaramo* is to re-learn 'Rwandan culture'. In the words of a student, *gitaramo* is included because 'it is the Rwandan culture. [In the past it used to happen] for the king or other leaders, they [would] tell stories, sing, provide entertainment.' Another reason seems to be the sense of togetherness produced by a mass of bodies joined in song, joined by a single rhythm, movement, utterance and shared enjoyment. A student told me how 'in Rwandan culture, when we sing that means we are one'. Others explain *gitaramo* simply as 'entertainment'.

Though *ingando*'s *gitaramo* certainly bears a parallel to the pre-colonial dynastic tradition of learning 'high culture' by the chosen groups of *itorero* (Bale 2002: 37), the contents of songs clearly reveal that a rather contemporary unity-building agenda is being served first and foremost. The refrain of one of the Nkumba songs has already been reproduced above. Another song from Nkumba espouses a similar message: 'The real man is the one who fulfils the duties that he has been mandated; we support unity and reconciliation, even those boys want it, we support unity and reconciliation.' A song from *ingando* for released prisoners (reproduced in Cacioppo 2005: 10) again promotes a very programmatic message:

> This is what we want: unity, reconciliation, brotherhood, and peace …
> This is the time for guaranteed peace and the time for joy –
> Whoever does not want to unite should be removed from amongst us.
> This is the time for joy –
> Whoever does not want *gacaca* should be removed from amongst us.
> This is the time for joy –
> Whoever is not happy should be removed from amongst us.

The Main Goal of *Ingando*: What Are the Camps 'All About'?

'According to you, what is the main objective of *ingando*?' This was the question I posed most consistently, with the hope of answering another, a slightly more pointed query: Where does unity building come in? Or else, what is unity building according to these responses? Interestingly, and as already insinuated, consensus emerged as one of the key themes. The notion of bringing people 'to accord' or 'on the same line' appeared repeatedly. Convergence was unity, and unity-as-convergence was the end point of the process of reconciliation. The story of the past represents one such key consensus. The main objective of *ingando*, I was told by a former participant, 'is to have the same ideas about the history of our country'.[58] The revisited and standardized historical narrative is indeed the centrepiece of *ingando*. Overall, the word 'convergent' might eventually be more fitting than the word 'consensual' in describing the learning experience of *ingando*: the key *ingando* narratives have not been arrived at through a free public debate resulting in agreement and are not open to public critique or rejection.

While waiting by the side of the road outside Kabuga in the Eastern province, I was approached by a bespectacled primary school teacher, currently 'begging for a job'. Suddenly and swiftly he pulled out a rolled teaching certificate from inside his shirt sleeve through the tight cuff and pointed to the valley where he had just visited a school. The teacher told me his version of history and *ingando* history teaching. He fled with the masses of other Hutu to the DRC in 1994. Back in Rwanda, after years of work, '*gacaca* accused him' and he was imprisoned. After seven years he was released because 'they realized I was innocent'. He attended an *ingando* for returnees in Nyagasambu in 1997 and described it in a dismissive way: 'What can you teach me on top of what I know? What do you want to teach me about co-habitation, I know how to coexist, I know my history ... These people [teaching me] who have come after I even left my country'.[59] The new official history inspires distrust and cynicism for the same reasons that the unity and reconciliation project as a whole draws them. Coexistence and unity among Rwandans are being narrated, implemented and overseen by a narrow elite presiding over an authoritarian regime.

The theme of convergence reaches beyond history. Convergence is even built into the *ingando* reconciliation imaginary. An *ingando* coordinator explains that 'people cannot be reconciled if they have not talked together ... [In *ingando*] people sit together, sort differences, see things in the same way'.[60] In a passionate and lengthy explication, the coordinator continued to draw out the political dimension of convergence. The students destined for *ingando*, he emphasized, need 'one way of looking at things, especially government policy'.[61] *Ingando* is there, after all, to teach participants how 'to defend the country and the policy of the country'.[62] In this rendering, the love of nation is being conflated with allegiance to the policies of the government.

Ingando camps are indeed a fundamentally politicized form of education, not only because politics and specific policies are part of the curriculum ('in *ingando* the government makes its programme known'), or because convergence and the 'defence' of policies of the ruling party are being openly cultivated, thus solidifying its grasp on power, but also because the state takes a keen interest in these specific groups and their transformation into an 'ideal citizen'. Interestingly, the value and faith placed in the transformation process makes *lavage de cerveau* (brainwashing) an ambiguous term in Rwanda. While some Rwandans use the term *lavage* to automatically dismiss *ingando*, others see the same process as an intended and necessary 'cleansing of people's minds'.[63] 'Mindset change', after all, has become a true stock phrase of the government, referencing the 'taking out' of bad mentalities and their 'replacement' by constructive ideas and attitudes.

With the above in mind, we can now better 'place' the component of military training. To simply conclude that *ingando* are 'military training camps' is perhaps to miss the bigger picture. Such a conclusion overlooks the political, and within it the transformative and the conformative that is essential to Rwandan governmentality. Today, the Rwandan government uses the space of the *ingando* camp primarily to try and effectuate a desired transformation – to create what they call a new citizen, but which in effect is an ideal government subject. The RPF believes it has created the contours of a New Rwanda, and now it needs to transmit the attitudes, behaviours and knowledge that underlie it. Through the lens of *ingando* and civic education more broadly, nation building and consent building are indeed inseparable.

Notes

1. The typical day is reconstructed on the basis of forty interviews with students at the National University of Rwanda (Huye Campus) in February 2009.
2. *Ingando* was described to me as a unity and reconciliation tool even in my first interview with the administrator of Nkumba *ingando*, 23 March 2008.
3. A Rwandan working in the legal profession at the international level. The court document was accessed on 20 June 2014.
4. See NURC website: http://www.nurc.gov.rw/index.php?option=com_content&view=article&id=50&Itemid=12
5. Interview with the director of programmes at the National Youth Council, 13 January 2009.
6. Local NGO of elderly community members aiming to revitalize Rwandan culture (in Gashanana 2005: 9).
7. This was suggested by General Rusagara, an *ingando* camp instructor (NTK, 1 March 2006).
8. Interview with the Muhazi camp coordinator, 28 January 2009.
9. Interview with the Ombudsman, 14 January 2009.
10. Ibid.
11. Interview with an 'independent consultant' and author of a manuscript on RPF history, 22 January 2009.
12. Ibid.
13. Ibid.
14. Ibid.

15. Interview with an 'independent consultant' and author of a manuscript on RPF history, op. cit.
16. Kagame reminiscing on the late 1990s (in Kinzer 2008: 215).
17. New Vision Uganda, 2008, 'District Officials to Train at Kyankwanzi'.
18. New Vision Uganda, 23 June 2014, 'Judiciary explains why magistrates went to Kyankwanzi'.
19. The Independent, 14 February 2014, 'How Museveni "ambushed" Mbabazi campaign camp'.
20. Interview with the director of programmes at the National Youth Council, op. cit.
21. Ibid.
22. Ibid.
23. Ibid.
24. Interview with the director of a language centre at a Rwandan university, 10 March 2009.
25. Interview with the Muhazi camp coordinator, 28 January 2009.
26. Interview with a communications adviser at the RPF Secretariat, 23 March 2009.
27. Interview with Bernard, 13 February 2009. Bernard participated in one of these *ingando* camps.
28. About 6,000 university entrants pass annually through Nkumba *ingando* alone; in the years 2009–2012 NURC estimated that 50,000 students would have gone through the camps (NURC 2009a).
29. NURC collaborates with the ministries of Education, Foreign Affairs, Defense and the Student Financing Agency of Rwanda (SFAR).
30. While there is no law requiring attendance, it is far from voluntary. According to HRW (2000), participants attend because they feel obliged to do so or have been told by the authorities that they must. Returning refugees would be unable to find a job without attending, and students on government scholarships cannot proceed to university without civic education in the camps. A NURC employee told me students have to show their *ingando* certificate before entering university.
31. The amount of 'schooling' per day might vary, and is in fact inversely proportional to the length of the camp, with longer *ingando* having less intense daily education programmes.
32. Interview with Bernard, 13 February 2009.
33. Naturally, retreats are used all around the world by large and small corporations to create a sense of 'togetherness' among people.
34. Interview with an employee at the East Rwanda Association of the Adventist Church, 21 January 2009.
35. Visit to Kageyo *ingando* at the Tanzania border, op. cit.
36. Interview with an employee at the National Youth Council and former *ingando* organizer, 13 January 2009.
37. Ibid.
38. The administrator of Mutobo camp: '[The plan is] by 2020, everyone has passed there'. The administrator of the Nkumba camp: '*Ingando* is for all Rwandese ... but not all attend due to money and time constraints'. Mgbako (2005: 209): 'The NURC National Plan is for every Rwandan of majority age to attend *ingando* at some point during his or her life'.

39. Interview with the Muhazi camp coordinator, op. cit.
40. By 1997, 44,000 'new-caseload' refugees passed through solidarity camps (AFP, 19 November 1997).
41. Interview with the Nkumba camp coordinator, Kigali, 26 March 2008.
42. Interview with a Nkumba *ingando* participant, Butare, 6 February 2009.
43. Interview with another Nkumba *ingando* participant, Butare, 4 February 2009.
44. 'The police associate hawking ... and the wandering way of doing business with social evils' (Barigye for NTK, 29 December 2008).
45. Interview with 'Association de Solidarité des Femmes Rwandaises' (ASOFERWA) employees, 3 November 2008.
46. Ibid.
47. Ibid.
48. Interview in Kigali, 16 February 2009.
49. Ibid.
50. A short interlude by one of the caretakers/teachers at the Rwamagana *ingando*, 16 March 2009.
51. Observation, informal discussions, semi-structured interviews and questionnaires gathered from very different types of participants – university students (who completed *ingando*), adult ex-combatants (undergoing *ingando*), and released prisoners (undergoing *ingando* wa TIG).
52. Interview with Bernard, a MINALOC employee, 12 March 2009.
53. Interview with the head of the Conflict Management Centre, Butare, 4 February 2009.
54. Interview with the Muhazi camp coordinator, 28 January 2009.
55. Interview with one of the coordinators of the TIG *ingando* at Gasabo, 4 March 2009.
56. Interview with the head of the Centre for Conflict Management, op. cit.
57. Interview with the Muhazi camp coordinator, op. cit.
58. Interview with a researcher at the Office of the Ombudsman, 14 January 2009.
59. Informal discussion at Kabuga ka Musha, 28 January 2009.
60. Interview with the Muhazi *ingando* coordinator, 28 January 2009.
61. Ibid.
62. Ibid.
63. Interview with the director of the language centre at a Rwandan university, 10 March 2009.

9

Rights of Passage
Liminality and the Reproduction of Power

Following instructions from the previous day, I get off the bus at the Kabuga ka Musha crossing, close to the town of Rwamagana. I wait for a long time at the side of the road, intermittently peering into the valley and glancing at the feeder road with the sign 'RDRC Child Ex-Combatants Rehabilitation Center, 9km'. Finally, Theo arrives in his pick-up truck and signals with his lights for me to come over. 'Sorry for being so late but I was cleaning the car, you see yesterday I was bringing some kids over from the Mutobo camp and they threw up, they are not used to travelling in the car and all those curves.' Theo was referring to the new group of *ingando* participants, boys recently demobilized from DRC-based militias and housed temporarily in a camp up north. 'Why is the camp located at the lake?' I ask as we gently bump forward on the dirt track. 'It is to avoid distraction. If the camp were at the side of the road say, then we are trying to give them one direction, and the outside is pulling them in another. We are trying to create a circle, we are trying to settle their mind.'[1]

Ingando is not just a 'school', a set of lessons and a type of instruction. The camp is meant to be a more wholesome transformatory tool drawing on symbolic, spatial and performative aspects of experience. Camping is meant to do the desired work not only through contents but contexts, not only through what participants learn in class, singing sessions or military parades, but where, with whom and how these take place. Using a spatio-temporal analysis and combining *ingando*'s two salient features in this respect – separation and transition – the chapter theorizes the camp as a strategic liminality, a state-tailored rite of passage to the official rules, ideologies and desired roles of RPF-led Rwanda. The aim is to demonstrate how multiple registers of a person's experience are used in an effort at transformation, and as such, the varied ways in which liminality as 'dislocated temporality'

(Ramadan 2012) and suspension of the common in 'a life in brackets' (Turner, S. 1999) is deployed in the working of state power. In contrast to a typical understanding of liminality (Turner, V. 1969 and 1967; Gennep 1960), *ingando* is not chiefly about rupture and transition. Though disruption is certainly intended and enacted in multiple ways from physical to symbolic, ultimately this is meant to serve the broader purpose of 'incorporation' of a person into a political system and consolidation of a particular state-citizen bond. *Ingando*'s liminality then arises as a complex social field – a concrete space of both temporary de-structuring of routine and a hyper-structure of new rules – and a broader tool that, far from 'representing' anti-structure or inter-structure (Turner, V. 1969), in fact represents an additional and perhaps unique form of social structuring. As will be shown, the camp's spatial and symbolic aspects are meant to serve as additional devices in the reproduction of a particular political order.

A Crucial Ingredient: The Spatial and Performative Nature of *Ingando*

The goals of *ingando* are transition and transformation. But why is camping chosen? Why this particular form of experience? What are the effects of camping that other forms of 'schooling' cannot achieve? Separation and concentration are perhaps the most salient spatio-temporal aspects 'put to work'. But besides the de-structuring aspect of removing a person from routine experience, *ingando* is also noteworthy for its almost hyper-structured time and space. Last but not least, the camp is a space of symbolic enacting – a space for staging the desired metaphorical exchange between body and mind whereby physical leaving, dislocation and enaction are meant to induce conceptual 'leaving' and adoption. Hence it is essential to try and read the camps' particular spatial and performative 'traffic in symbols' (Mortland 1987). The symbols also communicate the key values and meta-metaphors of the political system. It is through the experiential incorporation of this symbolic order (a *sous-texte* to lectures) that, in turn, a broader socio-political incorporation is meant to happen.

A Camp: Separation and Concentration

Ingando's participants are 'distanced' from the outside in different ways. The camp is a bounded space in a remote location. For the incoming group, the place is 'far away from home'.[2] Participants are not familiar with the surroundings, the people ('you go with people you don't even know'[3]) or the style of life. Altogether, people are 'out of their element'. The attempt is to create a complete separation from the outside and from the before.

Remoteness assures a lack of distractions and concentration on the goal.[4] It creates the possibility of undivided attention ('outside the camp everyone is in his business, here we concentrate'). A good example is the *ingando* for ex-combatants constructed nine kilometres off the paved road at one of the multiple crevices of Lake Muhazi with the explicit purpose of 'removing' the *ingando* participants from contact with society. An Adventist church functionary suggested that in their tented camps 'participants are protected from the bad influences of their parents because they are far'.[5]

Concentration is key in yet another sense – a camp is a concentration of people. This has two governance functions. First, it is logistically easier to sensitize people en masse ('it becomes easier for many people to know many things in the same place'[6]). It is also the most expedient way to separate out a social segment for tailored sensitization ('you have to bring them together to shape their mind'[7]). Second, *ingando* camps that mix different social groups (perpetrators, victims, returnees, etc.) are meant to serve as 'laboratories of coexistence'. 'You cannot reconcile people if they are not together [in direct contact],'[8] an *ingando* participant explains to me. 'People cannot be reconciled if they have not talked together,' a camp organizer echoes the same idea.[9] But since *ingando* are not spontaneous but orchestrated concentrations, they constitute 'simulated communalities'. Participants nonetheless have to communicate and interact. *Ingando* forces them to 'be together' in the most extreme sense – to live together in close proximity, sharing aspects of life normally shared only within the family context (e.g., dining, hygiene, sleeping quarters, sometimes beds). Finally, concentration is key from the viewpoint of content as well. Every *ingando* has a tight schedule packed with activities and lessons; it is meant to be *l'école accélérée*,[10] an intensive course.

The proximity and face-to-face contact that *ingando* engineers are believed to be significant from the viewpoint of transformation. In general (and this is relevant to all sensitization activities), the belief is that 'the message gets in better when they can see you [the speaker]'.[11] Singing and dancing in particular are believed to create mutual confidence and openness. On my visit to the TIG camp, an administrator called for an ad hoc *igitaramo* session, explaining: 'You will sing and dance a little with them, this will motivate them, this will open them to you, after that you can ask them anything and they will do it'. I did not resist but seeing the men walk slowly back to the camp after a morning of hard labour on the local road, my passive acceptance weighted heavily on my conscience. Soon my shame was covered in a cloud of orange dust stomped up by many feet. The energy of the song picked up and the circle of people swelled, there were soon two hundred of us clapping to the rhythm and singing, observing the *intore* troupe in the middle. The full paradox of this enforced togetherness, an imposed show of high culture on the back of sweat, was now visible and gnawing at me. Not only was this show directly my doing, I was there to introduce a further practice of extraction, with uncertain return to those around me.

Though dancing, singing, chatting and 'experiencing together' are part of the cultural repertoire of connection, and undoubtedly have the potential to create fraternality and familiarity with strangers however durable or fleeting, the challenge might be precisely to extend that potential across the social divisions that today are most pervasive. Naturally, there are important limits to 'building bridges' through song and dance in spaces such as *ingando*. A Hutu government employee confessed that 'when you dance with people [normally] they open up, so [before asking questions] at Mutobo *ingando*, we tried that but it did not work … They [the ex-combatants] have strategic information. [These men] they looked at us as if we were from a different world.'[12]

Internal Structure: Order and Hierarchy

Inside the camp, physical space and time are highly structured, reflecting the importance of order and rules, hierarchies and authority. Every camp has a detailed time schedule, which breaks the day down almost to the hour. Most *ingando* camps also assure order and indirect control by organizing participants according to a military hierarchy, dividing them into companies,[13] platoons and sections, with leaders called *kapita*. The camp is carefully divided into administrative quarters, dorms for participants, a common dining area, a clearing for physical exercise or other types of gathering, and a centrally-located spacious amphitheatre, in some cases called the 'Pentagon' (sometimes made in the form of a pentagon) or *l'école* where participants gather for classes and the evening *igitaramo*.

The 'Pentagon' of the TIG camp in Gikomero is an impressive feat of makeshift wooden architecture – a round enclosed arena with a rising scaffolding of benches, in front of which rises a balcony, a pulpit really, where the administrators and teachers deliver their lessons and oversee the evening *igitaramo*. Even in the tented and makeshift Adventist *ingando* lost among the hills of the Akagera Park, space is carefully ordered. An improvised revolving wooden door gives way to the area of the 'political headquarters' (administrators' area) with the main tent referred to as the 'White House'. In front of a large clearing rises a wooden tribune where the administrators or invited speakers deliver their message. The centrality of the lecture theatre in the spatial order further underlines the centrality of the transformation project itself.

More broadly, legible and structured order 'makes it easier for the government to come and teach', explains an *ingando* participant.[14] Order is directly linked to governmentality objectives through its effects of easing surveillance and increasing control. Space and time are disciplined as must be the 'being in them' of participants. 'Discipline is key for us', an *ingando* administrator tells me, pointing to hundreds of young people gathered on a grass clearing in front of the makeshift stage, 'See, all of them have numbers, and they cannot move from the spot unless allowed'. In her speech at that same *ingando*, NURC's Director of Civic Education highlighted lack of discipline as one of the reasons for genocide.[15]

Despite the neat divisions and ordering, *ingando* and especially the central platforms from which lessons and orders emanate bring forth a distinct blurring of boundaries. Military, religious and political realms blend into each other in interesting and unobvious ways. In the Akagera *ingando* for Adventist youth, the religious figures dressed in tracksuits speak of discipline, direct the camp from a 'White House' and invite the politicians to the podium, who in turn use religious similes and symbolisms, likening their work to preaching ('I am like a preacher,' proposes a speaker from NURC to the *ingando* gathering, 'I evangelize on unity and reconciliation'). At Nkumba *ingando* for university students, the military order harnesses political learning, and at the end of a long lesson unworking God and 'idealist' thought, the lecturer hailing from the Ministry of Defence playfully calls the perplexed gathering to pray. *Ingando* is a live interaction of three powerful domains.

Enaction: Experiencing through Simulation

Enacting specific roles and experiencing certain scenarios is meant to be educative and transformative. 'One thing [is] to be told that you are Rwandan, that it is more important than other identities,' a professional for good governance at MINALOC tells me, 'but another thing to feel it, to identify with that larger group'.[16] 'In general, we want actions rather than words, [we want] change by doing',[17] suggests the director of programmes at the National Youth Council. Depending on which *ingando* we focus on, there are two to three different simulations that overlap and seek to create specific 'unities' in the space of the camp: simulation of RPF military life during the 1990–1994 war, simulation of a community where diverse people interact and experience things 'side by side,' and finally simulation of a collective rite of passage through activities of separation and transition.

During an *ingando* lunch break, seated at the back of the communal kitchen and working away at our dish of beans, maize and rice (the simpler beans-maize version is nicknamed by the students *inkoko* – chicken), a participant excitedly shares his observations: 'They want us to go through what the soldiers went through, the training, the food, this is what RPF soldiers used to eat during the war.'[18] The military format is indeed essential and, as mentioned, tends to produce specific enactments of unity – us versus the other, uniformity and coherence. Sameness or uniformity are salient themes in *ingando* – the camps try to create an almost hyperbolic experience, an absolute erasure of differential treatment. Both organizers and students repeatedly highlight sameness as the core unity-producing strategy. Uniformity at the most literal level starts with wearing a uniform. In Nkumba and Gako this is military uniform, in TIG a work uniform. More generally, *ingando* produces a uniform experience. An excited participant recounts: 'We woke up at the same time, we ran together, our beds were made the same way, we wore the same clothes, we clapped the same way, and we marched together, we were *umoja* [unity in Swahili]'.[19] A similar observation comes from another student: 'We do the same things, drink the same thing, eat the same thing, we sit and we share'.[20] 'Why do they eat beans and corn in *ingando*?' I ask Florence, a friend of mine. 'It is to show that you and me ... we are at the same level, [there is] no difference, you might be rich and me poor but we eat the same thing, we are one people.'[21] Especially in difficult situations, there can be no differentiation: 'If a case arises of survival, of struggling, you all are supposed to [do your part] ... [The *ingando* administrators] find some [puddles of] water and we all go inside, we wallow in it like pigs [to show that] you and me, we are one.'[22] This common punishment is known as *kwiviringita* – rolling in mud.

Besides uniformity with its accent on equal treatment, *ingando* uses strategies that create a sense of coherence or oneness – of being an inseparable part of a larger unit, which itself is constituted as compact. Observation and interviews yield three distinct coherence strategies: collective punishments, body coordination and the rallying call. 'If someone makes a mistake, everyone is punished, there is a kind of connection in that',[23] explains a Nkumba participant. 'Everything you do, [you do] it as a team', explains another, 'If someone makes a mistake, they punish you as one, because you are one. For example, they shout "all of you down!" even if only one person does something wrong.'[24] Military parades also enact such a sense of oneness. The very movement of bodies and limbs in coordination is meant to make an individual part of a greater unit, not only of a physical regiment but also (even if only by a figurative extension) of an intangible idea, a larger imagined community. Coordination uses the physical to help experience the intangible. Finally, all *ingando* use the rallying call, which is perhaps the most 'concentrated' act in terms of combining different performative strategies of unity. The Nkumba call and reply (*kos!* and *umoja!*) is the best example: not only does the reply involve saying 'unity' (*umoja!*), but all have to respond in the same way (uniformity) and in unison (coherence/oneness).

Ingando's Simulations: Power in Heterotopia, Power of Heterotopia

In another understanding, *ingando* are experimental alterities, simulated polities enacting a concentrated order of rules and specific social imaginaries. The framework of heterotopia (Foucault 1986, 1980a, 1980b) thus might be a good entry point to a political analysis of *ingando*, and perhaps better fitted for the task than the concept of a 'total institution' (Goffman 1957). In one sense, *ingando* certainly fits the Goffmanian frame, it encompasses a person's 'whole being' and its total character is 'symbolized by the barrier to social intercourse with the outside'. In fact, *ingando*[25] fulfils all 'totalistic features' listed by Goffman (1957: 2).[26]

Surveillance, highlighted by Goffman, is certainly present too. While the *ingando* camp itself is hidden to the outside, inside the camp, there is strong oversight. The space is small, all follow the same schedule and all wear a uniform. Individuality is lost to the 'block management of people' (Goffman 1957: 2). In the TIG camp, a table on a blackboard offers the daily counts – it is literally divided into 'blocks' and represents a schematic symbol of oversight – *abahari* (those present), *abakore* (those working), *abarwaye* (those sick). The discipline and surveillance, however, can be escaped, and so can the camp. As we look at the TIG blackboard, the administrator informs me that there are currently forty-four 'deserters'.

But while surveillance – 'a seeing to it that everyone does what he has been clearly told' (ibid.) is present, the focus on relations of compliance might obscure the core aspect of many *ingando* – and namely that it is a simulation of a desired order, tailored to each participant group. Unlike Goffman's permanent structures of prisons, sanatoriums and boarding houses, *ingando* camps are short, intense and experiential (again, TIG is an exception here). The *ingando* camps effect a separation from the mundane and familiar and represent an intense experience of full immersion without respite. They involve the enaction of new roles, of different ways of being, in some cases the breaking down of barriers and interaction with new people. The complex experience is meant to communicate to the participant and habituate them in the desired eutopic order of the new Rwanda. In order to explore the type of 'social experiments' that these camps represent, I look at the set-up and intended effects of two very different *ingando* – one for young demobilized boys repatriated to Rwanda from the DRC, the other for the future elite. The focus on two distinct versions of a heterotopia is purposeful, because while the symbolic order remains the same in each case, and the ideal type of relation to the state is always that of consent, the place in that order naturally differs.

The Muhazi ingando: *Sovereignty and Indirect Control in a Simulated Social World*

The Lake Muhazi *ingando* for child ex-combatants is an example of a particularly intense and structured experience. Though the centre comprises only one administrator and fifty-six boys (aged 14–18), the intricate social organization within the camp is striking. The administrative divisions, information networks and surveillance, as well as the attempt to 'transform behaviour' are a concentrated reflection of key aspects of the Rwandan state and its governmentality project. The camp is also an interesting political entity – a simulated sovereign world unto itself, a pseudo-polity fitted with administrative, political and judicial 'systems' but where power is concentrated in the hands of one man – the camp administrator.[27]

A number of aspects help explain why this particular *ingando* is so intense. Not only are these 'children' who are thought to be 'malleable' and the 'nation of tomorrow',[28] there are also different types of transitions that these specific cohorts have to undergo. The participants grew up or spent a number of years living with an armed group;[29] hence they need to be 'corrected' and get accustomed to 'civilian life'. The administrator explains: 'We help them in terms of behavioural change because in DRC they adapted to behaviours that are not good, now they need to be reintegrated to society'.[30] Many boys never lived with a family, yet in Rwanda the aim is to reunite them with close or distant relatives. They are 'not familiar with activities commonly carried out at home, such as fetching water, firewood, helping with the young ones,' the administrator suggests, 'they do not know the duties, the roles of the child'.[31] Many boys have also spent all or most of their life abroad so they need to be updated on the rules and ideologies of the post-genocide government. One of the main goals thus, as in most *ingando*, 'is to give them a clear picture of their country'. The length of time spent in *ingando* adds to the intensity. On average, a child ex-combatant spends months in the camp; this however depends on how fast a host relative can be identified. There are two boys who have spent more than four years in *ingando*.

The ultimate goal is the transformation and 'preparation' of the young participants for their life in Rwanda. They need to be 'recovered and updated'.[32] The administrator uses the term 'psycho-social support' though his elaboration of the term suggests it is not trauma counselling he is engaged in, but rather behavioural modification:

> [Psycho-social support] is a tool of behavioural change. When the child comes, it has some behaviours that really need to be eradicated ... I approach the child, talk to it, and see how the child is answering, to see the extent of support that is required, that it requires this direction, orientation ... I do it in a parental way. Depending on the way they are behaving, I bring them from one direction

to another direction, I show the best way to cope with their lives, and then I continue to monitor how they are socializing with their fellows.[33]

'But how is that change to be achieved?' I asked. The camp administrator spent hours explaining the intricate system and multiple strategies he has created to assure control and monitoring, which, he believed, would in turn ease measurement and help consolidate the desired change in participants. The intricate system makes the Muhazi camp not only a unique case study of the use of separation, surveillance and indirect control in an effort to discipline and 'transform' participants, but also a useful case study of a complex simulated 'polity'.

To begin with, control is attempted through the system of 'ears and eyes'. 'To learn about the behaviour of a particular participant', the coordinator tells me, 'I talk to those already changed, [asking them] what is he doing, they tell me ... Then I call him in, he is surprised how I even knew [what he was doing]. But even if I am not here, there are so many eyes. That is one system.' Another system is that of indirect control. The camp is in fact a political system of sorts, equipped with an executive and a judiciary. 'They have leadership amongst themselves. It is actually a very complicated system which I have developed',[34] the coordinator suggests proudly. There is a leader – 'something like a prefect, he is in charge of all the children in the camp. The prefect keeps changing so that everyone can get a chance to be a leader, get experience with managing his own behaviour and helping others'. Below the rank of the leader is the disciplinarian, he is responsible for discipline of all including the prefect, this is 'so that the leader is not a dictator'. Below these posts, there is a person in charge of logistics and someone else in charge of sports. 'You see, it is like a cabinet,' the coordinator suggests. Additionally, he tells me, participants are divided into sectors (rather than military formations like in other *ingando*) and the camp's daily responsibilities such as sweeping are then rotated among these groups.

Besides an executive, there is also a judiciary of sorts:

> I created a *gacaca* [too] ... it is better if they can do it [disciplining] themselves, to see the change, if we do it for them, we cannot really see the change ... The prefect or those responsible for discipline identify you and the mistakes that have been done, and report to the prefect. The prefect delegates [the case] to the chairman of the *gacaca*, the prosecutor and the judges. The *gacaca* will then call you, and will call everyone, because judgement is done in front of everyone.[35]

After thorough investigation and a private judgement by the chairmen and judges, the punishment is announced:

> 'You, Mr B., have done a mistake, for that you will be punished ... sweeping the compound for five days, carrying five jerry cans of water. The case is closed.'
> ... If, however, the accused says 'I confess, I made a mistake, I will not repeat

it again', he gets [only] three days of sweeping because he confessed. This is to install unity, reconciliation.[36] ... It is a very complicated system. Everybody has an eye on his fellow, even the leader is looking [at] *gacaca*, *gacaca* is watching the leader, everyone is watching his fellow.[37]

The Muhazi *ingando* is not only an especially intense experience aimed at transformation and reintegration of young men, it is also unique for the simulated polity that it puts in place to foster such transformation. The Muhazi camp is thus a truly unique political heterotopia, neither completely 'outside', nor quite 'inside' the broader socio-political system, rather simply in a relationship, not quite mirroring but rather refracting the wider system into a modified and concentrated form. The wider Rwandan political dynamics that get translated into the space of the camp are the social control internalized in the social body through surveillance and a system of indirect control. The attempt is also to achieve greater docility by delegating 'responsibilities' in a system of indirect governance. Muhazi *ingando* is thus an experiment of sorts of an administrative 'divide and rule'. The administrator naturally remains at the top of the complex structure, approximating the figure of a sovereign – a person who remains both above 'law'/rules and has the power to make them. This society outside society, or perhaps a 'practice society', engineered by a quasi-sovereign and manipulated to achieve specific results, is a social experiment par excellence.

The Nkumba Production: A Convergent Elite?

My translator at the Nkumba *ingando* is a young Rwandan man with a distinctly Russian name and perfect English inflected with an American accent. He grew up abroad and the family only returned to Rwanda four years ago. As we sit on the steps of the *ingando* refectory after a lecture, he asks a girl genocide survivor sitting near us: 'Are you here because you want?' 'No!' she responds resolutely, 'I am here because I am patriotic!' 'Most people, I think', he turns to me 'are here because they must ... [after a pause] But in those evenings together, something powerful happens. You feel unity, that you can fight against whomever. When people come here, they don't want to be here, when the time comes to leave, they don't want to go ... Now if war comes, our parents get tickets to fly, but we can stand and defend the country'.

If the Muhazi *ingando* represented a simulated political system, both a 'practice polity' and a system of control, the Nkumba camp is a heterotopia of a different kind, it is centered around the simulation of a military camp fitted with political education. If the 'placing in order' in the Muhazi camp revolved around behavioural change and reintegration of demilitarized youth, the Nkumba site seeks to place in order the perceived future elite of the country. The focus in this section thus lies on Nkumba *ingando*'s simulations and the learning style accentuating convergence in knowledge and opinions. Though the theme of 'convergence' pertains to all types of *ingando*, the Nkumba participants bear a unique relation to the project. Since they are proclaimed to be the 'future leaders' of the country, very relevant questions regarding the reproduction of power and an acquiescent elite arise.

A student recounts the exalted feeling after ending *ingando* at Gako military academy: 'The ride to Kigali was nothing compared to the one to Gako [*ingando*]. All the students were interacting and singing patriotic songs, even those on the streets were cheering and smiling at us ... Our culture is the same, we all live on the same land, we speak the same language and we all hope for a better Rwanda, we are all *umoja* [one].' Some students might indeed turn into true zealots after *ingando*. For others, the intense feelings and camaraderie that they experience gradually dissipate. The 'apassionates', in any case, just as the open critics, the 'dodgers' or the 'leavers' seem to be a minority. In the majority of my interviews, participant responses were rather homogeneous, and were defined by a positive attitude and a lack of critique. The large pool of consensus naturally requires a careful analysis.

Leaving aside self-selection issues, the overall positive judgement and convergence in responses is structurally determined – on the one hand, we have the dynamic of suppression (of voice and certain opinion), on the other, the dynamic of co-optation (into agreement). The result is that it is extremely difficult to 'quantify' dissent. It is hard to know what was purposefully left out, and what was said because of clear incentives/disincentives but that otherwise would not be (i.e., co-option and deterrence). At the same time, not all who do criticize automatically speak the 'truth', while all those who agree might not be automatically 'parroting propaganda', hiding away a 'private' reserve of contradictory opinion.

Yet in order to demonstrate the differences in *ingando* experience and the issues of silencing of critique, it is useful to reproduce an opinion from another student, an orphan whose parents were allegedly killed by the RPF: 'I don't think that [*ingando* creates reconciliation]. You can show people that you agree, but in your head you think another thing ... You cannot tell it because otherwise you will be imprisoned ... so you prefer to close your mouth.' The student spoke at length about the unequal treatment of suffering, the distribution of resources to genocide survivors and the neglect of other victims of violence, with the distinct result of unequal educational opportunities. The tone, the phrasing and the narrative shuttle between 'I' and 'we' all suggested that he was speaking on behalf of others: 'Segregation, which the government creates results in a big problem ... we cannot show it, but we have it in our hearts'.[38] Even those who unequivocally support *ingando* are aware of disagreement: 'Some people are not happy about it [*ingando*, saying] it is just to teach about this government ... [they say] it is to promote the RPF line. [Well], it is to promote their line, but that is good!'[39]

Despite the existence of disagreement and its emergence on the researcher's transcript, the rather uniform spoken consensus, whether genuine or not, reflects a 'success' of *ingando*. The experience cultivates convergence and achieves it too. A small number of students evade *ingando*, another small minority never finishes it, and an unknown fraction has negative attitudes towards *ingando* or its aspects, or is disinterested, bored and participating because 'they have to'. Nonetheless, the unfailing ability to reproduce learned scripts and the homogenous response suggests again that a 'unified citizen corps' has been created, even if only on the surface. While the surface accord does not mean that the government has been successful in creating lasting social harmony or agents who will sow long-term peace, it does manage to form a friendly social cohort that will take over economic and political power. The students' understanding of and alignment with the government's programme is thus crucial in power's smooth reproduction.

In other words, there are not only disincentives to disagreement but structural incentives to agreement. The students are told that they are the intelligentsia and the future leadership of the country. They are made to see themselves in those who come to teach them, and it is the government staff including high officials who come to the north to deliver their message. 'Tomorrow we will be ambassadors, ministers, presidents', a girl tells me, trying to explain why university-going youth need to undergo *ingando*. Overall, the structural dynamics in contemporary Rwanda are such that greater alignment is a strategy of success (loyalty is rewarded) whereas non-alignment (of 'dodgers', 'leavers' or 'objectors' such as Jehovah's Witnesses and open dissenters) is visible and stamps people with a question mark.

Importantly, being co-opted and brainwashed are two distinct phenomena that should not be conflated. 'Brainwashed' is a derogatory term laden with assumptions (of permanent enforced change, for example) and one that overlooks the reasons for and contexts of changed behaviour. It also puts *ingando* participants in an extremely passive position. In private or outside of Rwanda, even the 'right hands of the government' might speak differently. In a Leipzig bar, a Rwandan student did precisely that: 'In Rwanda just after the genocide, I worked for the government in Gikongoro area with youth, not just in *ingando*, also in communities as a trainer. I worked with youth persuading them about how good the RPF are'. Part of the reason why my informant did this was 'because it was a job. I saw that RPF had problems, I did not agree with it on everything, but neither did I agree with the other parties. I also did it because I wanted to know what they [youth] think and to teach them patriotism.'[40] The short excerpt is meant to demonstrate the complex dynamic and numerous reasons underlying what we witness as co-optation. In politically tense and controlled settings, people's motivations, perceptions and beliefs cannot be judged as unchanging and one-sided just because their public expression (in an unchanged regime) is.

The Nkumba heterotopia is thus again a refraction and condensation of a political order, one adjusted specifically to shape this crucial social segment – a loyal elite – that will foster rather than undermine the system and its values of discipline, regimentation and alignment, loyalty and self-sacrifice for a greater goal. The camp is both a refraction of the system and an enactment of its 'world view' through active and specific being with others in space and time.

Collective Rites of Passage to a 'New Rwanda': Liminality and the Reproduction of Power

While the framework of heterotopia is useful in extracting the political 'order' embedded within the liminal space of *ingando*, it does not help unlock another salient aspect of the camp experience – the symbolism of transition – and the ways in which transition and transience can have significance in political reproduction. The concept of 'rites of passage' can provide a useful framework, but one that needs to be interrogated and modified to fit a collective and state-engineered experience. In fact, three theoretical approaches can be combined to offer a stronger grasp on the types of rites that *ingando* camps represent – Gennep's (1960) concept of a rite of passage with three stages, Turner's (1969) analysis of rite of passage with special focus on liminality and 'communitas', and finally, Hobsbawm's (1983) concept of 'invented traditions' and their functionality in modern nation-states.

Fundamentally, both Gennep and Turner focus on rites of passage as 'tradition' in small 'face-to-face' societies (e.g., Turner's focus on Ndembu installation rites). As will be shown, their theories are nonetheless more widely applicable. Hobsbawm's (1983) brief exposé of 'invented traditions' might be more directly relevant to the dominant political ontology of the present day – the nation-state system – as it shows how 'traditions' (including 'rites of passage') introduced from above can serve socio-political purposes. *Ingando* seems to be precisely such a device, and needs to be placed within the broader proliferation of 'traditionality' in post-genocide Rwanda.

Most broadly, rites of passage are said to serve as devices to help an individual (or a group) to cope with and accommodate change ('of place, state, social position and age'; Gennep 1960: xiii). In Rwanda, we can talk of a 'social crisis' or 'collective crisis', and hence of 'collective rites'. Gennep himself refers to these in passing, calling them 'rites of intensification'[41] whose function he sees as the 'restoration of moral sentiments ... disturbed through changes in the social life of the group' (Radcliffe-Brown, in Gennep 1960: xiii) or the 'restoration of equilibrium where changes in social interaction impeded or had occurred' (Chapple and Coon, ibid.). But while *ingando* certainly emerged in the context of a post-genocide society and is narrated as a reconciliation and nation-building tool first and foremost, restorative of 'one' community, we have to read the 'equilibration' itself as political. *Ingando* is a strategic rite, a rite that is also a technology of power, a way to 'manage' incorporation of different segments of the population in a new, 'unified' political order.

The phased spatio-temporal structure of passage rites can help us further uncover the political nature of *ingando* and the ways in which the desired transformation is attempted in the camps. Rites of passage can be subdivided into rites of separation ('preliminal rites'), rites of transition ('liminal rites') and rites of incorporation ('postliminal rites') (Gennep 1960: 10). With regard to *ingando*, the very act of camping in an unfamiliar and faraway place is an act of separation. This is further strengthened by the restricted movement out of the camp and the lack of communication with the outside. Changes of clothes and other 'temporary differentiation' (Gennep 1960: 74) also represent separation. On this count, the street children undergo perhaps the most symbolic 'parting' of all – their tattered clothes are gathered and burnt collectively in a bonfire. The new clothes they are given, I was told, mean that the children can start anew, they signify the beginning of a new life.[42]

Separation rites such as these are meant to give way to the transformation that is to occur in the transitional state – liminality. Liminality is induced through separation and encompasses all the time spent in the camp. Turner wrote of the fundamental 'ambiguousness' of the liminal period in which a person 'passes through a realm that has few or none of the attributes of the past or the coming state' (Turner, V. 1969: 94). Though at one level this claim is apparently correct – there is the transient nature of camping, the hyperbole of equal treatment – we also have to remember that *ingando* is a state-organized rite, which, as discussed above, is permeated by and reflects wider political dynamics and power constellations, and is ultimately meant for specific social engineering purposes. In this sense, we need to approach critically the powerful metaphor of 'betwixt and between', 'neither here nor there' (Turner, V. 1969: 95) that so often describes liminality and conditions such as 'refugeeness'. 'Betwixt and between' might be decidedly unhelpful when trying to make sense of *ingando*.

Turner (1969) has famously argued that liminality brings about a state of 'communitas' or equality of condition – a space where people are stripped of all social markers ('disiquiliers') and submitted to 'authority that is nothing less than that of the total community', with cessation of 'society as a structured, differentiated, and often hierarchical system of politico-legal-economic positions, with many types of evaluation, separating men in terms of "more" or "less"' (Turner, V. 1969: 96). *Ingando*'s liminality might indeed bring forth physical and/or symbolic displacement and the cessation of common or known 'rules' or 'ways' of life. It might indeed be even a temporary state of 'uniform condition' (skilfully doubling as a nation-building tool in *ingando*), which includes sexlessness (e.g., the same uniform for all), anonymity (e.g., demarcation according to military nomenclature; a group name for all initiands such as *kos*) and equal treatment. Despite all this, the liminality of *ingando* is by no means a powerless and structureless state, and in fact is ridden and constructed around powerful symbols – military, political and cultural. These fuse together in a particular way and communicate an image of an order and one's expected place within it.

In *ingando*, rites of incorporation are not included though the camps as such are meant to be about incorporation of the citizen into their place in the new government-designed order. The end of *ingando* (and *itorero* as well) is marked by a long graduation ceremony and the receipt of a diploma or certificate. These are meant to serve both as closure, an end to a stage and a way to hasten identification with a new role or a different status. The certificate after all is a tangible 'proof' of 'graduation'.

The frame of passage rites capture the overall *ingando* project of 'incorporation' well. Using the 'territorial' imagination, in liminality one is said to 'waver between two worlds' (Gennep 1960) – one that initiands must forgo for another one. *Ingando* is meant as a 'threshold' and to cross the threshold is an attempt to 'unite [the initiand] with a new world' (Gennep 1960: 20). This can happen in a physical sphere (from outside to inside the country; from the prison to 'inside' the New Rwanda) and/or a symbolic sphere (from one status or way of being to another). The transformation is not meant to result only through the contents of what is being taught but also through contexts, the where and how of experience. In the space of liminality, participants are 'out of their element', they use different words and do unusual things. They are supposed to be reconstituted through this, to become someone else. In certain cases, participants are simply meant to become 'someone'. In the *ingando* for street children, the administrator points to the fidgety and buzzing gathering, 'they were no one and now they can be someone'.[43]

As novel re-appropriations of the past in service of a present goal, *ingando* may also be usefully interpreted through Hobsbawm's (1983: 1) concept of 'invented' traditions (although the term 'reimagined' might be more appropriate). Usefully, Hobsbawm suggests that new political regimes 'might seek to find their own equivalents for the traditional rites of passage', some form of a stylized acknowledgement of or an impetus for the desired transformation of their subjects (Hobsbawm 1983: 10). The Rwandan government's intensive production of 'traditionality' and collective rites reflects the broader attempt at 'separation' from its immediate past, and yet a simultaneous anchoring of the present in the pre-colonial era, which offers a sense of connection and thus a source of legitimacy.

It is here that we can finally come back to liminality as a tool in the reproduction of power. As a reinvented 'traditionality' and thus authenticized liminality, *ingando* harnesses official script reproduction and, ultimately, helps cement the cohesiveness of the current power arrangement. The reproduction in *ingando* does not hinge on making people 'believe'. The project is more surface-level but still potent – it is about the upholding of surfaces – public speech, behaviour, performance – but this is still functional for the government. So the answer to the question 'Is this all just an orchestrated show, an empty ceremony?' is 'hardly'. As Lisa Wedeen (1999) has shown with regard to the symbolic displays of Asad's public personality cult in Syria, even insincere and feigned public obeisance is 'constitutive', rather than merely 'reflective', of power. The symbolic order of *ingando* both reflects and constitutes the rules of its incorporation.

Overall, *ingando* emerges as a space of transition into the role of the 'ideal citizen' – overwhelmingly interpreted as person with obligations to rather than rightful demands on the state. In a post-genocide landscape of disruption and multiplicity, *ingando* has been indispensable to teach people what is expected of them in the 'New Rwanda Order' (Mbabazi for NTK, 14 September 2005). The camps are thus not only about participants' incorporation into their place in the new government-designed order, but also their role in defending rather than challenging a consensus about the past, the present and the future. The image of a desired subject reproduced in *ingando* is one of a person who is aligned and alignable, and as such 'one'.

The Politics of Liminality: An 'Inter-Structural' Space?

The close observation of *ingando* camps opens space for a renewed discussion of the notion of liminality itself, specifically its political dimension. This dimension has been overlooked, yet might offer a new perspective on received knowledge. *Ingando* reveals not only that liminality itself is structured by power (it is a heterotopia of a political order, a state's unique double), but that the experience as a whole is meant to have broader political effects. The academic literature is rather silent on the topic of effects, and contemporary common usage treats liminality in an uncritical manner as having the potential to build, consolidate or strengthen collective and corporate identities, to build a sense of community or nationality. *Ingando* shows that this perspective might be limiting, as liminality can similarly be about regime building, and the project of fostering commonality itself requires political analysis.

Liminality is posited to be an 'inter-structural' space (Turner, V. 1967). Again, while correct at one level, this perspective can be limiting. The study of *ingando* paints a picture of liminality as a unique structuring force first and foremost. The camps show that wider power arrangements can be reproduced directly through the deployment of liminality, and that temporary disruptions or dislocations on an individual level are still socio-political 'stabilizers' more broadly. *Ingando* hence makes us question anew the interconnection between the stylized 'in-betweenness' of camps and them being an 'interstructural' space (Turner, V. 1967: 93).

The discussion reaches much beyond *ingando* and Rwanda. Whether camps are located inside the nation-state, such as the 'internal' liminalities orchestrated in *ingando*, *itorero* or *chaka mchaka*, or are in fact extra-state, such as the 'external' liminalities of refugee camps, in neither case do these spaces represent a 'lifting of structure'. What happens instead is the reaffirmation, the very making of wider political orders through particular practices of inclusion and exclusion – into or from belonging, citizenship, roles and political 'place'. The distinction itself between 'internal' liminalities of camps aimed at incorporation, such as *ingando*, and 'external' camps marking exclusion gets blurred upon closer scrutiny. All liminalities – intra-state and extra-state alike – combine inclusion and exclusion, albeit to different degrees of depth and surface visibility. Internal spaces more vividly reproduce the elite programmes and policies of the state; but the expectations they thus consolidate leave equally clear spaces of exclusion – the citizen who is either undesirable or not (yet) desirable. External spaces mark exclusion at multiple levels, but a close study of refugee camps shows that 'inclusion' practices are present as well, even if these might be unwitting and indirect. For one, research has demonstrated how cultural hegemonies might be reproduced in the settings of the refugee camp (see Sagy 2008; Knudsen 1991; Mortland 1987 for powerful examples of this).

The lesson here is not that liminality of camps does not 'upset normalcy'. Rather, the point is that this stylized disruption on an individual level serves to cement the wider status quo of power. Lifting of certainties, extraction from habitus (Bourdieu 1977), estrangement from one's own practice of everyday life, even the state of communitas (Turner, V. 1967) might all be present in the space of the camp. But as Mortland (1987) wrote when interpreting 'enjoyment' at a refugee transition camp graduation party, the key question here is not 'whether or not these are "real" parties at which people have fun and enjoy being together; they usually do'. What is relevant is that each of these liminal happenings, however experienced, still 'state[s] ritually and symbolically the [ultimate] purpose and importance' of this social event (1987: 392).

Reading *ingando* in this way shows the camps are ultimately about propelling people on a particular path, they are about the cementing of particular social, cultural and political structures, rather than about their 'temporary dissolution'. Hence while *ingando* can in no way be read as anti-structure, it can be read both as a 'destructuring' space in the sense that it produces a dislocation from the ordinary, and certainly as 'hyperstructure' due to the meticulous organization of time, space and roles, and the dense presence of the symbolic repertoire making up the new political order.

The simultaneity does not mean balancing, however. Rather, both of these temporal dynamisms are deployed in the name of a broader social 'structuring'.

The analysis here thus goes against the typical interpretation of liminality as suspension of social structures and norms allowing 'room for alternative interpretations and potentially dangerous freedom from the convention of society' (Stepputat 1992: 35, cited in Turner, S. 1999: 7). The oft-celebrated effects of liminality – 'the undoing, dissolution, decomposition accompanied by growth, transformation, and the reformulation of old elements in new patterns' (Turner, V. 1967: 99) – might be taken advantage of for particular political purposes too, here the exigent project of social transformation, or perhaps 'formation' of a particular political subject(ivity). The liminalities of *ingando* are concentrated and stylized enactions of a post-genocide sociopolitical order and the role of any given 'member' within it – they are sites of structure, and structuring.

Notes

1. Visit to the Muhazi *ingando*, 28 January 2009.
2. Interview with an employee of the East Rwanda Association of the Adventist Church, Nyamirambo, Kigali, 21 January 2009.
3. Interview with a student *ingando* participant, Butare, 3 February 2009.
4. Interview with an *ingando* participant and ex-president of national SCUR Forum, 14 January 2009.
5. Interview with an employee of the East Rwanda Association of the Adventist Church, op. cit.
6. Coordinator of Muhazi *ingando* for child ex-combatants, 28 January 2009.
7. Interview with a Nkumba *ingando* participant at NUR, Butare, 2 February 2009.
8. Interview with a student *ingando* participant, Butare, 5 February 2009.
9. Coordinator of the Muhazi *ingando* for child ex-combatants, talking about *ingando* in general, op. cit.
10. Interview with RPF communications adviser, 23 March 2009.
11. An executive at the Ruhengeri prison referring to NURC's presentation during Unity and Reconciliation Week, 19 November 2008.
12. Interview with Bernard at the ministry after his visit to Mutobo *ingando* with a delegation from northern Uganda (seeking inspiration for activities for the conflict-affected northern region), 12 March 2009.
13. For example, the TIG camp has four companies: 'AC', 'BC', 'CC' and 'DC'.
14. Interview with a Nkumba *ingando* participant, Butare, 4 February 2009.
15. Visit to Kageyo *ingando* at the Tanzania border, 12 November 2008.
16. Interview with the 'professional for good governance', MINALOC, 12 March 2009.
17. Interview with an employee at the Rwanda National Youth Council, op. cit.

18. Visit to Nkumba *ingando*, 16 December 2008.
19. Interview with Nkumba *ingando* participant, Butare, 5 February 2009.
20. A student at NUR reflecting on the *ingando* experience, Butare, 5 February 2009.
21. Informal discussion with a NURC intern, 19 December 2008.
22. Interview with a Nkumba *ingando* participant, Butare, 5 February 2009.
23. Ibid., Butare, 6 February 2009.
24. Ibid., Butare, 4 February 2009.
25. Goffman does not mention camping retreats in his list of total institutions (interestingly he mentions a more restricted category of 'retreats from the world or training stations of the religious') but he does highlight that his list is not exhaustive.
26. 'All aspects of life are conducted in the same place and under the same single authority. Second, each phase of the member's daily activity is carried on in the immediate company of a large number of others, all of whom are treated alike and are required to do the same thing together. Third, all phases of the day's activities are tightly scheduled, with one activity leading at a prearranged time into the next, and the whole sequence of activities being imposed from above through a system of explicit formal rulings, and by a body of officials...' (Goffman 1957: 2).
27. '[Me:] How many people work here?' 'I am a manager but also a social worker, it is basically me.'
28. Interview with the Muhazi *ingando* coordinator, 28 January 2009.
29. Most of the participants come from the FDLR, but also Mai Mai, RCD Goma, Mongoli, RDD and 'other'.
30. Interview with the Muhazi *ingando* coordinator, op. cit.
31. Ibid.
32. Interview with the Muhazi *ingando* coordinator, op. cit.
33. Ibid.
34. Ibid.
35. Ibid.
36. This plays off the wider Rwandan legal system making provisions upon admission of guilt.
37. Interview with the Muhazi *ingando* coordinator, op. cit.
38. Interview in Butare, 4 February 2009.
39. Interview in Butare, 5 February 2009.
40. Interview with a Rwandan student at a University in Leipzig, Germany, 20 April 2009.
41. The term was originally used by Chapple and Coon (1942, cited in Gennep 1960: xii).
42. Discussion with one of the *ingando* administrators, Rwamagana, 16 March 2009.
43. Ibid.

Part IV
Conclusions

10

The Yeast of Change
Civic Education, Social Transformation and the New Development Corps

'Introduction to Philosophy' is a seven-hour *ingando* lecture whose inclusion on the camp curriculum might initially seem puzzling. Other *ingando* lessons focus on themes such as history, government programmes, Vision 2020 or military strategy. A philosophy lesson does not quite 'fit' with the rest of the course. The lecture I participated in was delivered at the Nkumba *ingando* camp by a member of the Ministry of Defense Headquarters on 16 December 2008. As usual, on the day of the lesson, the pentagon-shaped classroom set in the centre of the camp was filled with hundreds of *wanakosi* dressed in their military fatigues. The sea of chattering youngsters was disciplined by a number of young militaries and a 'facilitator' who, with his eagle eyes scanning the room, periodically stood up, pointed his finger and fixed the troublemaker with his stare. The lesson itself focused on two opposing approaches to knowing the world – 'idealism' and 'materialism'. In short, the speaker suggested that Rwandans are still very much idealistic and need a more materialist outlook on the world in order to progress. Rwandans need to break away from passivity and belief in destiny and higher powers, and to grasp opportunity through hard work.

The speaker threw to the audience a set of shocking propositions. In fact, the whole lesson was meant to shake and unsettle. 'It is not god who created people', he suggested plainly 'it is people who created god. If there were no people, there would also not be any understandings of god.' This immediately created a general uproar in the room, hundreds of voices rose up in protest. But the presenter continued his performance energized, taking on the Bible and sneering at the idea of the 'lasting fire', painting Christianity as an imposition on Rwandans. This was not only a critique, the string of well-crafted jokes made this performance into a lighthearted mockery. 'I only want people to think!' the speaker exclaimed.

Finally, the lecturer arrived at the idea of the Big Bang and evolution and suggested that 'we are all part of the animal kingdom, we all come from apes'. Yet another uproar resulted, and my translator whispered in my ear: 'This is so insulting, man!' A girl from across the aisle threw us a meaningful look from above her glasses. 'I need to get out', she whispered. The microphone stopped working with an abrupt screeching sound. 'Technology failed, it is time to pray', the lecturer commented with a smirk. At this point, a full revolt ensued with students getting up from their seats, breaking into religious songs, clapping and chanting 'I see Jesus on the Cross'.

'What is his purpose here?' I asked my translator. 'He wants to persuade us, to brainwash us. Most governments, as you know, believe in Big Bang theory.' The presenter did not tire in the face of protest, however. After the scene settled somewhat, he continued for hours on end, walking, squatting, lying on the table and lifting up his legs ('there is no "up"!'), not only to demonstrate but really to intensify the general sense of inappropriateness of the points he was making. Transgression was certainly intended. As the evening set in with a drizzle, the exhaustion in the room was palpable.

A longer stay in Rwanda, but also some pointers in the lecture itself suggested why this type of deep 'unhinging' and 'reorientation' is an intended part of an *ingando* performance. As mentioned before, mindset change is a key item on the government agenda – to spur development, mentalities need to be reformed first and foremost. The speaker himself called a particular way of thinking 'the superstructure', claiming that 'if you change the superstructure, you can change the infrastructure'. Rwandan idealism needs to give way because, the speaker suggested, it is a form of 'ignorance', not ignorance as illiteracy, rather ignorance as 'negative thinking' that hinders progress. The wholesale transformation of the conceptual superstructure reaches even the Rwandan 'meta-metaphor' of the heart (*umutima*):

> Love is not in the heart, man does not cry in the heart [as we say], it is just a pumping organ. *Mu mutima* means in the heart, *umutima nama* is consciousness, it means 'from the heart'. [But] instead of a heart, we can draw a brain – I brain Kagame. Brain is very important, you get confused because it is passive whereas the heart beats two times per second, but it is the most important part of you.

After a longer time spent in Rwanda observing the official unity and reconciliation process, this seeming 'misfit' of a lecture in fact turned out to be key in unlocking the logics that tie *ingando* as an instance of 'civic education' to multiple other such instances. It was this lesson that addressed and reflected most directly the key force that propels the 'application' of government in multiple spheres of social life, and namely the desired transformation of people's very outlook on the world. It is only such change, the logic goes, that can deliver Rwanda to its envisioned future. The notion of unity itself is closely tied to that aim, and the rest of the chapter explores why and how this might be the case.

Unity for Development, Development for Unity

> 'Cripple poverty. Make it wail and run with fear out of this country. Chase it from one hill to another, then another and then out of a thousand hills...'
> *Poet's Corner, Rwanda Dispatch, November 2008*

> 'We need to reach where other advanced countries are. We use unity to reach where you are.'
> *A university student and ingando participant*

The fever of 'development' is everywhere in 2009 Rwanda. Poems are composed about it, innumerable speeches are made in its name. The technocratic terminology permeates daily informal speak. 'Plans' and 'targets' and 'bottlenecks' are smoothly stitched into a newspaper opinion piece or a lunch conversation. And the language of development is undoubtedly English. A *moto* ride is an opportunity for a speedy English vocabulary boost. In the forex quarter right around NURC, as I enter a small exchange *biro* accompanied from the street by its owners, I see an English textbook opened on the wooden counter. No one wants to stay behind. Development is abstract and yet so concrete, it is as graspable and yet out of reach as the villas of Nyarutarama whose freshly painted façades glow into the dusk. Development has an uncanny gravity, pulling everything into its orbit.

As mentioned previously, activities of unity and reconciliation cannot be easily extracted from wider frameworks of power. Similarly, these activities are part and parcel of a broader transformative effort of the Rwandan government. In what follows, I argue that the dense state apparatus is used today to achieve the elusive and ambiguous beacon of 'development' through varied systems and processes of social transformation and that unity and reconciliation activities are merely additional platforms through which 'progress' is to be pursued. In an expeditious manner, the official discourse describes both unity and reconciliation as by-products of development and (in some minimal form) necessary for its achievement. This in turn reflects a larger dynamic whereby the government's coercive eutopia bends all other needs and goals, the present and even the past, to fit its needs.

From this perspective, unity and reconciliation activities are not 'failing'. The exercise simply has a different set of final objectives. What often appears as no more than 'official theatre' becomes a necessary surface-level enactment that is deemed minimal but potentially sufficient to achieve other aims – strengthening of control through and for the successful transmission of knowledge, with the ultimate aim of transforming participants into ideal catalysts for development. The social body needs to be moulded into a perfect development corps.

Development in Kinyarwanda is *iterambere* or *amajyambere* – 'the stuff of the future' (in deLame 1996: 285). The literal translation describes the government project well. Clinging to the past, getting stuck in memories, working slowly on transformation of feelings and relations do not fit within the predominant conception of development as a fast-paced, forward-bound transformation. The negative symptoms of the past in the present are to be contained in the name of progress. But the very notion of 'unity' also aids a smooth unrolling of multiple government reforms, activities and plans. By demonstrating the way in which development affects, moulds and appropriates unity and reconciliation, this chapter tries to better understand both the 'ideal development subject' that is to be created in spaces such as *ingando* and the type of development that is indeed unfolding in Rwanda.

The Transformation Process

> 'We need to be flexible for development'
> *A headmaster of a secondary school*

Besides understanding that a certain transformation is desired, it is important to see how such transformation is envisioned to occur. In this respect, 'flexibility' or making oneself amenable to change seems to be key. The insistence on and intensity of sensitization, represented by the multiplicity of state-ordained activities, is intended to make people more responsive to government's plans: 'After the prison visits, debates and *gacaca*, prisoners begin to open up … and even survivors become flexible to pardon the perpetrators.'[1] The concept of sensitization is imbued with notions of steerability, of relaxing one's beliefs, of letting oneself be directed and moved elsewhere.

The key in achieving both amenability and the desired change is the transformation of 'mentalities'. The government's philosophy of material transformation hinges on ideologies and mindsets rather than resources and aid. '"There is a saying", the philosophy instructor addresses the *ingando* class: "He who is sick but diagnosed with nothing is also healed with nothing".'[2] Poverty as such 'is often reduced to adopting a "good mentality"', observes Ansoms in her research (2009: 297). But this is in fact an overarching discourse, pertinent as much to reconciliation as to agricultural policy (see Ansoms 2009), suggesting that neither of these two can be easily separated.

The theme of 'mentalities' reappears in diverse arenas, including that of 'unity and reconciliation'. NURC's Executive Secretary tells assembled SCUR presidents that *itorero*'s aim is to 'change the behaviour of Rwandans, to change their mindset, for unity and reconciliation, and to create "agents of change"'.[3] But in fact it is the whole official and mainly unofficial education system – *ingando*, *itorero*, post-*umuganda* meetings, sector meetings – that is used to this end. A MINALOC employee explains that the idea is to have 'an integrated civic education policy just like there is an Integrated Development Programme (IDP). One of the issues there [in the IDP] is mindset change. We realize it is one thing to give farmers fertilizer, market, seedlings ... but if they [have the] same mindset as before, [they will] not make the best use as they could'.[4]

The transformation process centres on the 'passing on' of ideologies, hence the government's focus on schools and the family. The 2010 'Teacher's Day' in Rwanda was 'celebrated under the national theme [of] "developing teachers based on mentality change"' (Mutara for NTK, 5 October 2010). With regard to family, it is believed that just like trauma can be passed down through generations, so can 'contamination.' The urgent task is then to penetrate a relatively closed circle of flow – the family – and prevent the passing on of negative ideologies. Children are seen as pliable ('a tree can be still straightened while young'[5]) and this heightens the resolve of the state to 'distance' them from their parents on key issues. 'We have to identify with them [the youth] so that the message can seep through',[6] suggests the Minister of Youth Habineza. He judges the process has been successful, producing a 'right-minded' cohort: 'Youth are not intoxicated as the elderly ... [youth] are willing to work, cooperate and actively participate in peace-building'.[7]

The emphasis on active engagement is tied to the wider project of abandoning 'idealistic' predisposition cementing passivity, and embracing a more 'materialist' outlook centred on knowledge and active manipulation of one's life-world. 'Opportunities are there, you have to fight for them, they are not "given"',[8] stresses the *ingando* instructor in his lesson on materialism. Yet a paradox unfolds – at the same time as the government elaborates the image of an 'active citizen', it firmly cultivates subjection.

The Perfect Development Subjects

The bespectacled President of Rwanda, versed in economics and politics, has carefully worked against the popular Rwandan stereotype of a military leader taking over power – the *inkandagirabitabo* or literally 'one who marches over the books' – a dismissive reference to ill-educated soldiers in high positions of power. Nonetheless, the nature of RPF government and its approach to governmentality owes much to its guerrilla past. The past explains not only the high securitization of society but leads to co-legitimization and half-glorification of military culture and values in today's Rwanda that translate into and are reflected through most aspects of social life, including 'civic education', reconciliation and nation building, development and progress, among others, and in fact the very notion of 'citizen' as well. With a small degree of exaggeration, the Rwandan society is today harnessed as one harnesses a guerrilla army. There are three distinguishing features to a rule where 'soldiers changed their khakis for suits': strong discipline,[9] politicization of the masses through education, and the expectation of sacrifice for the greater good. Respect for authority and respect for hierarchies are also connected to the guerrilla-inspired political imagination.

It is then through the lens of history – the history of the expansionary Nyiginya kingdom and the current rulers' past as a tight-knit guerrilla group emphasizing discipline and submission to higher goals – that we have to see the resurgence of alternative mass education and re-education centres such as *ingando* and *itorero*. In pre-colonial Rwanda, it was the *milices* or 'social armies' (*armées sociales*) that had their own identities – names or *ibyivugo* and attachment to specific locations – and whose main (but not sole) reason for existence was the physical defence of the country (Kagame 1952). Today, cohorts graduating from *ingando*, and especially *itorero*, mimic these 'social armies' of the past. Their contemporary goal is to fight for and defend the government-drawn visions of progress. Besides pledging to pursue specific *imihigo* goals once back in their communities,[10] the *itorero* graduates (*intore*) are expected to become 'opinion leaders' and 'fighters of social change' managing the development corps, the masses. They need to facilitate 'change from bad [mentalities]' for which 'some people [were] trained in each village' (Niyonshuti for NTK, 17 November 2009). They are referred to as 'social cadres', even 'yeast'. At the Ministry of Local Development, I was told that the first graduates of *itorero* in each village 'become *intore* who ... like the *umusemburo* – yeast – will facilitate change' (ibid.).

In a more direct parallel with the past, today's *itorero* graduates assume *ibyivugo* – a group name and thus a distinct identity. For example, the health workers who graduated from *itorero* adopted the name *imbagukiragutabara*, which can be loosely translated as 'the people who assist recovery'. The diaspora cohorts join the *intore* group of *indangamirwa*, coffee growers become *indongozi* (leaders), and agricultural officers and veterinarians become part the 'social army' known as *ingamburuzabukene* (anti-poverty activists).

In a sense, today's *itorero* groups might be more true to their name ('social army') than they were during dynastic times. While participants do receive military training, their main aim is the catalysis of desired change and the defence of the politics of the state: '[the graduates] have been called upon to become catalysts and agents of change in their country's quest for social and economic transformation' (Niyonshuti for NTK, 17 November 2009). Paul Kagame affirms this in his speech to *itorero* graduates, saying that the programme is 'actively participating in mindset change of Rwandans about the economic and political revolution'.[11]

Looking at these 'chosen ones' – at the select groups undergoing special training – but also considering the enterprise of civic education in general, which finds its concentrated expression in the camps but permeates the society as a whole, we can finally pose the crucial question: Who is the Rwandan who is to be reconstituted in the liminality of *ingando* and *itorero*? In other words, what does the attempt at transformation, as glanced through specific activities, tell us about the 'ideal' that is to be forged? All in all, the goal seems to be the creation of an 'ideal development subject', defined by at least five characteristics: possession of knowledge deemed essential for development (because 'if one develops oneself, he develops our country'[12]) in addition to leaving two types of ignorance,[13] containment of undesirable thoughts, emotions and behaviours, subordination of individuality to the collective goal, a combative zeal in achieving prescribed targets, and loyalty.

When considered from the viewpoint of desirable knowledge, the ideal Rwandan is a collage of beliefs, theories and fragmented dictums comprising the ever-evolving thought-world of the development industry. The knowledge, however, is sifted and interpreted at the local seat of 'development' (still a 'centre' of power) and a distinctly contemporary Rwandan developmental modernity is produced from among the diverse discourses on literacy, hygiene, the importance of savings, discipline, 'service mentality', timeliness, to name a few.

Importantly, it is not only what one knows that is fundamental but also what one contains and displays. Social engineering in today's Rwanda can be understood against the notions of containment versus flow.[14] The perfect Rwandan is a person who contains the symptoms of trauma, feelings, discord and disagreement, any signs of disorder and dirt, so that money/capital can flow. Equally crucial is the subjection of the individual preference and right to the collective (the 'greater good') that is reflected through the accent on containment, docility, the surface displays, as well as the alignment and non-veering from a previously set consensus. But the ideal Rwandan needs to be both passive and active. While crucial containments are both explicitly prescribed from above and indicated by more implicit norms, the ideal subject needs to act with zeal in achieving development targets. At an *itorero* graduation ceremony, those assembled 'vowed [in front of the president] not to be lukewarm or average people but firebrands who will not step down amidst difficulty' (Kagire for NTK, 3 August 2009).

The very notion of 'Rwandanicity' has been recently explicitly refashioned to include new development-friendly aspects. On 26 January 2009, Kwibuka writing for the *New Times* reported: 'As the country prepares for the commemoration of the annual National Hero's Day on February 1 [2009], the government has decided to promote and instil cultural values in the Rwandan tradition to help speed up development goals ... We need a brand for Rwandans'. The minister [Habineza] specified 'speed and respect for time, customer service mentality, quality delivery, completion towards results, and self-respect for national pride as the five core values to be instilled in Rwandans of every corner of the country in order to realize the country's development agenda' (ibid.).

'Poverty Causes Conflict' and 'Riches Reconcile': 'U&R' in Service of Development

In what ways is the unity and reconciliation process intermeshed with the overall goals of development, and in what ways is it subsumed within this goal? As mentioned, all state activities, those of unity and reconciliation notwithstanding, are first and foremost to serve the overarching goal of development. Specifically, the vision of the government hinges on a demanding transformation scenario of the country from a low income to a middle income country by 2020 (MINECOFIN 2000) to be achieved largely through a comprehensive restructuring of the agricultural sector from a 'subsistence domain' into a 'productive, high-value, market-oriented sector' (ibid.). The state's intricate machinery finds everybody and everything relevant in pushing through its *gahunda* – programme – and its *icyerekezo* – vision. In this context, it is not only those working in unity and reconciliation but also, for instance, religious leaders who are urged to 'sensitize their followers on development'.[15] All need to align with and further the goals of the 'Vision 2020 *Umurenge*' (in addition to the MDGs and the five-year EDPRS). The annual contribution towards achieving the 2020 targets is to be captured in the *imihigo* contracts, which crosscut society both vertically and horizontally. But the subjugation of activities and events to the needs and discourse of 'development' go deeper than this.

As my fieldwork progressed, it became clearer that the government's central strategy of unity is in fact 'unity for economic development' ('the economic liberation struggle' (Munyaneza for NTK, 3 February 2009)). 'We all want development, however much our differences', proclaims President Kagame at the Sixth National Dialogue Conference (Karuhanga for NTK, 19 December 2008). 'We need to reach where other advanced countries are. We use unity to reach where you are', explains a student at the National University in Butare. The more general dictum seems to be to forget differences, grievances and suffering and to work hard for a goal that will benefit all. Analysis of the discourse also reveals the prevalence of another logic. Unity is not only necessary for development, but can be achieved through development. 'People get integrated when they work together',[16] I am told by a university employee commenting on the social utility of cooperatives and schools. Importantly, it is the very notion of unity that is implicated and helps aid a smooth unrolling of multiple reforms, activities and government plans. As we have seen, the official discourse, plans and performances speak of unity as consent, coordinated action, as non-veering from the line. Unity indeed 'aids' development.

A crucial show of how a goal of economic development has the power to mould a whole discourse, in this case the discourse of unity and reconciliation, is the increasing hold of the following claim: 'Poverty causes conflict'. This contestable (and contested) thesis is unquestioningly embraced and forms the core of the current policy towards unity and reconciliation. 'We [the government] think the cause of long, sustainable conflict is poverty', a female MP tells me, 'so now [we are] orientating [the unity and reconciliation strategy] on ... poverty reduction strategies, the IDPRS'.[17] On another occasion, a public servant at MINALOC announces that 'we discovered that poverty is the element which forces people to fight each other'.[18] Major international organizations such as OXFAM also toe the line. The peace-building and reconciliation manager suggests that 'we believe poverty is generating conflict'.[19] One of the key OXFAM projects in unity and reconciliation is providing decentralized funding (in the form of grants) to local *njyanama* councils.

In this discursive frame 'coming out of poverty is [becomes] another form of attacking discriminatory thinking ... [because] empty stomach thinks discriminatively', claims MP Bwiza.[20] Poverty reduction, she continues, then becomes 'another way of unity and reconciliation'.[21] In the words of the NURC director of peace-building and conflict management, reconciliation results as a 'by-product of poverty eradication'.[22] But opposing voices can sometimes be heard in public: 'Poverty is not the problem' suggests the chairman of *Itorero ry'gihugu* and a well-known Hutu politician at the NURC meeting with partners: 'Can we be angry at each other that there is no rain? No, that is god ... The problem is rich people imposing on poor people.'[23]

The subjugation of unity and reconciliation to development is also reflected through the content of the unity and reconciliation activities. Previous analysis shows 'interpenetration of themes' as a salient characteristic of these activities where lessons that have little to do with issues of justice, nation building or coexistence are being imparted on participants. *Ingando* and *itorero* curricula include lessons on family planning, hygiene and more directly on the economic development of the country. *Umuganda* and TIG sensitize the population to be part of savings cooperatives or to create *akarima kigikoni* (little kitchen gardens). At the meeting with SCUR presidents, Ndangiza does not fail to mention the 'economic revolution' and the 'green revolution', both centred on a comprehensive reform of land use, to which all need to contribute.[24] The

National Unity and Reconciliation Commission of course 'abides by Vision 2020'[25] and many of their activities incorporate messages about this ultimate overarching 'vision'. *Itorero* is perhaps the best example, as its stated goal is 'creating mindsets that help speed the development agenda'.[26]

The penetration of developmentalist themes inside the space of 'unity and reconciliation' activities is demonstrated well in an article entitled 'Health Workers Vow to Excel' (Kagire for NTK, 3 August 2009) describing an *itorero* graduation ceremony held at the Amahoro Stadium in Kigali where 'President Paul Kagame ... challenged practitioners in the health sector that their role now transcends beyond providing health services to playing a vital role in the economic development of the country ... [He] told the 45,210-strong group that they should not only provide health services to individuals, but also to the country saying it equally has life'. At the *itorero* for coffee growers, Fatuma Ndangiza of NURC urged the attendees 'to use the training acquired to sensitize others on the need to embrace the concept of economic transformation by the coffee growers and the relevance of such thinking in forging unity for development' (Mukombozi for NTK, 8 June 2009).

The Politics of Development in Rwanda: A Coercive Eutopia?

The dynamics of promise, hope and aspiration lie at the core of the development discourse. Development hinges on promises of improvement in quality of life and its tokens score political credit. Since in today's Rwanda development is presented as legitimation for a variety of taxations, loyalty and vote extraction notwithstanding, it is pertinent to ask: What concept of development is being pursued in Rwanda? What are the effects of pursuing this type of development? Can 'unity' and 'reconciliation' really be its by-products?

Based on the analysis thus far, it is clear that 'development as freedom' (Sen 1999) is not the triumphant approach in Rwanda where instead the political axis to transformation is thoroughly silenced. In its stead, development in Rwanda highlights the biopolitical (life, health and the benign care for well-being), the material (overcoming material lack and lag), and the notion of autonomy and independence, which are tied to *ishema* – pride. The new paradigm, enveloped in the *agaciro* spirit of Rwandan dignity, makes multiple inroads into daily life in the countryside, though not without resistance (Van Damme, Ansoms and Baret 2014).

This politicized giving from the ultimate *shebuja* (patron) – the state – has to be complemented by an analysis of the extractions the *shebuja* demands. The concrete tokens of development have to be measured against all the taxation executed in its name. The book has detailed the variety of state-mandated community activities, always 'local', 'traditional' and 'beneficial' but never optional or properly remunerated – *umuganda, ubudehe, imihigo*, and many more. The amount of activity is never enough, and the possibilities of mobilizing labour in yet other more potent ways dazzle the planner's imagination. The 'umuganda fantasy' or else the tendency to imagine how community labour can be maximized, is the perfect example. Mutara of NTK (19 December 2006) informs us that 'they [*ubusabane* and *umuganda*] are abused, if abuse can be used to mean people's failure to thoroughly exploit the rich resource and potential that is embedded in them'. In another NTK article (27 February 2008) entitled 'Taking *Umuganda* to a Higher Level', the author conjectures that 'with determination and focus there is no project that needs just sheer manual labour that cannot be undertaken and successfully completed [in *umuganda*] ... Under *Umuganda*, roads can be built'.

It is the Greek word *eutopia* that perhaps best captures the two salient notions embedded in development – the worth (*eu* – good) and the spatio-temporal aspect (*topos* – place) – the improved state that is both possible and not yet present. Besides the problem of creating a 'coercive eutopia' (or utopia, viz Jennings 2009) – deploying coercive power in the name of an aspiration – there are issues connected to how and by whom the aspiration itself is envisioned. Rwanda's development paradigm sidelines aspects of quality of life that make it worth living and make it a 'good one' – the ability to control and direct one's destiny, the guarantee of freedom and rights, the ability to lead a dignified existence, the empowerment that is needed to achieve this. In other words, 'poverty is about privation as much as about oppression' (Uvin 1998: 104). Development 'is a process of social change in which different aspects of people's lives cannot be separated – the economic from the social, the cultural from the political and the religious' (Hiebert and Hiebert-Crape 1995, in Uvin 1998: 136). It is hence important to recognize the silences and excisions that give the official Rwandan eutopia its shape, and further coercive vigour.

But how unique is the current approach when placed into a historical perspective? In fact, evidence suggests that the development exercise in Rwanda both before and after independence (Uvin 1998; Verwimp 2000) has been imposed, extractive, inequitable and often demeaning. During the Second Republic, despite Habyarimana's pro-rural rhetoric ('he championed the culture of an agrarian society'; Ansoms 2008: 10) and the ties that the pre-genocide elite retained with rural milieus through their hills of origin (De Lame 2005), several scholars highlight that there was nonetheless an anti-rural bias in Rwanda in the 1970s and 1980s (e.g., Marysse 1982; Rumiya 1985; Newbury and Newbury 2000). With regard to agrarian policies more specifically, Pottier showed (1992, 1989) how local agricultural officers often ended up imposing state policies and any interaction between them and cultivators 'boil[ed] down to a one-way, dogmatic delivery of textbook instructions' (Pottier 1992: 151). Traditional knowledge was neglected (Pottier 1989) in the name of 'standardizing and rationalizing agriculture' (Newbury and Newbury 2000: 856). Altogether, 'development' in agriculture became a 'coercive field' (ibid.).

According to Peter Uvin, if we incorporate three typically overlooked axes to our analysis of Rwanda before the genocide – equity/inequality, inclusion/exclusion and dignity/humiliation – 'the resulting diagnostic contrasts singularly with the almost idyllic dominant image of Rwanda as a nicely developing country. It shows that, for decades, Rwandan society was characterized by rising inequality, exclusion along social, regional, and ethnic lines, and structural humiliation' (Uvin 1998: 108). Yet how unique was Rwanda in this respect when compared to the region? 'While much of what has been said about the top-down, vertical nature of the relations between the state and its citizens has been observed all over Africa,' continues Peter Uvin, 'what is specific about Rwanda ... are the omnipresence and strength of the state and the development machinery. Thus, paradoxically, it is in the 'best' country – the developers' dream location, where things were implemented the way they were stated on paper by a strong, well-endowed state committed to development – that life most resembled a labour camp, with questionable benefits' (Uvin 1998: 135).

In contemporary Rwanda, the example of land reform should suffice to demonstrate the continuities with the past. Among the many envisioned state-led development transformations, this one is perhaps the most exigent, invasive and disruptive since the vast majority of Rwandans derive their livelihoods from land. As mentioned above, poverty eradication in today's Rwanda centres on the wholesale restructuring of the agricultural sector (MINECOFIN 2000; Pottier 2006; Ansoms 2008). The key aim is to 'reengineer the sector into a modernized vehicle for economic growth, with little place left for traditional smallholder agriculture' (Ansoms 2008: 7). Plots of land deemed too small and insufficient for sustainable development have to be either given up or consolidated. The fewer and larger consolidated farms are to implement mechanized monocropping of high-yield varieties; those pushed off the land are supposed to find off-farm employment in a growing service sector (Pottier 2006; Ansoms 2008).

A number of scholars of Rwanda's land reform (Bruce 2007; Pottier 2006; Huggins and Musahara 2005; Ansoms 2008) raise critical questions related to the feasibility of the government approach and its wider political implications.[27] To begin with, consolidation and monocropping seem to have questionable benefits (in general and in the case of Rwanda, see Huggins and Musahara 2005: 313; Bruce 2007: 22), while small farm size does not always spell lesser productivity (Bruce 2007: 30). Much more worryingly, the land reform is bound to create a large landless class – all those with farm sizes below one hectare or those unable to develop their land 'efficiently' will have it confiscated (Pottier 2006: 521). Yet the alternatives for this segment of population (estimated 35 per cent of all Rwandans) are less than clear. 'None of the interviewed Rwandan policy makers ... had a clear vision of the employment alternatives available to the foreseen "surplus" 35 per cent of the population [previously dependent on farm activities]' (Ansoms 2008: 23). As Pottier (2006: 527) observes, the failure to offer viable solutions to a large mass of landless people has the potential to translate into violent conflict in the future.

The dynamics further aggravating the situation are the high inequality in land possession in Rwanda, the increasing urban grasp on rural land, as well as the perceived dominance in acquisition by the urban-based Uganda Tutsi returnee elites. Connected to this is the sensitive issue of abolishing 'customary' land tenure. The problem lies in the selective definition of 'customary', which suggests political manipulation. In the official documents, 'customary' largely refers to the *ubukonde* system (where lineage heads allocate land) and which used to be the dominant system of tenure in the Hutu chieftancies before the spread of the Nyiginya influence (Pottier 2006: 521). Naturally, the ethnic dimension today is silenced (Huggins and Musahara 2005: 322; Bruce 2007: 31). On the other hand, the royal *isambu* system (where all land belonged to the king but lease agreements existed) is often praised today as an example of 'integrated' land tenure. Further, the rumours about the potential restoration of the *ibikingi* domains (royal cattle pastures where the king or his chiefs afforded rights to cattle grazing) add further to discontent (Pottier 2006: 530). Last but not least, the land access rights of the Twa (whose forests have been progressively encroached upon) are not mentioned in the government policy (Huggins and Musahara 2005: 322).

Overall, one of the most important questions is: 'How will the vast majority of Rwandans be made to execute the necessary change?' Specifically, the very pertinent concern is 'To what extent will this be an autonomous process for the families involved?' (Huggins and Musahara 2005: 312). Just as with the transformation process as a whole, land reform hinges on 'mindset change' and 'adopting a good mentality' (Ansoms 2008: 20; see also Huggins 2013). The problem of 'peasants' resistance to change' is reduced to their 'ignorance' and 'lack of vision' (ibid.) rather than any valid concerns they might have. The government says it will 'encourage' people but this is a euphemism for what is essentially a top-down, imposed process where local administrative elites possess sufficient discretion and power to enforce the desired changes. 'If the targets set out in the Vision 2020 document are to be achieved, it seems clear that the process will involve some degree of compulsion by the government' (Huggins and Musahara 2005: 316; see also Huggins 2013).

In this scenario, the ideal development subject is 'the resource poor farmer who "voluntarily" gives up his/her land in return for "the promise" of a better future' (Pottier 2011, personal communication). But since the voluntariness is most likely to turn into selective coercions (just as in the *imihigo* system) and the 'leap of faith' that the farmers are asked to undergo has such uncertain payoffs, what we face here is a potentially large pool of discontent.

The Effects of 'Development' in Rwanda

The first clear effect of 'development' in Rwanda is disempowerment through depoliticization, whereby various issues deemed 'developmental' are taken out of contestation, being thus relegated to a sphere of 'non-decision making' (Lukes 1974: 22). Yet accessing 'development' is a clear question of power, specifically of acquiescing to the political demands of the centre(s) of power, one of which is being a 'good citizen', and not being 'unpatriotic'. Through depoliticization, this dimension of development is discursively silenced. Development is also implicitly constituted as an unquestioned good. This automatically undermines acts of 'opposition' as uninformed and harmful to the collective effort. Since development rhetoric is present everywhere and aspires to change most aspects of life, the depoliticizing effect is far-reaching.

Development, when repoliticized, emerges as an ambiguous political promise that can excuse coercion and legitimize exploitation. The promise of future development is used by the centre to extract taxes in various forms (most often labour and loyalties) in the present. Further, there is a push to intensify taxation in order to accelerate the 'epic march towards modernity' (Kinzer 2008: 230). People need to *kwihutisha amajyambere*, to hurry up progress. The acceleration is fuelled by the preoccupation with resolving the tension between the aspiration for economic autonomy and the reality of dependence. As a result, people need to work more and better. '*Il faut travailler encore plus, s'organizer encore mieux* [we need to work even more, organize ourselves even better]' suggests Kagame.[28] '*Birashoboka!*' is the motto: 'Everything is possible'.

In view of this dynamic, it is hard not to note the imbrications of donors in Rwanda's coercive eutopia. Pointing to the success of the Asian Tigers, the development machine looks for similar solutions in Africa. Rwanda as a small and historically 'strong' state is the perfect staging ground for this new experiment. In the process, the development community either overlooks the authoritarian nature of the political system ('development has its cost') or openly condones it as 'benevolent dictatorship' (Moyo 2009; for critique see Easterly 2010 and 2013). Yet 'the normative specification that lower needs [i.e., security or material need] must be satisfied before attention is given to higher needs [i.e., political and social rights] could be used to justify deliberate inattention to non-material needs and to preserve an unacceptable status quo' (Fisher 1990, in Uvin 1998: 136). Further to this, counterposing economic needs and political liberties creates an illusory trade-off: 'Political rights, including freedom of expression and discussion, are not only pivotal in inducing responses to economic needs, they are also central to the conceptualisation of economic needs themselves' (ibid.). Easterly (2013) pushes the argument further, standing the claim of a beneficent authoritarianism on its head: 'The real cause of poverty [is] the unchecked power of the state against poor people without rights.'

Besides disempowerment, the practices and logic of the development machinery lead to mystifications in the conflict-development nexus. Analysis of Rwandan discourse of development shows how 'development' is implicitly presented as a good unquestioningly benefiting all. Government officials and foreign enthusiasts draw their optimism from absolute levels of income increase (i.e., overall GDP rise) but rarely focus on how these gains are redistributed. Detailed empirical studies provide strong evidence that, in fact, inequality has risen in Rwanda since the genocide (UNDP 2007; Ansoms 2009). Evidence points to a growing rural-urban divide and a growing impoverishment of the countryside. Those at the bottom are taxed the most: 'Rwanda's high growth rates are deceptive in that they hide large and growing inequalities between social classes, geographic regions and gender ... Rwanda's recent growth has largely bypassed the rural poor, leading to a concentration of wealth at the top of the income distribution ... and a deterioration of living conditions at the bottom of the income distribution ... Growing inequality is not only an obstacle to poverty reduction and sustainable economic growth; it could also undermine social peace' (UNDP 2007: 5).

Why tie unity and reconciliation to development as materiality when it is proven that there is no easy causal connection between peace and income, and that in fact, economic transformation and accumulation is a contested struggle that often involves violence (e.g., Cramer 2006)? The political economy of aid resources can give us (at least part of) the answer – it is useful to tie development and conflict together in the extraction of foreign aid. First, the possibility of violent upheaval can be tacitly negotiated for foreign aid. In a discursive universe where violence/stability and economic progress are connected, the still vivid memory of the genocide is not only useful in extracting 'guilt capital' but also investments to prevent possible violence in the future. In a separate dynamic, strides towards peace are dangled as proof. The perfect example here are the so-called 'reconciliation villages' supported by the Millennium Village Project, where foreign workers and tourists (for a sum of money) can go and see 'unity and reconciliation' happen. Creating images of peace for the outsider is part of the extraction dynamic. The visit includes 'a presentation by a perpetrator and a victim and a testimony how they now live together in happiness'.[29] Creating this image is important both from the viewpoint of investment and as a reminder of how much can be lost if the situation reverts. This explains why seemingly 'shallow' ceremoniality of official activities, suppression of dissent, mere lack of voiced ethnicity ('here you do not talk about Hutu and Tutsi, you are so developed!'[30]) and multiple other containments and 'images of order' that these transmit, still generate political capital.

The government-designed eutopia is portrayed as a common bounty to be achieved, not as an uncertain process of transformation producing new inequalities and divisions, (dis)empowerment and possibly exploitation, struggles and resistances. Though there is no 'conflict-free' development, some attempts are more likely to entice violence than others. What is the verdict in the case of today's Rwanda? Which are the forces releasing the potential for organized violence and which are those that restrain it? In Rwanda, forces against (non-state) violence include the tight grasp of the state – the overbearing administrative structures and information networks, the resulting 'presence' in people's lives, the surveillance and indirect control, the display and use of informants, formal and informal police, the dominance and strength of the military, the resulting fear and suspicion. All of this, rather than 'quelling' some form of organized discontent, aims to prevent its emergence in the first place. Repression can, however, only assure negative peace (the absence of physical violence), not the absence of reasons for discontent.

The forces for violence include not only repression and political exclusion, but also the political legitimization of power based on promises of future development. Naturally, such assurances are not unique to Rwanda. We know that in Kenya, among other African states, 'the late colonial period was marked by developmentalist initiatives that among other things could justify colonial rule. These came with arduous physical demands, particularly on rural peoples, yet simultaneously raised expectations for change and prosperity. In Kenya, for example, rural development projects to combat soil erosion contributed to the frustrations that boiled over in association with Mau Mau' (Bay and Donham 2006: 5). In Rwanda, the story could be narrated in an eerily similar way. Developmentalist initiatives are being used to justify an authoritarian, highly controlling and exacting political system. The government's coercive eutopia thus has to be seen against both its promises and its costs.

Peter Uvin (1998: 1) opens his book on pre-genocide Rwanda by noting what he calls a 'profoundly disturbing contradiction'. The well-planned and massively executed genocide, the culmination of a long process, Uvin notes, starkly contrasted with the perception[31] of Rwanda at the time as a '"well-developing" country, seen as a model of development in Africa, with good performance on most of the indicators of development' (ibid.). Uvin's analysis of the 'signs' of social decomposition is validated *ex post* by the genocide itself. Today, rather than being lulled by overt calm, we have to read the signs of instability under the façade of economic growth and absence of large-scale physical violence. We should not wait for violence to occur in order to start analysing its nature, its causes and its prospects. But neither should we simply stay attuned to the possibilities of acute violence. It is the structural violence underlying the political system that we need to acknowledge and address in its own right.

Conclusion

After the genocide, the RPF-led government has not only embarked on an exigent plan of social and economic transformation of the country, it has also carefully elaborated and begun cultivating an ideal 'citizen role' fit for the task. The evolving and increasingly complex civic education programme is a potent show of the importance of instilling a particular relation to the state in the population. The type of future that Rwanda strives for is inseparable from the Rwandan who is meant to deliver it, and here being a 'good citizen' means squarely being a 'true friend' of the government.

The analysis above also points to powerful continuities across time, both in terms of the type of development that unfolds and the nature of state-society relations produced through that process. The unique dynamic in the post-genocide state is perhaps the verve with which development is reappropriated in the official discourse as a force for the very healing of a scarred society. The 'gravitational pull' of development in post-genocide Rwanda is remarkable as it is able to warp whole discourses around its universe of objectives. The 'talk' on unity and conflict demonstrates this well. Unity as alignment is presented as a key ingredient for development, unity as social cohesion is presented as its unquestioned product. The exigencies of the development project are also offset with a delicate politics of hope, which revolves around powerful 'temporal displacements'.

The images of the eutopic order and the narratives of development are a displacement and distraction of a kind – an imaginary 'moving away' from the present to the yet to come. More broadly, the unity the government cultivates hinges on Rwandans being repeatedly transported to a particularly renarrated past and being repeatedly displaced to a particular image of a future. Meanwhile, the space of the present is the space of containment and obligation, a responsibility to actualize 'potentials' referenced in both sets of temporal tales.

Notes

1. Discussion with members of 'Tuvindimwe UYAGI' (United Youth Against Genocide Ideology), 6 March 2009 at the Munyinyia Sector office, Eastern Province.
2. Lecture on the 'Introduction to Philosophy' delivered by a representative of the Ministry of Defence Headquarters, Nkumba *ingando*, 16 December 2008.
3. Ndangiza's speech to SCUR presidents at the Les Mamans Sportif, Kacyiru, Kigali, 26 January 2009.
4. Interview with a professional for good governance at MINALOC, 12 March 2009.
5. From the Rwandan saying *igiti kigororwa kikiri gito* (the tree can still be straightened when it is young).
6. Kyamutetera (2006) interviews the Minister of Youth, Sports and Culture.
7. Ibid.
8. Lecture on 'Introduction to Philosophy', op. cit.
9. Kagame always maintained strict discipline within the RPA and there was a detailed code of conduct that all soldiers had to abide by (Kinzer 2008).
10. Interview with a professional for good governance at MINALOC, op. cit.
11. Itorero Strategic Plan, 2009–2012, Republic of Rwanda, available online at http://www.rwandapedia.rw/archive/itorero
12. Interview with the street children unit coordinator at MIGEPROF, op. cit.
13. 'The population is still primitive, not primitive of not knowing how to write and read but other, that is "primary ignorance", then there is "negative thinking" that they cannot use well what they learned.' Lecture on 'Introduction to Philosophy', Nkumba *ingando*, op. cit.
14. 'Flow' was proposed by Christopher Taylor (1992) as an overarching cultural theme in Rwanda. Though Taylor is a medical anthropologist and connected flow to 'healing', the concept, he argued, applied more widely. Based on my own study of the government's projects of social engineering, I found 'blockage' and 'containment' equally important – certain containments are necessary if certain flows are to be produced.
15. TV Rwanda, evening news, November 10, 2008.
16. Interview with a director of language centre at a Rwandan university, op. cit.
17. Interview with Connie Bwiza of the Chamber of Deputies, Parliament of Rwanda, 23 March 2009.
18. Interview held on 30 January 2009.
19. Interview with a project manager at OXFAM Rwanda, October 30 2008.
20. Interview with Connie Bwiza, op. cit.
21. Ibid.
22. Africa Lutheran Communion (AFC) news update, 13 April 2008.
23. NURC meeting with partners at Hotel Novotel, 26 March 2009.
24. Fatuma Ndangiza addresses SCUR presidents, Kacyiru, Kigali, 26 January 2009.
25. Ndangiza at NURC meeting with partners, op. cit.
26. Interview with professional for good governance, MINALOC, op. cit.

27. Naturally, not all is negative; there are aspects to the Rwandan approach that have been lauded by analysts, particularly the accent on and progress towards gender equality. Daley and Englert (2010) and Daley, Dore-Weeks and Umuhoza (2010) show how, since the passing of the transformational Succession Law of 1999, women's access to land in Rwanda has improved (measured both in terms of equal inheritance and shared land ownership). 'Rwandan women [are] increasingly starting to claim their land rights and [are] increasingly succeeding in this as the notion of gender equality in marriage and inheritance has taken popular hold' (Daley and Englert 2010: 10).
28. Interview by Soudan for La Jeune Afrique N2514 (2009: 46).
29. A friend (development worker for the GTZ) reflects on her visit to a Millennium Village, 10 April 2009.
30. A SCUR president relays impressions of a 'visitor to Rwanda', 26 January 2009.
31. Not everyone shared this perception. Just as today, the outward, donor-oriented projection often diverged from what was happening on the ground and what many anthropologists and researchers observed during fieldwork.

11

What Kind of Unity?
Prospects for Coexistence,
Social Justice and Peace

Inzira y'ubumwe ni urugendo rurerure – 'the path of unity is a long journey', begins a short written piece on the Nyamaseke district webpage, in a characteristically evocative yet vague manner.[1] Unity in this popular formulation becomes a concrete presence that simply requires nurture to come to life at a later point in time. Yet what is perhaps more easily ascertained is the path leading backwards, the genealogy of unity as a political project that shows a similarly long trajectory. The disembedded opening statement is, after all, part of that very path as it is 'placed' within a government website, and its appeal to stock knowledge is used to produce authority.

Placing unity into a politico-historical context and the sphere of ideology is certainly an important opening to analysis. This book, however, has tried to delve beyond this and understand the 'life' of unity after a genocide when the notion gains special salience, currency and hence a unique form. It also tried to eschew a simple analysis of political instrumentality by focusing instead on the manner in which different actors and institutions deal with unity's semantic ambiguity and political ambivalence, it tried to look at the manipulation, playfulness and transfiguration of the concept as it develops and makes its appearance. The book traced unity to actors and expressions, to words but also actions sanctioned under its rubric.

Ultimately, the book itself tried to appropriate the term's allusional latitude and imaginative power, using it as a frame to explore the way in which a state formulates and executes an extremely challenging socio-political project of 'coexistence', and beyond that, how that project and the frame fit within the wider dynamics of post-conflict governance and state-society relations, the political imaginary of a new social order. The book has thus tried to make a case for a methodology of 'tracing', a tool to demonstrate how power holds together and propagates by analytically 'consuming' and combining all material with a 'trace', however disparate. As such, the analysis outlines the 'formation' of unity, beyond simply a 'discursive formation' (Foucault 1972), it traces a web of words, actions, attitudes, but also emotions, symbols, spatio-temporal orientations and placements. It traces the political dimension of unity building through transient spaces and extraordinary moments, through camps and retreats, as much as through the mundane, the happening on the street and the office. The tracing of the official unity discourse is unique for the powerful paradoxes that it lays bare. Its appeals to inclusion help reproduce exclusion, its orientations to togetherness and the social body help consolidate a narrow regime and further proliferate social bads.

It is certainly not correct to claim that there is no unity being built in Rwanda. Rather, we need to pay careful attention to the type of unity and togetherness that is officially being produced through the varied interventions of the Rwandan government-cum-state as a resource. Unity is not a singular concept, but is rather 'multiply meaningful'. Alternative conceptions exist, some of which have been briefly outlined – the social togetherness highlighted by many categories of people, the shared suffering emphasized by the psycho-social community and the artists, the nationalist vision promoted by the government. But even in the official sphere, unity is multi-referential in strategy and fragmented in policy pursuit. In the end reading nonetheless, unity both is and is not many things since a very concrete version of *ubumwe* is 'empowered' at the national level. It is unity as a disciplined, coordinated form of being together, as sameness and consent in the social body. The aim is to create one out of many, homogeneity (associated with order) out of diversity, convergence (drawing on the value of discipline) out of divergence (associated with dissent and loss of focus on a common goal). As such, unity both reflects and performs political work for the government's coercive eutopia.

Unity is involved in 'political work' at two key levels, firstly through the intersection of the unity and reconciliation project with the state-building project, and secondly through the concept's discursive incorporation into the 'grand equation' of post-genocide governance, as well as through the concrete work of political reproduction that results. Two questions thus remain to be answered: How is unity building also state building? And how is unity building also regime building? Rwandan society has become further etatized after the genocide; the state itself becoming denser and more present at a very local level. The post-conflict paradigm of reconstruction, securitization, developmentalism, as well as reconciliation and transitional justice, has opened a wider space for the application and hence 'presencing' of the Rwandan state. It is in this sense that unity building in contemporary Rwanda is also state building. The process has proliferated multiple platforms at the lowest of administrative levels that double as spaces of presencing of the state and as spaces of governmentality. The official activities of unity and reconciliation help disseminate the dominant consensus and reproduce official narratives, they help unwork open contention and serve as a symbolic affirmation of power.

But the 'state effect' is wider yet. The urge to police meaning and enaction reaches beyond the spaces that the state creates (and subsequently discursively disconnects from itself by labelling them 'traditional') to multiple other, local activities of healing and reconciliation, which cannot escape the broader strictures of politics. Importantly, the analysis here is not meant to obscure the achievements of local actors and the forgiving and healing that happen in different ways and to different degrees across the country. Similarly, by emphasizing the political nature of social challenges – the political rather than essentialist roots of past and present conflict, the political costs that explain relative non-dissention rather than 'obedience', the anxieties and logics that legitimize a non-democratic regime rather than any innate predilections – the analysis here in no way 'takes hope away', nor agency. Political dynamics are key, and they can be altered.

The grand equation of post-conflict governance refers to the underlying logic that joins politics, security, development and unity building together. The discursive equation today places development and security above participatory politics, and unity in the service of both. In this logic, unity as consent is necessary for development and stability while liberalization divides and destabilizes. But development is also predicated on change, on a vast social transformation effort, on the change of mentalities and attitudes and the acquisition of useful knowledge and behaviours. In the effort to 'incorporate' a person into the new political order, accent lies on spatio-temporal placement and displacement, both across time (useful promises and remembrances) and space (camps). This then explains the observed primacy of civic education, sensitization and re-education, the work of moulding the perfect development subject. In other words, it is this overarching equation that 'shapes' our subject of study – the 'what' of both purpose and actual happening that at times defies labels. It explains the observed interpenetration of themes, the insertion of the developmental 'work' into all types of platforms, including those of unity and reconciliation.

In Rwanda, unity building thus becomes regime building in different senses. The logical tangle whereby unity as consent is legitimized by its putative connection to stability and development is the first sense in which unity building becomes regime building. The actual staging of unity building through multiple institutions, activities and events also produces power for the regime. The effects might be shallow but are no less 'real', they serve as tokens of intention and even success that can be exchanged for extraverted legitimacy, thus further reproducing the regime-as-is.

But why does all of this matter? Should we not weigh the greater etatization and the consolidation of authoritarian rule against the effects in whose name they operate – the dividends of the developmental *eutopia*? Is this not both a necessary and a worthy price? Rwanda poses important questions for the study of post-conflict states more broadly and specifically for the 'social transformation' projects that they set out to pursue: Firstly, does the unique governance equation work? Can securitization and development be the driving forces of social cohesion? Can unity be development's 'by-product'? Secondly, what is the actual power of a 'strong' state across war and peace? Is such a state uniquely equipped to fulfil its policy objectives, whatever these are?

With regard to the logic of trade-offs, there is no doubt that Rwanda has seen positive developments in terms of economic growth, education and health. But there are equally no qualms about the top-down and coercive nature of development administered by a narrow elite. The dominant discourse paints these as inevitable trade-offs: political participation comes at the cost of wholesale betterment. The discursive set-up however falters on two points. It obscures the negative 'work' of the coercive eutopia, and it obscures the feasible alternatives to authoritarian-led transformation in Rwanda.

First, the notion of development as peace-, stability- and prosperity-producing is based on an erroneous model of conflict. What matters more than actual resources and absolute growth rates is perceived inequality, injustice, political exclusion and oppression – questions of access, right, distribution. Arguably, the same process that produces promising indicators comes at a cost that is more relevant from the viewpoint of conflict dynamics. The RPF-led government both fails to resolve past grievances through the process of partial justice and continues to accumulate new ones through exclusion, extraction and perceptions of oppression (see also Chakravarty 2014). Together with the structural violence that the state produces, this is a process that fundamentally undermines stability and social justice. The tight social control and the cost of dissent hold the state together. Hence the question is not merely one of 'balancing' the production of public goods like healthcare and infrastructure with public 'bads' such as the loss of political rights, but it is also fundamentally about adjusting the conceptual models of their 'weighting'.

Another fundamental precept arising from the development-first paradigm is the thorough depoliticization of social transformation – the onus lies squarely on the individual and their 'mentality change', the acquisition of appropriate knowledge, rather than on broader structural and political dynamics. Coercion today merely precedes the inevitable acceptance-after-results. Liberalization is presented as both dangerous and unnecessary. Yet the empirical record suggests something else altogether about danger and necessity. An imposed and closed system of rule not only accumulates grievance, it forecloses peaceful mechanisms of contestation; the divisions and divergences in the interpretation of the past and present are suppressed rather than dialogued with, while the top-down visions of the future excuse coercion, extraction and exclusion. The building of 'Rwandanness' is certainly a positive aspiration, but it must be constructed on the basis of a more inclusive political membership rather than on the alignment with roles, duties and visions set out and imposed from above. Twenty years after the genocide, a careful political opening is both possible and necessary.

But the key question of the unique efficacy of a 'strong' state in pushing its plans and visions through still remains. Does the combination of state reach and density, control and resolve assure the success of the government's transformation objectives, whether these be social destruction and physical annihilation (as in the genocide) or, conversely, physical flourishing and social welfare? Scott Straus (2006: 223) ventures to argue that in Rwanda 'once a state-backed policy crystallizes, that policy has tremendous force, even if government orders are to kill'. Do policies in peacetime then have similar force? An apparent puzzle also arises: How can we avoid treating society as a 'malleable putty' in the hands of the state (Migdal 2001: 106) and explain the mass mobilization for the genocide achieved unquestionably with the aid of state structures? Answering these questions demands that we carefully specify the type of power that a 'strong' state such as Rwanda actually produces across both war and peace.

In short, a state apparatus built on social control might extract multiple actions and contributions, yet it might still struggle to effect a deeper transformation. In Rwanda, a 'far-reaching governance of daily life' (Migdal 2001: 102) is certainly present. Most aspects of a person's life activity – agricultural, political, social, medical, sexual, even philosophical – become targets of the transformation drive. And while results are visible – people enter cooperatives and saving schemes, participate in activities and even engage in the appropriate speak – what results is a powerful moulding of surfaces. More broadly then, we can say that the Rwandan government has been extremely active and effective in a mode of transformation that can best be called 'surfacing' – producing reforms, laws, campaigns, institutions, activities, restructuring and construction, and extracting varied contributions from society towards these ends. The pace of change 'on the surface' is palpable, and it is certainly 'additive' change – more public order, more growth, more access to healthcare, more policing and securitization, more infrastructure. Hence 'surfacing' is doubly useful as a term – it does not presume 'deep' work of transformation at the level of opinion or belief, acceptance or legitimacy, and it also references a social contract where surfaces are publicly upheld even if privately 'unworked' (Purdeková 2013). This is a system in other words that, albeit shallow, is not without its utility to the current government, or one in fact that would not produce 'utilities' for its citizens. This is also not to say that deeper change is never achieved, or that in fact the state does not penetrate the very intimate registers through which a person relates to the world (i.e. fear and anxiety today; the manipulations of fears and anxiety during the 1990–1994 civil war). But if we expand beyond the 'infrastructural power' of the state (Mann 1984), we see that the social control model is based on a trade-off of powers – between repressive control and legitimacy (already noted by Arendt 1969) – and, as such, it can be both self-serving and self-defeating for the government that oversees it. In other words, 'surfacing' is power, just of a very particular kind. This explains why actions and results can be successfully extracted by a government for starkly opposed ends – production of death in genocide and fostering of life after it – and yet why such a state, when overseen by an authoritarian political system, might still struggle to assure social cohesion and transformation of conflict, legitimacy or long-term stability.

Rwanda thus poses different questions to the 'state-building' literature, questions not only about the negative impacts of state overreach or contestation over 'insertions' of the state into society, but also about more fundamental 'limits' of state power, especially (though not exclusively) if wielded by non-democratic regimes. The case of Rwanda also usefully shows that 'institutional infrastructure' is an important but insufficient concept if we are to understand the true extent of state power, which overspills its institutional bounds.

Is the Rwandan state unique in Africa when compared to other states with similar political geographies or state reach such as Burundi or Eritrea? Is the extent of social control in Rwanda unparalleled? And are the observed differences ones of degree, of qualitative nature, or both? Answering these questions will first require the development of a proper comparative framework. What seems certain is that research on the African state needs to shift from the study of absences to the study of presences of the state, and not only in the sense of studying the 'controlling' practices of states such as surveillance, but 'incorporative' ones as well, such as civic and political education. In this sense, the present project hopes to be an inspiration for further research on topics such as civic education, re-education and reintegration practices, as well as the use of camps and retreats for such 'incorporation'. With regard to political education camps, much more work is needed to trace their use and genealogies across time and space, and beyond Eastern Africa. What precedents inspired particular camps, and in what manner? The tracing of a practice can open to view the historical exchange, dialogue and interaction that tie countries and regions together, thus pushing beyond the imaginative and conceptual constraints of political borders.

Besides the tracing of practices, the tracing of key words and concepts synchronically and diachronically can also be useful, especially when it comes to words with political potency and incorporative appeal, words that governments put to intense use on the ground such as solidarity, unity, development, progress, among others. Such tracing can offer a unique window into the social 'ties' that are to be created, and that elsewhere have been explored under the heading of citizenship, political subjectivity, or nation building. Exploration of this kind can also offer insight into alternative pools of meaning, the exchanges, modifications and silencing that might occur, and finally the effects, political or otherwise, that result.

Notes

1. Accessed 29 June 2014 on the government's website: <www.nyamasheke.gov.rw/index.php?id=2469&tx_ttnews%5Btt_news%5D=2922&cHash=ccdab16936f5258e1fe50d621bb4c5e2>.

Bibliography

Africa Lutheran Communion (ALC). 2008. 'Inter-denominational Youth Gathering Concludes in Kigali, Rwanda [Online]', Posted on April 16. Accessed 15 January 2010, www.africa-lutheran.org/index.php?option=com_content&view=article&id=110%3Ainter-denominational-youth-gathering-concludes-in-kigali-rwanda&catid=32&Itemid=38&lang=en.

Afrol News. 2004. 'Rwandan Parliament Lashes out at "Genocide Groups"'. Afrol News, 2 July. Available at http://www.afrol.com/articles/13550.

Agamben, G. 1998. *Homo Sacer: Sovereign Power and Naked Life*. Stanford: Stanford University Press.

Agence France Presse (AFP). 1997. 'Last Reeducation Camps in Rwanda Closed'. *Agence France Presse,* 19 November.

———. 2003. 'Thousands of Rwandan Genocide Suspects Set for Reeducation'. *Agence France Presse,* 27 January.

———. 2005. 'Rwandan Genocide Prisoners Prepare for Freedom at Solidarity Camps'. *Agence France Presse,* 12 August.

Alexander, J. and J. McGregor. 2006. 'Veterans, Violence and Nationalism in Zimbabwe'. In States of Violence: Politics, Youth and Memory in Contemporary Africa, Bay, E. and D. Donham (eds). University of Virginia Press.

Alexander, J., J. McGregor and T. Ranger. 2000. *Violence and Memory: One Hundred Years in the 'Dark Forests' of Matabeleland*. Oxford: James Currey.

Allen, T. 2010. 'Bitter Roots: The "Invention" of Acholi Traditional Justice'. In *The Lord's Resistance Army: Myth and Reality*, Allen, T. and K. Vlassenroot (eds). London: Zed Books.

Allen, T. and A. MacDonald. 2013. 'Post-Conflict Traditional Justice: A Critical Overview', *The Justice and Security Research Programme Paper* N. 3, February.

Alusala, N. 2005. 'Disarmament and Reconciliation: Rwanda's Concerns'. *Institute for Security Studies Paper* 108, June.

Amnesty International (AI). 2010. 'Safer to Stay Silent: The Chilling Effects of Rwanda's Laws on "Genocide Ideology" and "Sectarianism"'. Available at www.amnesty.org.

———. 2012. 'Rwanda: Shrouded in Secrecy: Illegal Detention and Torture by Military Intelligence'. London, October.

Anders, G. and O. Zenker. 2014. 'Transition and Justice: An Introduction'. *Development and Change* 45(3): 395–414.

Anderson, B. 1981. *Imagined Communities: Reflections on the Origin and Spread of Nationalism*. London: Verso.
Ansoms, A. 2008. 'A Green Revolution for Rwanda? The Political Economy of Poverty and Agrarian Change'. *Institute of Development Policy and Management Discussion Paper* 2008.06.
———. 2009. 'Reengineering Rural Society: The Visions and Ambitions of the Rwandan Elite'. *African Affairs* 108(431): 1–21.
———. 2012. 'Dislodging Power Structures in Rural Rwanda: From "Disaster Tourist" to "Transfer Gate"'. In *Emotional and Ethical Challenges for Field Research in Africa: The Story Behind the Findings*, Thomson, S., A. Ansoms and J. Murison (eds). London: Palgrave, pp.57–69.
Apa-Kigali. 2010. 'Over One Million Rwandan Refugees Face Forced Repatriation from Uganda'. *APA Kigali*, 16 May.
Arendt, H. 1958. *The Human Condition*. Chicago: University of Chicago Press.
———. 1969. 'A Special Supplement: Reflections on Violence'. *The New York Review of Books* 12(4).
Asiimwe, A. 2009. 'Why Our Own "Imihigo" Outshines World Bank's "Doing Business"'. *The New Times Kigali*, 11 September.
Autesserre, S. 2010. *The Trouble with the Congo: Local Violence and the Failure of International Peacebuilding*. Cambridge Studies in International Relations series. New York: Cambridge University Press.
Bagilishya, D. 2000. 'Mourning and Recovery from Trauma: In Rwanda, Tears Flow Within'. *Transcultural Psychiatry* 37(3): 337–353.
Bale, J. 2002. *Imagined Olympians: Body Culture and Colonial Representation in Rwanda*. Minneapolis: University of Minnesota Press.
Barigye, T. 2008. 'Kigali Hawkers in Cat and Mouse Game with Police'. *The New Times Kigali*, 29 December.
Bay, E. and D. Donham (eds). 2006. *States of Violence. Politics, Youth, and Memory in Contemporary Africa*. Charlottesville: University of Virginia Press.
Begley, L. 2009. 'The Other Side of Fieldwork: Experiences and Challenges of Conducting Research in the Border area of Rwanda/Eastern Congo'. *Anthropology Matters* 11(2).
———. 2012. 'The RPF Control Everything! Fear and Rumour under Rwanda's Genocide Legislation'. In *Emotional and Ethical Challenges for Field Research in Africa: The Story Behind the Findings*, Thomson, S., A. Ansoms and J. Murison (eds). London: Palgrave, pp. 70–83.
Bell, C.H. 2009. 'Transitional Justice, Interdisciplinarity and the State of the "Field" or "Non-Field"'. *International Journal of Transitional Justice* 3: 5–27.
Berglund, A. 2012. 'A Local Perspective of the Vision 2020 Umurenge Program and the Land Tenure Regularization Program'. Kigali: SIDA. Accessed 2 May 2014, http://www.swedenabroad.com/ImageVaultFiles/id_7075/cf_52/Government_policies_from_a_local_perspective_Oct_2.PDF.
Bergman, T. 2004. 'The Politics of Reconciling Rwanda: Progress and Problems', [unpublished manuscript].
Bertocchi, G. and A. Guerzoni. 2010. 'Growth, History, or Institutions? What Explains State Fragility in Sub-Saharan Africa'. *IZA - Institute for the Study of*

Labour Discussion Paper No. 4817, March 2010. Accessed 22 May 2010, http://ftp.iza.org/dp4817.pdf.
Besteman, C. 1996. 'Violent Politics and the Politics of Violence: The Dissolution of the Somali Nation-State'. *American Ethnologist* 23(6): 579–596.
———. 1999. *Unraveling Somalia: Race, Class, and the Legacy of Slavery*. Philadelphia: University of Pennsylvania Press.
Betancourt, T. 2010. 'Rwandan Protective Processes and Resilience in Rwandan Children and Families Affected by HIV/AIDS'. Conference Presentation at the 'Children and HIV: Family Support First' Symposium in Vienna, Austria on 16–17 July 2010. Accessed 6 November 2010, http://www.ccaba.org/resources/vienna2010/Theresa_Betancourt2.pdf.
Bhatia, M.V. 2005. 'Fighting Words: Naming Terrorists, Bandits, Rebels and Other Violent Actors'. *Third World Quarterly* 26(1): 5–22.
Bierschenk, T. and J.-P. Olivier de Sardan. 1997 'Local Powers and a Distant State in Rural Central African Republic'. *The Journal of Modern African Studies* 35(3): 441–468.
———. 2003. 'Powers in the Village: Rural Benin between Democratisation and Decentralisation'. *Africa* 73(2): 145–173.
———. (eds). 2014. *States at Work: Dynamics of African Bureaucracies*. Leiden: Brill.
Bigo, D. 2002. 'Security and Immigration: Toward a Critique of the Governmentality of Unease'. *Alternatives* 27 (Special Issue): 63–92.
Blommaert, J., M. Bock and K.M. McCormick. 2006. 'Narrative Inequality in the TRC Hearings: On the Hearability of Hidden Transcripts'. *Journal of Language and Politics* 5(1): 37–70.
Boege, V., A. Brown, K. Clements and A. Nolan. 2008. 'On Hybrid Political Orders and Emerging States: State Formation in the Context of "Fragility"'. Berlin: Berghof Research Centre for Constructive Conflict Management.
Booth, D. and F. Golooba-Mutebi. 2012. 'Developmental Patrimonialism? The Case of Rwanda', *African Affairs* 111(444): 379–403.
Bouka, Y. 2012. 'Nacibazo, "No Problem": Moving Behind the Official Discourse of Post-Genocide Justice in Rwanda', in Thomson, S., Ansoms, A. and Murison, J. (eds), *Emotional and Ethical Challenges for Field Research in Africa: The Story Behind the Findings*, London: Palgrave, pp. 107–122.
Bourdieu, P. 1977. *Outline of a Theory of Practice*. Cambridge: Cambridge University Press.
Bozzini, D.M. 2011. 'Low-Tech Surveillance and the Despotic State in Eritrea'. *Surveillance and Society* 9(1/2): 93–113.
Bozzoli, B. 2006. 'Memory, Forgetting, and the Alexandra Rebellion of 1986.' In *States of Violence: Politics, Youth and Memory in Contemporary Africa*, Bay, E. and D. Donham (eds). University of Virginia Press.
Brubaker, R. 2004. *Ethnicity Without Groups*. Cambridge: Harvard University Press.
Bruce, J. 2007. 'Drawing a Line under the Crisis: Reconciling Returnee Land Access and Security in Post-Conflict Rwanda'. *Humanitarian Policy Group Working Paper*, June 2007.
Brugière, J.L. 2006. Tribunal De Grande Instance De Paris. 'Issuance of International Arrest Warrants. Ordonance de Soit-Communique [Order

to Execute]'. Document in English at http://nangamadumbu.tripod.com/nikozitambirwa/BruguiereReport_English.pdf

Buckley-Zistel, S. 2006. 'Dividing and Uniting: The Use of Citizenship Discourses in Conflict and Reconciliation in Rwanda'. *Global Society* 20(1): 101–113.

———. 2008. 'We Are Pretending Peace: Local Memory and the Absence of Social Transformation and Reconciliation in Rwanda'. In *After Genocide: Transitional Justice, Post-Conflict Reconstruction and Reconciliation in Rwanda and Beyond*, P. Clark and Z. Kaufman (eds). London: Hurst, pp. 153–171.

———. 2009. 'Nation, Narration, Unification? The Politics of History Teaching After the Rwandan Genocide'. *The Journal of Genocide Research* 11(1): 31–53.

Burnet, J. 2012. *Genocide Lives in Us: Women, Memory and Silence in Rwanda*. Madison: University of Wisconsin Press.

Cacioppo, C. 2005. 'Report on Education and Reintegration of Former Prisoners in Rwanda'. Report prepared for LDGL Kigali in October 2005. Available at www.christinacacioppo.com/content/publications/EducationAndReintegrationOfFormerPrisoners.pdf

Carrier, N. and G. Klantschnig. 2012. *Africa and the War on Drugs*. London: Zed Books.

Chakravarty, A. 2012. '"Partially Trusting" Field Relationships: Reflecting on Field Work on the Gacaca Trials in Rwanda'. *Field Methods* 24(3): 251–271.

———. 2014. 'Navigating the Middle Ground: The Political Values of Ordinary Hutu in Post-Genocide Rwanda'. *African Affairs* 113(451): 232–253.

Chemouni, B. 2014. 'Explaining the Design of the Rwandan Decentralisation: Elite Vulnerability and the Territorial Repartition of Power'. *The Journal of Eastern African Studies* 8(2): 246–262.

Clark, P. 2010. *The Gacaca Courts, Post-Genocide Justice and Reconciliation in Rwanda*. Cambridge: Cambridge University Press.

Clark, P. and Z. Kaufman. (eds). 2009. *After Genocide: Transitional Justice, Post-Conflict Reconstruction and Reconciliation in Rwanda and Beyond*. New York: Columbia University Press.

Collins, B. 2004. 'Rewriting Rwanda'. 7 April 2004. Accessed 22 February 2009, http://www.spiked-online.com/articles/0000000CA4BD.htm.

Contractor, N.S. and M.C. Ehrlich. 1993. 'Strategic Ambiguity in the Birth of a Loosely Coupled Organisation: The Case of a $50-Million Experiment'. *Management Communication Quarterly* 6(3): 251–81.

Cornwell, N. 2006. *Christophe's Story*. London: Frances Lincoln. Excerpt accessed 29 November 2009, www.nickicornwell.com/RESOURCEPACKforTEACHERS.doc.

Cramer, C. 2006. *Civil War is not a Stupid Thing: Accounting for Violence in Developing Countries*. London: Hurst.

Crewe, E. and E. Harrison. (eds). 1998. *Whose Development? An Ethnography of Aid*. London: Zed Books.

Curtis, D. 2013. 'The Limits to Statebuilding for Peace'. *South African Journal of International Affairs* 20(1): 79–97.

Daley, P. 2006. 'Ethnicity and Political Violence in Africa: The Challenge to the Burundi State'. *Political Geography* 25, 657–679.

Daley, E. and B. Englert. 2010. 'Securing Land Rights for Women: Changing Customary Land Tenure and Implementing Land Tenure Reform in Eastern Africa'. Paper presented at the African Studies Association Meeting, 16–19 September 2010, Oxford.
Daley, E., R. Dore-Weeks and C. Umuhoza. 2010. 'Ahead of the Game: Land Tenure Reform and the Process of Securing Women's Land Rights'. *Journal of Eastern African Studies* 4(1): 131–152.
Das, V. and D. Poole. (eds). 2004. *Anthropology in the Margins of the State*. Oxford: James Currey.
Davenport, C. 2007a. 'State Repression and Political Order'. *Annual Review of Political Science* 10: 1–23.
———. 2007b. 'State Repression and the Tyrannical Peace'. *Journal of Peace Research* 44(4): 485–504.
Davies, C.A. 1999. *Reflexive Ethnography: A Guide to Researching Selves and Others*. New York: Routledge.
De Certeau, M. 1984. *The Practice of Everyday Life*. Translated by Steven Rendall. Los Angeles: University of California Press.
De Lame, D. 1996. *Une Colline entre mille ou le calme avant la tempête, Transformations et blocages du Rwanda rural*. Tervuren: Musée Royal de l'Afrique Centrale.
———. 2004. 'Mighty Secrets, Public Commensality, and the Crisis of Transparency: Rwanda through the Looking Glass'. Canadian Journal of African Studies 38(2): 279–317.
———. 2005. *A Hill Among a Thousand: Transformations and Ruptures in Rural Rwanda*. Translated by Helen Arnold. Madison: University of Wisconsin Press.
Deleuze, G. and F. Guattari. 1987. *A Thousand Plateaus: Capitalism and Schizophrenia*. Minneapolis: University of Minnesota Press.
Demertzis, N. (ed.). 2013. *Emotions in Politics: The Affect Dimension in Political Tension*. London: Palgrave Macmillan.
Deng, F.M. 1995. *War of Visions: Conflict of Identities in the Sudan*. Washington, D.C.: The Brookings Institution.
Des Forges, A. 2011. *Defeat is the Only Bad News: Rwanda Under Musinga, 1896–1931*. Madison: University of Wisconsin Press.
Desrosiers, M-E. 2011. 'Rhetorical Legacies of Leadership: Projections of Benevolent Leadership in Pre- and Post-Genocide Rwanda'. *Journal of Modern African Studies* 49(3): 429–453.
Easterly, W. 2010. 'Foreign Aid for Scoundrels'. *New York Review of Books*, 25 November 2010. Accessed 3 January 2011, http://www.nybooks.com/articles/archives/2010/nov/25/foreign-aid-scoundrels/?pagination=false
———. 2013. *The Tyranny of Experts: Economists, Dictators and the Forgotten Rights of the Poor*. New York: Basic Books.
Eisenberg, E.M. 1984. 'Ambiguity as Strategy in Organisational Communication'. *Communication Monographs* 51(3): 227–242.
———. 2006. *Strategic Ambiguities: Essays on Communication, Organization, and Identity*. London: Sage.
Eisenberg, E.M. and H.L. Goodall. 1993. *Organizational Communication: Balancing Creativity and Constraint*. New York: St. Martin's Press.

Elkins, C. 2000. 'The Struggle for Mau Mau Rehabilitation in Late Colonial Kenya'. *International Journal of African Historical Studies* 33(1): 25–57.
———. 2005. *Imperial Reckoning: The Untold Story of Britain's Gulag in Kenya*. Henry Holt/Jonathan Cape.
Eriksen, S.S. 2005. 'The Congo War and the Prospects for State Formation: Rwanda and Uganda Compared', *Third World Quarterly* 26(7): 1097–1113.
Escribà-Folch, A. 2013. 'Repression, Political Threats, and Survival under Autocracy', *International Political Science Review* 34(5): 543–560.
European Report on Development (ERD). 2009. 'Overcoming Fragility in Africa'. Accessed 15 January 2010, http://erd.eui.eu/erd-2009/.
Evans Pritchard, E.E. 1940. *The Nuer: A Description of the Modes of Livelihood and Political Institutions of a Nilotic People*. Oxford: Oxford University Press.
Fairclough, N. 1989. *Language and Power*. New York: Routledge.
Ferguson, J. 1990. *The Anti-Politics Machine: 'Development', Depoliticisation, and Bureaucratic Power in Lesotho*. Minneapolis: University of Minnesota Press.
———. 1999. *Expectations of Modernity. Myths and Meanings of Urban Life on the Zambian Copperbelt*. Berkeley: University of California Press.
Finnström, S. 2008. Living with Bad Surroundings: War, History and Everyday Moments in Northern Uganda. Durham and London: Duke University Press.
Focus Media (Kigali). 2008. 'Rwanda: Ready to Embrace Shakespeare'. *Focus Media (Kigali)*, 21 October.
Foucault, M. 1972. *The Archaeology of Knowledge*. London: Routledge.
———. 1975. *Surveiller et Punir. Naissance de la Prison*. Paris: Gallimard.
———. 1980a. *Power/Knowledge: Selected Interviews and Other Writings*. Colin Gordon (ed.). New York: Pantheon Books.
———. 1980b. 'Space, Knowledge, Power', in J.D. Faubion (ed.) (2000), *Power: Essential Works of Foucault*. New York: The New Press.
———. 1982. 'The Subject and Power'. In Faubion, J.D. (ed.) (2000), *Power: Essential Works of Foucault* 1954–1984, Volume Three. New York: The New Press, 326–348.
———. 1986. [1967] 'Of other spaces'. *Diacritics*, (16): 22–27.
———. 1991. 'Governmentality'. Reprinted in Sharma, A. and A. Gupta. (eds). 2006. *The Anthropology of the State: A Reader*. Oxford: Blackwell.
Freedom House. 2014. 'Rwanda: Freedom of the Press 2014'. Available at www.freedomhouse.org.
Fujii, L.A. 2009. *Killing Neighbors: Webs of Violence in Rwanda*. Ithaca: Cornell University Press.
———. 2010. 'Shades of Truth and Lies: Interpreting Testimonies of War and Violence'. *Journal of Peace Research* 47(3): 231–241.
Games, D. 2009. 'Congo-Kinshasa: Intervention no Substitute for Good Governance [online]', *All Africa,* 16 February. Available at allafrica.com/stories/200902160086.html.
Gashanana, S. 2005. 'Le Role des "Ingando" dans le Processus d'Unité et de Reconciliation Nationale au Rwanda. Cas de la Ville de Kibuye'. Undergraduate thesis [unpublished], November 2005, ULK Library.
Gaventa, J. 1980. *Power and Powerlessness. Quiescence and Rebellion in an Appalachian Valley*. University of Illinois Press.

George, T. 2006. 'Smearing a Hero: Sad Revisionism Over Hotel Rwanda'. *The Washington Post,* 10 May: A25.
Gennep, A. 1960 [1909]. *The Rites of Passage.* Chicago: University of Chicago Press.
Gerschewski, J. 2013. 'The Three Pillars of Stability: Legitimation, Repression, and Co-optation in Autocratic Regimes'. *Democratization* 20(1): 13–38.
Global Youth Connect (GYC). 2008. 'Rwanda Program Report'. Accessed 15 April 2010, http://www.globalyouthconnect.org/pdf/rwanda_jan08.pdf.
Goffman, E. 1957. 'Characteristics of Total Institutions'. In Symposium on Preventative and Social Psychiatry. Sponsored by the Walter Reed Army Institute of Research, the Walter Reed Army Medical Centre and the National Research Council, Washington, Government Printing Office, 1957, pp. 43–93 (revised version of 'Interpersonal Persuasion', revised in: *Asylums,* pp. 1–124) Accessed at http://www.markfoster.net/neurelitism/totalinstitutions.pdf.
Goodwin, J., J.M. Jasper and F. Polletta. 2001. *Passionate Politics: Emotions and Social Movements.* Chicago: University of Chicago Press.
Graham, J. 2008. 'Nyagatare: *Umuganda,* Gardens and Guerilla Photo Exhibits', entry on the author's blog 'Umva [Listen]', 2 June 2008. Accessed 27 March 2009, http://umva.ca/?m=200806.
Grauvogel, J. and C. von Soest. 2013. 'Claims to Legitimacy Matter: Why Sanctions Fail to Instigate Democratization in Authoritarian Regimes'. *GIGA Working Paper* No. 235, October 2013.
Gready, P. 2010. '"You're Either With Us or Against Us": Civil Society and Policy Making in Post-Genocide Rwanda'. *African Affairs* 109(437): 637–657.
Great Lakes Centre for Strategic Studies (GLCSS). 2006. 'Rwandan Diaspora Political Parties Encouraged to Return to Build Nation', GLCSS 5 July 2006. Accessed 22 May 2007, www.bloggernews.net/2006/07/rwandan-diaspora-political-parties.html.
Green, L. 1999. *Fear as a Way of Life: Mayan Widows in Rural Guatemala.* New York: Columbia University Press.
Hagmann, T. and D. Péclard. 2010. 'Negotiating Statehood: Dynamics of Power and Domination in Africa'. *Development and Change* 41(4): 539–562.
Halfon, R. 2008. '*Umuganda*', Blog entry from August 1, 2008. Accessed 2 February 2009, http://conservativehome.blogs.com/centreright/2008/08/umuganda.html.
Hall, S. (ed.). 1997. *Representation: Cultural Representations and Signifying Practices.* London: Sage.
Hammersley, M. and P. Atkinson. 2007. *Ethnography: Principles in Practice.* Abingdon: Routledge.
Hampson, D. 2004. '"It's Time to Open Up". Ten Years After the Genocide in Rwanda: A Christian Aid Report on Government Accountability, Human Rights and Freedom of Speech'. *Christian Aid,* March 2004.
Hatzfeld, J. 2005a. *Into the Quick of Life: The Rwandan Genocide: Survivors Speak.* London: Serpent's Tail.
–––. 2005b. *Machete Season: The Killers in Rwanda Speak.* New York: Picador.
–––. 2007. *A Strategy of Antelopes: Rwanda after the Genocide.* London: Serpent's Tail.

Hayner, P.B. 2010. *Unspeakable Truths: Transitional Justice and the Challenge of Truth Commissions.* New York: Routledge.
Hayward, C. 1998. 'De-Facing Power'. *Polity* 31(1): 1–22.
Herbst, J. 1996. 'Responding to State Failure in Africa'. *International Security* 21(3): 120–144.
———. 2000. *States and Power in Africa.* Princeton: Princeton University Press.
Hilker, L. 2009. 'Everyday Ethnicities: Identity and Reconciliation among Rwandan Youth'. *Journal of Genocide Research* 11(1): 81–100.
———. 2012. 'Rwanda's "Hutsi": Intersections of Ethicity and Violence in the Lives of Youth of "Mixed" Heritage'. *Identities: Global Studies in Culture and Power* 19(2): 229–247.
Hills, A. 2014. 'Somalia Works: Police Development as State Building'. *African Affairs* 113(450): 88–107.
Hintjens, H. 2008. 'Reconstructing Political Identities in Rwanda'. In *After Genocide: Transitional Justice, Post-Conflict Reconstruction and Reconciliation in Rwanda and Beyond*, P. Clark and Z. Kaufman (eds). London: Hurst.
———. 2009. 'Post-Genocide Identity Politics in Rwanda'. *Ethnicities* 8(1): 5–41.
Hirondelle News Agency. 2003. 'Thousands of Genocide Suspects Released From Solidarity Camps', *Hirondelle News Agency/All Africa Global Media,* 6 May.
Hobsbawm, E. and T. Ranger. 1983. *The Invention of Tradition.* Cambridge: Canto.
Hogg, N. 2010. 'Women's Participation in the Rwandan Genocide: Mothers or Monsters?' *International Review of the Red Cross* 92: 69–102.
Huggins, C. 2009. 'Agricultural Policies and Local Grievances in Rural Rwanda'. *Peace Review* 21(3): 296–303.
———. 2013. 'Seeing Like a Neoliberal State? Authoritarian High Modernism, Commercialization and Governmentality in Rwanda's Agricultural Reform', PhD Dissertation, Carleton University, MN, USA.
Huggins, C. and H. Musahara. 2005 'Land Reform, Land Scarcity and Post-Conflict Reconstruction: A Case Study of Rwanda'. Accessed 20 May 2011, http://www.iss.co.za/pubs/Books/GroundUp/6Land.pdf.
Human Rights Watch Rwanda (HRW). 1992. 'Rwanda: Talking Peace and Waging War. Human Rights since the October 1990 Invasion'. *Africa Watch* 4(3)
———. 1995. 'Rwanda: The Crisis Continues', 1 April 1995, A701. Accessed 23 August 2009, www.unhcr.org/refworld/docid/3ae6a7f50.html.
———. 1999. 'Hostile to Democracy: The Movement System and Political Repression in Uganda'. Available at http://www.unhcr.org/refworld/country,,HRW,,UGA,456d621e2,45dad0c02,0.html
———. 2000. 'Rwanda: The Search for Security and Human Rights Abuses'. Accessed 22 January 2007, http://www.hrw.org/reports/2000/rwanda/.
———. 2001. *Uprooting the Rural Poor in Rwanda*, 1 May 2001. Accessed 23 February 2010, www.unhcr.org/refworld/docid/3bd540b40.html.
———. 2002. 'Preparing for Elections: Tightening Control in the Name of Unity', *HRW Briefing Paper,* May 2002. Accessed 8 November 2009, www.reliefweb.int/library/documents/2003/hrw-rwa-8may.pdf.
———. 2003. 'Lasting Wounds: Consequences of Genocide and War for Rwanda's Children', March 2003, vol. 15, no. 6. Accessed 3 November 2008, www.hrw.org/sites/default/files/reports/rwanda0403.pdf.

———. 2007. "There Will Be No Trial" Police Killings of Detainees and the Imposition of Collective Punishments', July 2007.
———. 2008. 'Law and Reality: Progress in Judicial Reform in Rwanda', 24 July 2008, Available on HRW website at http://www.hrw.org/en/node/62097/section/1.
———. 2009. 'Burundi: Stop Deporting Rwandan Asylum Seekers'. *Human Rights Watch*, 2 December 2009.
———. 2010a. 'Rwanda: Silencing Dissent Ahead of Elections'. *Human Rights Watch Press Release*, 2 August 2010.
———. 2010b. 'Rwanda: Stop Attacks on Journalists, Opponents'. *Human Rights Watch Press Release*, 26 June 2010.
———. 2012. 'DR Congo: M23 Rebels Committing War Crimes'. *Human Rights Watch Press Release*, 11 September 2012.
———. 2014. 'Rwanda: Spate of Enforced Disappearances'. *Human Rights Watch Press Release*, 16 May 2014.
Humanitarian Policy Group (HPG), Overseas Development Institute (ODI). 2007. 'Returnee Land Access: Lessons from Rwanda', *An HPG Background Briefing*, June 2007. Accessed 4 September 2010, http://www.odi.org.uk/resources/download/3187.pdf.
Hutchinson, S.E. 1996. *Nuer Dilemmas: Coping With Money, War and the State*. Berkley: University of California Press.
Huyse, L. and M. Salter (eds). 2008. *Traditional Justice and Reconciliation After Violent Conflict: Learning from African Experiences*. Stockholm: International IDEA.
Ingelaere, B. 2009. 'Does the Truth Pass Across the Fire Without Burning?' Locating the Short Circuit in Rwanda's Gacaca Courts'. *Journal of Modern African Studies* 47(4): 507–528.
———. 2010. 'Do We Understand Life After Genocide?' Centre and Periphery in the Construction of Knowledge in Post-Genocide Rwanda'. *African Studies Review* 53(1): 41–59.
———. 2014. 'What's on a Peasant's Mind? Experiencing RPF State Reach and Overreach in Post-Genocide Rwanda (2000–2010)'. *The Journal of Eastern African Studies* 8(2): 214–230.
Institute for Justice and Reconciliation (IJR). 2005. 'Evaluation and Impact Assessment of the National Unity and Reconciliation Commission (NURC)'. Accessed 12 January 2009, www.nurc.gov.rw/documents/researches/Impact_assessment_of_NURC_Sammary.pdf.
International Crisis Group (ICG). 2002. 'Rwanda at the End of the Transition: A Necessary Political Liberalisation'. Accessed 23 February 2007, www.grandslacs.net/doc/2555.pdf.
Internews. 2003. 'Over 20,000 Freed Genocide Perpetrators Taken to Solidarity Camps'. *Internews*, 31 January. http://business.highbeam.com/3548/article-1G1-97127671/over-20000-freed-genocide-perpetrators-taken-solidarity.
———. 2003. 'When Killers and Their Victims Meet', *Internews/All Africa Global Media*, 26 February.
Integrated Regional Information Networks (IRIN). 2008. 'Rwanda: Sustainable Peace Key to Post-Genocide Reconciliation', 26 August.
Jackson, R.H. and C.G. Rosberg. 1982. 'Why Africa's Weak States Persist: The Empirical and the Juridical in Statehood'. *World Politics* 35 (1): 1–24.

Jackson, S. (undated). 'Relief, Improvement, Power: Motives and Motifs of Rwanda's Villagisation Policy'. International Famine Centre (IFC). Accessed 20 February 2009, http://www.ucc.ie/acad/sociology/rip/essays/rwanda.htm.

Jefremovas, V. 2002. *Brickyards to Graveyards: From Production to Genocide in Rwanda.* Albany, NY: SUNY Press.

Jennings, M. 2009. 'Building Better People: Modernity and Utopia in Late Colonial Tanganyika'. *Journal of Eastern African Studies* 3(1): 94–111.

Johnson, D.H. 2003. *The Root Causes of Sudan's Civil Wars.* Oxford: James Currey.

Joint Governance Assessment (JGA): RWANDA. 2008a. 'First Draft: Volume I', March 4, 2008, Prepared by a team of consultants from *The Policy Practice*, UK.

———. 2008b. 'The JGA Report Endorsed by Cabinet on 12/09/08', 8 October 2008.

Jones, M. 2007. *An Introduction to Political Geography: Space, Place, and Politics.* New York: Routledge.

Kabeera, E. 2011. 'Itorero to Extend to Village Level'. *The New Times Kigali*, 21 January.

Kagame, A. 1952. *Le Code des Institutions Politiques du Rwanda Précolonial.* Brussels, Royal Academy of Overseas Sciences, Moral and Political Sciences Section, no. 26, Belgian Royal Colonial Institute.

Kagame, P. 2003. 'Speech by Paul Kagame on the Occasion of the International Water Day'. Rebero, Bwisige, Byumba, 31 March 2003. Accessed 30 October 2009, http://rwandanet.tripod.com/bwisige31march2003.html.

Kagire, A. 2009. 'Emulate Heroes – Kagame'. *The New Times Kigali*, 1 February.

Kagire, E. 2009. 'Health Workers Vow to Excel', *The New Times Kigali*, 3 August.

———. 2010. 'Home Grown Ideas Working for Rwanda – Kagame'. *The New Times Kigali*, 8 February.

Kailitz, S. 2013. 'Classifying Political Regimes Revisited: Legitimation and Durability'. *Democratization* 20(1): 39–60.

Kaiza, G. 2003. 'From a Past of Hostilities to a Future of Partnerships', *African Church Information Review*, 18 March 2003.

Kakimba, M. 2006. 'Poverty to be Discussed on Umuganda', *The New Times Kigali*, 29 September.

Karuhanga, J. 2008. 'Development Takes Centre Stage as National Dialogue Begins', *The New Times Kigali*, 19 December.

Kerekezi, A., A. Nshimiyimana and B. Mutamba. 2004. 'Localizing Justice: Gacaca Courts in Post-Genocide Rwanda'. In *My Neighbor, My Enemy: Justice and Community in the Aftermath of Mass Atrocity*, Stover, E. and H. Weinstein (eds). Cambridge: Cambridge University Press.

Kezio-Musoke, D. 2008. 'MPs in Bid to Stamp Out "Genocide Ideology"', *The New Times Kigali*, 18 January.

King, E. 2009. 'From Data Problems to Data Points: Challenges and Opportunities of Research in Post-Genocide Rwanda'. *African Studies Review* 52(3): 127–48.

Kinzer, S. 2008. *A Thousand Hills: Rwanda's Rebirth and the Man who Dreamt It.* New Jersey: John Wiley and Sons.

Knudsen, J.C. 1991. 'Therapeutic Strategies and Strategies for Refugee Coping'. *Journal of Refugee Studies* 4(1): 21–38.

Kuperman, A. 2001. *The Limits of Humanitarian Intervention: The Genocide in Rwanda.* Washington, D.C.: The Brookings Institution.

Kuran, T. 1995. *Private Truths, Public Lies: The Social Consequences of Preference Falsification.* Cambridge: Harvard University Press.
Kwibuka, E. 2008. 'Children Pledge to Fight Genocide Ideology', *The New Times Kigali,* 14 November.
———. 2009. 'Hero's Day to Focus on Reviving Cultural Values for Development', *The New Times Kigali,* 26 January.
Kwinjeh, G. 2008a. 'Smart Politics – Country Geared for Parliamentary Female Domination'. *The News Times Kigali,* 23 August.
———. 2008b. 'Abanyarwanda Register for New IDs'. *New Times Kigali,* 26 July.
Kwizera, C. 2008. 'Churches Have Big Role in Nation Building – Mushikiwabo', *The New Times Kigali,* 15 October.
———. 2009. 'Rwanda: Over 30,000 Have Passed Through Ingando'. *The New Times Kigali,* 2 August. Accessed 15 April 2009, http://allafrica.com/stories/200908030592.html.
Kyamuterera, M. 2006. 'Reconciliation through Sports', October 5.
Lefort, R. 2010. 'Powers- *Mengist-* and Peasants in Rural Ethiopia: The Post-2005 Interlude'. *The Journal of Modern African Studies* 48(3): 435–460.
Leggat Smith, Y. 1995. *Rwanda. Not So Innocent: When Women Become Killers.* African Rights.
Lemarchand, R. 1992. 'Uncivil States and Civil Societies: How Illusion Became Reality'. *Journal of Modern African Studies* 30(2): 177–191.
———. 1994. *Burundi: Ethnic Conflict and Genocide.* Cambridge: University of Cambridge Press.
———. 1997. 'Patterns of State Collapse and Reconstruction in Central Africa: Reflections on the Crisis in the Great Lakes'. *African Studies Quarterly* 1(3): 1–15.
———. 2007. 'Consociationalism and Power Sharing in Africa: Rwanda, Burundi, and the Democratic Republic of the Congo', *African Affairs* 106(422): 1–20.
———. 2009. *The Dynamics of Violence in Central Africa.* Philadelphia: University of Pennsylvania Press.
Lemke, T. 2000. 'Foucault, Governmentality, and Critique'. Paper presented at the Rethinking Marxism Conference, University of Amherst, 21–24 September 2000. Available at www.andosciasociology.net/.../Foucault$2C+Governmentality$2C+and+Critique+IV-2.pdf.
Leonardi, C. 2011. 'Paying "Buckets of Blood" for the Land: Moral Debates over Economy, War and the State in Southern Sudan'. *Journal of Modern African Studies* 49: 215–240.
———. 2013. *Dealing with Government in South Sudan: Histories of Chiefship, Community and State.* Oxford: James Currey.
Levi, P. 1989. *The Drowned and the Saved.* New York: Vintage Books.
Lewis, I.M. 1988. *A Modern History of Somalia: Nation and State in the Horn of Africa.* Boulder, Colorado: Westview Press.
Lischer, S.K. 2005. *Dangerous Sanctuaries: Refugee Camps, Civil War and the Dilemmas of Humanitarian Aid,* Ithaca: Cornell University Press.
Longman, T. 2010. 'Trying Times for Rwanda: Reevaluating Gacaca Courts in Post-Genocide Reconciliation'. *Harvard International Law Review* 32(2): 48–52.
Longman, T. and T. Rutagengwa. 2004. 'Memory, Identity, and Community in Rwanda'. In *My Neighbor, My Enemy: Justice and Social Reconstruction in Rwanda*

and the Former Yugoslavia, Weinstein, H. and E. Stover (eds). Cambridge: Cambridge University Press.

———. 2006. 'Memory and Violence in Postgenocide Rwanda'. In *States of Violence: Politics, Youth and Memory in Contemporary Africa*, Bay, E. and D. Donham (eds). University of Virginia Press.

Lukes, S. 1974. *Power: A Radical View*. London: Palgrave Macmillan.

Lundy, P. and M. McGovern. 2006. 'The Ethics of Silence: Action Research, Community "Truth-Telling" and Post-Conflict Transition in the North of Ireland'. *Action Research* 4(1): 49–64.

Lyons, T. and A.I. Samatar. 1995. *Somalia: State Collapse, Multilateral Intervention, and Strategies for Political Reconstruction*. Washington: Brookings Institution.

Malkki, L. 1995. *Purity and Exile: Violence, Memory and National Cosmology among Hutu Refugees in Tanzania*. Chicago: University of Chicago Press.

Mamdani, M. 1996. *Citizen and Subject: Contemporary Africa and the Legacy of Late Colonialism*. Princeton: Princeton University Press.

———. 2001. *When Victims Become Killers: Colonialism, Nativism, and the Genocide in Rwanda*. Princeton: Princeton University Press.

———. 2007. 'The Politics of Naming: Genocide, Civil War, Insurgency'. *London Review of Books* 29(5): 5–8.

Mann, M. 1984. 'The Autonomous Power of the State: Its Origins, Mechanisms, and Results'. *Archives Europeénes de Sociologie* 25: 185–213.

———. 1986. *The Sources of Social Power*. Cambridge: The University of Cambridge Press.

Manning, C. 1998. 'Constructing Opposition in Mozambique: Renamo as Political Party'. *Journal of Southern African Studies* 24(1): 161–89.

Marcus, G.E. 2000. 'Emotions in Politics'. *Annual Review of Political Science* 3: 221–250.

———. 2003. 'The Psychology of Emotion and Politics', Chapter 6 in Sears, D.O., L. Huddy and R. Jervis. (eds). *Oxford Handbook of Political Psychology*. Oxford: Oxford University Press.

Marysse, S. 1982. 'Basic Needs, Income Distribution and the Political Economy of Rwanda', Paper 82/55 in the series of the Centre for Development Studies, Antwerp, University of Antwerp.

Maundi, M.O., W. Zartman, G. Khadiagala and K. Nuamah. (eds). 2006. *Getting In: Mediators' Entry Into the Settlement of African Conflicts*. Washington, D.C.: United States Institute of Peace Press.

Mbabazi L. 2005. 'Released Prisoners No Angels After All!', *The New Times Kigali*, September 14.

Mbembe, A. 2001. *On The Postcolony*. London: University of California Press.

Mboyo, D. 2009. *Dead Aid: Why Aid Is Not Working and How There Is a Better Way for Africa*. New York: Farrar, Straus and Giroux.

McConnell, J. 2009. 'Institution [Un]Building: Decentralising Government and the Case of Rwanda', Report for the European University Institute, 15 May 2009. Accessed 5 December 2009, http://erd.eui.eu/media/mcconnell.pdf.

McEvoy, K. 2007. 'Beyond Legalism: Towards a Thicker Understanding of Transitional Justice'. *Journal of Law and Society* 34(4): 411–440.

McGregor, J. 2013. 'Surveillance and the City: Patronage, Power-Sharing and the Politics of Urban Control in Zimbabwe'. *Journal of Southern African Studies* 39(4): 783–805.

McNamara, R., T. McGinn, D. Lauro and J. Ross. 1992. 'Family Planning Programs in Sub-Saharan Africa: Case Studies from Ghana, Rwanda and the Sudan'. *World Bank Policy Research Working Paper: Population, Health and Nutrition*, no. 1004, October 1992.

Meagher, K. 2012. 'The Power of Weak States? Non-State Security Forces and Hybrid Governance in Africa'. *Development and Change* 43(5): 1073–1101.

Melvin, J. 2013. 'Correcting History: Mandatory Education in Rwanda'. *Journal of Human Rights in the Commonwealth* 1(2): 14–22.

Menkhaus, K. 2008. 'The Rise of a Mediated State in Northern Kenya: The Wajir Story and its Implications for State-Building'. *Afrika Focus* 21 (2): 23–38.

———. 2010. 'State Fragility as a Wicked Problem'. *Prism* 1(2): 85–101.

Mgbako, C. 2005. '*Ingando* Solidarity Camps: Reconciliation and Political Indoctrination in Post-Genocide Rwanda'. *Harvard Human Rights Journal* 18: 201–224.

Migdal, J. 1988. *Strong Societies and Weak States*. Princeton: Princeton University Press.

———. 2001. *State in Society: Studying How States and Societies Transform and Constitute One Another.* Cambridge: Cambridge University Press.

Minow, M. 1998. *Between Vengeance and Forgiveness: Facing History After Genocide and Mass Violence.* Boston: Beacon Press.

Minow, M. and A. Chayes. 2003. *Imagine Coexistence: Restoring Humanity After Violent Conflict.* San Francisco: Jossey Bass.

Mironko, C.K. 2006. 'Ibitero: Means and Motive in the Rwandan Genocide'. In *Genocide in Cambodia and Rwanda: New Perspectives*, S.E. Cook (ed.). New Brunswick, NJ: Transaction.

Mortland, C.A. 1987. 'Transforming Refugees in Refugee Camps'. *Urban Anthropology* 16: 375–404.

Mugabe, R. 2009. 'ULK Students Cautioned Against Divisionism'. *The News Times Kigali*, 20 February.

Mukarutabana, R.-M. 'Gakondo: The Royal Myths'. Accessed 1 December 2008, http://webspinners.com/Gakondo/en/Myths/index.php.

Mukombozi, B. 2009. 'Focus on Economic Transformation, Musoni Urges Coffee Growers', *The News Times Kigali*, 8 June.

Mulindwa, E. 2003. 'Rukokoma Keeps the Opposition Fire Alive'. *Ugandanet*, 19 August. Available at www.mailarchive.com/ugandanet@kym.net/msg06082.html.

Muller, T. 2008. 'Bare Life and the Developmental State: Implications of the Militarisation of Higher Education in Eritrea'. *Journal of Modern African Studies* 46(1): 111–131.

Munyaneza, J. 2009. 'Grappling with Heroes' Day Biggest Question', *The News Times Kigali*, 3 February.

Musoni, P. 2003. 'The End of the Transition Period: Prospects and Challenges', prepared for the Workshop on Citizenship and Social Reconstruction in the Aftermath of the Genocide, The National University of Rwanda. Accessed 5 May 2009, http://www.minaloc.gov.rw/IMG/doc/goodgov/1/butare_university_paper_uk.pdf.

Mutara, E. 2006. 'Ubusabane, Umuganda Not Fully Exploited'. *The New Times Kigali,* 19 December. Available at http://allafrica.com/stories/200612190851.html.

———. 2010. 'Teachers Seek Salary Increment' *The News Times Kigali,* 5 October.

Nagy, R. 2008. 'Transitional Justice as Global Project: Critical Reflections'. *Third World Quarterly* 29 (2): 275–289.

Naniwe-Kaburahe, A. 2008. 'The Burundian Conflict'. Chapter 6 in Huyse, L. and M. Salter (eds). (2008) *Traditional Justice and Reconciliation after Violent Conflict. Learning from African Experiences.* Stockholm, International IDEA, pp. 149–179.

National Assembly. 2003. 'Report of the Parliamentary Commission put in place on the 27th of December, 2002 to Investigate the Problems of MDR', accepted by the National Transitional Assembly on 14 April 2003.

———. 2004. 'Rapport de la Commission Parlementaire ad hoc crée en date du 20 Janvier 2004 par le Parlement, Chambre des Députés, Chargée d'Examiner les Tueries Perpetrées dans la Province de Gikongoro, l'Idéologie Génocidaire et ceux qui la Propagent Partout au Rwanda', accepted by the National Assembly on 30 June 2004.

———. 2007. 'Rapport d'Analyse sur le Problème d'Idéologie du Génocide Evoquée au Sein des Etablissements Scolaires', December 2007 [translation from Kinyarwanda by HRW].

National Democratic Institute (NDI). 2003. 'Assessment of Rwanda's Pre-Election Political Environment and the Role of Political Parties', 3–11 August 2003. Accessed 14 October 2009, http://pdf.usaid.gov/pdf_docs/PNADD285.pdf.

National Unity and Reconciliation Commission (NURC). 2005. 'Raporo Y'Ibikorwa Umwaka W'I 2004 [Report on Activities in Year 2004]'. Available at http://www.grandslacs.net/doc/3872.pdf.

———. 2006. 'Impact of the Solidarity Camps/*Ingando* on Unity and Reconciliation of Rwandans, 1996–2006'. Available at www.nurc.gov.rw.

———. 2007. 'The National Policy of Unity and Reconciliation', printed by PROGRAPH s.a.r.l.

———. 2008a. 'A Concept Paper on Unity and Reconciliation Week'.

———. 2008b. 'Social Cohesion in Rwanda: An Opinion Survey'.

———. 2009a. 'Strategic Plan of the Unity and Reconciliation Committee, 2009–2012'.

———. 2009b. 'Strategic Plan 2009–2012 of Itorero ry'Igihugu'.

———. 2012. 'List of Itorero Groups'.

Navarro-Yashin, Y. 2012. *The Make-Believe Space. Affective Geography in a Postwar Polity.* Durham, NC: Duke University Press.

Ndangiza, F. and A. Mugabo. 2008. 'The Process of Unity and Reconciliation in Rwanda', *Peace and Conflict Management Review* 1(1), Article 10. Available at: URL <http://scholarcommons.usf.edu/cgi/viewcontent.cgi?article=1009&context=pcmr>

Ndaruhuye, D.M., A. Broekhuis and P. Hooimeijer. 2009. 'Demand and Unmet Need for Means of Family Limitation in Rwanda'. *International Perspectives on Sexual and Reproductive Health* 35(3), September 2009.

Ndekezi, V. 2006. 'Experiential Learning for Conflict Resolution and Peace Building in the Great Lakes Region', Presented at the Outward Bound World Conference, Cape Town. Accessed 15 January 2007, www.outward-bound.org/conference/presenters/docs/Experiential%20Learning-Rwanda.pdf.

Neuman, R.W., G. Marcus, M. MacKuen and A.N. Crigler. 2007. *The Affect Effect: Dynamics of Emotion in Political Thinking and Behavior.* Chicago: University of Chicago Press.

Newbury, C. 1988. *The Cohesion of Oppression: Clientship and Ethnicity in Rwanda 1860–1960.* New York: Columbia University Press.

Newbury, D. 2001. 'Precolonial Burundi and Rwanda: Local Loyalties, Regional Royalties'. *The International Journal of African Historical Studies* 34(2): 255–314.

Newbury, D. and C. Newbury. 2000. 'Bringing the Peasants Back In: Agrarian Themes in the Construction and Corrosion of Statist Historiography in Rwanda'. *American Historical Review* 105(3): 832–877.

New Times Kigali (NTK). 2006. 'Rwanda: NURC; the Facilitator to Participatory Conflict Management', *The New Times Kigali*, 1 March.

———. 2006. 'Rwanda: Cabinet Reshuffle: What Could Have Cost Them Their Jobs?' *The New Times Kigali*, 22 March.

———. 2007. 'Health Insurance Defaulters Locked out of Market', *New Times Kigali*, 15 March.

———. 2007. 'RPF Polls Successful', *New Times Kigali*, 9 July.

———. 2008. 'Upcountry Insight: Lessons from Imihigo', *New Times Kigali*, 10 November.

———. 2008. 'Religious Leaders to Adopt Performance Contracts', *New Times Kigali*, 24 June 2008.

———. 2008. 'Taking Umuganda to a Higher Level', *New Times Kigali*, 27 February.

New Vision Uganda. 2008. 'District Officials to Train at Kyankwanzi', *New Vision Uganda*, 10 November.

Ngabonziza, D. 2008 'Two Primary School Girls Jailed Over Genocide Ideology'. *New Times Kigali*, 13 September.

———. 2009. 'Local Leaders Tough on Umuganda Dodgers'. *The New Times Kigali*, 12 August.

Niyonshuti, I. 2009. 'Cadres Urged to Foster Change'. *The New Times Kigali*, 17 November.

Nkurunziza, S. 2009a. 'Consultant Calls for Children's Commission, Parliament', *The New Times Kigali*, 8 May.

———. 2009b. 'Ingando – Inculcating Unity and Reconciliation into Locals'. *The New Times Kigali*, January 17.

Nordstrom, C. 1997. *A Different Kind of War Story.* Philadelphia: University of Pennsylvania Press.

Nordstrom, C. and A. Robben (eds). 1995. *Fieldwork Under Fire: Contemporary Studies of Violence and Survival.* Berkeley and Los Angeles: University of California Press.

Ntaganda, G. 2010. 'Umuganda is a Healing Tool'. *The New Times Kigali*, 6 August.

Ntambara, P. 2007. 'Be Good Citizens, Ex-Inmates Advised'. *The New Times /All Africa Global Media*, 28 February.

O'Farrell, C. 2005. *Michel Foucault.* London: Sage.

Office of the President of the Republic. 1999a. 'Report on the Reflection Meetings Held in the Office of the President of the Republic from May 1998 to March 1999'.

———. 1999b. 'The Unity of Rwandans – Before the Colonial Period and Under the Colonial Rule, Under the First Republic', Kigali, August 1999.

Oomen, B. 2006. 'Rwanda's Gacaca: Objectives, Merits and Their Relation to Supranational Criminal Law'. In *Sentencing in Supranational Criminal Law*, R. Haveman et al. (eds). The Hague: Intersentia, pp. 161–184. Accessed 22 January 2007, http://www.ceri-sciencespo.com/themes/re-imaginingpeace/va/resources/rwanda_gacaca_oomen.pdf.

Organic Law. 2003. 'Organic Law No. 16/2003 of 27/06/2003 on Governing of Political Organizations and Politicians'.

Organization for Peace, Justice, and Development in Rwanda (OPJDR) 2001. 'OPJDR Rejects March 2001 Rwandan Local Elections', 15 March 2001, Available at http://www.inshuti.org/opjdr5.htm

Pambazuka News. 2010. 'Forced Repatriations Taking Place in Uganda'. *Pambazuka News Issue* 496, 17 September.

Pankhurst, D. (ed.). 2008. *Gendered Peace: Women's Struggles for Post-War Justice and Reconciliation*. Oxford: Routledge.

Pells, K., K. Pontalti and T.P. Williams. 2014. 'Promising Developments? Children, Youth and Post-Genocide Reconstruction under the Rwandan Patriotic Front (RPF)'. *Journal of Eastern Africa Studies* 8(2): 294–310.

Penal Reform International (PRI). 2004. 'From Camp to Hill: The Reintegration of Released Prisoners'. Accessed 3 March 2007, http://www.penalreform.org/research-on-gacaca-report-vi-from-camp-to-hill-the-reintegration-of-released-pris-3.html.

———. 2007. 'Transitional Justice in Rwanda: The Limitations of the Popular Gacaca Courts', *PRI Newsletter* 60(4). Accessed 15 January 2010, http://www.juvenilejusticepanel.org/resource/items/P/R/PRINewsl60_07_EN.pdf.

Phillips, N. and C. Hardy. 2002. *Discourse Analysis: Investigating Processes of Social Construction*. London: Sage.

Pinchotti, S. and P. Verwimp. 2007. 'Social Capital and the Rwandan Genocide: A Micro-Level Analysis'. *HiCN Working Paper*, 30 March 2007.

Pottier, J. 1989. '"Three's a crowd": Knowledge, Ignorance and Power in the Context of Urban Agriculture in Rwanda'. *Africa* 59(4): 461–477.

———. 1992. 'Intolerable Environments: Towards a Cultural Reading of Agrarian Practice and Policy in Rwanda'. In *Bush Base: Forest Farm*, J. Parkin and L. Croll (eds). London: Routledge, pp. 146–168.

———. 1993. 'Taking Stock: Food Marketing Reform in Rwanda, 1982–1989'. *African Affairs*, 92: 5–30.

———. 2002. *Re-Imagining Rwanda. Conflict, Disinformation and Survival in the Late Twentieth Century*. Cambridge: Cambridge University Press.

———. 2006. 'Land Reform for Peace? Rwanda's 2005 Land Law in Context'. *Journal of Agrarian Change* 6(4): 509–537.

Prime Minister's Office. 2009. 'National Agricultural Extension Strategy [Draft]', Available at www.primature.gov.rw/index2.php?option=com_docman&task=doc_view&gid=901&Itemid=95.

Prunier, G. 1995. *The Rwanda Crisis: History of a Genocide*. New York: Columbia University Press.
———. 2009. *From Genocide to Continental War: The 'Congolese' Conflict and the Crisis of Contemporary Africa*. London: Hurst and Company. 1995. *The Rwanda Crisis: History of a Genocide*. New York: Columbia University Press.
Purdeková, A. 2008a. 'Building a Nation in Rwanda? De-ethnicization and its Discontents'. *Studies in Ethnicity and Nationalism* 8(3): 502–523.
———. 2008b. 'Repatriation and Reconciliation in Divided Societies: The Case of Rwanda's *Ingando*'. *Oxford Refugee Studies Centre Working Paper*, no. 43.
———. 2009. 'New Identity Politics for Post-Genocide Rwanda: Deconstruction of Identity Discourse, Reconstruction of a Political Community'. Paper presented at the 2009 UK Development Studies Annual Conference (DSA) entitled 'Current Crises and New Opportunities' held at University of Ulster, Northern Ireland.
———. 2011. '"Even If I Am Not Here, There Are So Many Eyes:" Surveillance and State Reach in Rwanda'. *Journal of Modern African Studies*, 49(3): 475–497.
———. 2012. '"Civic Education" and Social Transformation in Post-Genocide Rwanda: Forging the Perfect Development Subjects'. In *Rwanda Fast Forward: Social, Economic, Military and Reconciliation Prospects*, Campioni, M. and P. Noack (eds). London: Palgrave Macmillan.
———. 2013. 'Rendering Rwanda Governable: Order, Containment and Cleansing in the Rationality of Post-Genocide Rule'. *L'Afrique des Grands Lacs Annuaire 2012-2013*.
Rabinow, P. 1977. *Reflections on Fieldwork in Morocco*. Los Angeles: University of California Press.
Radio Rwanda. 1997. 'President Launches Campaign to Integrate Returning Refugees', *BBC Monitoring Service Africa*, Excerpts from Radio Rwanda broadcast on 25 May (0515 GMT).
Raeymaekers, T., K. Menkhaus and K. Vlassenroot. 2008. 'State and Non-State Regulation in African Protracted Crises: Governance without Government?' *Afrika Focus* 21(2): 7–21.
Ramadan, A. 2012. 'Spatialising the Refugee Camp'. *Transactions* 38(1): 65–77.
Reid, R. 2009. *A History of Modern Africa: 1800 to the Present*. Oxford: Blackwell.
Reed, C. 1995. 'The Rwanda Patriotic Front: Politics and Development in Rwanda'. *Issue: A Journal of Opinion* 23(2): 48–53.
———. 1996. 'Exile, Reform, and the Rise of the Rwanda Patriotic Front'. *Journal of Modern African Studies* 34(3): 479–501.
Renner, J. 2014. 'The Local Roots of the Global Politics of Reconciliation: The Articulation of 'Reconciliation' as an Empty Universal in the South African Transition to Democracy'. *Millennium: Journal of International Studies* 42(2): 263–285.
Reno, W. 1998. *Warlord Politics and African States*. Boulder: Lynne Rienner.
Republic of Rwanda, Eastern Province, District Of Ngoma. 2009. '*Imihigo* Report 2008'. Accessed 23 January 2010, http://www.primature.gov.rw/index2.php?option=com_docman&task=doc_view&gid=794&Itemid=95.
Rettig, M. 2008. 'Gacaca: Truth, Justice, and Reconciliation in Postconflict Rwanda?' *African Studies Review* 51(3): 25–50.

Reyntjens, F. 2004. 'Rwanda, Ten Years On: From Genocide to Dictatorship'. *African Affairs* 103(411): 177–210.
———. 2006. 'Post-1994 Politics in Rwanda: Problematising "Liberation" and "Democratisation"'. *Third World Quarterly* 27(6): 1103–1117.
———. 2009. 'Rwanda: A Fake Report on Fake Elections'. Accessed 31 January 2009, http://survivorsnetworks.blogspot.com/2009/02/rwanda-fake-report-on-fake-elections.html.
———. 2011a. 'Constructing the Truth, Dealing with Dissent, Domesticating the World: Governance in Post-Genocide Rwanda'. *African Affairs* 110(438): 1–34.
———. 2011b. *The Great African War: Congo and Regional Geopolitics, 1996–2006*. Cambridge: Cambridge University Press.
———. 2013. *Political Governance in Post-Genocide Rwanda*. Cambridge: Cambridge University Press.
Roth, K. 2009. 'The Power of Horror in Rwanda', *Los Angeles Times*, 11 April. Available from HRW website at URL <http://www.hrw.org/en/news/2009/04/11/power-horror-rwanda>
Ruburika, S. 2009. 'Unity and Reconciliation Not Possible Without Development', *The New Times Kigali*, 13 December.
Rumiya, J. 1985. 'Ruanda d'Hier, Rwanda d'Aujourd'hui'. *Vivant Univers*, no. 357: 2–8.
Rwanda Dispatch. 2008. '98% Turnout. Uniquely Rwandan', Issue 02, October 2008.
Rwanda Ministry of Agriculture (MINAGRI). 2006. 'A Proposal to Distribute a Cow to Every Poor Family in Rwanda', May 2006, Available at URL: <http://www.rarda.gov.rw/IMG/pdf/ONE_COW_JULY2006_1_-2.pdf>
Rwanda Ministry of Finance and Economic Planning (MINECOFIN). 2000. 'Rwanda Vision 2020'. July 2000. Accessed 24 February 2008, http://www.gesci.org/assets/files/Rwanda_Vision_2020.pdf.
———. 2010a. '2010–2013 Budget Framework Paper', April 2010.
———. 2010b. 'Annex [to the Budget Framework Paper]: State Revenues 2010–2013', Document Accessed 7 January 2011, http://www.minecofin.gov.rw/squelettes-dist/budgetdocs/index.php?dir=1. National+Budget%2F1. Annual+State+Finance+Law%2FCurrent+Year+Finance+Law%2FOriginal+Budget%2FRevenue+Annexe%2F.
Rwanda Ministry of Local Government, Community Development and Social Affairs (MINALOC). 2006. 'Mechanisms for Participation and Accountability at Community and Decentralized Levels in Rwanda', MINALOC, Available at http://www.minaloc.gov.rw/IMG/pdf_Microsoft_Word__doc_sur_la_part_b_m.pdf.
———. 2008. 'Good Practices on African Policy Reforms which promote Transparency, Accountability, and Participation in Municipal Public Expenditure Management and Service Delivery', paper presented by Musoni Protais at RSA Durban. Accessed 22 October 2009, http://www.minaloc.gov.rw/IMG/pdf_African_good_practices.pdf.
———. 2009. 'National Values to Promote Progress to Vision 2020 – *Indangagaciro Zafasha Kugera Kuri Vision 2020*'. Accessed 24 January 2010, http://www.minaloc.gov.rw/IMG/pdf_INDANGAGACIRO-2.pdf.

———. 2010. 'Concept Paper on *Imihigo* Planning and Evaluation'. Accessed 10 September 2010, http://minaloc.gov.rw/IMG/pdf_Imihigo_Concept_Note_22_feb_2010_1_.pdf.
———. 2012. 'Volunteerism Policy Paper'. Accessed 10 June 2013, http://www.minaloc.gov.rw/fileadmin/documents/Minaloc_Documents/VOLUNTEERISM_POLICY_.pdf.
Rwanda Ministry of Sports and Culture. 2004. *Intwari Z'U Rwanda*, Kigali.
Rwanda Monitoring Project (RMP). 2003. 'Tell Our Government It Is OK to Be Criticized!' Report accessed 9 January 2009 at the *Great Lakes Initiative on Human Rights* Library.
Rwanda Youth Gathering. 2008. 'Inter-denominational Youth Gathering Concludes in Kigali, Rwanda', posted on Rwanda Youth Gathering Weblog on 13 April. Accessed 6 March 2009, http://rwandayouthgathering.wordpress.com/.
Sabiiti, D. 2007. 'Ecstasy as Ex-Prisoners Begin Ingando', *The New Times Kigali*, 28 February.
Sagashya, D. and English, C. 2009. 'Designing and Establishing a Land Administration System for Rwanda: Technical and Economic Analysis', *World Bank Paper*, February 2009. Accessed 5 January 2010 www.fig.net/pub/fig_wb_2009/papers/sys/sys_2_english_sagashya.pdf.
Sagy, T. 2008. 'Treating Peace as Knowledge: The UNHCR's Peace Education as a Controlling Process'. *Journal of Refugee Studies* 21: 360–379.
Schatz, E. (ed.). 2009. *Political Ethnography: What Immersion Contributes to the Study of Power*. Chicago: University of Chicago Press.
Scheper-Hughes, N. 1992. *Death Without Weeping: Violence of Everyday Life in Brazil*. Los Angeles: University of California Press.
Schmitt, C. 1927. *The Concept of the Political*. Chicago: The University of Chicago Press.
Scott, J. 1985. *Weapons of the Weak: Everyday Forms of Peasant Resistance*. New Haven: Yale University Press.
———. 1990. *Domination and the Arts of Resistance: Hidden Transcripts*. New Haven: Yale University Press.
———. 1998. *Seeing Like a State: How Certain Schemes to Improve the Human Condition Have Failed*. New Haven: Yale University Press.
Sebasoni, S. 2007. *Le Rwanda: Reconstruire une Nation*. Imprimerie Papeterie Nouvelle.
Sen, A. 1999. *Development as Freedom*. Oxford: Oxford University Press.
———. 2001. 'Democracy as a Universal Value'. In *The Global Divergence of Democracies*, L. Diamond and M. Plattner (eds). Baltimore: Johns Hopkins University Press, pp. 3–17.
Senate of Rwanda. 2006. 'Genocide Ideology and Strategies for Its Eradication'.
Sezibera, V. 2009. Presentation on 'Artificial Families'. *The International Symposium on Genocide*, Serena Hotel, Kigali, 4 April.
Sharma, A. and A. Gupta. 2006. *The Anthropology of the State: A Reader*. Oxford: Blackwell.
Shaw, R., L. Waldorf and P. Hazan. 2010. *Localizing Transitional Justice: Interventions and Priorities after Mass Violence*. Stanford: Stanford University Press.

Shyaka, A. 2007. 'Home Grown Mechanisms of Conflict Resolution in Africa's Great Lakes Region'. *Global Studies Review* 3(1), Available at http://www.globality-gmu.net/archives/893.

Sluka, J. (ed.). 2000. *Death Squad: The Anthropology of State Terror*. Philadelphia: University of Pennsylvania Press.

Smaker, M. and M.C. Johnson. 2014. 'State Building in De Facto States: Somaliland and Puntland Compared'. *Africa Today* 60(4): 3–23.

Smyth, M. and G. Robinson (eds). 2001. *Researching Violently Divided Societies: Ethical and Methodological Issues*. London: Pluto Press.

Sogge, D. 2009. 'Repairing the Weakest Links: A New Agenda for Fragile States'. *FRIDE- A European Think Tank for Global Action*, October 2009. Accessed 15 January 2010, http://www.humansecuritygateway.com/documents/FRIDE_RepairingWeakestLinks_NewAgendaFragileStates.pdf.

Soudan, F. 2009. 'Paul Kagamé: Nkunda, Kabila, la France et Lui', *La Jeune Afrique* N2514, 15–21 Mars, p. 46, Available also online at URL<http://www.jeuneafrique.com/Article/ARTJAJA2514p042-047.xml0/-Paul-Kagame-interview-NkundaKabilalaFranceetlui.html>

Southcott, D. 2011. 'State of Exception: An Agambenian Perspective on the Detention of North Koreans in South Korea'. *Refugee Law Initiative Working Paper No. 2*.

Ssuuna, I. and S. Nkurunziza. 2009. 'Ugandan Officials under Probe in Rwandan Refugees' Scam', *The New Times Kigali*, 19 May.

Stearns, J. 2011. *Dancing in the Glory of Monsters: The Collapse of the Congo and the Great War of Africa*. New York: Public Affairs.

Stewart, A. 2001. *Theories of Power and Domination: The Politics of Power in Late Modernity*. London: SAGE Publications.

Stockton, N. 1994. 'The Great Lakes Crisis and the Humanitarian Contract Culture'. RSC Documentation Centre (Grey Literature Collection), Oxford (unpublished).

Stoler, A.L. 2010. *Along the Archival Grain: Epistemic Anxieties and Colonial Common Sense*. Princeton: Princeton University Press.

Stover, E. and H. Weinstein. 2004. *My Neighbor, My Enemy: Justice and Community in the Aftermath of Mass Atrocity*. Cambridge: Cambridge University Press.

Straus, S. 2004. 'How Many Perpetrators Were There in the Rwandan Genocide? An Estimate'. *Journal of Genocide Research* 6(1): 85–98.

———. 2006. *The Order of Genocide*. Ithaca: Cornell University.

Straus, S. and R. Lyons. 2006. *Intimate Enemy: Images and Voices of the Rwandan Genocide*. New York: Zone Books.

Straus, S. and L. Waldorf. 2011. 'Introduction: Seeing Like a Post-Conflict State'. In *Re-Making Rwanda: State Building and Human Rights after Mass Violence*, S. Straus and L. Waldorf (eds). Madison: University of Wisconsin Press.

Strauss, A. 1987. *Qualitative Analysis for Social Scientists*. Cambridge: Cambridge University Press.

Sumich, J. 2011. 'The Party and the State: Frelimo and Social Stratification in Post-Socialist Mozambique'. Chapter 7 in Hagmann, T. and Peclard, D. (eds) *Negotiating Statehood: Dynamics of Power and Domination in Africa*, Oxford: Wiley-Blackwell.

Taussig, M. 1984. 'Culture of Terror, Space of Death. Roger Casement's Putumayo Report and the Explanation of Torture'. *Comparative Studies in Society and History* 26(3): 467–49.
Taylor, C. 1992. *Milk, Honey and Money: Changing Concepts in Rwandan Healing.* Washington DC: Smithsonian Institution Press.
Telegraph. 2009. 'Rwanda Suspends BBC Broadcasts', *The Telegraph* 26 April 2009. Accessed 23 June 2009, http://www.telegraph.co.uk/news/worldnews/africaandindianocean/rwanda/5226512/Rwanda-suspends-BBC-broadcasts.html.
The East African Standard 2003. 'Freed Genocide Convicts Begin Journey Home', *The East African*, 6 April.
Theidon, K. 2001. 'Terror's Talk: Fieldwork and War'. *Dialogical Anthropology* 26(1): 19–35.
———. 2006. 'Justice in Transition: The Micropolitics of Reconciliation in Post-War Peru'. *Journal of Conflict Resolution* 50(3): 433–457.
Thomson, S. 2008. 'Rwanda'. In *Africa Yearbook 5: Politics, Economy and Society South of the Sahara 2008*, ed. A. Mehler, H. Melber and K. van Walrave. Leiden: Brill. Accessed 23 September 2009, http://susanmthomson.com/publications.html.
———. 2010. 'Getting Close to Rwandans since the Genocide: Studying Everyday Life in Highly Politicized Research Settings'. *African Studies Review* 53(3): 19–34.
———. 2011. 'Whispering Truth to Power: The Everyday Resistance of Rwandan Peasants to Post-Genocide Reconciliation'. *African Affairs* 11(440): 439–456.
———. 2013. *Whispering Truth to Power: Everyday Resistance to Reconciliation in Post-Genocide Rwanda.* Madison: University of Wisconsin Press.
Thomson, S. and R. Nagy. 2010. 'Law, Power and Justice: What Legalism Fails to Address in the Functioning of Rwanda's *Gacaca* Courts'. *The International Journal of Transitional Justice* 5: 11–30.
Tilly, C. 1985. 'War Making and State Making as Organised Crime'. In *Bringing the State Back In*, P. Evans, D. Rueschemeyer and T. Skocpol (eds). Cambridge: Cambridge University Press.
Tindiwensi, M. 2009. 'Gishwati Residents Uproot Rwf 210 Million Worth of Forest', The New Times Kigali, 25 May.
Titeca, K. and T. De Herdt. 2011. 'Real Governance Beyond the "Failed State": Negotiating Education in the Democratic Republic of the Congo'. *African Affairs* 110(439): 213–231.
Tronvoll, K. 1998. 'The Process of Nation-Building in Post-War Eritrea: Created from Below or Directed from Above?' *The Journal of Modern African Studies* 36(3): 461–482.
Tronvoll, K., C. Schaefer and G. Alemu (eds). 2009. *The Ethiopian Red Terror Trials: Transitional Justice Challenged.* Oxford: James Currey.
Turner, S. 1999. 'Angry Young Men in Camps: Gender, Age and Class Relations among Burundian Refugees in Tanzania'. *UNHCR New Issues in Refugee Research Working Paper*, no. 9.
———. (2007) 'The Precarious Position of Politics in Popular Imagination: The Burundian Case', *Journal of Eastern African Studies* 1(1): 93–106.

Turner, V. 1967. *Forest of Symbols: Aspects of the Ndembu Ritual*. Ithaca: Cornell University Press.
———. 1969. *The Ritual Process. Structure and Anti-Structure*. New Jersey: Rutgers.
UN News Service. 2005. 'UN Remains Concerned by Burundi's Forced Repatriation of Rwandan Refugees', 16 June.
UN Development Programme (UNDP). 2007. 'Turning Vision 2020 into Reality: From Recovery to Sustainable Human Development'. Accessed 6 March 2009, http://planipolis.iiep.unesco.org/upload/Rwanda/Rwanda%20HDR%202007.pdf.
———. 2008. 'Support to the National Unity and Reconciliation Commission: Summary', Document received through e-mail from a UNDP employee on 14 December 2008.
UN Office of the High Commissioner for Human Rights. 2010. 'Democratic Republic of the Congo, 1993–2003. Report of the Mapping Exercise Documenting the Most Serious Violations of Human Rights and International Humanitarian Law Committed within the Territory of the Democratic Republic of the Congo between March 1993 and June 2003', August 2010.
UN Security Council (UNSC). 1998. 'Report of the Investigative Team Charged with Investigating Serious Violations of Human Rights and International Humanitarian Law in the Democratic Republic of Congo', S/1998/581, 29 June 1998, no. 96.
———. 2001. 'Report of the Panel on the Illegal Exploitation of Natural Resources and Other Forms of Wealth of the Democratic Republic of Congo', Mrs Safiatou Ba N'Daw (ed.), New York, April 2001.
———. 2008. 'Report of the Group of Experts on the Democratic Republic of the Congo', 12 December 2008, S/2008/773.
U.S. Agency for International Development (USAID) Rwanda. 2008. 'Women and Vulnerable Groups in Land Dispute Management: A Plan to Ensure That They Fully Participate and Benefit', June 2008. Accessed 17 October 2009, http://pdf.usaid.gov/pdf_docs/PNADM809.pdf.
U.S. Department of State (US DoS). 2009. '2008 Human Rights Report: Rwanda', 25 February 2009 by the Bureau of Democracy, Human Rights and Labour, US DoS.
———. 2014. '2013 Country Reports on Human Rights Practices – Rwanda', US DoS, 27 February 2014.
Uvin, P. 1998. *Aiding Genocide: The Development Enterprise in Rwanda*. West Hartford, Connecticut: Kumarian Press.
———. 1999. 'Ethnicity and Power in Burundi and Rwanda: Different Paths to Mass Violence'. *Comparative Politics* 31(3): 253–271.
Uvin, P. and A. Nee. 2009. 'Justice, Silence and Social Capital'. In *Life after Violence: A People's Story of Burundi*, ed. P. Uvin. London: Zed Books.
Van Damme, J., A. Ansoms and P.V. Baret. 2014. 'Agricultural Innovation from Above and from Below: Confrontation and Integration on Rwanda's Hills'. *African Affairs* 113(450): 108–127.
Vandeginste, S. 2014. 'Governing Ethnicity after the Genocide: Ethnic Amnesia in Rwanda versus Ethnic Power-Sharing in Burundi'. *Journal of Eastern African Studies* 8(2): 263–277.

Vansina, J. 1985. *Oral Tradition as History*. Oxford: James Currey.
———. 1994. *Living with Africa*. Madison: University of Wisconsin Press.
———. 2004. *Antecedents to Modern Rwanda: The Nyiginya Kingdom*. Madison: The University of Wisconsin Press.
Verwimp, P. 2000. 'Development Ideology, the Peasantry and Genocide: Rwanda Represented in Habyarimana's Speeches'. *The Journal of Genocide Research* 2(3): 325–361.
Vidal, C. 1991. *Sociologie des Passions. Cote-d'Ivoire, Rwanda*. Editions Karthala.
Vincent, J. (ed.). 2002. *The Anthropology of Politics: A Reader in Ethnography, Theory and Critique*. Oxford: Blackwell Publishing.
Waldorf, L. 2006a. 'Rwanda's Failing Experiment in Restorative Justice'. In *Handbook of Restorative Justice. A Global Perspective*, ed. D. Sullivan and L. Tifft. London and New York: Routledge.
———. 2006b. 'Mass Justice for Mass Atrocity: Rethinking Local Justice as Transitional Justice'. *Temple Law Review* 79(1): 1–87.
———. 2011. 'Instrumentalizing Genocide. The RPF's Campaign against "Genocide Ideology"'. In *Remaking Rwanda: State-Building and Human Rights After Mass Violence*, L. Waldorf and S. Straus (eds). Madison: The University of Wisconsin Press.
Watkins, S.E. 2013. 'Review: Genocide Lives in Us. Women, Memory and Silence in Rwanda by Jennie Burnet, 2012, University of Madison Press'. Oral History Forum 33 (2013), Special Issue on 'Confronting Mass Atrocities'.
Watkins, S.E. and E. Jessee. 2014. 'Good Kings, Bloody Tyrants, and Everything in Between: Representations of the Monarchy in Post-Genocide Rwanda'. *History in Africa* 41 (June 2014): 35–62.
Wedeen, L. 1999. *Ambiguities of Domination: Politics, Rhetoric and Symbols in Contemporary Syria*. Chicago: The University of Chicago Press.
———. 2008. *Peripheral Visions: Publics, Power and Performance in Yemen*. Chicago: The University of Chicago Press.
Wendt, A.1999. *Social Theory of International Politics*. Cambridge: Cambridge University Press.
———. 2004. 'The State as Person in International Theory'. *Review of International Studies* 30(2): 289–316.
West, H.G.2005. *Kupulikula. Governance and the Invisible Realm in Mozambique*. Chicago: The University of Chicago Press.
———. 2007. *Ethnographic Sorcery*. Chicago: University of Chicago Press.
West, H.G. and T. Sanders (eds). 2003. *Transparency and Conspiracy: Ethnographies of Suspicion in the New World Order*. Durham: Duke University Press.
Whaites, A. 2008. 'States in Development: Understanding State Building', *DFID Working Paper*, Governance and Social Development Group. Accessed 5 October 2008, http://www.fias.net/ifcext/fias.nsf/Attachments ByTitle/Taxationgrowthandgovernanceprogram_taxandgovernanceworking paper/$FILE/StateBuildingWkgPaper.pdf.
Whitaker, B.E. 2002. 'Changing Priorities in Refugee Protection: The Rwandan Repatriation from Tanzania'. *Refugee Studies Quarterly* 21(1&2): 328–344.
White, L. 2000. 'Telling More: Lies, Secrets and History'. *History and Theory* 39(4): 11–22

Widner, J. 1995. 'States and Statelessness in Late Twentieth Century Africa'. *Daedalus* Summer 1995: 129–153.

Willum, B. 2001. 'Foreign Aid to Rwanda: Purely Beneficial or Contributing to War?' PhD Book [unpublished]. Accessed 5 October 2010, www.willum.com/book/6foreignaidwareffort.pdf.

Wilson, R.A. 2000. 'Reconciliation and Revenge in Post-Apartheid South Africa: Rethinking Legal Pluralism and Human Rights'. *Current Anthropology* 41(1): 75–98.

———. 2001. *The Politics of Truth and Reconciliation in South Africa: Legitimizing the Post-Apartheid State.* Cambridge: Cambridge University Press.

Women Without Borders (WWB). 2004. 'Connie Bwiza Sekamana (Rwanda) – We are No Flowers!' [Interview], 9 March. Accessed 2 December 2009, www.women-without-borders.org/news/archive/10/.

Wynter, A. 2009. 'Rwandan Red Cross: An 'Imihigo' for Risk Reduction [online]', 17 June. Accessed 14 November 2009, http://www.preventionweb.net/english/professional/news/v.php?id=10151.

Xinhua News Agency. 1998. 'Former Rwandan Soldiers in Political Training', Xinhua News Agency, 18 February.

———. 2004. 'Nearly 500 Ex-Genocide Prisoners Escape Solidarity Camps in Rwanda', Xinhua News Agency, 23 April.

Yates, S. 2003. *Doing Social Science Research.* London: SAGE.

York, G. and J. Rever. 2014. 'Assassination in Africa: Inside the Plots to Kill Rwanda's Dissidents'. *The Globe and Mail*, May 2, 2014.

Zartman, W.I. 1995. *Collapsed States: The Disintegration and Restoration of Legitimate Authority.* Boulder and London: Lynne Rienner.

Zorbas, E. 2004. 'Reconciliation in Post-Genocide Rwanda'. *African Journal of Legal Studies* 1: 29–52.

———. 2009. 'What Does Reconciliation After Genocide Mean? Public Transcripts and Hidden Transcripts in Post-Genocide Rwanda'. *Journal of Genocide Research* 11(1): 127–147.

Zraly, M. 2008. *Bearing: Resilience among Genocide Rape Survivors in Rwanda,* PhD Dissertation, Case Western University.

Index

A

administrative apparatus 90–99
   administrative web, intricacies of 91–2
   district *(akarere)* as main political-administrative unit 92
   hierarchies in 90–93
   lateral administrative structure 95–6
   levels of 90–92
   political administration, strength and intricacy of 90, 91–2
   public bads 24, 120
   regime building and building of state power 246
   "regime goods" 24
   responsibilities of administrators, multiplication of 96–7
   vertical administrative structure 90–93
advancement, donor-pleasing language of 135–6
affective embodiment 113
agency 48, 114, 246
aid, ethnography of 10
alignment, efforts in 195–6
   multiplicities of unity, ambiguity and 135
   performance, power in 163
ambiguity
   ambiguous communication 133
   brainwashing *(lavage de cerveau)*, ambiguity of 194, 200, 214, 226
   effects of 133, 149
   multiplicities of unity, ambiguity and 135
   politics of 8–9, 133–4
   semantic ambiguity 244
   strategic ambiguity, Eisenberg's concept of 9
   unified diversity, concept of 137
   see also multiplicities of unity, ambiguity in
amplified silence 49
Arap Moi, Daniel, President of Kenya 78–9
Arusha Accords (1993) 6, 82
associational identity 105
attitudes, landscape of 118–22
authenticity, tyranny of 156
authoritarianism
   authoritarian legitimation 64
   developmentalism and authoritarian rule 247
   hidden in pluralism 63, 76–7

B

Bagaza, President Jean-Baptiste 16
Banyarwanda identity 10, 40, 183
Barre, Siad, President of Somalia 17
Base of Unity *(Intango y'ubumwe)* 154
Bizimungu, President Pasteur 79, 189
brainwashing *(lavage de cerveau)*, ambiguity of 194, 200, 214, 226
Brugière, Jean Luis 37, 165
Bumaya, Andre Habib 30, 32n9
Buyoya, President Pierre 16–17
Bwiza, Connie, MP 233

C

camps 22–3, 26, 33, 38–9, 175–7, 245, 246
   Adventist youth *ingando* camps 26, 185–6, 187, 205, 206, 207
   camp-based education 22

Index

Chaka Mchaka political education camps in Uganda 22, 181
Community Work or Service (TIG) camps 48, 104, 125, 148, 160, 164, 186, 192, 194, 196, 205, 206, 209
dimensions, symbolic and performative, of 24
education camps 176, 181, 249
encamped experiences 176
FRELIMO re-education camps in Mozambique 22
Gako *ingando* camp 184, 192, 208, 213
Gihembe refugee camp 102, 187
Gikomero sector, TIG labour camp in 125, 186, 206
Gishari refugee camp 182, 191
graduation ceremony, Nkumba *ingando* camp 159–60
in-depth study of 21–2
intorero schools and *ingando* camps, contrasts between 188, 198, 219, 230, 233–4
Kiziba refugee camp 102
Kucikiro *ingando* camp 190
Kyankwanzi military camps in Uganda 181
labour camps 43, 48, 125, 148, 150n6, 160, 164, 192, 236
Mau Mau 'rehabilitation' camps in Kenya 22
military or militarized camps 79, 181, 193, 200, 212–13
Mutobo *ingando* camp 47, 138, 144–5, 150n22, 192, 194–5, 201n38, 203, 206
Nkumba *ingando* camp for university students 212–15
Nyagasambu *ingando* camp 199
participant observation in 26
peace and leadership camps 177
political camps 22, 176, 249
power arrangements, reproduction of 218–19
refugee camps 22–3, 38, 79, 80–81, 181–2, 186, 189, 219
liminality of 187
reintegration camps 22–3, 24–5, 138
reorientation camps 176
scout camps 187
social engineering and 22
social experimentation in 209
social laboratories, *ingando* camps as 187
solidarity camps 136, 176
training camps 186, 188
transformation, political camps for 22
transit camps 22, 186
vacation camps 136
work camps 4, 138, 187
see also ingando camps
censorship 121, 135
characterization 6–7
character fronts, maintenance of 153–4
issues of 154–5
political economy of 153–6
Charter of National Unity (1991) 16
citizenship 48, 78, 80, 82, 130–31, 187, 196, 219, 250
citizen and regime, circularity between 113
civic education, shaping citizenship and 176, 195–6
dutiful and responsive citizens, government need for 162–3
ideal citizen 23, 200, 218
ideal development subjects 166, 228, 231, 237–8
incorporative practices 249
sovereign inclusion 23
state and citizens, top-down relationship between 11, 98, 100, 109, 127, 140, 162, 236, 237, 247–8
civic education (or political education) 6, 21–2, 47, 108, 176
complex nature of programme of 241
consent building and 200
decentralized structure of 187–8
ingando camps drive for 22–3
integrated policy of 229
itorero and, aims of 187–8, 229, 231, 233–4
lessons in *ingando* camps on 194
nation building and 200, 230
primacy of civic education 246
re-education and 246, 249
reconciliation process and 226–7, 230
sensitization, re-education and, primacy of 246
society in general, transformatory aim and 231
state tutelage and 108–9

transformational aim of 108–9
see also ingando camps; National Unity and Reconciliation Commission (NURC)
co-optation 95–6, 96–7, 115, 213
coercion 79, 94, 97, 98, 110n2, 114–15, 116–18, 121, 127, 169
coercive *eutopia*, framework of 24, 209, 227, 234–8, 240, 241, 245, 247
coexistence 244–50
  mechanisms of 169, 170
  multiplicities of unity and 139, 141
  path of unity, long journey of 244
  social justice 247
cohabitation, theme of 141
cohesiveness
  coherence, allusion of 137
  cohesive society, conceptualization of 140
communal mutuality, localized activities of 155
communication 64, 68, 119
  ambiguous communication 133
  communication rules 179
  communication studies literature 9
  of consent and alignment 115
  culture of 44–5
  lack of 161, 185, 216
communitas, liminality and creation of 216–17
community festivals *(ubusabane)*, performance for 4, 6, 14, 25, 43, 152, 158–9, 161, 164, 165–6, 235
community policing
  Community Policing Committees (CPCs) 71
  information gathering and 101
Community Work or Service (TIG) 39, 48, 50, 98, 104, 125, 205, 206, 208, 209, 233
  headquarters for 26
  ingando camps, nation building and 185, 186, 188–9, 192, 194, 195, 196, 197
  multiplicities of unity, ambiguity and 145, 146, 148, 150n6
  performance, power in 160, 164, 168, 169
compliance
  factors influencing 118

obedience and 122–3
state reach, surveillance and 104
through coercion 169
complicity 39, 68
containment 123–4
  state reach and aim of 106–8
contestation 14, 114, 120, 122
  direct contestation, absence of 123
  political concept of 114
  unworking of 113–14, 120, 126–7, 238
convergence
  convergent elite, aim of Nkumba *ingando* camp 212–15
  notion of 140
  as unity 198–9, 199–200

D
de-ethnicization
  contradictions in 85
  legitimation narratives, power and 82–5
  meaning, politics and policing of 40
decentralization 99
  civic education, decentralized structure of 187–8
  state reach and 90
decontestation 70, 119, 127
development
  coercive *eutopia*, framework of 24, 209, 227, 234–8, 240, 241, 245, 247
  'common vision' of 148
  development corps 228, 230
  developmentalism, post-conflict paradigm of 245–6
  economic development, circulation of messages of 165–6
  in legitimation corpus 73
  schemes of *(ubudehe)* pressures of work for 96, 103–4
  standardized language of 155
  subjugation of unity and reconciliation to 233–4
disempowerment 48, 96, 114–15, 120, 238, 239
displacement 10, 22–3, 176
  forced migration as political tool 78–9
  internal displacement 38
  symbolic displacement 216–17
  temporal displacement 241, 246
dissent
  compliance or, question of 122–6

internal 'flight,' dissent strategy
    of 125–6
Local Defence Forces (LDFs) and 125
rule dodging, dissent in strategy
    of 124–5
shades of 105–6
umuganda community, dissent
    strategies within 124
distrust 119
    at organization of *ingando* camps 182
    and suspicion within NURC 44
divisionism
    accusations of 41
    definitional vagueness on 69–70
    security against 68–9
duplicity 119–20, 167
    indeterminacy and 51
    proverbs concerning 45

E
economic growth 236, 239, 240–41, 247
emotive spectrum 119–20
exclusion, politics of 80–82
expropriation 39, 107, 121, 128n16

F
fear
    comfort and fear, interplay
        between 65
    governmental lack of immunity to 72
    politicization of 118–19
    rumour and fear, information control
        and 120–21
    threat and fear, rule of 71–2
    uses of 64–72
Finance and Economic Planning,
    Ministry of (MINECOFIN) 73,
    86n5, 148, 232, 236
fragmentation 133–8
    National Unity and Reconciliation
        Commission (NURC) and 11, 130,
        133–8
    unity, fragmented concept of 136
friend-enemy distinction 67–71

G
gacaca court system 6, 13, 14, 21, 39, 70, 71,
    119, 130, 136, 185, 199, 211–12, 228
    conspiracy of silence, *gacaca* process
        and 50, 105–6

ingando camps, nation building
    and 155, 157, 168, 169, 170–71
    literature on 5
    state reach, surveillance and 90, 91–2,
        96, 98, 103–4, 109
Gakumba, Jomba 189–90
Gender and Family Planning, Ministry of
    (MIGEPROF) 26
    Street Children Unit 191
genocide
    geopolitical shift following 37–8
    interpretations of 'genocide against
        Tutsi' 40–41
    political dynamics and 36–7
    scale of 5
genocide ideology 67, 68–9
    definitional vagueness on 69–70
government
    consensual politics, benefits to
        government of 77
    dutiful and responsive citizens,
        government need for 162–3
    Foucault's perspective on 115
    governability, governmentality
        and 106
    governmentality and 106, 110, 171
    helpful partners of 163–5
    organized 'unity and reconciliation'
        activities 152, 154
    power, government styles of 115–16
    research on impacts of
        performance 168–9
    of RPF, nature of 229–30, 241, 247–8
    sponsored ceremonies, community
        interaction and 161
Government of National Unity (GNU) 145
    establishment of (1994) 15–16
governmentality
    containment, aim of 106–8
    governability, governmentality
        and 106

H
Habineza, Joseph, Minister for
    Youth 229, 232
Habyarimana, Juvenal 37, 74, 80, 99,
    156, 168, 235
heterotopia, power in and of 209–15
hierarchies
    in administrative apparatus 90–93

elaboration in *ingando* camps of 186
official ceremonies, hierarchized space of 161–2
HIV/AIDS 109, 174, 176, 194
Human Rights Report on Rwanda (US DoS, 2009) 168
Human Rights Watch (HRW) 117, 180–81, 189, 201n30
legitimation narratives, power and 68, 69, 71, 75, 77, 87n26
state reach, surveillance and 93, 94, 107–8, 109

I
identity
  ethnicity and 40
  in politics 82–5
  politics of 83, 137, 152–3
imithigo 96–9
inclusion
  issues of 154
  politics of 80–82
incorporation, political 10–11, 118, 126–7, 204, 245, 249
  forced incorporation 38
  ingando project and 216–18, 219
  simultaneity of disconnect and 113
indeterminacy
  dealing with 54–5
  politics of 34–5, 50–55
indirect control
  state reach and 95–6
  technology of 115–16
information management 100–101, 120
  meaning, politics and policing of 46–7, 47–8
information sources, official voice and 46–7
informational asymmetries 55–6
informers
  perceptions of ubiquity of 101
  recruitment and training of 100
ingando camps 21–4, 24–5, 174–200
  activities, categories of 186
  aims of 183
  alignment, efforts in 195–6
  anxieties about attendance at 182–3
  attendance rates 185
  brainwashing *(lavage de cerveau)*, ambiguity of 200

camp architecture 206
civic education drive and 22–3
clandestine meetings and retreats, organization of 179
collective imaginary, movement and 175–6
communication rules 179
components, interpretation and analysis of 191–8
concentration, key notion of 205–6
consensus building, objective of 183–4
consolidation of, national programme and 181–2
convergence as unity 198–9, 199–200
cultural cohesion, fostering of 184
curriculum 196
daily routine 174–5
discipline, accent on 184
distrust at organization of 182
experience through simulation in 207–8, 209–15
face-to-face contact, advantages of 205–6
family resemblance, system of 185–6
influences in the diaspora 178–9, 180–81
ingando, definition of 175
internal structure of 206–7
Itorero graduates and 187–8
judiciary and judgements in 211–12
lectures, lecture theatres and 186, 193–4, 196
lessons taught, diversity of 194
liminalities of 175–6, 219, 231
link to *ingando* of past, tenuous nature of 178
military nature of camps, contradictions in 176–7
military training, militariness and 186, 192–3
mindset change, aim of 187–8, 195, 200
nation building objective of 175–7, 183–4, 185, 187–8, 190, 194, 195, 196, 197
National Resistance Movement (NRM) and 179, 180, 181
new citizen role, cultivation of 184, 195
official scripts, transmission of 189, 190
order and hierarchy in 206–7

organization of 26, 182, 191–2
origins of name *ingando* 178
performative aspects 185–6
personal recollections of life in 175, 182–3, 196–8
political education, aim of 178–84, 198–200
political schools, organization of 179–80
politicization 179–80, 184
predecessors in the diaspora 178–9
prison overcrowding, easing of 189–90
reorientation, exercises in 189, 190
as research spaces, complicated nature of 26, 28–9
selective targeting of candidates 188–91
separation and distancing of participants in 185–6, 204–6
simulation in 207–8, 209–15
social gathering 185–6
social situation of *ingando* 185–8
symbolic and ideational movement 175–6
target groups 181, 185, 188–91
transformation, ultimate goal of 210–11, 212
transience of 175–6
unity and reconciliation and use of 21–4, 24–5, 174–200
insecurity
export of 66
production of 72
Institute for Justice and Reconciliation (IJR), impact assessment from 156
institutional performance of NURC on unity and reconciliation 133–49
intelligibility, politics and 34–5
inter-structural space 218–20
interaction, conceptual versions of 138–43
internal displacement 38
International Criminal Tribunal for Rwanda (ICTR) 5
itorero
aims of, civic education and 187–8, 229, 231, 233–4
graduates, *ingando* camps and 187–8
graduation ceremonies 161, 165, 217
ingando camps and *intorero* schools, contrasting of 188, 198, 219, 230, 233–4

liminalities of 219, 231
music troupe 60, 159
schools 6, 14, 96, 108–9, 135, 146, 152, 155, 177, 188
social armies of graduates 230–31

J
Jeunesse Ouvriere Catholique (JOC) 187

K
Kabuye, Rose 37, 102, 112n52, 148
Kagame, Abbé Alexis 15
Kagame, President Paul (formerly Minister of Defence) 48, 99, 120, 148, 165, 172n12, 180, 189, 226, 229–30, 232, 234
legitimation narratives, power and 65, 68, 76–7, 80–81, 84, 86n1
Kinyarwanda 3, 11, 30, 39–40, 80–82, 100, 109, 121, 170–71, 172n12, 228
multiplicities of unity, ambiguity and 136–7, 138, 141, 144, 145–6, 150n7
knowledge
elicitation of 51
'knowing,' symbolic struggles over 33–4
knowledge-based economy, importance of ICT and 166
voice and, politics of 35
Kwinjeh, Grace 74, 143–4

L
land reform, scholarship on 236–7
language
advancement, donor-pleasing language of 135–6
context and 8–9
development, standardized language of 155
incorporative appeal, use of words with 249–50
legitimacy, languages of 63–4
political potency, use of words with 249–50
political power, language of voice and 50
unity and reconciliation, non-contestation and language of 127
of unity and reconciliation (*ubumwe n'ubwiyunge*) 95, 127

see also Kinyarwanda
legitimation narratives, power and 63–86
  authoritarian legitimation 64
  authoritarianism hidden in pluralism 63, 76–7
  Community Policing Committees (CPCs) 71
  de-ethnicization 82–5
  divisionism 68–70
  exception, triggering of states of 67–8
  exclusion, politics of 80–82
  fear 64–72
  forced migration as political tool 78–9
  Forum of Political Parties, legal activity and membership of 75
  friend-enemy distinction 67–71
  genocide ideology 67, 68–9, 69–70
  hatred, perpetuation of 68–9
  identity in politics 82–5
  identity politics 83
  inclusion, politics of 80–82
  insecurity 66, 72
  irredentist discourse 81
  judiciary 77
  languages of legitimacy 63–4
  legitimation narratives 63–4
  Local Defence Forces (LDFs) 71
  local democracy 75–6
  morality, operation of 65–6
  multipartyism, 'feigned plurality' in 74–7
  names 70–71
  Neighbourhood Watch programme 71
  ordering and control 67–71
  political parties, registration of 75
  political power, exclusions from 83–4
  powers, alignment of 76–7
  prosperity, development and 72–7
  Rwandanness, blurred borders of 80–82
  security 64–72
  segregation 83
  silent engineering 82–5
  social harmony, political unity and 78–85
  sovereign exception 68
  state securitization 67–71
  threat and fear, rule of 71–2
  transformative identity politics 82–3
  unity, building of 85–6
  violence, justification of 65–7
  voting management 75–6
liberalization 246, 247
  political liberalization 16
liminality 23
  'dislocated temporality' of 203–4
  ingando camps, liminalities of 175–6, 219, 231
  politics of 218–20
  see also reproduction of power, liminality and
Local Defence Forces (LDFs) 101, 125, 159
  dissent and 125
  legitimation narratives, power and 71
local democracy 75–6
Local Government, Community Development and Social Affairs, Ministry of (MINALOC) 96–7, 117, 155–6, 171n1, 207, 229–30, 233
localization, trope of 157–8

M

Mao Tse Tung 95–6
Maquet, Jacques 15
meaning, politics and policing of 33–57
  academic narratives, divided nature of 35
  amplified silence 49
  complicity 39
  conspiracy of silence, *gacaca* process and 50
  de-ethnicization 40
  disclosure, political economy of 36
  dispersion, effects of 39
  disruption, mass movements of people and 38
  distortion and partiality in research encounters 52
  distrust and suspicion within NURC 44
  divisionism, accusations of 41
  duplicity 45, 51
  ethnic markers 41
  'faith in unity,' divisiveness and 33
  genocide 37–8, 40–41, 3607
  human rights, critical reports on 37
  identity, ethnicity and 40
  image, appearance and 34–5
  indeterminacy, politics of 34–5, 50–55

information management 46–7, 47–8
informational asymmetries 55–6
intelligibility, politics and 34–5
internal displacement 38
'knowing,' symbolic struggles over 33–4
literature, interconnected and overlapping 34
meaning making, political context of 42
metadata 53–4
narrative credibility 54, 55–6
official narratives, defensiveness over 48–9
official voices, counter-narratives to 47, 52–3, 56–7
outsiders, positives and negatives in positions of 51–2
plurivocality 53–4
post-genocide present, narrative disunity in 36–44
power asymmetries 52
press control 42
public interest, personal interest and 43
public silence, structural nature of 49, 50–51
public voice 44–50
racial body maps 41
repression, effects of 45–6
returnees, multiple groups of 39–40
signification, struggle over 33–4
silence, stated preference for 47–8
silence breaking, challenge of 50
silence pervading Rwanda, finding voice in 44–50
social divides 43
speech prudence, ethnic references and 41
state anthropomorphism 44
transgressive performance, deployment of 45–6
transitional space, characteristics of 45
validation of official narratives 49–50
'variability of voice,' nature and meaning of 29, 53, 55–7
voice and power, critical method for study of 55–7
written narratives, divergence from reality in 47

metadata diversity 53–4
military, power of 91–2
Military Intelligence, Department of (DMI) 100–101
Millennium Village Project 239–40
mindset change
  aim of 187–8, 195, 200
  role of *itorero* in 187–8, 229
Mitchell, Andrew 56–7
morality, operation of 65–6
multipartyism 74–7
multiplicities of unity, ambiguity and 12, 133–49
  advancement, donor-pleasing language of 135–6
  ambiguity, effects of 133, 149
  censorship 135
  cleansing 142, 183, 200
  coexistence, unity and 139, 141
  contamination, use of idioms of 142–3
  cultural homogeneity, strategy of 146–7
  deniability, fostering of 133
  diversity of interests, accommodation of 133, 136
  fragmentation 133–8
  heterogeneity of unity 137–8
  identity politics 137
  interaction, conceptual versions of 138–43
  intoxication, use of idioms of 142–3
  mentality change 229, 247
  mutual understanding 139–40
  National Hero *(Intwari z'u Rwanda)*, cult of 146, 232
  performance indicators 134–5
  performative strategies of unity 148–9
  pre-colonial unity and harmony, historical re-reading of 144–5
  reconciliation 4, 5, 7, 13, 14
    concept of 140
    differences in understandings of 141–2
    ex-combattants' perceptions of 138–40
    social interaction and 140–41
  redemptive history, concept of 145
  restoration, notion of 142–3
  Results Based Matrix (RBM) 134, 135–6

social togetherness 3, 4–5, 13, 137, 141
solidarity, official impressions of 135, 136
strategies, alternative paths of unity 143–9
success, images of 134–5
threat, real or imagined, invocation of idea of fighting against 147–8
unity
  ex-combattants' perceptions of 138–40
  fragmented concept of 136
  as operationalized category 135–6
  socially interactive conceptualization of 140
  vagueness, strategies of 136
Museveni, Yoweri 179, 180, 181
mutual forgiveness *(kubabarirana)*, process of 140–41
mutual understanding 139–40

N
names and naming 70–71, 153–6
narrative credibility 54, 55–6
nation building
  civic education (or political education) and 200, 230
  key aim of *ingando* camps 175–7, 183–4
  unity building and 12, 176–7, 184, 195–6, 198
National Academy *(Itorero ry 'Iguhugu)* 22, 175, 187–8, 233
National Chancellery on Heroes and Medals 146
National Congress for the Defence of the People (CNDP) 36, 102
National Coordinator for Decentralization 99
National Democratic Institute (NDI) 48, 94
National Dialogue Conferences 172n12, 232
National Habitat Policy (1996) 107
National Hero *(Intwari z'u Rwanda)*, cult of 146, 232
National Leadership Institute 181
National Policy of Unity and Reconciliation (2007) 154, 162–3

National Programme of the Newly Repatriated Refugees (NPNRR) 181–2
National Resistance Movement (NRM) 179, 180, 181
National School of Political Education 180–81
National Unity and Reconciliation Commission (NURC) 3, 4, 26–7, 28–9, 124, 152, 185, 187, 227
  Andrew Mitchell's visit to 56–7
  Arusha Accords (1993) and 6, 82
  awareness, *ingando* camps and raising of 178–9
  ceremonial 'theatres of unity and reconciliation' 158–61
  Civic Education
    Director of 27, 41, 112n40, 154, 167–8, 172n11, 207
    key department of 108, 135, 176, 206–7
  civic education, transformational aim of 108–9
  Databank of Unity and Reconciliation Organizations 154
  development, subjugation of unity and reconciliation to 233–4
  discourse of, manipulable nature of 167–8
  fragmentation 11, 130, 133–8
  impact assessment of *ingando* camps 181–2
  information source, official voice and 46–7
  ingando camps 26, 183, 191–2
  Institute for Justice and Reconciliation (IJR), impact assessment from 156
  institutional performance on unity and reconciliation 133–49
  interaction, conceptual versions of 138–43
  Juvenal Habyarimana, President 37, 74, 80, 99, 156, 168, 235
  mandate for, Article 178 of Constitution of Rwanda 136–7
  measurement of achievements of 168–71
  mindset change, role of *itorero* in 187–8, 229

mutual forgiveness *(kubabarirana)*,
  process of 140–41
names and personal narratives,
  dangers in 70–71
National Policy of Unity and
  Reconciliation (2007) 154, 162–3
National Programme of the
  Newly Repatriated Refugees
  (NPNRR) 181–2
official partners of 154
oppositional constitution, strategy
  of 147–8
peace building, conflict management
  and 233
planning, working and 133–8
post-genocide society, reflection of
  tensions within 42–3
responsibilities of 136–7
Results Based Matrix (RBM) 134,
  135–6
scrutiny of, party agendas and 163–5
silence among prisoners, problem of 50
strategies, alternative paths of
  unity 143–9
Student Clubs for Unity and
  Reconciliation (SCUR) 134, 163–5
Unity and Reconciliation Weeks 43,
  157, 158–9, 161, 162, 169, 173n26,
  232–4
National University of Rwanda
  (NUR) 104, 144, 163, 232
National Youth Council 183, 188, 207
nationalism 12, 14, 15, 17, 108, 137, 142,
  175, 177, 183, 184, 189, 245
nationalist unity 143, 148–9
Ndadaye, President-elect Melchior 16
Ndangiza, Fatuma 42–3, 83, 92, 93, 96,
  104, 136–7, 147, 151, 154, 158, 159,
  160–61, 167, 168–9, 185, 193, 229,
  234
Neighbourhood Watch programme 71
new citizen role, cultivation of 184, 195
New Times Kigali (NTK) 30, 143, 148,
  165, 168, 171–2n3, 172n12, 218
change, mapping developments
  for 229, 230–31, 232, 234, 235
ingando camps, nation building
  and 185, 187–8, 190
legitimation narratives, power and 68,
  69, 74, 86n1

power in Rwanda, embodiments
  of 117, 120, 123
state reach, surveillance and 93, 94,
  97–8
Nkunda, Laurent 36
Nyiginya monarchy 11, 91, 230, 237
  unificatory legacy claimed by 19–20,
  42

O

official ceremonies, hierarchized space
  of 161–2
official historical narrative, reproduction
  of 144–5
official narratives, defensiveness
  over 48–9
official scripts, reproduction of 170, 189,
  190
official voices
  counter-narratives to 47, 52–3, 56–7
  propagation of 46
opposition, suppression of 119–20
oppositional constitution 147–8
ordering and control 67–71
Organization for Peace, Justice,
  and Development in Rwanda
  (OPJDR) 76
outsiders, positives and negatives in
  positions of 51–2

P

participant observation 11–12, 25–6
participation
  ceremonial events, participation
    in 169–71
  levels of 135
  performance, power in 170–71
  political participation 247
  in state activities 103
  terminology of 157
performance, power in 152–71
  alignment as goal of activities 163
  authenticity, tyranny of 156
  ceremonial 'theatres of unity and
    reconciliation' 158–61
  character fronts, maintenance of 153–4
  characterization 153–6
  coexistence mechanisms 169, 170
  community festival *(ubusabane)*,
    performance for 158–9

desired impacts of performance, measurement of 168–9
effects of performances, claimed and actual 168–71
feelings, access to closed-off domain of 166–8
football, 'bringing people together' through games 160–61
fundraising, naming and political economy of 153–4
government-organized 'unity and reconciliation' activities 152, 154
graduation ceremony, Nkumba *ingando* camp 159–60
grassroots activities 157–8, 163
hierarchized space of official ceremonies 161–2
identity, politics of 152–3
impacts of performance, measurement of 168–9
participation 157, 170–71
party agendas 163–5
performances, actual effects of 169–71
power and performance, naming and 156–66
sensitization 157, 162
stages for performance, appropriation of 158–61, 163–5
Student Clubs for Unity and Reconciliation (SCUR) 163–5
subjects, transformation of 165–6
theatre of 'unity and reconciliation' 158–62
themes, interpretation of 165–6
'traditionality' discourse of 155–6
personal threats, harassment and 117–18
plurivocality 53–4
police, power of 91–2
political administration, strength and intricacy of 90, 91–2
political manipulation 45–6, 153, 156, 237
political potency, use of words with 249–50
political power
  entrenchment of 23–4
  exclusions from 83–4
  language of voice and 50
  performance activities as insertion points for 171

political schools, organization of 179–80
political subjectivity 10, 22, 250
politicization 14, 184
  objective of 179–80
  politicized information 53
  power interests, reproduction through 24
  regimes and development of 14–15
politics
  anthropology of 21
  Schmitt's perspective on 61
  Wedeen's, perspective on 33–4
possibility, principle of 115, 121
post-conflict governance
  dynamics of 244–5
  logic of 246
post-genocide society
  governance and unity in 245–6
  narrative disunity in 36–44
  politicization of 34–5
  reflection of tensions within 42–3
poverty 48, 73, 104, 108, 121, 194, 227, 228
  conflict and 232–4
power 113–27
  affective embodiment 113
  agency 114
  alignment of powers 76–7
  arbitrary nature of application of 115, 121
  attitudes, landscape of 118–22
  co-optation 96–7
  coercive strategies 117
  compliance 118, 122–3
  containment 123–4
  contestation 14, 114, 120, 122
  unworking of 113–14, 120, 126–7, 238
  decontestation 70, 119, 127
  deterrence, principle of 115
  direct contestation, absence of 123
  disempowerment 120
  dissent or compliance 122–6
  embodiments of 117, 120, 123, 127
  emotive spectrum 119–20
  fear, politicization of 118–19
  feelings, landscape of 118–22
  government, Foucault's notion of 115
  government styles of 115–16
  indirect control, technology of 115–16

indirect power, operation of 116–17
inscription of 118–22
internal 'flight,' dissent strategy of 125–6
liminality as tool in reproduction of 217–18
Local Defence Force (LDF), dissent and 125
loyalty, simulation of 123
micro-effects of 121–2
non-contestation, administrative intricacies and 115–16
opposition, suppression of 119–20
performance and, naming and 156–66
personal threats, harassment and 117–18
political threats 115
possibility, principle of 115, 121
relationships, landscape of 118–22
repression and control, effects of 123, 126–7
repressive systems, productiveness of 118–19
rule dodging, dissent in strategy of 124–5
rumour and fear, information control and 120–21
self-limiting behaviour, generation of 113
silence 119–20, 123
state and citizens, top-down relationship between 11, 98, 100, 109, 127, 140, 162, 236, 237, 247–8
strategies of 115–18
styles of 115–18, 126–7
suppression, systemic nature of 123–4
surveillance 116, 124
unnoficial contestation 123
voice, asymmetries of 120
see also legitimation narratives, power and; performance, power in; meaning, politics and policing of; reproduction of power, liminality and; state reach, surveillance and; unity, state power and
pre-colonial unity and harmony, historical re-reading of 144–5
President of the Republic, Office of 15–16, 32n5, 163, 165
Presidential Protection Unit (PPU) 100–101
prison overcrowding, easing of 189–90
Prison Reform International (PRI) 98, 146, 178, 182, 188
productiveness, performance and 169–70
Programme for Strengthening Good Governance (PSGG, UNDP) 177
prosperity, development and 72–7
Protais, Musoni, Minister for Local Development 171n1
public interest, personal interest and 43
public silence, structural nature of 49, 50–51
public voice
 management of 44–50
 political regimes and 44–5
 see also voice

R

racial body maps 41
reconciliation 4, 5, 7, 13, 14
 concept of 140
 differences in understandings of 141–2
 ex-combattants' perceptions of 138–40
 process of, civic education and 226–7, 230
 social interaction and 140–41
 see also unity and reconciliation
reconstruction, post-conflict paradigm of 245–6
redemptive history, concept of 145
refugee camps, liminality of 187
relationships, landscape of 118–22
reorientation, exercises in 189, 190
repression
 control and, effects of 123, 126–7
 effects of 45–6
 literature on 113
 repressive systems, productiveness of 118–19
reproduction of power, liminality and 203–20
 collective rights of passage and 207, 215–18
 communitas, liminality and creation of 216–17
 convergent elite, aim of Nkumba ingando camp 212–15
 enaction, experience through simulation 207–8
 heterotopia, power in and of 209–15

ingando camps
    camp architecture 206
    coherence, uniformity and 208
    compliance, focus on relations of 209
    concentration, key notion of 205
    concentration on aims in 205–6
    connection, cultural repertoire of 206
    control, direct and indirect within system 211
    experience through simulation in 207–8, 209–15
    face-to-face contact, advantages of 205–6
    internal structure of 206–7
    judiciary and judgements in 211–12
    oneness, enactment of sense of 208
    order and hierarchy in 206–7
    remoteness and lack of distraction 205
    separation and distancing of participants in 204–6
    simulation in 207–8, 209–15
    surveillance in 209
    transformation, ultimate goal of 210–11, 212
inter-structural space 218–20
liminality
    'dislocated temporality' of 203–4
    politics of 218–20
    power reproduction and 217–18
Muhazi *ingando* camp for child-combattants 194, 210–12
Nkumba *ingando* camp for university students 212–15
power, liminality as tool in reproduction of 217–18
research
    distortion and partiality in research encounters 52
    encounters in Rwanda, stakes involved 29–30
    government work on impacts of performance 168–9
    ingando camps as research spaces, complicated nature of 26, 28–9
    questions for, emergence of 30–31
restoration, notion of 142–3
Results Based Matrix (RBM) 134, 135–6

returnees, multiple groups of 39–40
rites of passage
    accommodation to change in 215–16
    concept of 215
    incorporation, *ingando* project and 216–18, 219
    officialdom, entry to 203–4
    separation rites 216
    spatio-temporal structure of 216
root burning, metaphor of 143
Rutaremara, Tito 16, 179
Rutayisire, Professor Paul 16
Rwagasore, Prince Louis 16
Rwanda
    appropriation of memory for narrative closure in 17–18
    civic education drive in 22–3
    decentralization in 19–20
    'densification' of state in 20
    developmentalism in 19–20
    genocidal disruption in, scale of 5
    inter-ethnic unity in, promise of 15
    interconnections between state building and unity building in 7–8
    meaning, politics and policing of characterization of 35–6
    opposed dynamics within 42
    mundane stateness in day-to-day lives 20
    nation building and 'solidarity' tools in 7
    neo-traditionality in, post-genocide production of 14
    oneness of people of 12
    politicization of reconciliation in 7
    politics of unity in, historical perspective on 15
    population density in 89
    reconstruction and the 'application' of state in life of 19–20
    research encounters in, stakes involved 29–30
    societies of, profound changes for 10–11
    state in, consolidation of 19
    ubumwe project in, key state asset 20
    unity, deployment in public realm of 9
    unity and reconciliation activities in, multiplicity of 14

Urugwiro Meetings 15–16
see also power in Rwanda
Rwanda Alliance for National Unity (RANU) 15, 179
Rwanda Demobilization and Reintegration Commission (RDRC) 26, 159, 203
Rwanda Monitoring Project (RMP) 69
Rwanda Patriotic Front (RPF) 22, 30, 33, 36–7, 56–7, 62, 69, 84, 101, 103–4, 105–6
  awareness, campaigns for raising of 178–80
  coercive might of 118
  'cross-ethnic unity,' political programme of 80
  disrupted and 'displaced' country, inheritance of 38
  forced recruitment 94–5
  government dominated by 6
  government of, nature of 229–30, 241, 247–8
  ingando camps after takeover by 181, 183–4
  inter-ethnic unity, promise of 15–16
  'liberator,' representation as 74–5
  loyalty to, *ingando* and inspiration of 189, 214
  membership (and price of) 94–5
  military life of, simulation of 207–8
  militia 177
  multiparty framework, agreement to work with 77
  official narrative of 144–5, 146
  parallel structures of 93–5
  peaceful order, credit for restoration of 64–5
  political discourse 78–9
  pressure to join 76
  Secretariat of, symbolic power of 42
  security production 67
  structure as fund-raising mechanism 95
  victims of crimes of 39, 49, 66, 154, 213
Rwandan Academy of Language and Culture 147
Rwandanness
  blurred borders of 80–82
  cultural tradition and 6, 21–2, 80–82, 83, 143–4, 145–6, 147, 176, 184, 197, 248
  fostering of 184
  patriotism and 145–6
  positivity in building of 248
  unity building and 143–5
Rwandicity, re-invention of 146–7
Rwigema, Fred Gisa 146, 180

S

scout jamborees 187
security
  discourses of 64–72
  divisionism
    accusations of 41
    definitional vagueness on 69–70
    security against 68–9
  friend-enemy metastructure and 69–70
  genocide ideology 67, 68–9
    definitional vagueness on 69–70
  internal and external threats 66–7
  legitimation and discourses of 64–5
  partial endeavour of production of 71–2
  securitization, post-conflict paradigm of 245–6
  state securitization 67–71
segregation 83, 213
selective targeting 188–91
self-control, value of 45
self-help, objective of 179
self-limiting behaviour, generation of 113
semantic ambiguity 244
sensitization
  performance, power in 157, 162
  primacy of, state power and 246
  re-education and 246
  state reach, surveillance and 109
settlement patterns, disruptions in 38–9
signification, struggle over 33–4
silence
  breaking silence, challenge of 50
  conspiracy of silence, *gacaca* process and 50
  coping strategy of muteness and 123
  prisoners' silence, issue of 50
  public silence, structural nature of 49, 50–51
  silent engineering 82–5
  stated preference for 47–8
  surveillance and 119–20

voice finding in pervasive silence 44–50
social control, extent of 249
social diversity, ethnicization of conflict and 78
social divides 43
social harmony, political unity and 78–85
social justice 19, 24, 32, 83, 90, 247
social laboratories, *ingando* camps as 187
social re-engineering 181
social situation of *ingando* 185–8
social space, saturation by state of 109–10
social togetherness 3, 4–5, 13
   imaginary of 137
   official production of 245
   unity and reconciliation as 141
social transformation 21–2, 31–2, 90, 127, 134, 220
   aims of convergence and 140, 147
   depoliticization of 247–8
   effort on, state power and 246, 247
   effort towards, vast nature of 246–7
   government tools for large-scale 155
   ingando camps and aim of 175–6, 195
   logic of 4
   politicization of goals for 156–7
   power preservation and 106
   processes of 227–8
   social togetherness and, state imaginary of 4–5
   'strong state,' social transformation and notion of 19
   theatres for unity and reconciliation, appropriation for 166
solidarity, official impressions of 135, 136
sovereign exception 68
sovereign inclusion 23
speech protocols 41
speech prudence, ethnic references and 41
Sports and Culture, Ministry of 146–7
state
   aims of state power 106–9
   appropriation of unity and reconciliation processes by 17
   counterweights to 104–6
   effects of control and state reach 248
   etatization, process of 18, 19–20, 24, 156, 245, 247
   inflexibility of 92
   mundane stateness in day-to-day lives 20
state anthropomorphism 44
stateness in Africa, meta-narrative of 89
strength in, notion of 19
state reach, surveillance and 89–110
   administrative apparatus 90–99
   administrative structure, levels of 90–92
   civic education, state tutelage and 108–9
   community policing, information gathering and 101
   decentralization 90, 99
   development schemes *(ubudehe)* pressures of work for 96, 103–4
   district *(akarere)* as main political-administrative unit 92
   enclosure, Foucault's concept of 107
   hierarchies in administrative apparatus 90–93
   imihigo 95–9
   indirect control 95–6
   information apparatus 100–101
   informers 100–101
   intricacies of administrative web 91–2
   labour-exacting duties 103
   lateral administrative structure 95–6
   local administration, problems of effectiveness for 92–3
   locally traced intelligence 101
   management of civil society 105
   military, power of 91–2
   Military Intelligence, Department of (DMI) 100–101
   mobilization of citizens by state apparatus 102
   national priorities, mainstreaming of 98–9
   participation in state activities 103
   police, power of 91–2
   political administration, strength and intricacy of 90, 91–2
   power, non-territorial nature of 89
   Presidential Protection Unit (PPU) 100–101
   responsibilities and responsibilisation 95–6
   responsibilities of administrators, multiplication of 96–7

sensitization 109
social space, saturation by state of 109–10
state-led activities 102–4
suppressions of the non-state 105
surveillance, ubiquitous nature of 100–101
target achievement, pressures of 98
taxation, alternative forms of 102
top-down directives of power 92
transformation, aim of 108–9
vertical administration structure 90–93
state-society relations in Africa 20–21
stateness in Africa, meta-narrative of 89
strategic ambiguity, Eisenberg's concept of 9
strategic characterization 136
Striving for Unity *(Duharanire Ubumwe)* 154
Student Clubs for Unity and Reconciliation (SCUR) 134
performance, power in 163–5
subjects, transformation of 165–6
suppression
of non-state, state reach and 105
systemic nature of 123–4
surface enactments, repetition of 170
surveillance
intricate systems of 46
irreverent compliance in face of 124
role of perceptions of 116
ubiquitous nature of 100–101

T

theatre of 'unity and reconciliation' 158–62
Think Africa Press 56
threat
fear and, rule of 71–2
real or imagined, invocation of idea of fighting against 147–8
Tilly, Charles 64–5
top-down
directives of power 92
state and citizens, relationship between 11, 98, 100, 109, 127, 140, 162, 236, 237, 247–8
transformation
aim of, state reach and 108–9
civic education, transformational aim of 108–9
political camps for 22
process of 228–9
restoration and, idioms of 145
state power, transformative 'surfacing' and development of 248–9
transformative identity politics 82–3
see also social transformation
transgressive performance, deployment of 45–6, 226

U

ubudehe scheme 6, 96, 103–4, 152, 165, 235
unified diversity, concept of 137
United Nations Children's Fund (UNICEF) 182
United Nations Development Programme (UNDP) 47, 134, 177, 182, 239
United Nations High Commission for Refugees (UNHCR) 66, 79, 80–81, 182
United Nations Security Council (UNSC) 66
unity, state power and
authoritarian rule, developmentalism and 247
deployment of discourses in Africa of 9, 12, 16–18, 26–7, 31–2
developmentalism, post-conflict paradigm of 245–6
economic growth 247
ex-combattants' perceptions of unity 138–40
grievance, closed rule and accumulation of 247–8
imaginative power of idea of 244–5
incorporative appeal, use of words with 249–50
inequalities, perceptions of 247
infrastructional power and 249
legitimation of consent 85–6
liberalization 247
local achievements in promotion of 246
meaning, policing of 246
political potency, use of words with 249–50
political work on, levels of 245–6
politico-historical context 244
'politography' of unity 10–13

post-conflict governance 244–6
post-genocide governance and 245–6
re-education, primacy of 246
reconstruction, post-conflict paradigm of 245–6
regime building and building of 246
Rwandanness, positivity in building of 248
securitization 245–6
sensitization, primacy of 246
social challenges, political nature of 246
social control, extent of 249
social togetherness, official production of 245
social transformation effort 246, 247–8
socially interactive conceptualization of unity 140
state reach, effects of control and 248
structural violence, production of 247
surface-level engineering on unity 17
suspicions of discourses on unity 17
togetherness and, official production of 245
transformative 'surfacing' and development of 248–9
unity as operationalized category 135–6
see also multiplicities of unity, ambiguity and
unity and reconciliation *(ubumwe n'ubwiyunge)* 3, 49, 111n13, 129, 167–8, 227–8
Unity and Reconciliation Weeks 43, 157, 158–9, 161, 162, 169, 173n26, 232–4
unity and unity building
  characterization, politics of 6–7, 153–5
  civic education, shaping citizenship and 176, 195–6
  commemoration months, problems during 167
  community festival *(ubusabane)*, performance for 158–9
  depoliticization, politics of 13–18, 153–6
  development goals and 232–4, 239–40
  effects of, measurement of claim and actuality 168–71
  effects of performances, participation *(ubwitabire)* and 169–71

football, 'bringing people together' through games 160–61
government-sponsored ceremonial, community interaction and 161, 162
graduation ceremony, Nkumba *ingando* camp 159–60
hierarchized space of official ceremonies 161–2
ingando camps and 21–4, 24–5, 174–200
  interpretations of 140–42, 143–4
  language of 95, 127
local *gacaca* courts 6, 90
  meaning of 140–41
memorials, burial sites and 66
National Unity and Reconciliation Strategy (2007) 135, 154, 162–3
official activities, myriad of 7–8, 14, 21–2, 28, 148–9, 152–3, 154
participatory activities 6, 156–7
political dynamics and 31, 62, 129, 130, 135–6, 245–6
power, state and 6–8, 152–71
processes of, government elites and appropriation of 17–18
reconciliation, concept of 129–30, 138–9, 140–41, 142
Rwandan 'tradition' of, presentation of 155–6
social interaction, invocation of 138–9
staging and performance of 158–62
state, societal presence of 18–21
Student Clubs for Unity and Reconciliation (SCUR) 134, 163–5
thematic interpenetration of activities 165–6
top-down nature of activities 161–2
transformation process 228–9
unity, politics and conceptionalization of 8, 11, 85–6, 135–6, 138–9, 163, 244
unity building *(kubaka ubumwe)* 62, 85, 135, 143, 153, 155, 176–7, 184, 195–6, 198
  homogeneity and difference in 11
  ingando camps, nation building and 176–7, 184, 195–6, 198
  state power and 4–6, 7–8, 9, 11–15, 17–18, 20, 23, 30–32, 245–6, 246–7

US State Department (DoS) 71, 75, 76, 77, 100, 117, 145

V

vagueness
  on policy content 162–3
  strategies of 136
validation of official narratives 49–50
Victims of Genocide Fund (FARG) 38
violence
  death by violence, differential treatment of 66
  justification of 65–6
  in post-genocide security 65–7
  retaliatory violence against Tutsi people 86m2
  structural violence, production of 247
Vision 2020 40, 57n17, 97, 148–9, 174, 191, 194
  change, mapping developments for 225, 232, 234, 237
  performance, power in 158, 165–6, 173n27
voice
  asymmetries of 120
  control over 48
  information sources, official voice and 46–7
  power and, critical method for study of 55–7
  'variability of voice,' nature and meaning of 29, 53, 55–7
voting management 75–6

W

World Bank 99
World Health Organization (WHO) 182
World Relief 182
written narratives, divergence from reality in 47

X

Xaveriens Group 187

Y

Youth Action Plan (Ministry of Youth) 81
Youth and Associative Movement, Ministry of (MIJEUMA) 182
youth vanguard building 184

www.ingramcontent.com/pod-product-compliance
Lightning Source LLC
Chambersburg PA
CBHW072145100526
44589CB00015B/2101